# Best Sermons 2

## CONTRIBUTING EDITORS

# Best Sermons 2

*James W. Cox, Editor*

*Kenneth M. Cox, Associate Editor*

*1817*

Harper & Row, Publishers, San Francisco

New York, Grand Rapids, Philadelphia, St. Louis
London, Singapore, Sydney, Tokyo, Toronto

*Designed by David M. Hamamoto*

**Library of Congress Cataloging-in-Publication Data**

Best sermons 2.

Includes indexes.
1. Sermons, American.   I. Cox, James William.   II. Cox, Kenneth Mitchell.   III. Title: Best sermons two.
BV4241.B42   1988   252   87-45696
ISBN 0-06-061612-1

90 91 92 93 HC 10 9 8 7 6 5 4 3

# Contents

## III. DOCTRINAL/THEOLOGICAL

## IV. ETHICAL

# Preface

Today there are important signs of a renewal of interest in preaching. In the past few years, several major textbooks on the art and craft of sermon making have appeared. Also, a number of provocative monographs have stimulated excitement among practicing clergy. Perhaps sermons are listened to with more attention as preachers are discovering the relevance of the Bible for our times and our personal living and are bringing that revelance to creative expression in a variety of forms. At present, there may be fewer much-discussed pulpit heroes than there were a generation or two ago, but there might be so many more preachers who are as competent as those heroes were that they get lost in the crowd. The sermons in this volume can help one to judge for himself or herself whether this is true.

In this collection the reader will find sermons commissioned for the most part from well-known preachers or from not-so-well-known preachers whose outstanding gifts and achievements have been recognized by persons who know a good sermon when they hear it. These contributions are diverse and clearly uphold the tradition of good preaching.

We also received many fine entries in the second annual Best Sermons competition, and we are grateful to those who were willing to take part in the project. The twenty-four winning sermons included in this volume were chosen by a panel of six authorities in the field of preaching. For the encouragement of those whose contributions did not get to the winner's circle, we may point out that at least one unsuccessful competitor in last year's judging was a winner this year.

You will note that the book is divided into six categories. These categories are not precise; some overlap. For example, an expository sermon might fulfill the requirements of any of the other categories. However, the categories follow a logical path of personal and corporate religious progression and development. Evangelism makes possible the church. The church so gathered has to be taught the Scriptures through exposition. The church instructed in the Scriptures must understand what they mean in terms of doctrine. Doctrine calls for specific ethical response. Living a moral, Christian life requires guidance and sympathetic pastoral reassurance. Finally, the inspiration and aspiration for it all are found through personal and public devotion and service.

We have been privileged to see that preachers are taking preaching seriously and are helping congregations of worshiping Christians all over the world in their spiritual journeys. To have a small part in recognizing and encouraging this is deeply satisfying to us.

We look forward to reading more of your best sermons.

JAMES W. COX
KENNETH M. COX

# I. EVANGELISTIC

# 1. This Is the Church's Hour

## Charles Colson

*Text:* Matthew 5:13–16 NIV

RECENTLY I came across a cartoon that captures what's happening, I think, in American life today. It's a Bloom County strip, which I'll describe for you. I don't always read the comic pages, nor do I always find truth there, but sometimes you find it there as well as on the front pages. In this particular strip, Opus the penguin is standing there and it says, "Last Tuesday Opus was suffering a general crisis of faith." Opus is standing and looking at the television set and saying, "I believe in our government." And the television announcer is saying, "Today the president admitted sending a personally inscribed copy of Leo Buscaglia's *Living, Loving and Hugging* to Qaddafi." Opus kind of shakes his head and walks into the next room and in the next box he says, "Well, I have faith in the forces of capitalism." Someone is reading a newspaper, which says, "Today on Wall Street, everybody but the wiener vendors were busted." Into the next frame comes Opus, who stands there and says, "Well, there's always religion." And someone is reading, saying, "Says Oral Roberts strangled Jimmy Swaggart and ran off with Tammy Bakker's drug counselor." Opus walks out on the front porch of his house, and looks

*Charles Colson* is a native of Boston, Massachusetts. Educated at Brown University and George Washington University, he was special counsel to President Richard M. Nixon from 1969 to 1973. He is president and founder of Prison Fellowship and author of *Born Again,* *Life Sentence,* and *Loving God.*

up with this marvelous plaintive expression and says, "What can a fellow believe in anymore? Are there no more bastions of purity?" Great question! Opus walks out on the front porch, looks around, and here comes a very pregnant woman and Opus runs over, leans up against the pregnant woman, and says, "Ah . . . motherhood!" And the woman looks down and says, "Surrogate."

What can a fellow believe in anymore? Are there no more bastions of purity? You look around us today and you will see, I think without precedent, at least in modern times, evidence all around of a breach of trust. I was a captain in the Marines and I remember the day that they pinned those bars on my shoulders and I put on the globe and anchor of the United States Marines, a proud military tradition, and I can remember how excited I was to be a Marine. And yet, last year a Marine embassy guard who traded secrets for sexual favors, dishonored his Corps and his country. Stockbrokers, fiduciaries—many of you in this room are probably in the investment business, and you know what I'm talking about. A fiduciary was once a very honored position in our society, and today fiduciaries take that inside information and trade it for millions of dollars of personal profit. Record numbers of indictments of people in high public offices, two presidential candidates who could not maintain their candidacy because of character flaws, one of whom could not restrain his glandular passions long enough to maintain a candidacy for the presidency. And perhaps the most egregious breach of trust of all is ministers of the gospel with a sacred, holy calling betraying that trust. Unthinkable!

Are these just isolated instances? Are these just a rash of bad events that have all taken place at one time? No. I think it's part of a general trend, a breakdown in our culture of values. People cannot live without values, society cannot exist without values. For twenty-three centuries in Western civilization, going back to when Cicero wrote, "Without God there could not be justice and concord in society." For twenty-three centuries the moral heritage of Western civilization is that we have always defined our responsibilities first by looking to God and then deciding how man related to his fellow man by first considering our relationship with God. And what is unique about the decades in which we live—and make no mistake about it, these are unique times in which we live—is that we have decided for the first time in Western civilization that we can live our lives without a transcendent standard, without a reference to God. We're seeing fulfilled in our times, I believe, the prophecy of a philosopher, a German, who was syphilitic and eventually insane but one of the brilliant minds of modern times, Friedrich Nietzsche. More than a hundred years ago, Nietzsche peered into the twentieth century, and he said, "The twentieth century will be a time in which"—he coined the phrase—"God is dead." Not that there wouldn't be a God; Nietzsche was too smart for that. Nietzsche could look up and see the stars and the planets and the galaxies all in perfect harmony and order and he knew that life was no accident; he knew that there was a force beyond man. What Nietzsche said is that man, because of his own desire for power, his own will, will kill God. He will kill him by living his life as if God does not exist. If there ever was a prophecy for the latter part of the twentieth century, it was that which Nietzsche rendered, that man would kill God.

What happens when there is no God is that men and women do one of two things. Blaise Pascal, a great philosopher and theologian of three centuries ago, once said that when man is separated from God, he either seeks to be God himself—and that's what's happening in a lot of the world—or he seeks the gratification of his senses—and that's exactly what's happening in our society today. There was a study recently by the secular sociologist Robert Bellah, entitled *Habits of the Heart*, in which he tried to figure out what's happening in American life. He surveyed hundreds and hundreds of people in depth, and decided that there were two overriding life goals that Americans have. One is personal success; and the other, vivid personal feelings. And Bellah asked people what they expected to get out of the institutions of life. He asked them what they expected to get out of marriage, and people answered, personal development. No wonder marriages are in trouble. He asked them what they expected to get out of work, and they said, personal advancement. He asked them what they expected to get out of church, and they said, personal fulfillment. Find that for me in the Bible. Find where God says that if you come to church you're going to get personal fulfillment. Precisely the opposite. You're going to pour yourself out as a living witness of God's work among men and women. Everything today is so self-centered.

I had eleven years' experience in government, four years in the office next to the president of the United States, and I have seen the world really through two lifetimes—one rising in secular power, ending up in one of the most powerful positions in the world, and then in the last several years in Christian service. If I were to look over the times in which we live and ask, What is the greatest crisis we face today? it would not be the threat of nuclear annihilation or ecological disaster. It would not be the collapse of the stock market. It would not be the trade deficit or the budget deficit. If I would pick the greatest crisis that we face today, it would be a crisis of character.

The question we have to ask ourselves is, What values shall we live by? The question that was put to the people of Israel was, How then shall we live? By what standards shall we live? Interestingly enough, even the secular world recognizes the crisis that we face. Jesse Jackson in his presidential campaign constantly talked about education and drugs, and less about institutional issues and moral issues, which is one of the reasons that people listened to him. Bill Bennett, the recent secretary of education, talked about the breakdown of values in our school system. Allan Bloom wrote an extraordinary book from a secular perspective entitled *The Closing of the American Mind.* What he says in the first paragraph is that there is one thing of which a professor at a university in America today can be absolutely certain, that every student who arrives on campus as a freshman believes that values are relative and there is no absolute truth.

What can a fellow believe in anymore? *Time* magazine described it in an insightful cover story on the moral malaise of our time, about the fact that we have no values upon which we can agree. A friend of mine who was in government and had recently retired endowed a chair at the Harvard Business School for thirty million dollars to teach ethics, because he was so alarmed at the breakdown of ethical standards in American life. So at Harvard Business School today they are trying to decide how to teach ethics. But they can't make up their minds on how to do it. They can't decide what values undergird ethics in a society that has eliminated God from our deliberations. We live as if he does not exist. We will kill God, Nietzsche said, because we will live. We will raise our families. We will go to work. We will construct our public institutions as if there is no God while we'll come in on Sunday mornings and pay lip service to the fact that there is a God.

Well, my friends, this crisis in our culture today ought to be the greatest opportunity for the church of Jesus Christ. If you stop and think about it, there really are only two places in which values are formed in a society, fundamentally. One is the family. Sociologists tell us today that the causes of crime—and I know this from working in the prisons—trace back to the character development and the moral development of young people from one to six years old. The job of the family! And one of the most appalling statistics and reflections upon American culture today is that only one out of five families in America today is what we call a traditional family, that is, the mother taking care of the children, the father working, and a two-parent family. One in five! The minority. There's one place where the church has a job to do, which is to model for this culture what a Christian family is. What a godly family is. What it means to train our young people in the ways of the Lord—early.

The second institution that affects moral values in society is the church. Business can't do it. Labor unions can't do it. The military can't do it. Our schools aren't doing it today.

Where else is it going to come from? It is the church of Jesus Christ that must model the values of the kingdom of God for a sick and decaying world. That's our opportunity. As we come here on Sunday mornings to worship and to love the Lord and to take our communion, let us never forget that the whole purpose of being here is that we are to be equipped to be the people of God, to go out these doors and to live as the salt and the light and to make a difference in the world, that the world might see that there is a better way, that the world might see that there is hope. The world is crying out, like Opus the penguin, What can a fellow believe in anymore? This is the church's hour.

What must we do? I'd like to leave you with six points on what I think the responsibility of the church is today in modern American culture. The first is to get serious in your own life with God. And when we close this morning I'm going to lead you in a prayer, and if for some reason you never have really made a commitment to Christ, don't go out of this church today without doing something. Maybe some of you came here this morning because you heard I was going to be here and you wanted to hear what kind of a strange duck is that fellow who was in the White House and now preaching, so you came out of curiosity, or maybe somebody dragged you here this morning, or maybe you've been sitting in a pew for years and years and never really made that decision, that surrender, that totality of commitment that is what it means to be Christian. Sitting in church will not do it. Sitting in a church won't make you a Christian any more than sitting in the garage will make you an automobile.

So many people in America—it's tragic—so many people in America say they are Christian. George Gallup says that 81 percent of the American people will say that they are Christian. Oh, they grow up in America, and it's a Christian country, not Jewish; they go to church twice a year, so they must be Christian. I was like that. But that's not what's involved. What's involved is a recognition that Jesus Christ died on the cross for your sins and your forgiveness, and that you come to Him and ask forgiveness of those sins and you surrender your life to Him and commit yourself to live under his lordship and make a difference in the world. Fifteen years ago, in the driveway of a friend's home, in the midst of Watergate, toughest of the Nixon tough guys, I couldn't drive my automobile out of my friend's driveway because I was crying too hard, calling out to God. I wanted to know him. All I knew was that I was blind, and suddenly I could see. And the whole world laughed and scoffed, and I don't blame them. I kept the cartoonists of America clothed and fed for at least one full month. Cartoons were all the same: Chuck Colson in a monk's habit kneeling in front of the White House with a big sign that said, "Repent," and Nixon looking out saying, "Help, call Billy Graham, Colson's got religion." And all the incredulous stories of the White House tough guy turning to God. But I can stand here today, fifteen years later, and tell you that I am more certain today of the reality of Jesus Christ than I am of my own life. My faith has deepened with every passing day. I wouldn't trade the worst day of the last fifteen years—and that includes seven months in prison, and the time in serious surgery for cancer a year ago when I wondered if my life was slipping away—I wouldn't trade the worst day of the last fifteen years for the best day of the forty years that went before it. Don't miss that. Get serious with God. If you don't know him and the Holy Spirit is touching you this morning, surrender. We'll be singing a hymn, "I Surrender All," and that's exactly what the Christian life means.

Second, to be Christian and to make a difference in today's world means that we've got to be a repentant people. Preachers don't like to preach about repentance because people like to be told that everything is fine in your life and all you have to do is come in here and we'll make you feel good and then you can go out and be inspirationally lifted for the rest of the week. Nonsense! Before the good news of the redemption from sin has to be the bad news of the conviction of sin. Before that night in my friend's driveway, I always had thought I was a pretty good guy. I had done as well as anybody else in life and I hadn't done things other people hadn't done or any worse. In politics I hadn't done anything that Democrats hadn't done before me. I figured that God, like any good college professor, grades on a curve and on a curve I'd be fine. But he doesn't grade on a curve. Look into your own heart and you'll see that. There was terrible evil in my life, much worse than the stuff that got into the newspapers. To become a Christian means that you see your own sin. I think it was Bishop Fulton Sheen who said that the doctrine of original sin is the only philosophy empirically validated over two thousand years of human history. You don't have to look very far—just look around in the world today. Understand how we need to be conscious of our sin. What the word repentance, *metanoia*, means in the Greek is a change of mind. It means you turn from your ways to God's ways. I think it was no accident that the gist of the ninety-five theses of Martin Luther, nailed on the door at Wittenberg, was that when God calls, he calls a man to come and live a repentant life. Sometimes, particularly with our big television ministries and our celebrity-oriented ministries, we put ourselves up on pedestals and sometimes we Christians get really smug and say, We're saved and we don't care if the rest of the world is going down and crashing around us . . . we're saved. No, that's arrogant and hubristic. The attitude of the Christian is a repentant attitude, with sorrow over our sins and wanting to change and be different.

Third, it is vital that we Christians take our stand at the only place we can take it—on the Holy Word of God. I know this is a controversial area, but I have to say that after fifteen years of studying and reading everything I could get my hands on I have come to the conclusion that the Bible is precisely what it says it is—the Word of God—with authority over our lives, authored by him and without error: inerrant. That's what it is. I didn't start out believing that; I started out as a lawyer reading this book—and I know a lawyer and a Christian is an oxymoron—from cover to cover, and I thought to myself, I've really got to see; could this possibly be what it says it is? It says it's the Word of God, but it's a whole lot of old legends handed down from ancient times and it can't really be true. I have to confess to you that I read it through three times looking for the one verse of scripture I've known all my life by heart, the only one I knew by heart: "God helps those who help themselves." I went through the Bible three times looking for that, but couldn't find it. In fact, I discovered quite the reverse. Is this not what it means to know me? God said. He cared for the poor, the oppressed, and the hurting. But as I read this book through cover to cover I came to the most amazing conclusion. This book was written over hundreds of years, by many different authors, yet with incredible integrity, with prophecies that were fulfilled in the most amazing ways. As you begin to discover the archeological evidence that has been accumulated over the years, you begin to see that everything that has been printed in this book is exactly borne out by discoveries. The most recent text we have of anything Aristotle wrote was a thousand years after he was dead, yet no one would question that Aristotle said the things he said. We have seventy manuscripts now, pieces of manuscripts from the first century in England that actually can be dated back, studied in all the great classics courses in college, and yet scholars still say, Could this really be what Jesus said? Preposterous! There's an eminent scholar today by the name of Paul Johnson, probably the greatest living historian in modern times on the history of Christianity. He started out as sort of a liberal in his view but has become very conservative and very open about it. He gave a speech recently in which he cited all of the historical evidence for the Bible being exactly what it is and represents itself to be, and he said that it is no longer the men of faith but the skeptics who have reason to fear the course of scientific discovery. The evidence of this book is that Jesus was raised from the dead, and how do we know Jesus was raised from the dead? We have the eyewitness accounts of the eleven apostles who were with him and who for forty years never denied that they had seen Jesus raised from the dead. They were beaten, persecuted, whipped, thrown in prison. Let me tell you something, this book is exactly what it says it is, and my own experiences in Watergate more than anything else convinced me of that. I was in the middle of Watergate and the first time that President Nixon knew completely what was going on was March 21, 1973, when John Dean walked in and said, "There's a cancer growing on your presidency," and laid it all out for him. And it was not even two weeks later that John Dean went to the prosecutors, not to save the Constitution, he wrote in his memoirs, but to save his own skin, turning state's evidence against the president to try to keep from being prosecuted himself. The moment he did that everybody else ran to save themselves. The twelve most powerful men in the world couldn't maintain a lie for more than two weeks. The evidence for the resurrection of Jesus depends upon eleven apostles who were powerless, who had nothing, who in forty years never once denied him. Humanly impossible. The apostle Peter would have been just like John Dean. He would have turned state's evidence. He'd already done it three times. But they had seen Christ raised from the dead, and because he was raised from the dead he has the authority, as God's witness to man, to say, Thy word is truth, and we Christians had better take our stand on the scripture. And we had better take our stand on the historic orthodox confession of the Christian faith. One of the appalling things today is the cheap grace that's preached in so many churches. Praise the Lord that the gospel is preached faithfully here in this pulpit. But that isn't so everywhere. We see things like the PTL collapse, and people say, Isn't that awful, that greed and sexual lust and all those things? No—the real root problem was the lack of orthodoxy; they simply were preaching that if you came to God he'd give you anything you want. And so they began to believe that, to live that way. That's why Jim Bakker's PTL collapsed. Now take your stand on the historic confession of truth, of the Christian faith.

Fourth, it's absolutely vital that we think as Christians. As you think will determine the way you act. Too many people think that being Christian means that they come in on a Sunday morning, listen to the message and take part in the church service, but that's not true. To be a Christian means that at all times you look at the world through God's eyes and not through your own and begin to think in a Christian manner and apply Christian truth in every walk of life. It's amazing what happens when you do this. I'm often invited to address state legislatures and to meet with public officials because of our work in the prisons and prison fellowship, and last year I was invited to address the Texas legislature. It was an interesting experience, because they passed a resolution inviting me to come and speak to the legislature for twenty minutes on prison reform. And when I walked into the assembly chambers, it was just bedlam. Most state legislatures are chaotic, with some poor fellow standing up there with a microphone trying to talk, everybody running around to their chairs and talking in their little groups, the humdrum of activity all over the floor of the assembly. Of course the galleries are full with kids looking down and getting their civics lesson. Nobody on the floor was paying any attention and when I walked in the speaker said to me, "Mr. Colson, I don't know what I'm going to do." He said, "I guess I'll just bang the gavel and it's up to you to try to get their attention. George Bush was here two weeks ago to address the legislature and he never did get their attention, so don't get discouraged if they don't listen." I said, Okay. I figured I had spoken in hundreds of prisons, and in football and baseball locker rooms, so I could take on the Texas legislature, I guess. So he banged the gavel on the table and I started and it was interesting how about a couple of minutes into my speech little groups came and sat down here and there, and eventually the whole room assembled and everybody in the legislature was sitting in rapt attention. It wasn't my oratorical skills; it was the fact that politicians have a growing interest in prison. Sometimes personal. My favorite cartoon is one of two convicts sitting in a cell with striped suits, and one looks at the other and says, "The food was better here when you were governor." The Texas legislature didn't laugh at that one.

As I was talking that morning it gave me a wonderful opportunity to share my own Christian witness, to tell what

Christ had done in my life. I also had to explain why I was there. I talked about the need for a moral law beyond the law of man to govern our relations, and then I ended up talking about the need for restitution. Texas had a 10,000-bed shortage of space in its prisons and a five billion dollar deficit. And half the prisoners were there for nonviolent offenses. I think we ought to take those nonviolent, nondangerous people out of prison, where they are each costing the taxpayers fifteen thousand dollars a year, and put them out on the streets, working to pay back their victims. After my address to the legislature I went to a little room and maybe fifteen or twenty of the members of the legislature came to me and said, "Hey, Mr. Colson, that's a great idea, that restitution. Why hasn't someone tried that before?" I said, "Do you have a Bible at home?" And they said, "Yeah, I got a Bible." I said, "Well, you go home and dust it off and turn it to Exodus 21:22 and you'll see exactly what God told Moses to do on Mt. Sinai, exactly what Jesus did with Zacchaeus." That's the biblical answer. If we begin to think Christianly, we will begin to bring Christian truth to bear in public debate, and that doesn't mean just in the legislature, that means in your businesses, that means in your homes, that means in your country clubs, to bring Christian truth by taking biblical truth. Your job here is to guard this church as purveyors of truth in a society that has given up on truth.

The fifth point is that it is crucial that we learn that the heart of Christian life is obedience. I went into a prison in Peru a few years ago, the bloodiest prison in the world, with 7,000 inmates, nine murdered the week before I went there. The army had sealed off the prison. I went into this incredible place where my feet were just sliding on the open sewage. I saw the slime coming out of the cells and the dead eyes of the men. I'd walk those cell blocks and every now and then a man would grab me and he'd haul me into his cell and he'd point up at the wall. There would be a certificate saying that he had graduated from a prison fellowship or prison seminar, and he'd point to it and say, "Me, me." He would be so full of joy and, though he didn't speak any English and I didn't speak any Spanish, I'd grab that brother and just hug him. Then we met with about a hundred men who had come to Christ in the very pit of hell.

Never when I go into those places—and I have been in hundreds and hundreds around the world—never do I fail to think of the great paradox in my life. God has used my life to touch the lives of who knows how many people locked away in prison—to give them new life, to give them hope. But what is it God has chosen to use in my life? The fact that I won academic awards and scholarships to Ivy League universities and graduated with a doctorate in law, served as a captain in the Marines, and wrote laws in the United States Senate and wrote laws in the White House? All of these great things are admired, but no. No—what God has chosen to use out of my life is the fact that I was a convict who went to prison. My one great failure. The only thing in which I could not rejoice in my own life. The time that I lost. God uses that time. What's the lesson? The lesson is that it's not as important what we do in life as what God chooses to do through us. What he wants from us is our obedience. Obey him. "If you love me you will keep my commandments." That's the heart of the Christian life.

Finally, my friends, be holy. When I say holy, I'm not talking about smoking and drinking and dancing and all the legalisms of the church. Those things can be important for our witness. But I'm talking about having a heartbeat for God. Caring about the things of God. Caring about justice and righteousness. Doing the good works that God calls us to do, not because they are good works but because they are manifestations of our faith that the world might see the invisible kingdom of God made visible in our midst. Across America last year at Christmas 57,000 kids had daddies in prison, with mommies on welfare, and those kids wouldn't have had a Christmas, but Christian people went out and bought them Christmas presents and delivered them to their homes and witnessed to them, and all over this country today there are families in church who wouldn't have been there otherwise. That's what Jesus said: Be the salt of the earth. Be the light that goes into the darkness. In the Hebrew culture meat would spoil when left out in the sun, so the Jews rubbed salt into the meat, not for flavor, but as a preservative. Christians need to be the salt that is rubbed into our society. When you rub in the salt it becomes invisible, and when you don't rub in enough salt the meat spoils. Our whole job is to be the salt, to go from this place and to make a holy witness, caring about the things of God and doing what God calls us to do. You *can* make a difference. We were in Africa a couple of years ago and we met a professor of etymology, named Pascal, from the University of Madagascar. There was a Marxist coup and he was thrown in prison. Pascal told us that in prison he had been a nominal professing Christian in a largely Moslem country, but as an academician he had rejected God. In prison Jesus came to him. In his cell he began to preach the gospel to the prisoners and began to build a large Christian fellowship. When he was released he started a little business, but he went back to that prison week after week, preaching the gospel. One day he was there visiting the infirmary and he saw fifty or sixty bodies lying on the porch. Dead bodies. He said to the nurse, "That's terrible! Is there a plague?" "Oh no," she said, "That's the number of people who die here every week from malnutrition." She said that the prison had rations for just 2,500 inmates, but the prison housed 5,000. Sixty, seventy, even sometimes a hundred died every week. There was no relief organization, there were no big Christian operations, no big churches, so Pascal went home that night, he and his wife prayed, and they did the only thing they could do—they started cooking in their own kitchen. Today that little man goes into the prison preaching the gospel week after week bringing food to keep 700 inmates alive. I went up to him and I said, "Pascal, is there anything we can do to help you?" (That's a cardinal sin for anybody in the first world visiting a third-world prison—you know you'd better get out your checkbook.) Pascal looked up at me with the most radiant expression and said, "No, no, our God is sufficient for all." That's the kind of people we need to be, who do the gospel and make a difference. Yes, 700 people are alive in a prison today in Madagascar, an island off the coast of East Africa, because one man is feeding them. One by one—that's the way in which we give a witness to the world that there is something we can believe in.

What can a fellow believe in anymore? The good news that Jesus came and died on that cross for your sins. And if you don't know him, this morning as I leave you just pray a simple prayer with me. An easy prayer, but don't pray it lightly; pray it only if you mean it. Give your life to Christ, surrender your life to Christ. The rest of you who have made that decision and who have professed that kind of commitment, pray that God will renew your hearts this morning to be a holy and righteous people. To be the salt and the light and to go into this world and make a difference, so that the world can see that there is hope and that there's something that a fellow can believe in.

For those of you who do not know Christ or maybe you're in doubt, pray a simple prayer. When I did it fifteen years ago it was just calling out saying, God come into my heart. I want to know you. Pray with me now:

Father God, we thank you for your son Jesus, who died on the cross, in my place. Forgive me my sons. Jesus, come into my life, make me the person you want me to be. Lord God, let your spirit descend on this place. I sense a holy hush, a holy sign as we reflect in our own hearts whether we are truly a repentant people prepared to think Christianly and to be obedient and to live for you as a shining light. Father, give us that courage to be truly Christian, to offer hope to a world that is crying out for help. Make us your people. We surrender to you. We pray in the mighty and powerful name of the one you sent to die on the cross in your place, our Lord and Savior, Jesus Christ. Amen.

## 2. Who Is on Trial Here?

*Thomas G. Long*

John 19:12–16

IN A SERMON not long ago, a minister friend of mine told his congregation the story of an unusual event that happened in a Broadway theater. It seems that it was Friday night, and the theater was packed for a performance of Tennessee Williams's *The Night of the Iguana,* starring the notable actress Dorothy McGuire. Just before the curtain was about to rise, a woman in the audience—an overweight, middle-aged woman in a blue print dress—startled the audience by suddenly shouting, "Start the show! Start the show! I want to see Dorothy McGuire! I love Dorothy McGuire!" The people sitting next to her quickly moved out of their seats, not wanting to be associated with this madwoman. Ushers and the house manager descended to try and reason with the woman. Then they reached out for her, but she pulled back and continued to shout, "I want to see Dorothy McGuire! Start the show!"

After a moment of shocked silence, the people in the audience decided they had a maniac in their midst and began to get

*Thomas G. Long* was educated at Erskine College, Erskine Theological Seminary, and Princeton Theological Seminary, where he received his doctorate. Dr. Long has been a pastor and currently teaches preaching and worship at Princeton Theological Seminary. He is co-editor of *Journal for Preachers* and general preaching editor of *Homiletic.* He is author of *Shepherds and Bathrobes, The Senses of Preaching,* and *Preaching and the Literary Forms of the Bible.*

ugly, booing the woman and laughing derisively. Somebody shouted, "Listen you old bag, get out!" "Throw her out. Start the show!" somebody else yelled. The woman turned to the shouters, "All I want to see is Dorothy McGuire," she said, "and then I will leave." More laughing and booing—things were edging toward chaos.

And then . . . then, from behind the curtains, Miss McGuire herself appeared. She crossed the stage over to the place where the woman was sitting and, with remarkable poise, and grace, and kindness, extended her hand toward her. Quietly, willingly, the woman took her hand, and Miss McGuire led her gently toward the exit. As they reached the edge of the auditorium, Miss McGuire paused, turned toward the audience, and said, "I'd like to introduce you to another fellow human being."

The audience was stilled, their shouts and taunts silenced by Miss McGuire's compassion and by the recognition of what they had just done. They had put a fellow human being on trial, convicted her, and sentenced her to abuse. But now they knew that they were really the ones who had been on trial, and their silent shame was a sign of their guilt.[1]

If there is one question that reverberates throughout John's story of the trial of Jesus, it is the question: Who is really on trail here? A court reporter would quickly say that it was Jesus, of course, who was on trial. He was the one being held by the police. He was the one who had to answer to the charges. He was the one accused and placed on the stand and interrogated. Jesus was the one on trial. Nothing could be plainer than that.

But listen to the way John tells the story, the way he uses irony, the way he depicts the ambiguities in the accusers of Jesus, the way he unfolds the court record, keeps switching our perspective in the courtroom until we are no longer sure who is actually on trial. The prosecutor's table begins to look more and more like it is really the prisoner's dock, and the accused Jesus appears less and less like the defendant and more and more like the true judge.

For example, listen to the exchange between Jesus and Caiaphas, the religious district attorney. I picture Caiaphas leaning back on two legs of his chair. You know when people are sure of themselves, relaxed, comfortable . . . they sometimes lean back in their chairs. I can picture calm Caiaphas doing that, crossing his arms, smiling confidently, and asking, "So, Jesus tell us about your teaching." In other words, here is a piece of rope long enough to hang you. Wrap it around your own neck. Tell us about the heresies you proclaimed. Tell us about the laws you undermined. Tell us about the treason you breathed. Just a simple, little open-ended question. "Tell us about your teaching," he said, leaning back in his chair.

"Everything I said," replied Jesus, "I said out in the open. I taught in the synagogue. I taught in the Temple. Everybody heard what I said. My motivations were clear, but what about yours? Why do you ask me this question?" No doubt Caiaphas's chair thudded back to four legs. Who is on trial here?

Then they transferred the trial to the federal court, and there is confused and weary old Pilate, leafing through Jesus' folder, looking for the list of charges. He was probably muttering to himself that sometimes he would rather be a file clerk in Rome than deal one more day with these crazy Jews. "I apply for Iconium and what do they give me? Jerusalem." Finally he finds the paragraph he is looking for. "Are *you* the King of the Jews?"

"Is this your question," said Jesus, "or did someone else put you up to it? Is this someone else's idea, or do *you* want to know?"

"Do *I* want to know? Look at me. Do I look Jewish to you? Do *I* want to know? . . . Do I *want* to know?" Who is on trial here?

Perhaps you know the legend which circulates in the art world about the inexpensive painting purchased in a second-hand shop. Cheap art, but it would at least add a little color to a drab wall. The new owner, before hanging it on the wall, decides to clean the painting, so out come the cotton balls and the solvent. But as the owner begins to clean, the surface paint itself dissolves, and underneath there is another painting. A professional art restorer is brought in, and as the surface paint is washed away there is gradually revealed the work of a master. So it is with the Gospel of John. It is impossible to read this story carefully without discovering that beneath the cheap theatrics and cosmetics of Jesus' trial there appears another picture. In this picture, it is not Jesus on trial, but Caiaphas. It is not Jesus on trial, but Pilate. It is not Jesus on trial, but the world . . . all of us. Like the audience in the Broadway theater that night, we discover that we are, all of us, on trial.

Ever seen one of those game shows on television? The contestant is standing there trembling with excitement. He has just won the luggage and a trip to Hawaii, and now the emcee wants to know if he will risk it all for the sailboat and the convertible. His brow wrinkles with uncertainty, and the audience begins to cheer, "Go for it! Go for it!" And we're with them. A new car, a sailboat. Go for it! Go for it!

Jesus said, "My kingdom is not of this world. Do not labor for the food which perishes, but for the food which endures to eternal life."

"Shall I crucify your King?" asks the emcee.

"We have no King but Caesar," we say, eyeing the sailboat. "Go for it!"

When they found Mary Ann Cardell she had been dead for several hours. Mary Ann was an elderly woman who lived alone in an Atlanta welfare hotel, and her only two comforts in life were a bottle and a pen. With the bottle she eased her pain; with the pen she wrote about her thoughts and feelings. Eventually the bottle became more demanding than the rent, and one day she was evicted from her room. She tried to find a place to spend the night, but there was alcohol on her breath, and no one would take her in. When they found her, her body was in a litter-filled field of weeds, cold and blue, and there was a note beside her. Mary Ann had written, "I have nowhere to go, and there is no one to understand. God is not dead. He is only sleeping, but sleeping very soundly."[2]

Jesus said, "This I command you, to love one another."

"Shall I crucify your King?" we are asked again.

"We have no King but Caesar," we reply, and all of the Mary Ann Cardells are left once more to believe that God sleeps through their cold nights.

When we stand at the foot of the cross, we look at the condemned man, and then we look inside ourselves, and we know who is truly worthy of being condemned. We hear his voice saying, "Let not your hearts be troubled. You believe in God, believe also in me." But our troubled hearts let us know who is really on trial here.

As the old hymn has it:

> Who was the guilty?
> Who brought this upon Thee?
> Alas, my treason, Jesus, hath undone Thee!
> 'Twas I, Lord Jesus, I it was denied Thee:
> I crucified Thee.

So, there we stand in the courtroom, and the verdict rings out, "Guilty!" There is no escaping this judgment, and we have now only one hope. It is this: The Jesus whom we crucified is now the judge of all time, and our only hope is in the mercy of this judge. "Who is to condemn?" asks Paul. "It is Christ Jesus, who died, yes, who was raised from the dead, who is at the right hand of God, who indeed intercedes for us . . . " (Rom. 8:33). As the old hymn continues:

> Therefore, kind Jesus, since I cannot pay Thee,
> I do adore Thee, and will ever pray Thee,
> Think on Thy pity and Thy love unswerving,
> Not my deserving.

NOTES

1. From a sermon by the Rev. Patrick Willson, Shades Valley Presbyterian Church, Birmingham, Alabama.

2. As recorded by Ed Loring in *Hospitality 3*, no. 5:3, the newsletter of the Open Door Community, Atlanta, Georgia.

# 3.  All of Us
## *Willard Scott*

THERE ARE A couple of things that I want to share with you this morning, two things in my life that have meant a lot to me.

Of course I love my job. I don't think there is anything that has any more impact on your life and, really, on the lives of others as when you enjoy what you do for a living, because you spend so much time at it.

But there are two *other* things, as I say, and one is that I always wanted to preach. I majored in religion in college. That comes as a great shock to a lot of people, and a lot of people in the religious order are very grateful that I chose to be a weather person instead of a preacher. But as I got a little older in life I made a deal with myself and the Lord that I would start going around and doing this sort of thing for free. After all, I got mine.

My grandfather had a dairy farm up in Maryland and as kids, four of us slept in one of those old horsehair beds, with chicken down, duck down, with chicken feathers for pillows,

*Willard Scott* was born in Alexandria, Virginia, and has a degree in philosophy and religion from American University. Since 1980 he has been the weatherman for NBC's "Today" program, and in 1985 he received an award from President Reagan for public service. He has written several books, including *The Joy of Living* and *America is My Neighborhood.* "All of Us" was preached at Mr. Scott's home church, the First Baptist Church, Alexandria, Virginia, on the occasion of the church's 185th anniversary.

and I slept better there than I've ever slept in my life. In the best hotels in the world I've never slept any better than I did up in Freeland, Maryland, on that old horsehair mattress. But at about 4 A.M., I used to hear my grandfather rummage around and get into his overalls and go out to milk his forty head of cattle, and I thought, my Lord, what kind of crazy person would do this for a living at this hour of the day? And here I am now, getting up at four o'clock every morning, slipping into my khakis to go out and milk the country. I figure I've made enough at that so I can preach for free.

The only other thing I do for free is play Santa Claus. I've played Santa Claus every year since I was fifteen, and I've had some of the greatest experiences in my life playing Santa Claus, especially for the National Park Service, where I play Santa Claus every year when they light the national Christmas tree.

Anyway, I truly love my job and I like working with the people I work with and I enjoy what I do for a living, but I also enjoy coming home. I have said that New York never looks better than it does from an Eastern shuttle at 20,000 feet as you are headed toward Virginia. I've come home to Virginia almost every weekend since I've been up here, which is nine years. And they said it wouldn't last, which is a miracle story in itself.

By all rights, I shouldn't have made it. That's really what I'm here for this morning—to tell you that, to proselytize. I love that word, "proselytize." I used it in a commercial one time for a Mormon who was running for Congress. He'd been in Congress for, Lord knows, twenty years, and when I was reading the commercial—a half-hour political commercial—I hit the word "proselyte." I'm a Baptist, and I had never seen the word before. Sounds a little risqué to me, to be honest with you. I asked the producer, "What does this mean?" He said, "Well, Mormons proselytize, they give two years of their life and they go out, you know, to preach the gospel, and to preach their particular type of religion." So I read the commercial and unfortunately, the guy lost the election, first time in twenty years, and he died six months later. So I guess, if you're in politics, that's your cue. Don't bother to use me as one of your political spokesmen. Let me do my thing and you do yours.

But I've always wanted to get up and tell people that I believe that I was put on the "Today Show" for a purpose. I think the good Lord placed me there, because there are so many things that shouldn't have worked that did. And nothing that I've ever done in connection with that program— whether to stay on the show, or to get around and do the things that I've been able to do, to appear at various functions and affairs and to represent what I believe in around this country—none of those things could have been done without some superhuman power. And that supernatural, superhuman power is the love of Christ that put me there. I am convinced of that, with all my heart and soul.

It is so interesting to go places and be a part of the scene, so to speak. I remember specifically out in California, little Willie Scott was at a press conference. "Entertainment Tonight" was there, we had *People* magazine, and we had the press. It was for "Valerie's Family," a nice little family sitcom, and I was there being presented as a new member of the cast for this show. And here's little Willie Scott, from Alexandria, Virginia, at the in place to be in Hollywood. I couldn't believe it. Here I am at this press conference and one of these guys comes up to me who had bleached his hair. I knew he was over fifty. He had the open shirt and the gold chains, but he hadn't tinted his chest hair. It was a dead giveaway to the fact that he was an old dog, you know, 'cause you can always tell old dogs by looking at their muscle and their teeth. He was the quintessential showbiz Hollywood-Sweetheart-Baby California type, you know, that you associate with my business. And he came up to me with his gold chains, his open shirt, and his pink trousers and he said, "Willard Scott, you're the only Gentile I trust on television." Which I know is a great line anyway. And I said, "What is that?" He said, "Well, you're real, and you seem to enjoy what you do, and you have a good time doing it, and you don't seem to let things bother you, and you always are talking about nice things." He said, "What makes you so happy? Why are you happy?" Almost like it bothers him. This has happened so many times. Everything that happened after that was so predictable. And I said, "Well, you're not going to believe what makes me happy." He said, "Tell me. Try me. What is it?" And I said, "Because I'm saved. I love the Lord Jesus Christ. I believe that I will find home, a home in Heaven. I believe in the redemption of forgiveness of sins and the resurrection of the body, and I believe I will go home, and I believe in Jesus Christ." Happens every time. "Oh, yeah. Okay baby. Crazy."

He didn't really want to hear that for an answer, did he? I mean, we are cuckoo a little bit, we're fanatics. Man, we're, you know, fundamentalists. Of course, we're not all as fundamental maybe as some others. But basically it's very simple, it's fundamental to say that you love Jesus Christ. And it's fundamental to say He loves you. And it's fundamental to say that you are happy because of that. What else can you say? You can't back off and apologize for it. But people want to hear anything else but that.

What I find, though, is people who are basically so darn good and so full of love, who are really waiting for that little bit of love that comes sometimes in just the least thing that you say. How do I know what that man thought when he left me? How do I know to this day where he is? He could still be in his hot tub with his German shepherd. I don't know what he is doing today, but how do you know that what I said hasn't made a difference? Because I believe with all my heart and soul that "I need Thee every hour, every hour I need Thee." We do definitely, there's no question about it. We need religion. We need Almighty God. We need Jesus Christ as our personal savior.

But did you ever think, brothers and sisters, that He needs us? I think when He sat down and figured the whole thing out, after He had invented the world and gotten us all organized, He probably thought He'd have been better off if He'd have given his divine love to dogs. Because they're infinitely more faithful and obedient and they require a lot less attention and they are so forgiving and kind. If you ever stop and think about it, dogs really are what the message is all about. And if people could be more like dogs, I think we'd be just a little better off. And so would He; He'd be a little bit happier. The truth is that He needs us. He needed Joan of Arc. He needed the apostles. He needed my old friend Johnny Appleseed, John Chapman. I love Johnny Appleseed with all my heart and soul. One of the great American heroes who was a little bit, they thought in writing about him, a little bit strange. He wore a pot on his head and he walked all over Ohio and Indiana and he planted apple trees. That was his thing. One of the great lines is about Johnny Appleseed just before his death. He heard God say to him, "You know, Johnny, we are a little short on apple trees up here. And we need you to come home." Basically, that's what it's all about, the fact that we are so important to the scheme and plan of what Jesus Christ had in mind for the world. We are the keys, the instruments to salvation.

Ronnie Reagan, God bless him. For better or for worse, whatever went on over there at the summit in Moscow, we all want to think that good things will come of it. Maybe out of necessity, after fifty or sixty years with their Marxist philosophy and their economic policies, everyone will realize it's been a disaster. The Russians have done some good things, they've done some beautiful things, and there are a lot of things they can build on. But one thing Karl Marx knew was that there was a problem in religion. I'm not sure he knew where the problem was. I'm not sure whether he really thought religion was just something that was going to soak up people's emotions or whether he was afraid of it. I'm not really sure. But the fact is, the people over there are longing to be free, not just economically and socially, but to be free religiously. Good old Ronnie Reagan, our beloved Irish president, I don't care what your political affiliation, I like the man. I love the man, and I love Nancy. (I called her before I came over here today, and she said Leo was in Aries, and it was a good morning for me to preach!) But almost 90 percent of every film clip or videotape bite that you saw from the summit was Reagan going into a church, Reagan meeting with dissidents who wanted one thing only—to be free religiously. That will kindle a flame. It's already in the process of happening over there right now. There are no two ways about it, in my mind. But the point is that Jesus Christ used Ronald Reagan, the president of the United States, to go over and help promote belief in God and the practice and freedom of religion.

One of my favorite pulpit stories demonstrates this in a way. Maybe you've used it, or maybe you've heard it, but I love it. It was used in an Episcopal church at home. The rector told the story one Sunday about this pious preacher. (He wasn't a Baptist, he couldn't have been a Baptist preacher since he simply was a little bit pious.) Anyway, there was an old man in town that this preacher tried to get to join the church for years. And on his way home from one Sunday service this preacher passed the old man, who had a marvelous garden. The garden was sensational. Every row was straight, and there wasn't a weed in it. It was absolutely perfectly cared for and nurtured and had been fertilized and watered and everything was right. This same spot one year before had been a dumping place for old refrigerators and trash, and brambles and honeysuckles had just engulfed this mess. But now it was a magnificent garden and the preacher figured he'd get a shot in here, pour a little salvation and bring the man home to glory. He said to him, "My goodness, John, my goodness, you and the Lord have made such a beautiful spot out of this place that was once a disaster." And old John, with a little tobacco juice trickling down his cheek, said, "Lord, you should have seen this place when the man upstairs had it by himself." The fact is, it proves again that the combination is potent. What we do and how we work and how we affiliate ourselves in sometimes the seemingly simplest and smallest ways can make a statement, be a witness.

I recall a couple of other stories as well. One is a beautiful story to me personally, because it happened to me twenty years ago though I really hardly remember the incident. In a taxi the other day in Washington, the driver said to me, "I remember you when you were Ronald McDonald." And I said, "Oh, that's terrific." He said, "Yeah, I brought my little boy to see you." I said, "That's wonderful." He said, "It was over at Anacostia." And I said, "Yeah." And then I started to remember it was the week that Dr. King had been assassinated. I remember how we had debated whether or not to go since the police had advised us, because there was so much turmoil in the city, that maybe we shouldn't because we would draw a crowd, and that wasn't the best thing in the world to do. But the McDonald's people said, "We don't want to disappoint the people in the neighborhood, and they might think that we don't care and don't love them." So they took some precautions, and this is why I remember this particular incident. They took out a $100,000 insurance policy on me for that appearance, which made me feel a little bit funny. And they cut a hole in the security fence and backed the truck up to it with the platform where I was going to work, so that in case anything did happen I could get away.

The taxi driver mentioned this appearance to me to say that twenty years or so ago he had brought his little boy to see me as Ronald McDonald. And I thought, Well, that's nice. He said, "You know what I remember most?" And I said, "What's that?" He said, "I was a Black Panther at the time." A member of a militant group. He said, "I really hated white people." And he said, "In all the crowds of kids that came up, when my little boy came up to you, his shoe was untied. I remember you reached down and tied his shoe." I reached down and tied his shoe. I don't remember it. But whatever it was that triggered in that man the love, the feeling, he had remembered that. A simple act, a simple little movement, one simple little thing that that man had remembered for twenty years, because of my being kind to his child, and being considerate. It was an automatic reflex to me: The little child's shoe needed tying. The man loved me and he cared about me.

Some of the best friendships I've ever made are on airplanes, because they don't require any follow-up. Don't you like relationships like that? I mean, you sit there, and there is no obligation. You don't have to phone back. It's terrific. You sit there and you fly for maybe two hours, sometimes four if you are going across the country. And recently I sat next to this nice-looking man who was in his early forties. And as he sat there with me, he opened a book and started to read, and it was obvious he wanted me to see the book. Got it out of his briefcase, and he was holding it toward me. And it was the AA Book—Alcoholics Anonymous.

Well, I could tell the man wanted to talk a little bit. So as he was reading and flipping pages and moving the book closer to me, I said, "That's a marvelous book." And he said, "You bet." That's how people out in the Midwest talk, I picked that up. I use that to stroke them once in a while. "You betcha." It comes back from the old Swedes and the Norwegians who used to say, "Yah sure, you betcha." And now you meet people from the Midwest—Iowa, North Dakota, Minnesota—you bet, you bet. In fact, you'll say something like, "Nice day." "You bet."

So I'm sitting there with this man—I believe he was from North Dakota—and the book is getting closer and closer and I acknowledge the fact that this is a great book. I didn't know too much about the book. I had never read the book myself, but I appreciated it. He said, "I was in terrible shape. I was near death. I almost lost my family and my job. This book has saved me." And I said, "Well, I understand this is a great book. I don't know too much about it." And then I said to him, "You know, I have been drinking too much lately, the last two or three years."

I'm not a bad drinker. I don't want you to think that, and I'm not coming up here to pour my soul out to you, but the truth is, I was drinking too much. Sometimes even one drink is too much. We talk about drugs and marijuana and coke and crack and heroin, but let's be honest. It's taken me a long time to realize it, but with alcohol we're talking about a substance that can abuse your body and mind. We're talking about a drug. We're talking about something that can be addictive. And alcohol is right in there, baby. I mean, it's a nice drink for some people; it's a very relaxing, calming thing. But I noticed two things. One, as I got older, I couldn't drink like I used to. And two, I noticed all my friends around me who were past fifty were moving into a sort of semiretirement, and they were drinking and sometimes they even retired and expired six months later, half of them because they drank too much. And I was worried about myself a little bit.

And the man on the airplane said, after I told him this, "Take the book." I said, "I don't want to take your book." It had that look like it's grandma's beloved Bible. Every page had a fingerprint on it, kind of twisted and kind of knotted up. He said, "Take the book, I've got plenty of them at home. Take the book."

So I took the book and I took it home and I put it on my bar and left it there for maybe six months, and every night I would come home and I'd fix my two Jack Daniels that I love with all my heart and soul. I enjoy my Jack Daniels. And I really enjoyed those drinks, and the book was just there. I don't think I did it to be cynical or smart. It just happened to be there, and it stayed there. One night I drank much more than I normally did and I woke up in the middle of the night. I wasn't sure whether I had put the dog out. I wasn't sure whether I had gone to bed. And I remembered something about a rabbit. You ever do that? The next day, I realized that I had searched around and found an Easter bunny. I had had a chocolate attack, and I had eaten this rabbit and gone to bed. And all I remember was that the whole thing was jumbled up enough that I said, "You know, Willie old boy, you're smarter than that." And I picked up the book and I started to read it. And next month, it will be a year since I had my last drink. And I will never drink again.

We love that, don't we? That's our kind of stuff. We really get off on that. But the truth is, what a fantastic thing that was, a brief encounter on an airplane with a man who changed my life. And to this day, that man doesn't know whether I've stopped drinking or not, or whether or not what he did was something that had a lasting influence on my life.

Every single one of us is a messenger. We are all instruments. Everything we do, everything we say, every move we make says something about us and what we believe and how we feel. I hope that we realize that. Because sometimes we feel a little bit insignificant. And in this world that just turns and twists, with just so many humongous problems out there, we seem to be helpless even to come close to having an influence. But every moment, every moment that we live, and everything that we do, and everything that we say has a meaning. That's why I'm here this morning. Those influences have meant so much to me in the old Baptist church, with the love of the people who I recall in my youth had such a tremendous influence on my life. I don't see it written in stone anywhere in Washington in any monuments or museums, and it wasn't anything that you would say would go into some document or historical recollection. But it made a difference in my life. And we do make a difference, each and every one of us, through Christ's love and through our devotion to him and through the truth. Because it is the truth, and it's the only way.

It's awful to be so dogmatic, but it really is the only way. I've looked around, because sometimes I want to be a little more liberal and say, Well, of course you can do this and get there. No, only one way. There's only one way, and that's through the love of Jesus Christ and the sacrifice of Jesus Christ and the compassion of Jesus Christ. There is no other way. And to the guy in the hot tub in California, I hope he's thinking about it. And to the man out in North Dakota who gave me the book, I thank you very much. And to that lovely taxi driver who took me for a ride and reminded me that I'd done something one time in my life that helped somebody, thank you very much, wherever you are. God bless you all.

When do we eat?

# 4.  Who Is This Jesus Christ?

*William Powell Tuck*

Matthew 16:13–21

DESIRING TO GO apart from the crowds, Jesus and his disciples withdrew to a place called Caesarea Philippi. Caesarea Philippi was located about twenty-five miles northeast of the Sea of Galilee. Jesus and his disciples may have stopped to rest there for a while, or they may have camped there overnight. We don't know. While they were resting during the day or in the early part of the evening, Jesus asked his disciples two significant questions. The setting was charged with religion. Jesus and his disciples sat under the shadow of Mount Hermon, the mountain where many of the great religious leaders of Israel had experienced God's presence. Fourteen temples of Baal, where the Syrians worshiped their god, were located in this area. Outside Caesarea Philippi was a deep cavern that was supposed to be the birthplace of Pan, the god of nature.

Originally Caesarea Philippi was named Panias because of the impact this god had on the community. The source of the Jordan River was claimed to be located in a cave near Caesarea Philippi. This was the most significant river in the nation of

---

*William Powell Tuck* was educated at the University of Richmond, Southeastern Baptist Theological Seminary, and New Orleans Baptist Theological Seminary, where he received his doctorate. Dr. Tuck is currently pastor of St. Matthews Baptist Church, Louisville, and has served as professor of preaching at Southern Baptist Theological Seminary. He is the author of several books, including *The Way for All Seasons*.

Israel, and being near its place of origin would remind Jewish persons of their history. Herod had also erected a temple for the worship of Caesar at Caesarea Philippi. Later his son Philip decorated the temple more lavishly and then changed the name of the city from Panias to Caesarea—Caesar's town. He then added his name, Philip, to distinguish it from the Caesarea on the coast of the Mediterranean. So in the day of Jesus it was called Caesarea Philippi.

In this religious setting, the itinerant preacher Jesus turned to his disciples, a group some might characterize as a lower element of society, and asked them: "Who do men say that I am?" Can you see the eyes of the disciples as they quickly glanced from one to the other? "Oh, no. He has heard the rumors," they thought to themselves. "He has heard the rumors." "Some are saying that he eats with sinners, and has gone into the home of sinners. Why he even talked to a woman in public and let a woman touch him—anoint his feet and head in public! He has heard the rumors." "Birds of a feather flock together," some were saying. "We are known by the company we keep," others asserted. "Some of the religious leaders are saying he is unclean. He touches the blind, deaf, lame, lepers, and other outcasts of society. He eats without observing the proper ceremonial rites and does not eat kosher food."

"He has heard the rumors." "By what authority do you do these things?" the religious leaders asked. "Show us your seminary degree. Let us see your certificate of ordination. Where are your ministerial letters of reference? Do you belong to the Society of Biblical Literature? Are you a member of the Academy of the Professors of Religion? Are you listed in the Who's Who of Galilee? By what authority do you teach?" "He has heard the rumors," they thought. "By what authority do you heal? Is it by the power of Beelzebub the prince of demons? Show us your listing in the Medical Society of Galilee. By what authority do you heal people?"

"What gives you the authority to forgive sins? That is reserved only for God. Who do you think you are? Some folks think you are crazy." "Has he heard those rumors? His mother, brothers, and sisters have come to take him home, because the rumors were going around the countryside that he was 'beside himself.' He is crazy. Has he heard these rumors?"

"Who do men say that I am?" he asked. "Well," one of the disciples finally responds. "Some say you are John the Baptist. But we know better than that. He was your cousin. Because he was beheaded, some now think that you are John the Baptist who is risen from the dead. Others say that you are Elijah, who was one of the great prophets. Still others say you are Jeremiah. They have seen in you his tenderness, endurance, and national concern." "Some say you are a forerunner of the Messiah." I suppose that it is always easier to look for the Messiah to come than to believe that he has come.

After listening to what they said, Jesus then observed: "You have told me what other folks are saying, but what I want to know is, What do you think? Who do you say I am?" That question dropped like a silver dollar on a slate floor, and it has continued to ring down through the centuries. "Who do you say that I am?" On the walls of ancient catacombs of Rome before the end of the first century, symbols have been inscribed in response to that question. Vivid images of a lamb, a shepherd, a fish, a vine, a ship, an anchor, a lyre, and a cross were painted in answer to "Who do you say that I am?" Churches were constructed in the shape of a Latin cross as a nonverbal response to that question.

Scholars have not found much of a record about Jesus in ancient time outside the Bible. The Talmud has only a few references to Jesus, and they are late and slanderous. According to this record, Jesus practiced sorcery, ridiculed the religious teachers, led the common people astray, and was put to death on the eve of Passover. But the very fact that he was mentioned at all in the Talmud is interesting. Josephus, in his *Antiquities,* has only two references to Jesus. One of these records the stoning of "James, the brother of Jesus who was called the Christ." The other reference in Josephus is considered by almost all scholars not to be original but a later addition by a

Christian. There are three early Latin sources that have references to Jesus. These are Pliny, Tacitus, and Suetonius.

The Apostle Paul was the first person to write about Jesus, and his first letters were not written until about A.D. 50. The first Gospel was not written until later, somewhere around A.D. 65 to 70. This means that the first Gospel was not written until thirty years after the death of Jesus. But the only real records we have of the life and ministry of Jesus are found in the Scriptures. They are our chief source.

"Who do you say I am?" That question has continued to be asked through the centuries. This is not an answer but a question. We sometimes say that Jesus is the answer. But here Jesus is the question, and he is the questioner. "Who do men and women say that I am?" Most of the heresies of the Christian church have arisen in response to that question. "Who do men say that I am?" The Apostle's Creed came into existence in response to that question. The Councils of Nicaea and Chalcedon were called to respond to that question.

Christians through the ages have attempted to give a reply. His footprints have been seen across the pages of history. The answers continue to come to that question, "Who do men say that I am?" Listen to some of the replies. Ernest Rénan, a French writer, called Jesus a sentimental idealist. David Strauss saw Jesus as a fanatic, maybe psychopathic. William Hirsch said he conformed to a clinical picture of paranoia. Bruce Barton, an American businessman, said that Jesus was the greatest salesman who ever lived. Swinburne's bitter lines refer to Jesus as "the Pale Galilean" who has caused the world to grow grey from his breath. Richard Bucke claimed that Jesus had "cosmic consciousness." T. S. Eliot pictured "Christ the Tiger." James Cone called Jesus "The Black Messiah." Karl Rahner depicted Jesus as "a perfected human person." In South America he is seen as "liberator." John A. T. Robinson claimed he was the "human face of God." Edward Schillebecckx used the image of Jesus as "the sacrament of encounter." Paul Tillich called him "the New Being"; Richard Rawlingson wrote of Jesus as the "Religious Ultimate";

Dietrich Bonhoeffer saw him as "the man for others."Jürgen Moltmann asserted that he was "the crucified God." Norman Vincent Peale claims Jesus gives "peace of mind," while Robert Schuller says he gives us "possibility thinking." A musical drama was performed a few years ago portraying "Jesus Christ as Superstar." A religious organization in North Carolina depicts Jesus as the "curator" of a religious theme park.

Who is Jesus Christ? The answers seem to be "written in the wind." First this, and then another. "Who do you say that I am?" Is he simply a mannequin that we dress in whatever manner we like? Is he a lump of clay that we can mold any way we want? Is he an empty canvas on which we can paint any picture we desire? The variety of responses to him through the centuries makes one wonder if this is not the case. Who has seen his real face? Can he be whatever men and women want him to be?

"Who do you say that I am?" Roland H. Bainton, a former professor of church history at Yale Divinity School, felt that to end in skepticism about Christ because of the diversity of pictures of him is not warranted. He found a symbol of this struggle to know who Jesus is in a mosaic of Christ in a church in Constantinople. When the Turks invaded the city they plastered over the picture of Christ on the wall so it could not be seen. But centuries later the plaster has cracked, and one can see features of the face of Jesus Christ showing through the broken plaster. Maybe . . . maybe these varieties of images which people have given of Jesus Christ have some dimension of truth about him in each. Each separate image might contain some fragment of the reality of Jesus to which people have responded.

"Who do you say that I am?" Jesus asks. Jesus often first confronts us as disturber. Those who only want peace of mind will be shocked by his coming. When Jesus Christ comes into your life, he never leaves it the same—not if he really comes. Jesus disturbed the people of his day with words like, "I have come not to bring peace but a sword." And in another place: "I have come to cast fire on the earth." His coming is disturbing.

In Dostoevsky's *The Brothers Karamazov* there is a powerful story which Ivan recounts about "The Grand Inquisitor." The story takes place in Seville, Spain, during the time of the Inquisition. The Roman church was condemning persons to death because of heresy or disbelief. Suddenly one day a man appeared on the scene. He began to heal the sick, gave sight to the blind. The coffin of a child came by, and the crowd cried for him to bring the child back to life. He touched the child and she lived again. But the Grand Inquisitor, the cardinal, was in the crowd and had him arrested and thrown into prison. In the darkness of night, the Grand Inquisitor entered the dungeon cell where the "Stranger" was and closed the door behind him. After a few moments of gazing into his face, he sat his light on the table and asked:

> "Is it Thou? Thou?" but receiving no answer,
> he adds at once, "Don't answer, be silent. What
> canst Thou say, indeed? I know too well what
> Thou wouldst say. And Thou hast no right to
> add anything to what Thou hadst said of old.
> Why, then, art Thou come to hinder us? For
> Thou hast come to hinder us, and Thou
> knowest that. But dost Thou know what will be
> to-morrow? I know not who Thou art and care
> not to know whether it is Thou or only a
> semblance of Him, but to-morrow I shall
> condemn Thee and burn Thee at the stake as
> the worst of heretics. And the very people who
> have to-day kissed Thy feet, to-morrow at the
> faintest sign from me will rush to heap up the
> embers of Thy fire. Knowest Thou that? Yes,
> maybe Thou knowest it," he added with
> thoughtful penetration, never for a moment
> taking his eyes off the Prisoner.[1]

Then the cardinal went into a tirade about what the church had done, and how it had to move beyond what Jesus had accomplished by "correcting" his work. The masses of people want bread not freedom, he told him. They want mercy, mystery, and not authority. Jesus had refused once to rule over the kingdoms of earth and now others had to take his place. Why had he now returned to disturb them? But the Prisoner never said a word. He had listened intently, looking gently into his face. The silence weighed upon the Grand Inquisitor. He longed for him to say something even if it were bitter or terrible. But suddenly He walked over and kissed the bloodless aged lips of the cardinal. That was his only answer. Then the Grand Inquisitor shuddered, threw open the door, and said to the Prisoner: "Go, and come no more. . . . Come not at all, never, never!"[2]

Sometimes even the church of Jesus Christ has rejected its Lord. He comes first as disturber into our lives. He disturbs our sinfulness, challenges our prejudices, reorders our priorities, and redirects our values and standards for life. First we meet Jesus as disturber.

"Who do you say that I am?" Peter responded for the disciples. "You . . . You are the Christ." He was seen as the anointed one—the Messiah. The earliest Christian creed was "Jesus is Lord." They recognized that Jesus was not the forerunner but the Messiah. He was Lord. After the disciples first responded to him, they slowly began to discover that he was more than they ever dreamed he was. When they first spoke of him, they said that he was sent by God. Later they began to say that God was with him. Then following the resurrection, I believe they realized that God was in him. They came to believe that Jesus was Lord.

A group of small children were asked one day, "What do you think it means to say that Jesus is Lord?" "It means he is the big boss," they replied. That is right. For you to say that Jesus is Lord means that he is the boss of your life. He directs and guides you.

Jesus was different from other religious teachers of the past. You can have Buddhism without Buddha. You can have Confucianism without Confucius. But you cannot have Christianity without Christ! Jesus put himself at the center of his religion. He was not just the founder of a religion. He is its foundation. He is its source. "I, if I be lifted up," Jesus declared, "I will draw all men unto me." "I am the way, the truth, and the life. No one comes to the Father but by me." Jesus did not ask his followers, "Do you believe in God?" or "Do you think the Beatitudes are correct?" No! He put himself at the center of his message. "Come unto me." "Follow me." "Believe me." "Learn of me." "Preach in my name."

"Who do you say that I am?" The New Testament rings with the words that men said about him and claims Jesus made for himself. He is the Son of David, Son of God, Son of man, Messiah, the Servant of God, the Good Shepherd, the Divine Physician, the Savior, the Prophet, King, the Stone, Bridegroom, the Bread of Life, the Light of the World, the Door, the Vine, the Way, the Truth, the Life, the Resurrection and the Life, the Judge, the Lamb, the Scapegoat, the High Priest, the Just One, the Amen, the Alpha and Omega, the Beginning and End, the Head, the Image, the Christ of Creation, the Firstborn of Creation, the Bright and Morning Star, and others.

Who is he? He is Lord of your life, if you will open it to him. "Who do *you* say that I am?" The question demanded an answer. The disciples could not remain neutral. They had to decide. They had to choose. Whenever Jesus Christ comes into your life or my life, we can no longer remain neutral. We must either accept or reject him. He expects a decision and response. We cannot ignore him. "Who do you say that I am?" is now a question directed to you and me. Martin Luther once wrote: "I care not whether he be Christ, but that he be Christ for you!" Admiration is not enough. There must be adoration. When Christ confronts us, if we know who he is, we will fall at his feet and say with Thomas: "My Lord and my God."

I have seen people respond to Christ in many ways. Two college students sat in my church study one day. Neither of these young women had been to church before. They had started coming to our college church with some friends. Slowly they felt an attraction toward Christ. They asked for a conference and came by and talked with me. I spoke with them several times about Christ and gave them some books to read. Several weeks later they quietly gave their lives to Christ. When they knew who he was and met him, they had to respond. As a young college preacher, I sat nervously talking with a man whose skin had been darkened by long exposure to the sun. His rough-tough manner made me a little uncomfortable. But I talked to him about Jesus Christ over a cup of coffee. He listened but didn't say a word, didn't raise a question. I asked him if he would like to give his life to Christ and he said, "I would like to think about it." The next week he responded in our church service and gave his life to Christ. I have seen men, women, and young people, who in the quietness of my study, in their home, in a hospital room, in church, beside a lake at a retreat or in many other places, hear the gospel of Jesus Christ and respond by faith to the question: "Who do you say that I am?" It is not enough to hear reports about Jesus. Each of us has to decide who Christ is.

This question is shrouded in mystery, because people have found Jesus Christ in many different ways. We cannot confine him to the first century. He is not bound by time, space, or culture. His presence is continuously making itself known. He meets us in different ways and different places. He confronts us and asks us to follow him. Just imagine—the Man who never wrote a book has had thousands of books written about him. The Man who never published a song has had thousands of songs written about him. The Man who never built a house of his own to live in has had thousands of churches constructed in his honor. The Man who never painted a picture has had thousands of images of him and his church drawn. Gilbert Chesterson once wrote: "There was a man who dwelt in the East centuries ago and now I cannot look at a sheep or sparrow, or a lily or a cornfield, or a raven or a sunset, a vineyard or a mountain without thinking of Him." He has touched all of life.

When I was young, I used to go camping a lot. I remember one time when I was camping in the mountains of Virginia. I had built a fire and was sitting by its light in the darkness of the night. Off in the distance I heard thunder. Suddenly there was a flash of lightning and the mountainside around me, the valley below, and the mountains on the other side were visible just for a split second. For a moment, it was as light as day. The lightning flash revealed the reality of the world around me. Then darkness returned. Jesus Christ entered our world. His presence—life, ministry, death, and resurrection—were the lightning flash of God's revelation. Through the brightness of his life, we have seen something of the radiance of God. He didn't remove all of the darkness. But those of us who have seen the lightning-flash of his presence experience life differently. Having heard the question, "Who do men say that I am?" we respond to him and declare: "You are Christ the Son of the Living God."

Albert Schweitzer concluded his study, *The Quest of the Historical Jesus,* with these words:

> He comes to us as One unknown, without a
> name, as of old, by the lake-side, He came to
> the man who knew him not. He speaks to us the
> same word: "Follow thou me!" and sets us to
> the tasks which He has to fulfill for our time.
> He commands. And to those who obey Him
> whether they be wise or simple, He will reveal
> Himself in the toils, the conflicts, the sufferings
> which they shall pass through in His fellowship,
> and, as an ineffable mystery, they shall learn in
> their own experience who He is.[3]

Who do you say he is? Luther is right. "I care not whether he be the Christ but is he the Christ in you?" Is he?

## NOTES

1. Fyodor Dostoevsky, *The Brothers Karamazov* (Garden City, NY: International Collectors Library, n.d.), 230.

2. *Ibid.,* 241.

3. Albert Schweitzer, *The Quest of the Historical Jesus* (New York: Macmillan, 1961), 403.

# 5. The Inevitable Encounter
## *James R. Zug*

Psalm 139, Ephesians 1:9–10

THEY SAY THAT dreams can help us
  understand the emotional and spiritual
    struggles taking place in our lives.

I'd like to tell you a dream of mine.
  Yes, I agree it's very personal. But I want to tell you
    because I consider you to be my friends, and I know
      that you will understand what has happened to me.

And yet, I remain unconvinced
  that what I'm about to tell you was only a dream.
    The feelings of reality are still too strong to
      resign the experience to mere mental activity.

And although the dream was, at times, haunting . . . and
terrifying,
  I would hope that you, too, might encounter
    the persistent pursuit that I share with you.

And so, the dream . . .

---

*James R. Zug* is senior minister of Western Oaks Christian Church (Disciples of Christ) in Oklahoma City, Oklahoma. He is a graduate of Chapman College, and of Brite Divinity School of Texas Christian University. Zug was the co-founder and president of the board of Bethany House, Inc., a nonprofit organization in Tarrant County, Texas, providing residential living for mentally retarded adults, and he has been involved in community programs for the mentally disabled for more than twenty years.

For nights and days on end he followed . . .
    as though he had been paid to do so.
My initial reaction was that of curiosity.
    Who would want to follow me?
    And why?
      *Coincidence!*
      *Mere coincidence,* I said!

But soon I was aware that his pursuit
    was not mere idle chance.

I found that I could not elude him!
    Every path and street I traveled . . . he knew.

The alleys,
   the deceptive maneuvers,
     the diverting motions—
       all provided no hope of my . . . being alone.

He was on every highway—
   in every building—
     waiting outside every room.

He knew my destinations so well that often . . .
   when I thought I had finally lost him . . .
     he was there to meet me when I arrived.

He was my constant shadow . . .
   following at a distance . . .
     but never so far behind that his presence
     could not be keenly felt.
My curiosity turned to anxiety!
   I ran . . .
     I backtracked . . .
       I mingled with the crowd . . .
       I changed my itinerary . . .
         Still—he was there . . .
          Never visible—but always present.

"Was he following to report on my activities?" I thought.

Perhaps I was being investigated!
  *That's it. He's following the wrong person!*

But a sense about me knew that he wanted . . . *me.*
  And I became convinced that he wanted . . .
      *my . . . Very . . . LIFE!*

It was soon apparent that one day
  I would inevitably encounter this one who pursued me.
      *But I wasn't ready for that encounter.*

And thus . . . *I set upon my plan . . .*
  for *I MUST BE FREE!*
      I could not live as one of the hunted.
          *I WOULD HIDE.*
              I would conceal myself!

Outgoing as I was . . .
  I gave up all my friends . . .
      I no longer frequented my favorite places . . .
          I began eating alone . . .
              I moved about very little—I restricted
                  my activities to the cover of darkness.

I sat in darkness in my home.
  Though other laughed at me,
      I tried to work in darkness.
          "Let them laugh," I thought . . .
              but *I would not be overcome by a power*
                  *or spirit or being I could not see.*

Surely, my pursuer couldn't follow in the night.

My activities were such as to require brief trips.
  So I waited until night.
      But each time I ventured forth
          I knew he was there . . . just behind me.

And though I couldn't hear his feet
  *I once heard his voice say . . .*
      *"I am the light . . .*

*In me there is no darkness at all."*

And then it was
  that I knew the identity
    of that one who hunted me so.
But I also knew that God
  could not dominate me against my will.

"I am a free agent," I thought,
  "endowed with the freedom of making intelligent choices."
  *What right does God have to hunt me so?*

*And again I heard his voice saying . . . "I love, so I pursue."*

I had heard of his love.
  At times I even thought I wanted his love.
    Yet, I was afraid . . . desperately afraid.
      Afraid that in having him . . .
        I could have nothing else . . .
None of the things that meant so much to me.

But I had already embarked
  upon my next plan of action.
    *I would escape the pursuit of God*
      *in the labyrinth of intellectual pursuits.*

And so, I followed physics, wherein I found truth
  in the physical world that could be
    measured . . .
      weighed . . .
        tested . . .
          where forces could be seen and felt.

Here, in physics, there was no room for spirit.
          I felt at ease.

I followed biology and anthropology,
  wherein I came to know mankind as environmentally
  developed.
    I felt a new peace.

I followed philosophy, in which I found a system

of thought that needed no prime mover or first cause.
  I glowed in triumph.

I became enmeshed in psychology
  and the intricacies of the subconscious, the ego,
    the makeup of the psyche and the development of
    selfhood.
Through my intellect I designed a way of understanding life
  that provided all the meaning I needed
    for my own being and existence.

"Surely," I thought, "with meaning already established for
my life
  God would no longer pursue."

*But the voice still came . . . saying . . .*
  *"Love comes from one's total being . . .*
    *not just the mind."*
By now this invisible companion
  became my greatest challenge.

*"Why should I be the one pursued,"* I thought!
  This thought changed my course of action.

*"Now,"* I said, *"I will pursue."*

"I will gain mastery of this hunter . . . God.
  I will have this one in *my* grasp,
    by knowing the secrets he knew.
      His power over me will be gone
        when I know him for what he is."

Swiftly . . . I set about to unlock the hasp on nature's secrets.

Soon, I knew the swift movements on the face of the skies.
  I knew how the clouds arise.
    I stood in the spray of the wild and snorting sea.
  I gained the long-kept mystery of birth and death.
    I wept with dusk as the heart of day throbbed into sunset.
  I shared the confidence of evening
    when she lit her glimmering tapers.

I laughed with the morning
as she spread her pink and golden sun starts
through the glade and meadow.

*But . . . still . . . he followed . . .*
with steady pace,
deliberate speed,
unrelenting pursuit.

And . . . although the knowledge I had gained
helped my understanding . . .
I was still the hunted . . .
He was still the hunter.
I saw no escape.

*And then,*
*my mind recalled the words written by one of old . . .*

*"Though they dig into Sheol, from there shall my hand take them.*
*Though they hide themselves on the top of Carmel,*
*from there I will search out and take them . . .*
*Where can I go from thy spirit?*
*Or where can I flee thy presence?"*

I now knew the truth written by the ancient one.
*At some point in our lives*
*we must decide on a relationship*
*with that which is eternal*
*We cannot escape the encounter.*

*I came to understand that, in life,*
*if we are not reaching out toward God*
*we may be ignoring him . . . perhaps running from him.*

But I wasn't ready
to accept the idea that God
wanted me for a purpose that was good.
*My mind flashed back over my life.*

*It could well be that*
*I was an enemy of God . . .*

*that he wanted me solely out of revenge.*

Fear gripped me . . .
I had never had confidence
in things I could not see.

But, other than that
where was my sin?
*I became angered.*
*I began to yell . . .*
*Where is my crime?*
*SHOW ME MY SIN!*

*Wherein have I failed*
*that God would become an avenger*
*after my . . . Very BEING?*

I became convinced
that this is why God wanted me.
*For Revenge!*

*"If I am an enemy,"* I thought,
*"I will act like one."*

And so, *I stole,*
*I burned,*
*I plotted against my fellow man,*
*I became the carrier of hate, malice and prejudice.*

*I persecuted.*
*I incited.*
*I became everything that embodied evil.*

But . . . still . . . with deliberate step,
with patience,
he pursued.

He spoke again . . . *My love is for all who will accept it.*
*My fellowship is offered to you."*

His pursuit was more than I could endure.
When would it end?

Would he never give up?

My mind was confused.
    I trembled with fear and awe.
        My mouth was dry,
            My body was emaciated,
                My stomach churned.

Every particle of my being fought against being possessed
    by this one who had pursued me for so many years.

Then . . . suddenly,
    as though new understanding had come over me,
        I realized that
            *though I had thought I was free all these years,*
            *I really hadn't been.*

In my deep desire to avoid being related . . .
    and associated . . . and given over . . .
        to that which was spiritual . . .
            *I had become my own prisoner!*
            *And my prison was myself.*

My flight and fight
    to avoid the encounter with my pursuer
        had brought untold misery to myself . . .
            to my family . . . and to others.

The freedom I had so strongly believed in
    had now become only the mockery of myself
        against the inter-relatedness of all living things.

In trying to remain free
    (as I understood the word)
        I had kept myself from developing
            into what I could have been during
                those years of protest and bitterness.

I had run so far . . . and so fast . . .
    had tried to escape so that none could follow . . .
        that now . . . I was near death.

Mentally exhausted,
  physically near shock,
    I needed sleep desperately.

And then . . . everything went black.


*I awoke to the touch of radiant warmth—*
  *I was Refreshed . . . RENEWED!*

No longer trembling,
  I felt a vibrant strength.
    No longer tense,
      I was aware of a soothing peace.

*And with a burst of insight*
  *I knew two things:*
    *I knew I had seen myself*
      *and my immature ideas of freedom*
      *in a painful, but beneficial, light.*
*Then, too, I knew I could no longer run away . . .*
    *from myself . . .*
      *from God . . .*
        *wasting myself in rebellion*
          *against the eternal dimension in life.*

*Life is too short . . . too precious . . . too important*
      *for me to continue to disregard my own destiny.*


A dream? After telling it again I'm not so sure.
Those who have heard it
  before my relating it to you
    have said it isn't a dream at all.

They have said that what I dreamed
  is taking place in all of our lives—
    that some of us are running away from God,
  some are struggling with the spiritual dimension to life,
    some are sitting in the darkness, hiding,

afraid of the very one who can bring light
and joy into their lives.

I'm convinced that an encounter with God is inevitable.
One day it must take place in our lives.
*The encounter is part of God's plan in Christ*
*"to unite all things in Him—*
*Things in heaven and things on earth."*

*I encourage you—*
*Have confidence in the spiritual dimension of life,*
*Open your lives to God as never before,*
*And vigorously pursue "the inevitable encounter."*
*Hoping—praying—that it may happen to you!*

# 6. Jesus and the Woman at the Well

## *Gordon C. Stewart*

John 4:1–43

HERE IN THE encounter with the woman at the well we have all the dynamics usually present in the personal drama of salvation.

The initiative lies with God, not with us. We sometimes think that people search their way to God. But it isn't so. God is in search of us, and so intense and intimate is God's search that we can easily confuse it as our own. The conversation at the well is initiated by Jesus. The fact that he would even speak to the woman catches her by surprise. She is shocked! Why?

By speaking to the woman Jesus broke two prevailing behavioral patterns. He, a Jew, spoke to a Samaritan; and he, a man, dared to be alone with her, a woman, making himself vulnerable to false charges of impropriety, and then dared to have conversation with her. So the Samaritan woman was caught off guard by Jesus' initiative. She is going about ordinary chores when Jesus catches her attention, and once he catches it, there is no end to the need to know more.

The whole conversation ends with the Samaritan woman

---

*Gordon C. Stewart* is senior minister of Knox Presbyterian Church in Cincinnati, Ohio, a church known especially for its music program. A graduate of Maryville College, he received the master of divinity from McCormick Theological Seminary and the Charles E. Merrill Fellowship to Harvard Divinity School in 1981.

going to her friends with her testimony, "He told me everything I ever did!" He knows her through and through and
takes her seriously.

You remember in the synoptic Gospels how the men of the
city brought to Jesus a woman caught in adultery and proposed to stone her. And you remember how Jesus disarmed
them with his statement: "Let him who is without sin cast the
first stone."

Here too Jesus does not condemn but guides and gently
leads. He invites her to drink from living water, to quench the
thirst which has led her to be promiscuous, to drink from a
deeper well than cheap sex or serial relationships. "Go home,
call your husband, and come back," says Jesus. And the woman says, "I have no husband." "I know," answers Jesus,
"you've had five husbands and the man you live with now is
not your husband." He sees her need for relationship; he sees
her loneliness, her thirst, all of these basic human needs twisted and distorted, and he invites her to drink from a deeper
well, the well of living water. "For everyone who drinks this
water will never thirst, for the water I shall give will be an inner spring always welling up for eternal life."

The encounter with Christ is a saving experience, yet it is
also scary! And I suggest that if in some way it isn't scary, then
perhaps you have not yet met him at the well where he can
offer you his living water.

What's scary about it is that we can't at first believe that
there is anyone, let alone the Son of God himself, who would
accept us, would love us, if he knew everything about us. I
mean everything: your behavior in every nook and cranny of
your life. Your every thought. Your dreams. Your subconscious. Your unconscious, and your conscious life. Your
weaker and bleakest moments. We hide them behind the appearance of a better self. We hide our whole self not only from
others but also from ourselves. Deep down we may be troubled by it, but we tell ourselves we have to live with our sin
alone. Communities aren't real good about accepting people
who admit their faults and shortcomings. Like the woman at

the well, we can't at first believe that anyone would love us if they really knew everything we thought and did. The encounter with Christ is scary!

And because it is frightening, we do what the Samaritan woman did: We try to sidetrack the conversation. We try to get Jesus off the personal stuff to the theoretical. We try to remove the conversation from the depths of our being to a less engaging and less threatening discussion about where the appropriate place to worship is—Mt. Gerazim, as the Samaritans believed, or Jerusalem, as the Jews believed. But Jesus keeps bringing the conversation back to the depths where it belongs. "The true worshipers will worship the Father in the spirit and in truth. The Father seeks such to worship him. God is spirit and those who worship Him must worship in spirit and in truth."

We too try to sidetrack the Christ who encounters us. We engage in theoretical discussions with ourselves. For us it's not a question about Mt. Gerazim or Jerusalem. It's a question about religious relativism—about how one can possibly believe in Him when there are so many other religions to pick from, so many different religious expressions, and, even within Christianity itself, so many different denominations and so many different theories. Whether to baptize as infants or adult. Whether the Bible is infallible and written by God or is divinely inspired but written by humans. Whether the atonement is substitutionary to satisfy the wrath of an angry God or the revelation of the God of love appealing to us through the voice of the cross. Whether Jesus' resurrection was an actual resurrection of the body or a spiritual resurrection. Whether one should have communion every week or once a month or five times a year. Or where authority lies in the church: in the pope, or the presbytery, or in the individual conscience.

Important as these questions may be, they are like the topic brought up by the Samaritan woman to sidetrack the conversation with her Lord from the more personal encounter. They move us from the depths to the surface, from the scary to the safe, from the personal to the theoretical, from the confrontation with ourselves to the escape of safe speculation. And we do it all the time, don't we?

Yet Jesus keeps bringing us back to the reality and to the essentials: "Everyone who drinks of this water will thirst again, but whoever drinks of the water I shall give him will never thirst." Isn't it interesting that the disciples themselves don't seem to understand this encounter? Up until this point in the story Jesus and the woman have been alone. No one has heard their conversation. It is like the conversation you sometimes have with your Lord: personal, private, observed by no one, heard by no one, yet real and moving in the inner recesses of your own spirit and your own truth. Up until now the woman has been alone with Jesus.

But then the disciples, who have gone off to buy food in the town, return. And they are astonished! Astonished to find him talking with a woman. None of them is rude enough to ask her point-blank what she wants or to ask Jesus why he is talking with her, but their body language and their eyes speak their resentment and condemnation. So she leaves them and tells the people in the nearby town her story instead.

The same thing has happened again and again throughout the church's own history. When white members of St. George Methodist Episcopal church in Philadelphia dragged Richard Allen and other black Christians from their knees when they sought to take their rightful place as direct and equal partners in the conversation with their Lord back in 1787, they repeated the hostility of Jesus' disciples toward the woman at the well. When the church turns away people who are not from their social class, or who do not share their taste or their race or their ideology or whatever, they repeat the original sin of the disciples toward the Samaritan woman. When Christians gossip about others, they repeat the self-righteous sin and misunderstanding of Jesus' disciples at the well.

*Our Lord's love is so much greater than ours is.* So much more expansive. So much less judgmental. So much more welcoming. So much more gracious. So much more profound and deep is his love for every person!

Notice what happens when the disciples return. The disciples think they need to take care of their Lord!

The woman has gone off to the town and told her story. And we have this wonderful picture of the Samaritans from the town pouring out in droves to see Jesus. But listen to the disciples. "Rabbi, have something to eat." And when Jesus answers that he doesn't need their food, they still don't understand. "Can someone else have brought him food?"

Like the woman at the well early in the encounter, the disciples also do not understand. Just as the woman had been concerned only with physical water and immediate needs, the disciples do not yet understand. They think Jesus needs them, and have yet to see that it is not they who have the food but Jesus.

The church too is sometimes like that. Protective. Defensive. Exclusive. Shallow. Culturally religious but not yet affected by the real encounter, the personal encounter with a living Lord who doesn't need our protection, a living Lord who has the living water, an inner spring welling up for eternal life.

We are like that when we think we have to protect Jesus from atheists or from Moslem fundamentalists, and when we abandon his way of love and peace and the way of the cross in favor of what we think is our defense of him. We are like that when we come to church simply out of habit, the way we would go to a job about which we have no enthusiasm rather than because of our real need to receive from Christ what he alone can offer, the fresh waters that spring up from eternal life. We are like that when we confuse being born into a Christian family with being a Christian, when we confuse a cultural accident of birth with a personal, running conversation with a living Lord.

What is so helpful about this encounter of Jesus and the woman at the well is that it reminds us of where the action is. It's in our personal conversation with the living God. Like the people of the town, we first believe or consider believing because others tell us *their* story of an encounter with the living Lord: "He told me all that I ever did and loves me still!" But beyond that, the Samaritans pressed Jesus into staying with them and he stayed there two days. The initial testimony of another invites us to our own personal conversation with the Lord himself until we can say with the people of that blessed town: "It is no longer because of the testimony of another that we believe, for we have seen for ourselves, and we know that this is indeed the Savior of the world."

Christ invites you to a conversation with himself. A conversation that starts where you are, and which grows and develops, which brings you to deeper and deeper levels of spirit and truth until the water he gives becomes a spring within you welling up to eternal life.

Jesus says: "If anyone thirst, let him come to me" (John 37:7).

# 7. Standing in Someone Else's Sunshine

## M. Vernon Davis

Philippians 2:1–11

WHEN YOU LIVE very close together, it is easy to stand in someone else's sunshine. When you are struggling to claim your own place in the sun, a reminder that you are a steward of your own shadow can be quite irritating.

In Tokyo, Japan, 12 million people are crowded into the relatively small space of 800 square miles. As increasing numbers of people come to live in the city, there is no place for them to go but up. New skyscrapers are built, towering over existing tall buildings. As they rise, they block the sun from the adjacent buildings. People living in them find their environment increasingly dark and cold. Without much central heating people in the city depend heavily upon winter sunlight to help them keep warm.

The Japanese have developed a concept they call *nissho-ken*—the right of sunshine—in response to this situation. This principle has resulted in a law that requires a builder to com-

*M. Vernon Davis* is vice president of academic affairs, dean of the faculty, and associate professor of Christian theology at Midwestern Baptist Theological Seminary in Kansas City, Missouri. Formerly president of the Baptist General Association of Virginia, Davis has pastored churches in Virginia and Texas. He has written extensively for the Southern Baptist Sunday School Board as well as for other periodicals and journals.

pensate the people who are robbed of sunshine by his building. According to *National Geographic*, the Japanese have devised a complex formula that requires high-rise builders to give people whom they overshadow a one-time payment that can range from $420 to $1,260 for each hour of sunlight they lose on a winter day.[1]

*Nisshoken*. Perhaps there are other settings in which such a right to sunshine should apply. Consider Paul's words:

> Do nothing from selfishness or empty conceit,
> but with humility of mind let each of you
> regard one another as more important than
> himself; do not merely look out for your own
> personal interests, but also for the interests of
> others. (Phil. 2:3–4, NASV)

*Nisshoken* is an appropriate concept in Christian community, for even here we at times find it easy to build our own lives in someone else's sunshine and conduct our own ministry at someone else's expense.

The early church experienced similar crises in community that have plagued the people of God in advanced forms throughout history. They confronted problems for which they knew no precedents. They faced complex issues for which they had no guiding texts. They looked to the counsel of Paul and others, who sought to help them remember the example of Jesus and to understand the relevance of his teaching in their own circumstances.

Paul found much to commend in the church at Philippi. Yet he appears to have seen some disturbing signs in the fellowship. He had experienced the pain of churches where conflict had ripped the fabric of fellowship. He seems to have sensed the growing possibility that the church at Philippi could be moving toward a similar crisis. He looked at the ominous signs of "grumbling and questioning." He pleaded with two coworkers to find the way to solve their differences and live in harmony. He was disturbed by the members' concern to accumulate more things for themselves, and he called them to "be anxious for nothing."

Paul was troubled by a self-centeredness that expressed itself in a way of life that sought accumulation to oneself at the expense of others. To the Philippians, who were in danger of failing to trace the roots of original sin into their own lives, he held up the example of Jesus as the model for Christian behavior. The hymnic words of Philippians 2:6–11 convey the New Testament's most profound truth about the essential nature of Jesus and those who would follow him.

Theologians would later make careers out of speculation upon the meaning of this passage. In its phrase, "He emptied himself," *kenosis*, they discovered both the promise and problem of Christology. The phrase, which eloquently expresses the self-sacrificing nature of divine love, became a technical way of confronting the endless question concerning how the divine could become human.

However legitimate it is to use Paul's words to prove something that is unique to Jesus, we dare not forget that his intention in this passage was to teach us something about ourselves as Christians. He holds before us the example of Jesus as he talks about what it means to live as Christians in the fellowship of the church. He speaks not only of what Jesus did, but also of what he challenges us to do. "Have this mind among yourselves." The themes of humility and servanthood are unmistakable.

Paul spoke of Jesus as man. In the passages in his letters that focus upon Christ's humanity, the contrast with the humanity of Adam always lies close at hand. The Second Adam reverses the course of the First. Where Adam saw his status in the image of God as something to be clutched selfishly, Jesus took on himself the form of a servant. Where Adam sought his own way, Jesus became obedient to the will of God. Where Adam's self-centeredness disrupted relationships, Jesus' love created community.

In the Philippian hymn one begins to recognize a hauntingly familiar theme from the Servant Songs of Isaiah. It becomes an explicit commentary for Christians on words from Isaiah 53. The phrases "he emptied himself" and "he became

obedient unto death" give new meaning to the moving statement by the prophet: "He poured out his soul unto death."

Christians have always been more comfortable in applying
these texts to Jesus than they have to themselves. We would
rather see them speaking exclusively of something he did in
substitution for us rather than something he also did before us
as an example. The theme of servanthood is muffled in contemporary Christianity. In its place for many is a theology of
prosperity in which the goal of life is to get the things we want
with Jesus as the way to get them.

This self-centered and materialistic way of life reflects
more of the values of contemporary culture than the gospel.
Edward Dobson, writing in the *Fundamentalist Journal,* has
said that "prosperity theology is nothing more than secular
humanism controlling the church. It is secular—not religious." He contends that "America is addicted to 'self.' Sacri-
ficial living and compassion for others have given way to an
unbridled quest for self-actualization and self-gratification."[2]
How strange such a pursuit seems when considered against the
counsel of the apostle Paul.

In the penetrating analysis of contemporary American culture *Habits of the Heart,* Robert Bellah contends that "we have
committed what to the republican founders of our nation was
the cardinal sin: We have put our own good, as individuals, as
groups, as a nation, ahead of the common good."[3] We view
the meaning of our work as the pursuit of private aggrandize-
ment rather than public contribution. We think in terms of
our individual rights and freedoms rather than our commitments to community. The model of the one who "emptied
himself" in the service of love seems strikingly irrelevant in
such a world.

The self-centered pursuit of life finds expression within
the church in ways that disrupt community and deny the values of diversity. Consider the way this devastating self-centeredness can express itself as people seek to build theological
houses in which to dwell securely. A person discovers a splin-

ter of the truth and mistakes it for the whole plank. His insight grips him to such an extent that he not only wants to live in its light but believes that everyone else must live there also. He presses his point, often beyond the bounds of his own certainty and common reason. He is deaf to other voices and will not look at the light that has come through another's window. He chooses libelous labels for others, and he recoils when labels are applied to him. After all, he is only telling the truth. Thinking in this way, one too easily forgets the insight of Tennyson's lines:

> Our little systems have their day;
> They have their day and cease to be.
> They are but broken lights of Thee;
> And Thou, O Lord, art more than they.

Such persons forget that all human understanding is limited by one's peculiar perspective and personal sin. In the process of living they have shrunk the limits of the world to the dimensions of their own horizons. Wherever they happen to be standing becomes the center of the universe. What they see is what exists. Their own understanding is the measure of all things.

In the play *Fanny* by Harold Rome, the young man Marius has an idea of the world far different from that of his father, Cesar. The old man is a barkeeper on fisherman's wharf in Marseilles. He views all of the world from that perspective and appears to insist that everyone else see it his way, too. The young son accuses his father, "You think that Marseilles is the center of the earth!"

Cesar replies, "It is! That is north, this is south; that east, this west. I am here, the center!"

The bewildered young man shouts, "But there are others!"

And Cesar replies, "They are off-center!"

The principle of religious liberty in a free society is threatened when people seek to impose their own understanding of

God upon others. The spiritual stock market will not forever rise for evangelical Christianity or any other religious body if they deny to others the privileges they seek for themselves. The heritage of religious liberty is nurtured by the one who would not seek his own way, but gave his life to make many free.

Christian community cannot be created by people who insist upon having things their own way and denying to others their own right to live in unfiltered sunshine. Christian community is incompatible with what someone has called the "menace of meism." Where people are secure in their own power and confident in their own insight, the one who sings a servant song seems quaintly irrelevant.

The trappings of self-sufficiency, however, may prove to be an illusion. The cocksure confidence in one's own grasp of reality may be threatened by the gnawing, subterranean ache of unacknowledged doubt. Even success can hide a struggle of the soul. Many in our culture have come to the point, in Harold Kushner's phrase, "when all you've ever wanted isn't enough." He aptly describes the lives of many when he says, "We may have all the things on our wish list and still feel empty. We may have reached the top of our professions and still feel that something is missing. We may know that friends and acquaintances envy us, and still feel the absence of true contentment in our lives."[4]

When we have become disillusioned by the way we have chosen to live, we stand at the intersection of despair and hope. Life can dissolve into cynicism or can rediscover the resources of grace. Such moments can bring the soul to hear the gospel with new understanding. With broken models for living lying all around us, we may remember one we have been too ready to ignore.

The one who walks through the self-centered world as a servant continues to call all people to share his mind and embody his life. He invites us to the freedom that comes from walking in the light as he is in the light. And I think I hear him as well: Do you know where your shadow falls?

NOTES

1. William Graves, "Tokyo: A Profile of Success," *National Geographic* (November 1986): 614.

2. Edward Dobson, "Prosperity Theology," *Fundamentalist Journal* (October 1987): 12.

3. Robert Bellah, *Habits of the Heart* (Berkeley: University of California Press, 1985), 285.

4. Harold Kushner, *When All You've Ever Wanted Isn't Enough* (New York: Summit Books, 1986), 21.

# 8.   In Church on Christmas Eve
## *Terence C. Roper*

Text: Isaiah 9:2 "The people who walked in darkness have seen a great light."

TONIGHT I WANT to give you a Christmas gift, and if you will listen carefully to what I have to say, with great care and attention, I may be able to do it.

You see, mine is not a passive gift. I cannot just hand it to you like a tie or a bottle of perfume and watch while you look at it, hoping that you will like it, and accepting your thanks either way. I can't do that.

Mine is a gift that requires your cooperation, or you won't get it. It's not that I won't give it, it's that you won't get it, because my gift requires your active participation.

Some gifts are expendable. Soon after you get them they are eaten, gone, used up, spent, and worn out. Blazing like bottle rockets for a brief moment and over and gone in a flash. Great while they lasted, but soon gone, finished, forgotten.

Some gifts last. Those are the best ones. So lasting and meaningful are they that one's whole life may be changed by them. One is never the same again. My gift is like that.

If you could give the most valuable gift in the world to

---

*Terence C. Roper* was born in England and educated at King's College at the University of London. An Episcopalian, Roper has been Rector of the Church of the Transfiguration in Dallas, Texas, for the past thirteen years. He has also written articles for *The Living Church* and other periodicals. "In Church on Christmas Eve" was preached at the Church of the Transfiguration on Christmas Eve.

someone you love, your spouse, your child, your mother or father, you'd do it, wouldn't you? What would it be?

Some would say health because where are you without it? Some would say wealth, for then you can be sick in comfort! Others would say wisdom because with wisdom you may be able to get the other two! What would you say?

I'd say that my gift is better than any of these, better than all three put together, but you may not think so at first. As I said earlier, you are going to have to work on this to appreciate it properly.

You'll need to take the time to think about it. You'll need to evaluate it for yourself and decide for yourself. My fear is that you'll be in too much of a hurry or get distracted and not recognize it for what it is. You'll need to be careful about this, you know.

Why are you here tonight? Is it because you always come on Christmas Eve? Is it a habit? Have you come as a member of your family because on Christmas Eve you all go to Church together and afterward open packages? Is it a part of your family ritual at Christmas? Is it a thing you do as a member of your family, but not because you are a member of this family, the Church? Do you feel just a bit like a spectator at somebody else's party? Sort of allowed in but feeling left out? Do you come in order to please someone else, a parent, friend, lover but not really for yourself? Why are you here tonight?

Maybe my gift to you tonight is to tell you why you are here! You are here because almost two thousand years ago a man named Jesus rose from the dead. Whether you know it or not, that's why. You are here because he is calling to you personally, across almost two thousand years of time and space, calling to you to answer his call, respond to him and commit yourself to him. That's why you're here.

You thought you came because it's Christmas, didn't you? Wrong! You came here because of Easter.

If Jesus had not risen from the dead there would be no reason whatsoever to celebrate his birth. His birth would be no different from that of any other first-century Jewish child. But millions upon millions remember Jesus. And why? Because he rose from he dead. Without Easter there would be no Christmas. Who'd need it? What would be the point?

Tonight we gather around the manger scene, assembled at the four o'clock service by all the children in a sweet little ceremony, and we sing carols and hear the old, old stories about the child born in the stable, and it's nice. It's beautiful. It's sweet and lovely. But don't be fooled by all that stuff will you? It can distract you from the truth.

The truth is that the manger is empty. The child has gone, the shepherds have gone, the angels have gone, everything has gone! Gone forever, never to return! And that's not bad, that's good! Did you think it was bad? Wrong again!

The good news is that Jesus lives! That news never grows old, never pales, never ends. Jesus lives! That's the good news of the gospel. And that's what puts life into Christians; eternal life, no less! And I want you to know that. I want you to have that knowledge this Christmas as the greatest and best gift that you can have. I want you to have it deep down in the depths of your being. I want you to know and believe that.

So, if you came here this evening just to spend a pleasant couple of hours listening to a few ancient religious stories and to croon a few carols, do I have a deal for you!

You can take home with you the most valuable gift that this world affords: a personal knowledge of Jesus Christ as Saviour. That gift is here with your name on it.

Maybe you thought you knew Jesus already when you came in, but now you find that in your heart of hearts you really don't. You knew his story bud didn't know him. That happens, you know. But it's not an occasion for grieving, it's a time for rejoicing. Don't feel sad, be glad. This is the greatest moment for you. This is your night of rebirth.

If there is one gift above all gifts, it's God's gift to you. It's not really my gift to give at all, it's God's. I just have the privilege and joy to tell you about it.

This gift will not wear out or become tattered and torn.

You won't outgrow it either. God's gift lives and loves and lasts forever, beyond this world and into eternity.

If you want Christ to come into your heart and fill the emptiness that is there now, if you want Jesus to take possession of your life and fill you with the riches of his grace, there is no better time than now to invite him in.

In his divine humility, Jesus Christ always enters when invited; He never refuses, no matter how grubby he may find the new stable to which he comes as guest, and some are pretty bad. He always accepts and enters. He is not too proud for you. Are you for him?

Sometime during this love service, during one of the prayers, in a quiet time, when the choir is singing, whenever you feel it right, just ask him in and your prayer will be granted. The gift above all gifts will be given to you this night. Jesus will be born again in your heart.

Jesus Christ, the child once cradled in a manger, will come into your heart and dwell in you forever. All you have to do is to open your heart to him. He is not pushy and will not force himself upon you. Remember, I told you earlier, this gift requires your cooperation. You have to invite him, and if you do, you will never be alone and empty again.

That is what he has promised, that's the deal that God has made with his people, and that's the gift that is waiting for you tonight in this Church.

Christmas is not about the birth of Jesus of Nazareth, not really, it's about the birth of the Risen Lord Jesus Christ. The birth of Jesus has no meaning until we recognize that he is the Risen Lord, and we have no meaning until he is enthroned in our hearts as Lord of Life.

Every year at Christmas, great crowds gather in all the churches, just as they do in this one, and I know for certain that there must be many people filling the Christmas pews who do not really know the Risen Lord, and I do want them all to have that joy.

May God's gift to you this Christmas be the knowledge of

the resurrected Lord. My prayer for you this Christmas is that you never make the mistake of trying to put Jesus back in the manger, but will know him as he really is. He belongs not in the manger but in your heart as the Lord of your life. If all you offer him is a manger he will have to refuse because you have not allowed him his rightful place. He won't fit in the manger anymore, he's outgrown it. Have you? Have you outgrown the manger, or are you the one that really stuck in it? Is it you that hasn't outgrown the manger, long after Jesus has left it? He's way ahead of you if you are.

My Christmas gift to you this year is this. It's the golden opportunity of meeting Jesus, not as baby in the manger, but as Risen and Ascended Lord, Head of the church, Author of Salvation and Redeemer of Souls, and having him take over your life.

You will have received a gift this Christmas that is better than the whole world, and it will be your support in this life and into eternity. Just think of that! All you have to do is invite him in.

All around you in this Church are men and women like yourself, each one either struggling with the same decision that faces you or confident and joyful in the fact that they have already made it. In this life we have to take that road. Also all around you in this Church is the great invisible crowd of witnesses, the saints who have gone before us into heaven and who now live in Jesus in the eternity of God. They all know Jesus as Lord. They do not look for him in the manger, hoping to see the Infant King, because they know him as Lord—Risen, Ascended, Glorified Lord.

My prayer for you this evening is that you may be counted among that number, one of the Church, rather than one who attends Church on big days like Christmas and Easter. I want for you to be converted for Christmas into a living member of this community, the community of faith in the Living Lord.

Oh, no, I am so sorry about that, but there are no social memberships available. There never have been. It's an all-or-nothing deal.

Only you can decide, and I hope that you will, of course, because I want you to have this Christmas the most precious of all gifts, the knowledge of the love of God as shown forth to us in the face of Jesus Christ Our Lord. Better than that you cannot have. I know that for a fact. Words can never express the value of this gift of God that reaches across time and into eternity and is yours for the asking.

May Jesus Christ be yours this Christmas, and what is more important, may you be his forever. Amen.

# II. EXPOSITORY

# 9.   Incredible Freedom
## *Peter J. Gomes*

Luke 24:11

IT SEEMS a very long time ago that many of us began the long journey that culminates today: Ash Wednesday, weeks and weeks ago, promises and promises ago, ambitions and hopes ago, failures and frustrations ago. Ash Wednesday began with high hopes and ambitions, lives of self-denial and discipline, and the Sundays of Lent were punctuated by extraordinary Lenten discipline on your part, my Lenten Sunday series. I've often said that I ask the people of Memorial Church to take me on for Lent, even as I do you. But we've come to the end of all of that, and most of us, perhaps battered and scarred but not broken, in fact today rejoice in the Resurrection of Jesus Christ. Once again, that good news and that bright hope has brought us through all of this, the best and the worst of which we are capable.

So today we consider the incredible freedom of the Resurrection, and I take as my text the eleventh verse of Luke's twenty-fourth chapter, the summary of those marvelous Res-

---

*Peter J. Gomes* was born in Boston, Massachusetts. He was educated at Bates College and Harvard Divinity School, where he received his doctorate. A Baptist, Dr. Gomes has served since 1974 as minister of the Harvard Memorial Church and Plummer Professor of Christian Morals at Harvard University. He is the author of several books and was recognized in 1980 by *Time* as one of the outstanding preachers in the United States. This sermon was preached on Easter Sunday at Harvard Memorial Church.

urrection accounts: "But these words seemed to them an idle tale, and they did not believe them." Or, in the New English translation which is printed in the order: "The story appeared to them to be nonsense, and they would not believe it."

In St. Luke's Gospel, there is no Jesus, at least not yet. There is no Jesus in those first verses of chapter 24. There are no words of comfort, or reassurance or recognition from the risen Lord. He is not there to make it easier for those who are. He does not say, "Here I am!" as he does in certain of the other Gospels. He does not say, "Be not afraid!" There is no dramatic, thunderclapping, trumpet-blaring triumph of personality over circumstances in that twenty-fourth chapter, there is no Houdini emerging from the water tank to the applause of an audience delighted and relieved to be fooled. Not at all. Jesus is eloquently absent from these verses. St. Luke presents us first with a mystery, and it is a practical, sensible, Miss Marple kind of mystery. When the women reached the tomb on their errand of mercy to anoint the body of Jesus, they found the stone rolled away and the body missing. And they are described, as rightly they might be, as perplexed. Instead of the broken body of their late friend and Lord, they find two men in dazzling apparel, angels. Now perplexity is turned to fright. And what then happens? These innocent, frightened, well-intentioned women on their errand of mercy are subjected to the first Easter sermon, and in the words of the first Easter preachers, those two angels, this is what they say, this is the substance of the Easter Gospel: "Why seek ye the living among the dead? Remember how he told you, while he was still in Galilee, that the son of man must be delivered into the hands of sinful men, and be crucified, and on the third day rise." End of story, end of sermon. The first Easter message, the only Easter message. That's it: no tortured theology, no heavy-handed exegesis, no confutations of nature, no proclamations of the mystery of the empty tomb, no invitations to immortality. Just the reminder, *If you remember what Jesus said, you won't expect to find him here.* The first word at Easter, the first Easter sermon, the only Easter sermon is to remember what Jesus said.

And they did. St. Luke says of the women, "and they remembered his words," that's the hinge, "and they remembered his words." And we might say at that point, to those women, the risen Lord appeared, that is to say, he was made real to them, manifest to them, for they recalled him to their midst by his own words and actions. What Easter power is contained in those five little narrative words St. Luke ascribes to these women: "And they remembered his words." No thunder, no lightning, no *corpus delicti*: not even a metaphysical morsel to chew on. The truth of Easter was invoked for those women by the power of their memory of what the Lord said he was, and would do. That's the first thing to remember about the first Easter sermon: Take everything away and aside, all those wonderful details, that enchant and confuse us. Remove them all away and what you have left is: Remember what he said. He and his mission are at the center of the incredible truth and freedom of Easter.

But here we must needs be careful. For it is ever so easy to see the Easter gospel simply as memory and recollection. Press the button called "spiritual nostalgia" and it all comes back, so we imagine. Memory indeed is powerful, and we too know our dead by the power of memory. These flowers this morning and those in whose memory they are given, they have the power to evoke from the dead our loved ones whom we know by name. We have that power and we know what it is. We too remember, and, against that day when there is no one to remember, we erect our tombs and our memorials, we indeed build our endowments, we strike our epitaphs so that something remains when the last one who remembers is gone. And that reminds us that memory alone is not all that it's cracked up to be. But isn't that what they mean when they say of us here at Harvard that our graduates never die, they simply turn into buildings? Thayer, Wigglesworth, Canaday: Who are they? But there they are. Easter would be so much easier to understand if it were simply a springtime memorial service for Jesus, as it were, calling to mind, as we do in the Memorial Minutes of the Faculty of Arts and Sciences, the life and services of this good man, recalling to mind his occasional publications, his occasional discoveries and inventions, and filing him away for another year. Indeed, memory is good, it is very good, but for Easter, it is not good enough.

Memory is important on that first Easter, and for those women in particular, and they remembered his words. But the key to that morning, and to this morning, is not *that* they remembered, but *what* they remembered. What was the content of their memory? What was it that they remembered of his words? The Angels' sermon once again: "Remember how he told you while he was still in Galilee, that the son of man must be delivered into the hands of sinful men, and be crucified, and on the third day rise." *This* is what they remembered, and they were now witnesses to the truth of what they first heard and now remembered. They remembered *today* what Jesus had said *yesterday* about *tomorrow*. They heard *now* what Jesus said *then* about the *future*. And that about sums it all up.

And in that moment of recollection and remembrance, I submit to you that those women experienced that first incredible freedom of Easter, that is to say, they were freed at last of the incredible burden of their own responsibility for the sad duties of that morning. They were freed of the burden of the past, all of the things that they hadn't done, that they wished they had, all the things that they had done that they wished they hadn't done. They were freed of the burden of guilt and gloom of Good Friday, freed of the fear and the terror of the darkness of Holy Saturday, and more to the point: They were freed of the fear of a future without Christ, the most terrifying fear there is, that you and I will have to go into the dark future alone, by ourselves, with no one else. At that moment of Easter they were freed from all of those terrors and all of those fears, a freedom so incredible as to be almost too good to be true.

And here is the second message of Easter: It was not simply Jesus who was freed from the captivity of death on Easter day, it was not just Jesus. Jesus we can perhaps expect and understand in a curious sort of way to triumph on Easter morning.

That is how the script is written: Jesus is intended to win out, to defeat Satan and death. After all, being the son of God means never having to come in second, at least when all is said and done. We can give Jesus easy credit for the resurrection. In our flippant way, we would expect no less of one who could walk on the water, heal the sick, feed the hungry, do all those deeds of derring-do recorded in red in our red-letter Bibles. Jesus has finally done all those things he refused to do when we read about him at the start of Lent in the desert, those temptations, and with Satan. There he refused the reasonable entreaties of the Devil to do something, to do anything to prove himself. And then again, just on Friday last, he was taunted on the cross: "If thou be the Christ, save thyself and us," he was charged. We heard that cry, perhaps uttered it under our breath ourselves, and we were disappointed when he didn't respond. So on Easter, we finally have what we have long been coming to expect. Jesus finally does something we can understand. That is the heroic part of Easter, striding forward from the tomb, thrusting rocks aside, combination of Steven Spielberg and Jimmy Stewart, an incredible, decent freedom, such as befits the son of God. In our perverse sort of way all of that makes sense, in that sort of insensible world we set aside for religion and the Christian life. All of that works.

But can we posit that same incredible freedom to those ministering women at the tomb in St. Luke's gospel, women of whom we have no reason to expect very much, by the Gospel's account? Why, they never even saw the risen Lord, and there is a tremendous paucity of physical evidence. All they are given are the words of Jesus himself. And yet, could it be that the power of the resurrection for them and for us is not simply the affirmation of new life in Jesus Christ, important as that is, Jesus Christ who rose as he said he would. But could it be that the power of the Resurrection is indeed the affirmation of new life in them, new life in ourselves, a freedom because of Jesus, an incredible freedom from the bondage of past, present, and future, such as is the only true liberation, the only freedom worth having?

Such freedom is that of which Kierkegaard says in a lovely prayer when he writes these words:

> Father in heaven!
> Thou hast loved us first,
> help us never to forget that Thou art love
> so that this sure conviction might triumph
> in our hearts over the seduction of the world,
> over the inquietude of the soul,
> over the anxiety for the future,
> over the fright of the past,
> over the distress of the moment . . .

Think of it: Love is the incredible freedom that triumphs over the inquietude of the soul, that can calm those anxieties we all have for the future, that releases us from the fright, the guilt of the past, that gives us confidence to deal with the distresses of the moment. Doesn't that about sum everything up? Are we not all at some level or other hostage to past guilts and debts, terrorized about what the future will hold for us, anxious over the moment, and disquieted, troubled in soul and in mind? To be relieved of that, to be freed of that, would we not pay an enormous sum for that privilege? Would we not buy those books, take those pills, listen to those lectures, do those exercises if they could accomplish this for us? To know freedom from all of this is truly to be free to live life, perhaps for the first time, and to fear nothing, including the fear of death. For life is love, and love now is proven stronger than death. This is what that first Easter sermon says: For love Jesus lives; for love Jesus dies; for love Jesus lives again. And because of that "sure conviction" we too now shall live lives of incredible freedom, because of that love.

The message of the risen living Lord is simply this: We do not have to die to live, and to live that truth is to realize that death can no longer intimidate life. To know that truth is to know an incredible freedom in a world that is held hostage daily to doubt, to fear, and to death. And the key to all of that is to remember, that's what the angel said, to remember what

Jesus said: "Remember how he told you while he was still in Galilee, that the son of man must be delivered into the hands of sinful men, and be crucified, and on the third day rise." His resurrection *then* enables our resurrection *now*: that's incredible freedom.

And so, with that good news and that profoundest of Easter sermons and messages, what is the response? What is the response to the first gospel of Easter, the angelic sermon to those women witnesses? The women—Mary Magdalene and Joanna, and Mary the mother of James, and the other women with them—went and told all that they had heard and seen to the Apostles, the closest associates of the Lord, and, as St. Luke tells us, "but these words seemed to them an idle tale, and they did not believe them." For the Apostles were sensible men of affairs, the Apostles were practical people of human experience. The Apostles, those battered believers, believed that Jesus was now dead. His death was too true to be good, and his resurrection too good to be true. An idle tale: The superstitious prattling of women, unreliable witnesses to matters of fact.

And how much easier it is to believe credible bad news than incredible good news. Indeed, isn't our response to news that is too good to be true exactly that? You won the lottery: I don't believe it. You got into medical school: I don't believe it. Peace has broken out in the Middle East: That's incredible, I don't believe it.

We cannot be too hard on the poor old Apostles, easy as it might be to charge them with an insufficiency of faith on their first Easter morning. They didn't know it was their first Easter morning, they can't be blamed for that. Reality, credibility, sensibility, indeed common sense: These are the tools, the protective coloration that protect us from the consequences of too great an expectation. They secure us against disappointment, and we are taught early to arm ourselves with them: Expect little, accept less, and be grateful for anything. All of us, to some degree or another, hold fast to that simple Yankee creed. We're all honorary Yankees in that regard. And so, in thinking ourselves adult, responsible, sensible, and free, living securely within the fortress of our own limited experience, protected from doubt and disappointment, and too great an expectation, we find that rather than being free from all that, we are in fact hostage to all of that.

The householder who invests in the most sophisticated and complicated of electronic burglary devices sits in the shadows of his alarms and motion detectors and blinking red lights connected to the police station, thinking himself "free" from the fear of burglary. And indeed, while the burglar roams at liberty outside in the neighborhood enjoying the night air, the householder sits locked up inside, secure, perhaps, but one begins to wonder who is really free and who is in fact the hostage. "Don't trouble us with this nonsense about the resurrection. We must get on with the business of mourning our lost opportunity. We are used to pain and suffering and disappointment. Expect little and you won't be disappointed with less," practical advice from men of affairs to women up too early in the morning.

We know those disciples, for we are they, and our prayer for them as for ourselves is that wonderful prayer that asks that we be protected from the frailty of our own hearts, indeed, that we might be open to an experience that while it transcends our own experience, it also transforms our own. It is an experience that while it is not yet ours, enables all that is ours. This is the incredible freedom of the first Easter morning and sermon: that Jesus lives and therefore we might live, not in some blissful yet-to-be future, but here and now, in Cambridge, at Harvard, in the spring of 1988. Easter is not back there, nor is out there, it is here, now and you and I are the proof and experience of it.

The early church believed that the resurrection of Jesus Christ from the dead had a direct and immediate effect upon their lives. They didn't believe that somehow they would be spared death. No, that was not their conviction. And they didn't believe that they had to wait to die to experience the new life in Christ. They believed that because Jesus lives they too, in their own lives, their own ways, and their own times would experience newness, fullness of life, and that literally death would no longer have dominion over them.

It is the fear of death that corrupts and rules. It is the terror of death that terrorizes our lives, from the youngest to oldest; the notion that it's all going to go kaput is a terrorizing thing. Lives lived in fear of death are lives lived at the mercy of those persons and things that can prolong life and delay death. Time itself becomes our terrible enemy and Dorian Gray becomes our patron saint. The incredible freedom given us in the resurrection of Jesus is that we are now free to live our lives as fully and as freely as Jesus lived his, knowing indeed, as the French say, that the best revenge is living well. Not as hostages, not as prisoners, not intimidated, but knowing full well that life has been given for you to seize, and embrace, and to undertake because there is one who has given it to you by giving you his life.

Thus those early Christians, those who lived new lives because of the new life in Jesus Christ, were able to face up to the dangers and demons of this world as they found them. Think of the transforming power of the resurrection in their lives. Weak and denying Peter becomes a heroic apostle. His fellow believers, weak-minded, terrified souls driven to exile at the foot of the cross, were able to confront Romans and lions, scoffers and doubters alike. No kingdom on earth remains standing from the stable world order of the time of the early church, and yet the Easter faith is alive in the world today because of the transforming power of light in those lives. You, and I, for better or worse, we, friends, are the proof of that. For here you are, witnesses in your own way, to the promise of new life in Christ, responding as best you can to the incredible freedom which sets you free both from the fear of death, and for the living of the life you have been given.

You could be any number of other places today: getting an early croissant at the Harvest, watching television, in bed, and other places, but here you are. And there is something about the continuity and the contagion of that new life in Christ that infects you and affects you and if you take it seriously, enables you to live and to reclaim the life you have been given. The new life in Christ, the incredible freedom of the Gospel enables us to stick it out until the end. Not simply to endure, but to triumph. And to know that this sure conviction triumphs in our hearts over the seductions of the world which pass away so quickly, the inquietude of the soul, the fright of the past, anxiety for the future, and the distress of the moment.

We know all of this because of what we remember of what Jesus said, and we are freed from our fears to face past, present, and future, rejoicing not in nonsense or in an idle tale, but in the incredible freedom Jesus Christ gives by his life to live our lives here and now. You do not need to die to know the power of the resurrection; and when the power of the resurrection enters into your life, you will not need be intimidated by death.

Christ is risen: glory unmerited for all dispirited folk whose inherited needs are their prison. We have been broken out of that prison. Thank God for this incredible freedom, this liberation which we have in Jesus Christ.

# 10. The Burden of Love
## Page H. Kelley

Malachi 1:1–2, 6; 2:10; 3:13–17

SOMETIMES THE FIRST two or three sentences of a book set the stage for everything that follows. This is especially true of Malachi, the last book of the Old Testament. The first two verses of this little book read—and I am giving a literal translation—"The burden of the word of the Lord to Israel by the hand of Malachi. 'I have loved you—all of you' says the Lord. Yet you say, 'How have you loved us?' "

Some of you may find it strange that the word of God to Israel should be spoken of as a *burden*. A burden to Israel? No! But rather a burden to God himself. But why should God's word to Israel be a burden to him?

The answer is found in verse two: "I have loved you," says the Lord. Yet you say, "How have you loved us?" From this bit of conversation between God and his people we can understand why his word to them was a burden to him. He had loved them, as only God was capable of loving someone, and had declared his love to them, only to have them respond, *"Just exactly how have you loved us?"* God's burden was the burden of love, the burden of having loved his people with a love that could

*Page H. Kelley* was born in Hartford, Alabama, received degrees from Samford University and Southern Baptist Theological Seminary, and has studied at Harvard University and Cambridge University. Dr. Kelley is professor of Old Testament interpretation at Southern Baptist Theological Seminary in Louisville, and he has written extensively in his field.

only be described as lavish, and then hearing them respond, "*How* have you loved us, pray tell?"

Elizabeth Achtemeier, in her recent commentary on Malachi, has noted that God's love for us has always been a burden to him because of our rebellion, our hardness of heart, and our ingratitude. Listen to what she has to say, "Certainly that love has been a burden—from the very first. When we read the sacred story, his love for us seems to have given him nothing but sorrow and grief—grief in his heart over human wrong (Gen. 6:6); grief in the wilderness over disbelief (Ps. 78:40); grief over the rebellion of his children (cf. Hos. 11:8; Jer. 31:20); grief in his Holy Spirit (Isa. 63:10), over his beloved Jerusalem (Luke 18:40), and over the hardness of his people's hearts (Mark 3:5); until finally that grief is all gathered up, as it must have been, in his weeping at the sight of a cross." "And yet," Achtemeier continues, "before a cynical people who have hauled him into court, God defends himself with only that word of compassion, 'I have loved you, and I love you still.' "

I suppose some persons who are listening would find it hard to imagine that love could ever be a burden. Try to sell that to a teenager who has just fallen in love for the first time. Sweet misery—yes! But a *burden*? Never! But many of you can verify that some of life's heaviest burdens are those that come when you dare to reach out and love someone. Only those who choose not to love can avoid this kind of vulnerability.

I went to a small town in a neighboring state a few years ago to help a pastor friend of mine in a revival meeting. He had been pastor of the church only a short time and had not yet become personally acquainted with all the members. One morning during the week he and I went to visit a couple who were members of the church but who had not yet attended the revival meeting.

When we were invited in by this middle-aged couple, we were almost overcome by the pleasant aroma of hot foods. Seated in the combination living and dining room, we could see that the wife was preparing a veritable banquet of food.

Her table was filled with food, and from the kitchen came the smell of fresh-baked bread and all sorts of cakes and pies.

We made our visit short but before we left the pastor said, "You must be expecting a lot of company today." "No," the woman replied, "It's only our son." "Oh," the pastor said, "And where does your son live?" There was an awkward silence before the woman replied, "Pastor, our son has been in prison the past seven years. He's coming home today and I've cooked him all his favorite dishes." And I knew that this woman understood that the burden of love can sometimes be a very heavy burden indeed. She had borne this burden for seven long years.

But the question we have to answer is whether or not our Heavenly Father feels the pain of love as this mother and father had felt it. Some would deny that he does. Perhaps you have heard of the doctrine of the impassibility of God. It is a central teaching in some of the great world religions. Briefly stated, it argues that God exists in such a state of endless joy and perfection that he is incapable of experiencing grief or pain. Some have argued that such a doctrine as this is necessary in order to safeguard the person of God from all that is weak and finite.

But H. Wheeler Robinson is among those who would disagree. Listen to his words of warning: "The conception of a God who cannot suffer makes theology much more manageable, but leaves it high and dry, like the gods of the Epicureans:

> —who haunt
> The lucid interspace of world and world,
> Where never creeps a cloud, or moves a wind,
> Not ever falls the least white star of snow,
> Nor ever lowest roll of thunder moans,
> Not sound of human sorrow mounts to mar
> Their sacred everlasting calm!"

Surely our God is not so removed from our situation that he cannot feel the grief and pain of our sin. Robinson would remind us that whenever divine love meets human sin a cross is erected, and there God bears with us the whole burden of our finitude, our sinful wanderings and sorrows, and the suffering without which we cannot be made perfect. If the love of God is more than just a metaphor, then the suffering of God must also be regarded as real.

What had the Israelites done to make God's love for them a burden to him? Malachi mentions two things in particular. The first was that they had failed to honor and respect him as their heavenly Father. Listen to the words of Malachi 1:6: "A son honors his father, and a servant his master. If then I am a father, where is my honor? And if I am a master, where is my fear? says the Lord of hosts to you, O priests, who despise my name."

To despise God's name was to despise God himself. The following verses show that the Israelites had done this by making a mockery out of worship. The animals they offered in sacrifice were often sick, and lame, and diseased. It was as if they had offered a plate of rotten food to an honored guest. Malachi challenged them to try offering the same kind of gifts to their governor to see what his response would be.

God is always grieved when our attitude toward him is one of irreverence, indifference, and unconcern. Jesus taught his disciples that the greatest of all the commandments was this: "Hear, O Israel, the Lord our God, the Lord is one; and you shall love the Lord your God with all your heart, and with all your soul, and with all your mind, and with all your strength" (Mark 12:29–30).

D. T. Niles has reminded us of the cost of Christian discipleship in these words: "It is irresponsible . . . to think that Christians can find time and money and strength for everything that everybody else does, and that with spare money in spare time with spare strength they can serve the ends of God's kingdom. The great pearl is bought only by selling small pearls (Matt. 13:45–46). Where no pearl has been sold, there obedience to the demand of the kingdom has not begun."[1]

Could it be that we too have grieved the heart of God and added to the burden that he must bear? Have we failed to honor him and respect him? Have we repeated those words, "Our

Father which art in heaven, hallowed by thy name," and then lived in such a way as to make a mockery of our words?

God's love for us becomes a burden to him when we live as unfaithful servants and as disrespectful and disobedient sons and daughters.

But there is something else that we do that causes grief to our heavenly Father. It is explained in Malachi 2:10: "Have we not all one father? Has not one God created us? Why then are we faithless to one another, profaning the covenant of our fathers?" God not only wants his children to love him with all their heart, and soul, and strength, but he also wants them to love one another.

Isn't the same true of any responsible parent? After I had taught the book of Malachi recently to a group of pastors, one of them came to me and shared the joy that he and his wife had experienced in their three children. He told how kind and considerate the children were to each other and how protective they were of each other. In the Christmas season that has just passed, my wife and I were deeply moved not only by our three daughters' expressions of love toward us but also by their expressions of love toward each other.

And God also wants his children to love one another. And Malachi's question comes back to haunt us: "If we have one father, and if one and the same God created us, why then do we deal treacherously with one another?" Jesus said, "A new commandment I give you, that you love one another."

In Malachi's day those who called themselves the children of God, and who regarded God as their creator, were dealing treacherously and faithlessly with each other, thereby violating the covenant that God had made with Abraham and Isaac and Jacob and their descendants. Israelite society in Malachi's day was shot through with jealousy, hatred, deceit, and strife.

Contrast this situation with God's ideal for his followers as set forth in Psalm 133:1–3:

> Behold, how good and pleasant it is
> When brothers dwell together in unity!

It is like the precious oil upon the head,
running down upon the beard,
upon the beard of Aaron,
Running down on the collar of his robes!
It is like the dew of Hermon,
which falls on the mountains of Zion!
For there the Lord has commanded the blessing,
life for evermore.

Here blessing and life are inseparably linked to a fellowship of unity and peace. And let us not be deceived, my Christian brothers and sisters, God cannot afford to bestow his blessings upon us so long as we are bickering and fighting among ourselves. There is no sorrier spectacle than that of a church or a denomination whose fellowship is destroyed and whose credibility is undermined by internal strife and divisions.

God never condones our mean-spirited and underhanded ways of dealing with our Christian brothers and sisters, no matter how eloquently we preach or how piously we pray. John would remind us that "If anyone says, 'I love God,' and hates his brother, he is a liar; for he who does not love his brother whom he has seen, cannot love God whom he has not seen" (1 John 4:20).

I once attended a prayer service where those present were invited to express their praise in short, three-word sentences. One person said, "God answers prayers." Another, "God is love." Another, "I love Jesus." Finally, an elderly man whose speech had been seriously impaired by a stroke stood and haltingly spoke these words: "Jesus—loves—*me!*"

Not that we love Jesus—but that *he loves us*—this is the heart of the gospel.

But how easy it is for us to add to the burden of his love by failing to give him first place in our lives and by failing to relate to each other in brotherly love.

Wheeler Robinson, noted scholar and dedicated Christian, relates the story of his own conversion. He was a teenager when it took place. He had gone to church and had decided to while away his monotony during the sermon by practicing his shorthand. He would take down the preacher's sermon in shorthand. He was good at this and he managed to take down every word from beginning to end. But somewhere in the middle of the sermon his imagination was seized by the preacher's vision of the incomparable grace of Christ, and by our frequent attitude of indifference to him. He says, "As the preacher reached his end, I resolved to make my beginning as a disciple of Him who is still despised and rejected of men. For me it was the discovery of the great appeal of suffering grace, which is the very heart of the Gospel of divine love."

Wouldn't it be wonderful if as this sermon comes to an end, someone within the sound of my voice would resolve to make a new beginning as the disciple of him who loved us and laid down his life for us!

NOTES

1. D. T. Niles, *Preacher's Task and the Stone of Stumbling* (New York: Harper & Brothers, 1958), 114.

# 11. Herod—Peter—James
## Jan M. Lochman

Acts 12:1–11, 21–24

MY DEAR brothers and sisters:

The twelfth chapter of the Acts of the Apostles is an especially exciting and dramatic story. King Herod decides to liquidate the young church. He has all the power he needs to do it—and already the blood of the martyrs is flowing. James, the brother of John, is killed with the sword. And Peter, the first of the apostles, has been arrested and thrown into prison; he is awaiting his executioner. So Herod triumphs. To all appearances, it is over with the Christians, it is over with Christianity.

But the story in our chapter unfolds in a quite different way. At literally five minutes to twelve midnight, Peter is saved. By a real miracle he escapes from the grasp of the tyrant. And on the other hand, Herod, the great, proud ruler falls, quite unexpectedly, in the very moment when he appeared to himself and his courtiers as the very greatest, divine—indeed, as God. That is how the arrogant dictator ends up—however, the powerless "word of God grew and multiplied."

*Jan M. Lochman,* a native of Czechoslovakia, is a member of the Swiss Reformed Church. Dr. Lochman has been professor of systematic theology at the University of Basel since 1969 and is the author of a number of books, most recently *Christ or Prometheus: A Quest for Theological Identity.* This sermon was translated from the German by James W. Cox.

## Herod—or Arrogance and Fall of a Tyrannical Ruler

The powerful figure of Herod pushes its way from the beginning into the foreground of the scene. He is the one who sets the wheels of the plot in motion. He "lays his hands on." And he appears restored also at the end of the story—and indeed in his entire glory. Now, this Herod Agrippa was actually a strong king, a successful politician. In the view of the book of Acts, he is of course a sinister figure, arrogant before God and man. Before man: Beneath his throne flows blood—and that is an unlucky sign. A politician who builds up his authority by naked power and might, who treats the life of his people so roughly, who arrogantly rules and governs—such a ruler sooner or later, as the Bible views it, incurs judgment.

Herod incurs it all the more clearly because he not only acts arrogantly before people, but also before God. He places himself upon the final throne: He allows himself to be celebrated as a divine figure, he promotes a "personality cult" in the worst sense of the word. Our text shows this notorious temptation of blind political power with unforgettable clarity. In full royal raiment, high upon the throne, Herod begins to speak for the celebration and confirmation of his triumph; he delivers a solemn royal speech. And the courtiers and the people gathered for the occasion are beside themselves with rejoicing: "The voice of a god, and not of man!"

That is our Herod. There is no law above him—he is the ultimate one and the highest one; he plays God.

The fall comes blow upon blow: "Immediately an angel of the Lord smote him, because he did not give God the glory; and he was eaten by the worms and died." One can hardly speak more drastically than that. But this is precisely how drastic is the reality of the illusion of power. It is not within the province of man in his relationship to fellow man and God to overstep the bounds. There is on this earth no throne and no cathedral, perhaps even no family table, on which a "divine," unswerving, irrevocable authority may establish itself. There are in all these places only human voices. They have more or less authority, they deceive themselves more or less, but they are and remain human voices. It is well for us to let the biblical witnesses tell us this—considering the human authorities surrounding us, but this above all, considering our own temptations. Every "personality cult" in politics, but also in the church and in the family, is folly; every arrogance has its revenge. "Arrogance goes before the tumble," says a Czech proverb—and behind it stands biblical informed practical experience.

We need all this warning—in public and private life. How easily and often Herodian tendencies develop among people who have had authority over others suddenly thrust upon them! How many little "Herodettes" there are even among us where we work, in our marriage, family. Perhaps no blood flows, perhaps not even tears—but wherever fellow human beings are preplanned and manipulated by us as pawns in a game, wherever their roles are assigned—precisely there the "herodian leaven" is already at work. To warn of that—such is the classical accent of a biblically oriented political and personal ethic, especially in our Reformed tradition. "Soli Deo Gloria"—To God Alone the Glory. And therefore simply: no fear of "mighty Lords." And no desire of domination of people. The way of Herod never leads to the goal; it is the wrong way, deception, delusion. "Beware of . . . the leaven of Herod" (Mark 8:15): This is the first point of our text.

## Peter—or the Miracle of Freedom

The first story stands in sharp contrast to the second. Before us lies a man condemned to death and completely exhausted: in prison, behind solid walls, chained between two soldiers, and more guards at the door. A prisoner in a hopeless situation. A totally washed up man outwardly—and indeed inwardly as well. This prisoner did not behave as did other un-

Christian prisoners, about whom we have reports in the books of Acts. We think perhaps about Paul and Silas! They pray and sing—even during the night. Peter does not sing any more, nor does he pray. He sleeps. Worn out and depressed, he sleeps through what may be his last night.

And yet precisely at this dark point the gospel in our chapter blazes up. This hopeless case is not quite without hope. This worn-out and abandoned man is not totally forsaken. To begin with, Peter is not forgotten by his brothers and sisters: "Earnest prayer for him was made by the church." Dear brothers and sisters, here something of the true reality of the church emerges. What is that—the church? A society? An interest group or action group with limited responsibility? In the New Testament way of looking at things, it is much more. The church is a community of the Spirit, founded upon prayer and faithfulness to Jesus, renewed in the prayer and in the faithfulness of its members. Our Catholic and Free-Church fellow Christians understand this side of the church often better than we. So let us say to ourselves: Prayer is the life element of the church. Even where we in our life and faith are at the end of our rope with Peter, utterly defeated, finished: We are carried by the prayer of the church—even if it is only two or three who pray. This is the power of the Christian life—precisely in a situation like Peter's we are in prison, between two soldiers, separated from those near to us—and yet, "Earnest prayer for him was made to God by the church."

Our text has, however, still deeper things to tell us. The depressed and sleeping Peter would not even then have been abandoned and forgotten, if all his brothers and sisters had forgotten him, if the organized prayer of the church were long since exhausted. He abides in truer remembrance than the best and truest remembrance by human beings: He abides in the thoughts of God—therefore in the remembrance of the one of whom the Psalmist says, "He who keeps Israel will neither slumber or sleep." This illustrates precisely that remarkable event at night. "And behold," says Luke, "an angel of the Lord appeared." And this is what he does: He gives the sleeping one a blow on the side; wakes him up; makes the chains fall off; leads Peter right through the guard. The iron gate opens of its own accord, and they walk out—into freedom.

Dear brothers and sisters, I am aware that this miracle story in such garb is difficult for most of us to understand. An angel who strikes a man on the side, wakes him up, gets him dressed—who can believe such things today? And yet—let us be patient with angels. Angels—they are in the New Testament messengers of God, signals of the needed presence of God, sign and witness that God himself is at work where, by every human estimate, the end, nothingness, death reigns.

This concerns all of us moderns, who live and think differently, with getting our bearings by different means of representation. What Luke wants to attest for us in the story of Peter concerns us: The story of our life is not only what we experience and what we suffer, what we attempt to conquer, and what we often botch. Our story is not only Herod and prison and manifold dangers of death. We are not hopelessly abandoned and taken prisoner in the adversities and compulsions of our life. We live with our story at the same time in God's liberation story, taken up into the Easter story of Jesus and therefore, as Paul put it, not slaves, but sons—people meant for freedom, free. There are moments in which we can experience this especially clearly. There are miracles of liberation along our life's journey. This is attested for all of us through the miraculous story of Peter. This is its sign, its signal testimony: For freedom we have been set free.

## James—or the Blood of the Martyrs

But then we come upon a counterpoint in our text—in the third story. This third story stands altogether in the shade. What it says is conspicuously reticent: "[Herod] killed James the brother of John with the sword." Only a few words. Telegraphic in style. And yet—as is so often the case with telegrams—these words convey an important, essential message.

It would be too bad if we—perhaps in the light and glow of the story of Peter's going free—overlooked these words about James. The entire message of the chapter would come to us in a skewed, implausible perspective. To be silent about the fate of James would mean to transfigure the stark reality of human life in a shallow and false manner. The life of Christians—our story—is, to be sure, in no way only the story of miraculous deliverances and triumphs; the story of the church is no chain of victories over the Herods. Human life is even suffering and death, absurd rending of our plans and achievements. And the life of the church—that, also, is made up of surrenders and capitulations, blood and tears of martyrs (or apathy and boredom). To the contrary, the Bible is not silent on this state of affairs. That is why in this chapter James stands alongside Peter.

At this point the most difficult questions emerge. Our text places these questions before us: Why was Peter spared, but not James? Why is it that some people were helped in the nick of time, miraculously, while others waited in vain for help and deliverance? Where is God's justice on this earth? From Jesus we hear these words: Without the will of God, not a hair falls from our head. But then: Where was the angel who awoke Peter, when the executioner's assistants dragged James to his execution? Where was the God of justice then?

It is no wonder that precisely in view of such questions the conclusion for many people as the only honorable answer is simply: There is no God. In a world where Herod murders James, where innocent children are bombed and starve, indeed "only" in a world where cancer and other illnesses triumph over the best people: In such a world, to have faith—that seems for many absurd and dishonorable. God does not exist.

Dear friends, if we attempt to believe in terms of the New Testament, we know this: Such protest of the unbelieving concerns us, hits us. Faith suffers from the absurdity and perversion of the human lot no less than unbelief. The protest of the unbelieving is understandable. And yet—the other answer is possible. That is for the New Testament—and also for our story—the answer of the cross of Christ. Well do we mark: It has to do with the *cross*. No transfiguration or prettifying of the human sphere, no superficial retouching of its shadows; rather, the cross—therefore an apex to absurdity, an especially harrowing, perfidious suffering of an innocent one. But the cross of *Christ*: the event which in the New Testament is understood not only as blind fate, as a summit meeting of human treachery and inhuman absurdity, but as the final proof of the faithfulness and solidarity of God with us—up into the ultimate depth of human abandonment and agony. So the death of Jesus is attested in the New Testament in this way: *God* with us—even and precisely in the hopeless and absurd situation of the cross.

In this context the fate of James in our chapter is to be seen. This disciple of Jesus dies—prematurely, cruelly, meaninglessly. And yet: The same light which—first of all, in an altogether different manner, with an altogether different outcome—has illuminated the story of Peter, shines also on what happens here. James does not fall into the abyss. He is taken up into the same story of deliverance as Peter. Both, the one slain and the one miraculously set free, live and die under the same cross and in the light of the same resurrection. "None of us lives to himself, and none of us dies to himself. If we live, we live to the Lord, and if we die, we die to the Lord; so then, whether we live or whether we die, we are the Lord's" (Romans 14:7-8). The question, "Why Peter?" and "Why not James also?" we cannot answer. But we can direct both questions to this story. So there is no total forgetting, no final writing off, no irretrievably lost ones in the light of this story. There is participation in the death and in the life of Jesus Christ. He holds and carries—in life and in death.

Therefore the story of James is not simply deleted, definitely not. The old church fathers coined the expression: "The blood of the martyrs is the seed of the church." This is precisely what Luke wants to attest. His story concludes with the unmistakable point: "But the word of the Lord grew and multiplied." It says this in view of the story of Peter; however, it confesses this also in view of the story of James. And in this way it relates itself also to the story of every one of us: for days when we succeed brilliantly, but also for the hours in which we fail; indeed, for our last hours. The life that is grounded in the liberating story of Jesus does not perish. Amen.

# 12. An "I Am" Saying of Jesus
## Gardner C. Taylor

Jesus saith unto him, I am the way, the truth and the life, no man
cometh unto the Father but by me.—John 14:6

THE WHOLE THING was coming "down to the wire," as
they say in horse-racing circles. These men who had followed
Jesus, betting, so to speak, everything they had and were on
him now began to see some hazards and horrors for which
quite frankly they had not bargained. They had followed in
the confidence that here and now, in flesh and blood, Jesus
was to be the bringer of a new Kingdom, something to be
touched and felt and in which they could hold positions of
prominence and influence, some sitting on his right hand and
some on the left. So it may be safely said that from the very
beginning we who follow Christ have suffered from what has
come to be called "triumphalism," earthly grandeur, blowing
trumpets, with pomp and circumstance as the mission and destiny of the church.

Of late, their leader had been talking strange talk about his
approaching end. Slow-witted though the disciples were, they
were beginning to see for themselves that things were not going well for either their master or their cause. Disquieting rumors were coming to their ears of sinister and ominous plots

*Gardner C. Taylor* is a native of Baton Rouge, Louisiana. He has
been pastor of the Concord Baptist Church of Christ in Brooklyn since
1948. He has lectured and preached worldwide and has been referred
to by *Time* as "the dean of the nation's black preachers." In 1975 and
1976, Dr. Taylor gave the Lyman Beecher Lectures at Yale University.

against him being planned by the authorities. Jesus himself seemed to feel, from the way he talked to them, that his death was almost only an arm's length away now. There seemed to be a crack in their own solidarity, for Judas had been acting strangely of late. Simon Peter, so bold and forward, had been told that his loyalty was in question once the storm would break.

Bewilderment and consternation sat starkly on their faces. Looking at them, Christ shows the unbelievable patience of God himself. It was like a teacher drilling his students once again, and yet not irritably, over lessons the pupils should know by heart. And so he starts that fourteenth chapter, "Let not your heart be troubled. Remember how I have taught you and led you. You believe in God, believe also in me. Over at Father's House there are many rooms and I must go away. I will come back. I've told you so many times and in so many ways. You know where I go and you know the way. We have gone over it so many times."

Thomas could not take it any longer. This loyal man felt comfortable only with the rock of solid fact beneath his feet. Thomas cried out, "Lord we know not whither thou goeth, and how can we know the way?" Then the words that form the text: "I am the way, the truth, and the life, no man cometh unto the Father but by me."

How exclusive that seems, "No man cometh unto the Father but by me." That word seems to shut out so many people in so many parts of the world who have never heard of Jesus. Must they forever be barred from the endless sunshine and ecstatic joy of the Father's face? In another place, Jesus spoke of a "light which lighteth every man that cometh into the world." And elsewhere the New Testament says that God hath "left not himself without witness, in that he did good, and gave us rain from heaven, and fruitful seasons, filling our hearts with food and gladness." In lands and among people who, for whatever reason, hear not of Jesus, God has given other ways. A candle can give light in the darkness. At the same time a candle gives no light when daybreak and sunrise have come. For us who have heard of Christ we dare not close our eyes to that daybreak, holding on to any candle's light; for us no man cometh unto the Father but by Jesus our Lord.

"I am the way." Jesus is the way out. We are all captives and slaves. There is something wrong with our humanity. We feel a disquiet, a deep and true dis-ease. We are not satisfied with what we are; we sense that we are born for some spacious destiny from which we feel some how barred. We feel trapped and flail about, in our own refined way, longing to be free. Most recently we have thought that our way out is by acquisition, and so greed has become our new religion—prettified, to be sure, by nice-sounding political phrases uttered with a practiced unctuousness. This self- centeredness has been baptized and sanctified by the "health and wealth" TV evangelists in their worship of and service to mammon. All of this results in the greater transgression of becoming calloused to the needs of those most vulnerable in the society—the young, the old, the disabled, the disadvantaged.

What is saddest about all of this is that we are training our children to believe that worship at the altar of greed is the way out of our sense of unfulfilled destiny. A California university carried on a survey recently of more than 200,000 college students in America. More than 70 percent said that their purpose was to make money. Less than 30 percent of those surveyed said that they felt a meaningful philosophy of life to be of paramount importance. What a harvest of disillusionment and collapse of the civic contract we may expect in our country!

Jesus is the way out of our foiled sense of destiny and purpose. He declares us to have august connections, a relatedness to the eternal God, intimate and abiding. We are children of a Father's House and our ways may be ordered of the Lord. We are born for greater things than creature comfort; we are heirs of all that God has and wills. A person so believing walks with a firmer tread through the winding and often troubled ways of life. We are the children of the God who steadily leads us onward and upward to a destiny so worthful and so wonderful that the eye of man has not seen and the mind of man cannot imagine the final issue of our days and years. Christ is the way out!

"I am the way," says Jesus, and he is the way through life's hardness and harshness, its pain and its penalties, its fears and its failings. Jesus is the way through. Now we all know full well that there are many religions and philosophies and creeds which claim to be able to spare us, to get us around the pains and problems of life. Brand any religion as false which says that it can spare its adherent the burdens and cares which are the lot and legacy, the inheritance and portion of every person born of a woman. Laugh to scorn any religion which claims it can make you able to avoid hard trials and great tribulations. This is our lot, and it is far wiser to find out, if at all possible, how to deal with these things than how to avoid them.

"Life is real, life is earnest" sang Longfellow, and it is. Our days know hardness and harshness, fear and failings, sin and sorrow, sickness and death. It is, therefore, no wonder that a wistful, and frequently anguished note runs through the world's noblest literature and worthiest music. Brave truth incarnate, Jesus said it to us plainly, "In the world ye shall have tribulation"; then joining our paltry strength to his triumphant power, he added, "but be of good cheer. I have overcome the world." Following him, joined to him, we may do the same. How lustily ought we to be able to sing and to believe.

> When through the deep waters, I call thee to go
> The rivers of woe shall not thee overflow
> For I will be with thee, thy troubles to bless
> And sanctify to thee thy deepest distress

Christ is the way through!

Yes, and he is the way in. There was a play on Broadway years ago in which the distinguished actor Louis Jourdan starred. It was called *Tonight in Samarkand*. Sent into the village to purchase supplies for the estate, a servant is terrified at meeting death, who is dressed as a blond woman wearing a trenchcoat and a red kerchief around her neck. The servant is terrified and returns panting to the estate. With terror-filled eyes and voice quaking, the servant tells his employer of his experience and then desperately asks use of the fleetest horse in the stables that he might flee from this blond woman whose real name is "Death." Permission is granted and the servant frantically races off stage. The master of the estate calls out, "But where will you flee?" "To Samarkand," is the reply.

Later the estate owner goes into the village and meets the same woman. He asks her why she had terrified his servant. "Terrified him?" replied the trenchcoat-wearing person, "I was the one shocked—shocked to see him here in the village when I have a date with him tonight—in Samarkand." And so do we all. It may be that we are not too fretful about our "date in Samarkand," but we are greatly concerned about those whom we love and who love us, and surely about those dear souls we have "loved long since and lost a while," as Newman put it so unforgettably.

If Jesus told us anything at all, he told us that this world is not all, that we have dual citizenship. This we know now, for Christ taught and proclaimed that this present existence is but a narrow, cramped room hardly to be compared with what else God has in store for us. He gives us no intimate details, as if to say it is all too wonderful to submit to description. He did say that he is the way! The way home! The way to bright glory! The way to sunlit shores of an everlasting country! Still, this is not enough. Suppose the poor pilgrims cannot find the way, though it is said that "a highway shall be there, and a way, and it shall be called The way of holiness . . . it shall be for those: the wayfaring men, though fools, shall not err therein." Suppose we cannot find the way and cannot discover the path to glory? "I go to get things ready," said Jesus. Still, it may be we cannot find the way! Then, says the Lord, "I will come again, and receive you unto myself that where I am, there ye may be also."

So the Shepherd will search and find his sheep "and when he hath found it, he layeth it on his shoulders, rejoicing. And when he cometh home, he calleth together his friends and neighbors, saying unto them, 'Rejoice with me; for I have found my sheep which was lost.' "

# *13.* Dives and Lazarus: Neighbors Who Never Met
## *Joe E. Trull*

Luke 16:19–31

DIVES AND LAZARUS were neighbors. Daily they passed by one another at the rich man's front gate, yet the two never met. The reason is revealing. The wealthy Dives was so absorbed in his indulgent lifestyle, he never noticed a "beggar named Lazarus . . . at his door" (Luke 16:20).

The parable in Luke's gospel is a masterful drama in which Jesus wastes not a word in contrasting the lives of two men. Socially they are poles apart. Eternally a great gulf separates the two. Yet there is a lesson that links them together. The selfish use of possessions divides men, destroys lives, and determines destiny. That is the focal point of the parable.

Jesus addresses man's greed and godlessness. The theme of the story is stewardship, not eternal destiny. The lesson concerns money—how it can be used to help the needy or be selfishly hoarded.

This dramatic parable was probably precipitated by the attitude of certain Pharisees who were "lovers of money" (Luke

*Joe E. Trull* is associate professor of Christian ethics at New Orleans Baptist Theological Seminary in Louisiana. Formerly pastor of First Baptist Church, El Paso, Texas, Trull has written several books and articles for *Christianity Today* and other periodicals. He is a graduate of Oklahoma Baptist University and holds the Th.D. from Southwestern Baptist Theological Seminary.

16:14). When Christ shared with them a story about an unjust steward (Luke 16:1–13), these pious play-actors only sneered. Jesus' pointed word, "You cannot serve God and money" (Luke 16:13), must have upset them.

This led our Lord to tell a second story, a dynamic drama in three acts. To read this tale of two neighbors is to look in a two-way mirror. We first view ourselves, for rich Dives looks all too familiar. We also see images of our neighbors, for Lazarus the beggar reminds us of someone lying at our doorstep.

Today, as never before, the selfish use of possessions builds barriers instead of bridges. This morning the *Today* television newscast pictured street people sleeping on steaming street gates in front of the White House during subfreezing weather. Immediately the program shifted to Paris, where American socialites were selecting designer dresses at $15,000 per original. The contrast is obvious.

Jesus still looks upon our wealth and poverty with troubled eyes. His parable about two neighbors who never met speaks to our day also.

## *Act One: Contrasting Lifestyles*

The first act of Jesus' dramatic story is a tableau contrasting two men in life. They were in opposite extremes of the socioeconomic scale, their lifestyles completely different.

First we meet Dives (the Latin translation for "rich man"). Dives was the plutocrat of Palestine. Like Croesus, his name became a synonym for wealth and always appeared on the list of best-dressed. A connoiseur of exotic cuisine, Dives was the popular host of the rich and famous.

The description of him is opulent to the last detail. Dives "habitually dressed in purple" (verse 19), the color worn by royalty and the high priest due to the costliness of the purple dye, which had to be meticulously extracted from oyster shells. His underclothing was "fine linen" (verse 19), an expensive Egyptian product called "woven air," traditionally used to bind the mummified bodies of the Pharaohs.

Every meal was a banquet, for he "feasted every day brilliantly" (verse 19). The menu read like Antoines of New Orleans—pheasant under glass, oysters Rockefeller, beef Wellington, caviar, and perfectly aged wine. No food was too exotic; no table too lavish. The picture painted by Jesus is one of selfish indulgence.

The other character in this drama was a beggar named Lazarus. The Hebrew name means "God helps," probably indicating his utterly destitute condition. This cripple was literally "thrown down" (verse 20) before the high ornamental gate of Dives each day, there to seek survival. A mass of ulcers on his body no doubt indicated the diet deficiency which made him weak. Lazarus barely managed to stay alive by eating the crumbs of discarded bread, which banqueters at Dives's table used as napkins. Servants gathered these leftovers to throw to the waiting dogs in the street.

Too hungry to refuse the crumbs and too helpless to drive away the dogs, Lazarus could not keep the animals from licking his sores. Since most Jews disliked dogs, Jesus may have meant the mongrels gave weak Lazarus relief and were his only friends.

The lone connection between those two men was at the front gate, where Dives and his friends daily passed by Lazarus. Neighbors they were who never met, because Dives never noticed. The selfish use of possessions truly divides men in life. It also destroys men at death.

## Act Two: Surprising Reversal

The second scene suddenly shifts. Now we see two persons at the time of their death.

To no one's surprise, poor Lazarus died. "What a blessing! Now he no longer suffers," thought most. Immediately he was "carried away by angels" (verse 22) to the place of highest honor—next to Abraham, the father of Israel.

Rich Dives also died; but he was only "buried" (verse 22). Jesus shared no detail of his death. Surely the community was shocked. Certainly the news traveled throughout the countryside. Undoubtedly the day of his elaborate funeral was declared a state holiday—everyone who was anyone came to pay homage to Israel's multimillionaire.

But where was he? Jesus shared the shocking news: "in hell . . . in torments . . . afar off" (verse 23). Dives was now on the outside looking in, begging for mercy—just a few drops of water from Lazarus's finger. Only yesterday Lazarus had begged for a few crumbs from Dives's table!

What a striking reversal! The real reason for this turnaround is revealed in one word from Abraham—"remember" (verse 25). In his lifetime this Jewish Midas had lived purely for self, while a poor beggar died at his gate. Fastening his eyes on the "good things" of this word, he abused God's gifts, spending all on personal pleasures.

Not that he was necessarily irreligious. His cry "Father Abraham" (verse 24) may have meant he was a good Jew, praying and offering sacrifices at the Temple, perhaps even fasting and occasionally giving alms. But Dives's lifestyle and treatment of Lazarus showed he primarily lived in selfish indulgence, oblivious of God.

After death a complete and permanent "chasm" (verse 26) separated Lazarus and Dives. Who dug the ditch? Dives. It is the same gulf that separated the rich man in his affluence from Lazarus in his misery in life. The one thing Dives overlooked was that God was on the side with Lazarus. In shutting out Lazarus, he shut out God. Jesus always portrayed God as friend of the poor, helper of the weak, and compassionate toward the needy.

If a person lives without love, he digs a deep ditch between himself and humankind—and also God! On the day of death, the self-centered life scores zero on the final test. For to shut out human need with selfish indifference is to shut out God— and that indeed brings eternal failure. The Bible calls it hell!

## Act Three: Intentional Blindness

Scene three arrives without warning. After contrasting two men in life and at death, Jesus now juxtaposed these two in eternity.

Dives suddenly made a new request. "Send Lazarus to warn my five brothers," he pled (verses 27–28). The tormented Dives knew his family's selfish lifestyle would lead each to the same fate. Although on the surface the petition seemed considerate, the wish implied this man of means had not himself received fair warning.

Abraham's answer, like the rapier thrust of a swordsman, burned to the soul: "They have the writings of Moses and the prophets" (verse 29). God's revelation was available to the five brothers, as indeed it had been for the rich man. Both ignored the word from God.

Shouting an emphatic "No!" (verse 30), the rich man strongly rejected Abraham's response. "Only a supernatural event will deter them," he insisted. A warning from Lazarus, resurrected from the grave, surely would get their attention and cause them to repent!

Like their deceased brother, these five were traveling in the fast lane, panting after pleasure, drinking to the dregs every intoxicating cup the world offered. There was no time to hear or heed God's prophetic message.

Abraham observed a universal truth. People who are deaf to God's voice in the Bible will not be convinced by "signs." Further revelation is not needed. The Scriptures contain all the knowledge the brothers needed—their problem was not understanding, but attitude. Like deep-sea creatures who lose their sight through years of living in darkness, these five men intentionally blinded themselves by shutting their eyes to God's light.

For such persons signs never redeem; they may terrify, but are soon forgotten. When another Lazarus did rise from the dead, what happened? Witnesses only hardened their hearts in disbelief (John 12:10–11). When Jesus Himself was resurrected, what happened? Religious leaders would not believe the evidence; instead they concocted false stories to discredit the event (Matt. 28:11–15).

Genuine conversion, you see, is not the product of sensationalism. God does not coerce with signs, He appeals in love. Persons are not changed by spectacular miracles, they are persuaded by God's truth.

The curtain falls; the drama concludes. Do we grasp the point of Jesus' parable? What was the rich man's sin? Dives did not order Lazarus removed from the gate or object to his begging. Neither did he refuse the beggar bread. No, the wealthy nobleman did not deliberately mistreat the penniless pauper.

The sin of Dives was that he *never noticed Lazarus!* The beggar was just there, part of the street scene. Every day he and his friends walked past this charity case, maybe even stepping over the destitute man. Dives was so absorbed in selfish indulgence, he never saw a fellow human hungry and in pain. Because he never noticed this neighbor on his doorstep, he cut himself off from God and humanity.

What about us? The beggar is also on our doorstep. Needy persons surround us. Each year between 15 million and 20 million people die of starvation or hunger-related illness. About 12 million of them are children who die before they reach the age of five. This day over 40,000 will starve, 30,000 of them children.

Do we notice?

At least 1 billion persons on planet earth live in a state of absolute poverty. Some in our city.

Do we notice?

There are 5 billion souls who live in major urban ghettos, most without adequate food, housing or health care. By A.D. 2000 the number will increase to 6.5 billion.

Do we notice?

Latin America now has 40 million abandoned street children. By the turn of the century over 60 million young people will roam the metropolitan alleys, like packs of wild dogs, struggling to survive.

Do we notice?

Each year 250,000 children become blind due simply to vitamin deficiency in their diet.

Do we notice?

Our sin is not that we do *wrong* things, but that we, like Dives, do *no-thing*! He never noticed the neighbor at his gate. The beggar is on our doorstep. Do we notice? Do we?

Hear the word of Isaiah the prophet:

> I want you to share your food with the hungry
> and bring right into your own homes those who
> are helpless, poor and destitute. Clothe those
> who are cold and don't hide from relatives who
> need your help. If you do these things, God will
> shed his own glorious light upon you. He will
> heal you; your godliness will lead you forward,
> and goodness will be a shield before you, and
> the glory of the Lord will protect you from
> behind. Then, when you call, the Lord will
> answer. "Yes, I am here," he will quickly reply.
> All you need to do is to stop oppressing the
> weak, and to stop making false accusations and
> spreading vicious rumors!
>
> Feed the hungry! Help those in trouble!
> Then your light will shine out from the
> darkness, and the darkness around you shall be
> as bright as day. (Isaiah 58:7–10, LBT)

# *14.* Giving Birth to a Miracle
## *Martin B. Copenhaver*

Luke 1:26–55

THE STORY STARTS quietly, on an intimate scale. Before the crowded inn, before the chorus of angels, before the star, before the shepherds and the wise men, even before the child, there was the mother, who was not much more than a child herself, receiving word that she was to give birth to a child, bring forth a new life, and also receiving word that in some way through that child she was to give birth to the whole world and bring new life to all.

Every mother is not only a witness to miracle, but also in some way part of the miracle. But this mother was part of two miracles: the miracle of a new human life that stirred inside her and the miracle that in some special way God resided there as well. We can only wonder which miracle more occupied Mary's heart and mind, but I am quite sure that each miracle would have the power to prompt both fear and praise. Considered together the two miracles cannot help but make this simple country girl shudder with the fearsome wonder of it all.

We do not know much about who the angel Gabriel was or is, and we can only imagine how he made himself known to

---

*Martin B. Copenhaver* is senior minister of the First Congregational Church (United Church of Christ) in Burlington, Vermont. A graduate of Dickinson College, he received the master of divinity degree from Yale Divinity School and was the recipient of the Mersick Prize in Preaching from Yale in 1980. Copenhaver is the author of *Living Faith While Holding Doubts.*

Mary. But this I think we can say: He was not very subtle, even for an angel. He finds her and gets right down to business, with words that might startle a young woman even if they did not come from an angel: "Hail, O favored one, the Lord is with you! Blessed are you among women!" Maybe if you are an angel you know that there is no way to ease into a conversation with a human being, so you don't even try. Or perhaps Gabriel was so fluttering with the news he had come to share that he couldn't contain himself, like a winged obstetrician on his first case who is as eager and giddy as the parents are. That is to say, if, as the Bible records, Mary was greatly troubled at the greeting she received, we do not have to wonder why.

And then Gabriel, perhaps seeing the reaction he has stirred, quickly adds, "Do not be afraid." It is an appropriate reassurance to one who has just seen an angel. And it is also an appropriate reassurance to a young woman who is about to receive the news that she is soon to become a young mother. "Do not be afraid," a phrase that I am sure is often heard in the offices of earthly obstetricians. "Do not be afraid," even though you do not know what lies ahead. "Do not be afraid," even though you feel more like your mother's child than like a child's mother. "Do not be afraid," even though there is nothing in human experience that can prepare you for this moment.

"Blessed are you among women," said Gabriel. But it may be an unnecessary addition to the greeting, for it is the way of young mothers that they can feel especially blessed, and without any prompting from man, woman, or angel. "Blessed are you among women," because you are about to witness a miracle, and to be part of a miracle. "Blessed are you among women," because though the cycle of birth is as old as life, it is now to be renewed in you.

But also, "Blessed are you among women," in other ways too. "Blessed are you" in all the ways that God blesses people, not always through pleasure and prosperity, but also, perhaps especially, in the midst of sorrow and trial. God's blessing is also God's burden. The blessing is life in its fullness, and that is also the burden. It is the burden of life in all of its pain and complexity and in no life will that be more evident than in the life of Mary's child. The seeds of sorrow and trial are so surely in Mary's womb as is this new life. A mother, especially this mother of this child, must be prepared to give birth to both life and death, both joy and pain, for no life is without this uneasy mixture. To receive this blessing is to affirm life in spite of all its contradictions and limits and disappointments. And so, to receive this blessing is ultimately an act of faith.

There are traditions within Christendom that praise Mary as the one who loved Jesus more than any other person ever did or ever could. And there may be good reason to believe that. It does seem that no love for Jesus could be more remarkable than this love she had for him before his birth, for it was true unconditional love. After all, what love could be more unconditional than love that does not yet know what it is loving? Will he be tall or short? Will he be handsome or homely? Will he be attentive or cold? Will he reject me or love me in return? Somehow, in this miracle of unconditional love, such questions are not asked and need no answer. The love is love of the unknown, a personal devotion to another before that other is more than just a stirring and a promise.

In these ways, then, Mary's experience was not too unlike that of other women in other times and other places, women who learn that they are to give birth and respond with fear, and feel blessed, and who love their unborn child with an unconditional love.

Yet, in other ways, Mary's experience is as far from common human experience as is the very life of Jesus. We can only imagine, and then only barely imagine, what it would be like to know that the child you carry in the womb is also, in some way, at the same time, your parent, as God is the parent of us all, and thus even the parent of the one who is to give him birth.

And though every mother wants to know what kind of child she carries in her womb, how can we imagine receiving the word that Mary received: "He will be great," said Gabriel;

and though every parent might think that that would be most gratifying news, the message quickly gathers in such power that even a mother's imagination can no longer keep up with it. "And he will be called the Son of the Most High; and the Lord God will give to him the throne of his father David, and he will reign over the house of Jacob forever; and of his kingdom there will be no end."

Such news could have been cause for sheer dread, and I am sure that dread was at least part of what Mary felt. And yet whatever dread there might be was also coupled with faith and trust. We can catch only a glimmer of what this must have been like. Other mothers may recognize that though a child is their child, the world also lays claim to that same child. Other mothers may know that their desire to protect their child should not prevent the child from claiming his or her destiny. But to have so great a burden laid on one's child, a burden so complete and uncompromising that it does not even wait for the child to be born, no less wait for the child to grow older and stronger, why, that requires something else from a mother—a faith and trust that is almost as much a miracle as the birth itself.

And the story of Mary is different from our story in another way. It is common for us to see God at work in something exotic or distant or dim. But it can be more difficult to find God in the familiar and everyday. We may be willing to concede that God has acted in some remembered point in history, but it can be more difficult to affirm that God is acting today. We may grant that God is active in human lives generally, but, ironically, it is often God's actions in our own lives that are most difficult to trace. Our own days are too common, our own lives too familiar to sense the mystery of God pulse within them. We who may find it difficult to imagine that God could be somehow uniquely at work in the life of one man at one point in history, we cannot even imagine what it would be to know that man as a mother knows a son and still to be able to affirm the wild miracle of it. Mary could look at Jesus with a mother's sure familiarity—every hair on his head, every crease in his face, every turn of his smile. He was as familiar to her as the way home, as close as her own skin. And yet, she could see God there too, a God she could not only love, but also a God she could worship, and a God to whom she could entrust her life.

From Mary we learn about miracles and how to receive them. Mary understood that God is at work in unexpected places, in the life of a simple country girl through the promise of a child, and from her we can learn that God can be at work in perhaps the most unexpected place of all, in our own lives. After all, God's miracles are nowhere more difficult to see than when they occur in front of our eyes.

Before the crowded inn, before the chorus of angels, before the star, before the shepherds and the wise men, before even the child, there was the mother, who was not much more than a child herself, receiving word that she was to give birth to a child, bring forth a new life, and also receiving word that in some way through that child she was to give birth to the whole world and bring new life to all. She received the promise as a promise from God and thus in some way as a promise already fulfilled. And indeed, in time, the child was born, the Son of the Most High. It was a promise fulfilled first in the heart of one young woman, awaiting fulfillment in history. And for us the order has been reversed. The promise has already been fulfilled in history, and now it awaits fulfillment in our hearts.

# 15. A Finished Life
## C. David Matthews

Luke 2:22–35

WHEN I WAS a child, Christmas was always agonizingly slow in coming, and then was over much too fast. Do you remember waiting for Christmas, counting the days with almost unbearable expectation? Time seemed to drag almost to a standstill. Then, suddenly, the wonder for which you had waited came. And then, even more suddenly, it was over. Too quickly, life fell back into routines.

In church, too, the time right after Christmas can be a problem. Worship on the Sunday after Christmas seems anticlimactic, both for the preacher and the congregation. If you are the preacher, what do you say? What is an appropriate subject for this second-class Sunday?

Here in the afterglow of Christmas may be a good time to consider a largely forgotten figure from the story of Jesus' birth. In Luke's gospel we have traditionally quit reading the Christmas story with chapter two, verse twenty. Therefore, most people could not begin to tell you who Simeon was. Actu-

*C. David Matthews* is minister of the Church of the Good Samaritan in Orlando, Florida. He was awarded a master of divinity and doctor of theology from Southwestern Baptist Theological Seminary. He has been pastor of First Baptist Church, Greenville, South Carolina, and, before that, of churches in Texas and Oklahoma. Matthews gave the E. Y. Mullins Lectures on Preaching at Southern Baptist Theological Seminary in 1984, and he is the author of *Prayer Meeting Resources* and the composer of "Creative Praise," and "I Ask None Else of Thee." "A Finished Life" is a sermon for the Sunday after Christmas.

ally, he has a prominent place in Luke, even though he is obscure in our memory.

Simeon is a rare and precious spirit. The peace the angels announced at the Savior's birth is personified as profoundly in Simeon as in anyone. Let me tell you about this man and that part of the Christmas story that comes right after the shepherds and the angels.

What does a person want to see most before death comes and life ends? One may want to see one's reputation secure. One may want to see one's name honored. One may want to see one's children established and prospering.

Here is a man with a very different wish. He was not so focused on himself. Simeon wanted to see what was referred to in his day as "the consolation of Israel."

The Jews of Jesus' time lived with great messianic hopes. The Messiah would come and bring in a whole new age for Israel. The future fulfillment of all those hopes was sometimes called "the consolation of Israel." That is what Simeon wanted to see.

Moreover, this righteous and devout man had been promised that he would not die before he had seen "the Lord's Christ," which means the Messiah. Simeon, like Zechariah and Elizabeth in Luke's account, represented the highest qualities of Jewish faith and life. He was a genuinely saintly person. As devoted as he was to the ancient faith of Israel, however, in his soul he longed for the "new thing" he knew God would do. The one thing left, the one thing for which he now lived, was to look upon the face that had the light of God on it.

All of us know at some time, and some of you know now, what it is to live with one great wish, with one dominant desire that overrides all others. It is not the most pleasant way to live. To possess, or to be possessed by, some mighty hope or some magnificent obsession may give heavy meaning to your life. But it is far from the most comfortable way to live. Until that one powerful desire is either fulfilled or given up there is no real peace. Everything else may be going well, but at the center of your being there is a restlessness, a fundamental conflict.

I have know ministers, for example, who wanted more than anything else to build a great church building. For obvious reasons, of course: Buildings make nice monuments. For half a century or longer people can say, "We built this wonderful edifice when Dr. Fuddyduddy was our pastor."

This is a hard temptation for some ministers to resist, sinners that we are. Getting one's name on a cornerstone appears to some a very appetizing immortality. Some preachers would rather build a building than have a robe and a crown in glory!

Professionally religious people, I am saying, can get a lot of ego wrapped up in their work. When it is excessive, it is the most unfortunate thing that can happen in the ministry.

It has always been a problem. It was a problem at the time Jesus was born. Some of the religious leaders in Jerusalem back then were extremely self-seeking, and religion was every bit as subject to abuses by both clergy and laity as it is today.

But Simeon's ambitions were pure. He was not living for something he would accomplish himself. He was living to see what he believed God would do. Something was going to happen in Israel. A new day was going to dawn, and this aged man's great desire was to behold its first rays of light.

Simeon had apparently been waiting a long time. There must have been days of discouragement, days when he wondered if he would actually live to see it happen. There must have been times of perplexity, times when he almost despaired that nothing had happened. But there was always the unrest in his soul. No peace.

Then, one day, he was inspired to go into the temple. A father and mother were there with their infant child. In those days two religious rituals were very important approximately a month after the birth of a child. One was the rite of purification, which was primarily to take away the mother's "uncleanness." The Jews considered a woman ritually unclean after childbirth. The other was the rite of presentation, which had more to do with the dedication of the child to God.

Here was an ordinary couple doing an ordinary thing in Judaism. It was obvious from the sacrifice (two turtledoves, or young pigeons) that they were poor. No one would have seen much in this event. But the restless, watchful eyes of an old man saw something.

It is a poignant image, Simeon taking this little baby and holding him in his arms. Just a baby. And suddenly Simeon sees the dawning of the new day. He knows he holds the Messiah. This tiny infant, he knows, is the long-promised Savior.

Simeon had arrived at the moment for which he had lived. The ache in his heart became a fullness almost to bursting. The restlessness was resolved in a deep peace. Peace at last.

He spoke: "Lord, now lettest thou thy servant depart in peace, according to thy word; for mine eyes have seen thy salvation which thou hast prepared in the presence of all peoples, a light for revelation to the Gentiles, and for glory to thy people Israel" (2:29–32).

In the history of the church these words are called the "Nunc Dimittis." These are the first two words of the Latin translation of Simeon's response. This passage may have been circulated in the early church as a hymn. Luke's account of the first Christmas is full of such musical passages. There is the "Annunciation" of the angel Gabriel. There is the humble yet revolutionary "Magnificat" of Mary. There is the "Benedictus" of Zechariah, father of John the Baptist. And, of course, there is the "Gloria" of the angels. Luke sings the Christmas story.

Much of the greatness of Simeon's words is that they contain such a rare depth of insight concerning the nature of Jesus' messiahship. First, Simeon sees that this Messiah will have worldwide significance. He is not just for Israel, but for the Gentile world as well. Do you remember how long it took Simon Peter to come to that understanding?

Second, Simeon sees that this messiahship will involve suffering. "Behold," he said, "this child is set for the fall and rising of many in Israel, and for a sign that is spoken against" (2:34). And to Mary he said, "And a sword will pierce through your own soul also" (2:35). Popular notions of the Messiah had submerged any thoughts of him as a sufferer. A winner was coming! He would be triumphant in all the ways the world measures success.

But Simeon remembered his Bible. He had not forgotten what kind of Messiah was promised. And he saw the promise now in the face of a baby. Peace came to his tired heart. Peace at last. "Now lettest thou thy servant depart in peace."

Peace. Let's talk about peace a moment.

Nothing about the Christmas story in Luke has been more universally appealing than the angels' declaration of peace. Our world has longed for peace for a long time. It is our most recurring and most fleeting dream. So, maybe you come away from Christmas singing:

> . . . in despair I bowed my head;
> "There is no peace on earth," I said,
> "For hate is strong
> And mocks the song
> Of peace on earth, good will to men."

Yet we cannot give up our pursuits of peace. We pray for peace. We cry for peace. We work for peace. We negotiate for peace. Sometimes we even fight for peace.

We seek peace in international treaties, in law courts, in the back rooms of conventions, in the offices of marriage counselors and psychotherapists, in the books of pop psychology gurus, and in every expression of religion imaginable. We are serious about finding peace.

Simeon can help us. At least he can help us see what peace really is. He embodies true peace.

Peace is a word that is most commonly used in a rather negative sense. Peace means resolved conflict, or the cessation of hostilities. Peace, everybody knows, is when the fighting stops.

Remember the genius who said that the one good thing about wearing shoes that don't fit is that it feels so good when you take them off? This is peace as relief. And it's not a bad peace.

But if peace means merely the absence of conflict, then you are not going to have much peace in this world. Conflict is one of the facts of life. Some conflict is inevitable in every situation and every relationship.

That is not to say that conflict is to be passively accepted. Most conflict needs to be reduced, of course, and we must keep working on that. If we do not stop the nuclear madness, for example, in which our country and the Soviets are involved, we may forfeit the destiny God intends for us in creation.

In the Bible, however, peace is much more than the absence of conflict. It includes that, but it is much more.

The beautiful Hebrew word *shalom*, at the deepest level, means peace as fulfillment. It is peace as the realization or fulfillment of God's intention. The case can be made that this word for peace, *shalom*, has almost the same meaning as salvation, or even eternal life.

True peace is not sitting in front of the TV with your feet up, and your tummy full, and plenty of money in the bank, and no major worries. That's not bad. But the Bible knows a better peace.

It is the peace that comes to the person who is fulfilling God's purpose in his or her life. True peace comes with being, in this world of conflict and pain, a whole person, the person of the Creator's intention.

It is the peace of knowing who you are. It is the peace of knowing what really matters, and thus what doesn't matter.

It is the peace of integrity. It comes from remaining identified with what is true, and good, and godly, even when the world's on fire.

It is the peace even death cannot destroy. It is the peace that passes understanding (Phil. 4:7).

This is the peace found in all the truly great lives. This is the peace of the prisoner Paul, of the dying Stephen, of a Gandhi, of a Thomas More, of a Martin Luther King, Jr. These never knew much peace in the ordinary, popular sense. But they lived with a deep serenity of heart despite everything.

As a pastor, I have observed quite a number of people approach life's last experience, the experience of death. I find that those who have known something of this higher peace of which we are speaking are generally more accepting of that last passage.

It is easier to end a finished life than an unfinished one. By "finished" I do not mean nothing left to do. I mean a fulfilled life, a life full of what God intended for all of us.

Funeral services, I have found, are not all the same. Some are difficult almost beyond endurance. And some are almost easy. Some are occasions of tragedy and unbearable grief. And some are joyful.

What is the difference? It is not just a matter of how long a person has lived, or even whether death has come as a release from suffering. These things matter. But the determining consideration is whether or not we are dealing with a truly completed life, a finished life. That is, if a person has become something of the person God created all of us to be, whatever the age or circumstances, there may be found a triumphant dimension even in that person's death.

Conversely, we grieve most, I think, for those who have never really lived, no matter how many years they have existed. How tragic to die unfinished.

You have known people, old in years, who died with small, twisted souls. You have known people, young in years, who died with their hearts full of all the things that matter. Shalom, the peace of God, is to have a healthy soul and a heart full of good things.

We are all fascinated by famous last words, or the last words of the famous. Often they are a succinct summation of a person's life. Often they provide a crystal-clear glimpse into a person's character. Often they indicate whether a life has been truly finished or not.

We all know George Gipp's last words: "Someday, when things look real tough for Notre Dame, ask the boys to go out there and win one for the Gipper." The famous British admiral, Horatio Nelson, mortally wounded on board ship at the battle of Trafalgar, said, "Thank God, I have done my duty." The South African statesman and financier, C. J. Rhodes, a part of whose fortune endowed the prestigious Rhodes scholarships, died beset by personal scandals and discredited by the Boer War. His dying words were, "So little done, so much to do."

I have some lesser-known last words in my collection, which, frankly, I value more than these. As the Mexican revolutionary Pancho Villa lay dying, he said, "Don't let it end like this. Tell them I said something." Madame de Pompadour, mistress of Louix XV, as she lay dying, summoned her last strength and called to God, "Wait a second," and she dabbed her cheeks with rouge. Knowing he was about to die, the French philosopher Auguste Comte is reported to have murmured, "What an irreparable loss!" And my favorite may be from Oscar Wilde. One of several versions of Wilde's death has him staring from his death bed at his shabby Paris bedroom, and saying, "Either that wallpaper goes, or I do."

Seriously, though, we need to think about what our own last words might be, if they turned out to be a commentary on our living. What might they honestly be if you were required to speak them now? What would you like for them to be whenever they might have to be spoken?

I commend the words of Simeon to you. They represent a most worthy aspiration. They reflect a finished life, a life full of shalom, full of the peace of Christmas.

Simeon, therefore, is not only a good person with whom to conclude the Christmas season, he is also a good person with whom to begin the new year. I will say to you what I think he might say to all of us.

In this new year seek the peace that comes from living for those higher things God has revealed in Christ. Live for what God is doing in the world, not so much for things that are transient and do not satisfy. Live for what matters.

Then you will really live. Then you will know genuine peace. Then at the end of your living, even (God forbid) if that end should come for you during this year before us, you will be able to offer your own "Nunc Dimittis":

"Lord, now lettest thou thy servant depart in peace, according to thy word; for mine eyes have seen thy salvation . . ."

Amen.

# 16. A Marriage Made in Heaven
## Cindy Witt

John 4:5–42

DEAR FRIENDS in Christ,

> "The time has come," the Walrus said,
> "To talk of many things:
> Of shoes—and ships—and sealing wax—
> Of cabbages—and kings—
> And why the sea is boiling hot—
> And whether pigs have wings."[1]

The Walrus in that poem from *Alice in Wonderland* had some important topics to talk about—most notably, about "shoes and ships and sealing wax, of cabbages and kings, and why the sea is boiling hot and whether pigs have wings." These are, as the Walrus indicates, topics for which the time has come.

This morning, we, too, have some important things to talk about, most notably, about weddings and water . . . and no doubt these two topics sound just as strange to your ears as discussing why the sea is boiling hot. But, as the Walrus says, "The time has come."

*Cindy Witt* is a Ph.D. student at Claremont Graduate School in Claremont, California. A graduate of Luther Northwestern Seminary and member of the Evangelical Lutheran Church in America, she has been assistant pastor and interim pastor of churches in Minnesota and California. Witt has also coauthored articles for *SCOPE*, a publication of American Lutheran Church Women.

So . . . come along with me then, on a journey of sorts, to a time of wonder and delight.

We begin, "Once upon a time, in a land far, far away." Let's stop right there.

When I say, "Once upon a time in a land far, far away . . .", what kind of story comes to your mind? A news story from West Germany? A discussion of the relative merits of a warm Minnesota winter? No. In all likelihood what you would expect to hear would be a story of fantasy. "Once upon a time in a land far, far away" is the normal way for a make-believe story to begin. It lets us know that we are to hear about a world of fairy princesses, of frogs who turn into princes, of evil trolls who hide under bridges.

And that's as it should be, for the words, "Once upon a time in a land far, far away" are our entry tickets to the land of imagination. It is the traditional, conventional way most make-believe stories begin . . . and as soon as we hear those words, we come to expect some very specific things to happen. We expect:

- a very good, kind, wonderful person . . . maybe a princess or other image of "the good" to play a prominent role in the story that follows;
- we also expect to encounter "the bad"—the "evil" in the form of a wicked person, or a troll, or something like that;
- and we would expect a contest between the forces of good and the forces of evil . . . with the imminent threat of the evil winning out when, at the last minute, through some courageous effort, the good emerges victorious;
- and, of course, the story will end with "the good" living "happily ever after."

Those expectations we have of a story that begins, "Once upon a time in a land far, far away" are due to story conventions, that is, a skeleton structure upon which stories are woven. The idea of using a skeleton structure upon which to fashion a story is an ancient method of storytelling. It is a device that assists those who tell the story to relay it accurately;

and it enables those who hear the story to know what kind of story to expect in order that they can pay closer attention to the details they might otherwise miss.

The people of Israel were a people used to stories being told in a particular manner in order that they could hear and retell those stories from generation to generation.

One of the types of stories that were told were Betrothal stories—the stories of how their ancestors met and got married to one another. Those stories had particular things in common.

1. There was a young man who was not married. The eligible bachelor, so to speak.
2. He, or a representative, would make a trip to a foreign land.
3. While on the trip, he would stop by a well.
4. A maiden would come to the well, where the two would meet.
5. After a discussion or event that bonded them to one another, the maiden would run to tell her family about the events at the well.
6. The family would then extend hospitality to the stranger.
7. The marriage plans would be announced.

Isaac became engaged to Rebekah that way, Jacob became engaged to Rachel that way, Moses became engaged to Zipporah that way. It was the way Betrothal stories were told.

Listen to the story of Isaac and Rebekah.

1. *The eligible bachelor, or his agent, goes to a foreign land:* "And Abraham said to his servant . . . 'Go to my country and to my kindred, and take a wife for my son Isaac' . . . then the servant went to Mesopotamia, to the city of Hanor."
2. *The eligible bachelor, or his agent, stops at a well:* "And he made the camels kneel down outside the city by the well of water at the time of evening, the time when women go out to draw water. And he said, 'O Lord God . . . let the maiden to whom I shall say, "Pray, let down your jar that I may

drink" and who shall say, "Drink, and I will water your camels"—let her be the one whom you have appointed for your servant Isaac.' "

3. *The maiden comes to the well:* "Before he had done speaking, behold, Rebekah, who was born to Bethuel, the son of Milcah, the wife of Nahor, Abraham's brother, came out with her water jar on her shoulder."

4. *A bond is established:* "Then the servant ran to meet her, and said, 'Pray, give me a little water to drink from your jar' . . . and she gave him a drink. When she had finished giving him a drink, she said, 'I will draw for your camels also, until they have done drinking . . .' and she drew for all his camels."

5. *The excited running home to report the event:* "Then the maiden ran and told her mother's household about these things."

6. *Hospitality is extended:* "So the servant of Abraham came into the house and Laban ungirded the camels, and gave him straw and provender for the camels, and water to wash his feet and the feet of the ones who were with him. Then food was set before him to eat . . . "

7. *The engagement is announced:* "Then Laban and Bethuel answered, 'This thing comes from the Lord . . . Behold, Rebekah is before you . . . let her be the wife of your master's son, as the Lord has spoken.' "

So you see, just as we have particular ways our stories of fantasy are told, so also the Israelite people had particular ways their stories of their ancestors were told. If you were an Israelite, and someone began to tell you a story about a young, unmarried man traveling to a foreign land, who stopped by a well, and was approached there by a woman, there would be no doubt in your mind what was about to take place. Betrothal stories *always* seemed to take place that way.

Listen, then, to our gospel story for today with Israelite ears, remembering how Isaac came to marry Rebekah, how Jacob came to marry Rachel, how Abraham came to marry Zipporah—all as a result of encounters between a man and a woman at a well.

"So Jesus left Judea and departed again to Galilee. He had to pass through Samaria. So he came to a city of Samaria, called Sychar, near the field that Jacob gave to his son Joseph. *Jacob's well was there,* and so Jesus, wearied as he was with his journey, *sat down beside the well.* It was about the sixth hour. *And there came a woman of Samaria to draw water. And Jesus said to her, 'Give me a drink.'* "

Well . . . if you were listening to this story with Israelite ears, what do *you* think this story is going to be about, hmmm? You got it. A *betrothal!*

But—Jesus and a Samaritan woman? Why . . . such a thing was unthinkable! Scandalous! After all, Jews considered Samaritans unclean—even a slight contact with them made the Jewish people unable to participate in worshiping their holy God. To find Jesus, then, approached in a Betrothal-type story by a Samaritan woman was cause for astonishment, if not horror.

But it gets worse. This is not only a Samaritan woman—for goodness sake, she's not even a maiden. She's been married *five,* count it, *five* times and is currently scoping out the possibility for a *sixth* husband! This is hardly the unblemished rose with whom one might expect Jesus to be engaged.

It would be understandable how such a thing *might* happen, if Jesus didn't realize what kind of woman she was—but no, Jesus *did* know what kind of woman she was. He knew all about her, in fact; and yet, he persists in the scene, asking her for a drink and then offering living water to her instead.

It is here that the heart of the story is revealed—here in the story where the bonding between the maiden and the bachelor usually took place. Here it is that we discover that it is not her lineage that binds her to Jesus, nor her chastity. There is only one thing that binds her to him, and him to her: her thirst for life, for living water, for the messiah. The fact of her many husbands merely underscores how *very deeply* she was searching for wholeness and happiness, *unsuccessfully* searching for her whole unfulfilled life. Searching, that is, until Jesus enters her life, uniting himself to her through the gospel, the water of life, betrothing himself to her, to the thirsty, unclean one.

This story of water and wedding here in the book of John, no matter how often it is read, never seems to lose the radical impact of Jesus' gospel, Jesus' mission, Jesus' person. Imagine! Jesus and a Samaritan woman together in a traditional Betrothal-type scene! Imagine! Jesus with an outcast of Jesus' society! Imagine! Jesus identifying with, caring for, and offering the gifts of life and happiness to one such as she!

And so it is that the woman runs back to her townspeople, sharing with them her news of this person she'd met at Jacob's well—and they, too, come out to meet him, only to discover that they, too, receive from him the same gift of life that the Samaritan woman had received. Jesus was, they discovered, not only her salvation, but theirs as well. He betrothed himself, as it were, to *all of them.*

Which is, of course, the point of the story. As shocking as it is, this betrothal scene expresses the heart of the gospel of Jesus, a gospel that comes as a gift of life—not only to the Samaritan woman, but to the whole population of the town. Jesus' love embraces them all.

Jesus comes, the story tells us, to unite himself with the thirsty, unclean ones . . . ones just like the Samaritan woman, ones just like the Samaritan townsfolk . . . ones generations to come, ones just like you and me.

You see, dear people, this story of Jesus meeting the Samaritan woman at the well is not only her story. It is *our* story of relationship with Jesus. It is the classic story of how God reaches out to *all* of us with springs of living water, binding us to God's self forever, quenching our thirst for life, for love, forever.

In our case, we meet the messiah at the waters of baptism, where springs of living water flow for us, from which time we live in God's loving embrace.

Just as God's love reaches out to embrace this Samaritan woman, our foresister of faith, so also God's love reaches out to you, to me, to the townsfolk in Samaria, to the people of the world.

This is a love story for all time, for all places, for all people who thirst for wholeness, for life, for God. The thirsty ones will thirst no more. That is our story, our gospel, our life.

It is a love story, pure and simple. And as shocking as it may be to our sensibilities, it is a story that seeks to quench all of our thirst for life, for love, forever.

Jesus in a Betrothal story with a Samaritan woman?! Definitely. It is the way of God, is it not? It is the way of God with us.

## NOTES

1. Lewis Carroll, *The Adventures of Alice in Wonderland and Through the Looking Glass* (New York: Chanticleer Press), 193.

# III. DOCTRINAL/ THEOLOGICAL

# 17. Theodicy in the Library
## Thomas H. Conley

Psalm 86:11-17; Romans 8:18-25; and Matthew 13:24-30, 36-43

JAY HARDY pushed open the door to the church parlor and felt the rush of memories escape against him. In his ten-year stay with this Baptist congregation, how many times had he met in this parlor? Teas for new staff members; a women's meeting; a meeting with a group who were after peace and ready to fight to get it. Deacons' meetings he remembered, a growth group, an advanced theology seminar. They were all there and like ghosts they rose up to meet him as he stepped across the threshold.

He enjoyed getting away from the study and rambling about other parts of the church building. But this time he's to meet his wife here for a quick lunch before an afternoon of pastoral caring: counseling, visiting, and looking at bids with the business manager for someone to repair the sewer line. "Ah! The nobility of the office," he thought.

Jay was early—intentionally so—for his luncheon date with his wife. So, he sat and rested for a moment, scanning the room with a kind of peaceful and fulfilled sense that he was pastor here. Suddenly the door was ajar and there stood Marcie, seventeen, long blond hair, blue eyes, and a vivacious spirit.

*Thomas H. Conley* is a native of Jacksonville, Florida. He has served as senior minister of Northside Drive Baptist Church in Atlanta, Georgia, since 1976. Reverend Conley is a founding member and serves on the board of the Southern Baptist Alliance.

"Oh, I'm sorry Dr. Hardy. I didn't know anyone was here. I'll just . . . "

"No, Marcie, I'm glad to see you. Come in. Come in."

"I don't want to disturb you, I was just going to do some reading."

"A seventeen year old reading in the church parlor on such a lovely summer day? Sounds serious. Come on in and sit down."

"Well, I've had a lot of thinking to do recently. And . . . well, I wanted to get some things settled."

Marcie's parents had been in the church for years. Both were sensitive and caring people and Jay had watched Marcie grow from seven years of age and he felt like she was part his. She was at his house "hanging out" with his kids, and there was a mutual admiration and respect between the two of them. He thought Marcie's wit and good mind would take her far.

"What are you reading, Marcie, if I may ask?"

"Sure. Well, you've mentioned Leslie Weatherhead a lot in your sermons and so I got a couple of his books. *When Good Men Suffer* and *Salute to a Sufferer*. Are they good?"

Suddenly it clicked with Jay. He knew why she had those books. "They are fine, Marcie. Tell me, how did the funeral for Eric go last week?"

Eric was a friend of Marcie's. He lived on the outskirts of the city. He had been killed tragically the week before in a motorboat on Lake Fisher. A man who was drunk had driven into Eric's boat and cut it in half. Eric was injured and had drowned before anyone could rescue him. Jay linked Eric's death with Marcie's choice of the books she held in her hand.

"It was OK."

Marcie's voice was flat and her eyes fell to the floor.

"Just 'OK'?" asked Jay.

"Well, to be perfectly honest, I heard some things that really bothered me . . . about God and evil and death, and all. I mean, you know, Dr. Hardy, I've never been close to death before. My grandparents are still alive on both sides of my family. All my aunts and uncles are alive. I've just never really encountered death. And what some of them said . . . "

"What did you hear, Marcie?" Jay had a pretty good idea what she had heard. He knew the minister at the church where the funeral was held. He was a different breed from Jay in many ways.

"Well, some of the things people said at the funeral home really got to me. I mean, is there a purpose for everything, do 'things' work out for the best always? They kept saying, well, that Eric's death was for the best. Do you believe that?"

"No, Marcie. I don't believe that. I know the sentiment, and those people are sincere. They really believe it."

Marcie went on. "And some of them kept saying how the Lord was really with Jo Ann and Pete and Frances—they were with Eric. But wasn't God with Eric, too? Why would God let this happen to Eric and not the others? Do you think we have a time to go and was this Eric's time? If God stopped death from taking the other three, why didn't God stop it from taking Eric? What they were saying doesn't make any sense."

"Well, let's take those one at a time. No, I don't think we have a time to go, or that our number is pulled when God's ready for us. And I don't think everything always works out for the best. I know where those folks got the idea. It's from Romans 8:28: 'All things work together for good to them that love God . . . '

"The only problem with that, Marcie, is that the Greek says, 'In all things *God* works for good. . . . ' The subject is not things, but God. Well, I won't get technical with you, but suffice it to say that there are those who feel we are in some kind of cosmic predetermined plan for every single thing that happens to us. The evidence I see says no. If that is so, if 'things' are worked out and predestined, then our freedom is a farce and responsibility—which we all feel so heavily—really belongs to the one who drafted and oversees the plan. If someone else, namely God, is running my show and making me pay for it, then that plays havoc with the justice of God."

Marcie let out a big sigh and sank back in the thick chair she had chosen across from Jay.

"Oh, thank goodness! That makes so much sense. I just felt horrible when I heard those people talking like that. But why were the other three saved and Eric wasn't? Didn't God have the power to save Eric, too, or didn't God want to?"

"Well, that's a tough one, Marcie. And remember this is the way I've worked it out. Not everyone sees it this way. But to me the evidence is that God limits himself . . . "

"Hellooo, Hellooo. Oh, my, I do hope I'm not interrupting anything." A rather large but stately woman burst through the door and walked right through Jay and Marcie before Jay could catch his breath. It was Ella Mae Dimley and if his guess was right, Herbert, her dutiful husband, was not far behind.

"Come along, Herbert." Jay was right. In came Herbert burdened down with upholstery and drapery fabric, grunting as he pushed through the door and labored to dump the materials on the large couch on the south wall.

"Oh," said Ella Mae, placing her hand over her chest, "that was such a job."

"Yes. For Herbert it was," Jay wanted to add. But he didn't. Ella Mae Dimley was one of those women who knew exactly how everything ought to be done. Mention it, she would plan it. Plan it, she would execute it. She used to be on the decorating committee, but several years back everyone resigned and no one new came on. So, now, Ella Mae *was* the decorating committee. She busied herself here and there with swatches of cloth and paint samples punctuating her forays into all the church with her favorite words: "Oh, divine. Simply stunning. Absolutely striking" and she would hold the sample on the wall to wait for someone, anyone to give approval. Fortunately, Ella Mae did have taste and a sense of appropriate balance, so the church let her do her thing. Unfortunately today her thing was obviously going to be the church parlor.

Now if Ella Mae was pink enamel, Herbert was flat white. About half the size of Ella Mae, he was usually found at her left heel. He almost never spoke and when he did it was, "Yes, dear." Herbert had one disconcerting habit that drove Jay up the wall or the pulpit, whichever was appropriate. Today it would be the wall. Herbert had false teeth that didn't fit and he would click them, especially when he had feelings about something. Jay had analyzed that instead of speaking, Herbert let his feelings be known by clicking and grinding his teeth. He would sit in the second row at church and Jay knew when he had not stirred anything in Herbert—good or bad. No clicks. He also remembered that the one sermon when Herbert clicked all the way through was on women's liberation. Jay was sure, when he looked at Ella Mae, that he knew why.

"Am I interrupting anything?" Ella Mae asked.

"We were just discussing Eric Linden's tragic death on Fisher Lake, Ella Mae."

"Oh. How terrible that was. Well, we're just not to understand those things. Nor to question them. Come here, Herbert, and hold this."

Marcie, in a low voice, said to Jay, "That's another thing they said at the funeral home. We aren't to question these things."

"I understand, Marcie, but if we can't go to God with our questions and expect some answers, who can we go to?" said Jay in his normal voice.

Ella Mae glared over her shoulder but said nothing. She and Jay had never been on the same theological wavelength.

"Another thing I heard was that sin must have been related to this. Dr. Hardy, that made me sick. They just didn't know Eric. He was a good boy. Is that true? Does God punish us for our sins that way?" Jay noticed Ella Mae leaning in his direction.

"I don't think so, Marcie. Sins have their punishments, but God is in the forgiving business. I can't see him running down a teenage boy in a boat for whatever misdemeanors he may have done. That's ridiculous, Marcie, but I know a lot of people who still believe God works like this. I don't."

Ella Mae had worked her way over to Jay and Marcie's side of the room.

"How do you like this, Jay?" she asked. She spread a swatch of material over a badly worn chair.

"Fine, Ella Mae, fine. Whatever you think."

"I think, about that Linden boy, that it's hard to talk much about the whys and wherefores of it. If it's the will of God, then it's the will of God. And that's that."

"Not quite that simple, Ella Mae. How can we say it was the will of God?"

"Well it happened, didn't it?"

"Yes, it did. But why should we attribute to God things that a person would be put in jail for doing? The fellow who ran over Eric's boat is in the county jail now. If we believed it was God's will, then we ought to let him out and give him a citation for doing God's will."

Jay was faintly aware of a click, click, click. He looked over and Herbert was reading a *Home Life*. Jay had the feeling he was really listening.

Marcie spoke. "That's what the preacher said, that Eric's death was in God's will. I just couldn't believe that. You've always preached that God is love. I couldn't worship a God who did that to Eric."

"Neither could I, Marcie."

"But you were saying when Mr. and Mrs. Dimley came in something about God's limiting himself?"

"God's limiting himself?" exclaimed Ella Mae. "Really! Whatever are you teaching these sweet children, Jay Hardy? You preachers can get too smart for your own good, you know—and ours, too."

Jay sighed. He knew Ella Mae wouldn't hear him, but there was Marcie eager and hurting to know another way to see this thing. So he went with it.

"Well, the way I see it, Marcie, is that God has limited himself because he made us free. He made us free because coerced love, or faith, or anything else is not a tribute either to God or us. He presents us with choices and we choose and have to be responsible for those choices. We have the freedom to be right or wrong. When we choose what's best for us, God is pleased.

When we don't, well, I'm sure he wonders if that freedom idea was the best thing.

"If Eric's death was anyone's will, it would be the fellow's who ran over him. He chose to drink beyond his capacity and to try to drive a boat in that condition. Eric paid a price for that man's freedom and the man will pay a price, too—probably jail for many years."

"And how do you know *for sure* that God is that kind of God, Jay?" Ella Mae had dropped her paint sample and had her hands on her hips. "Where do you get those ideas, Reverend Doctor Hardy?"

"From the Bible, Ella Mae. From the Bible." Herbert started clicking loudly. "Do you remember in Matthew thirteen there is the parable of the wheat and the tares?"

"Yes. I taught that to my class two weeks back. I'm *well aware* of it," said Ella Mae.

Marcie nodded yes.

"Well, in that parable there is the wheat sown by the farmer and the tares sown by someone else. If God is the farmer, or his parallel, then we have a clear picture that it is not God (the farmer) who sows the tares, but someone else. In other words, evil, bad, tragic things, the tares, came from another source, not God. Granted, some of the Old Testament seems to believe that God wrought evil on people, but Jesus seems to have gone beyond that in this parable."

"Oh, that makes me feel so much better about God," said Marcie. "I just knew he couldn't have done that to Eric."

"But there's another point here. We know best who God is by looking to the Christ. Remember he told us that he and God were one. So, if we can take Jesus at his word, the way he related to us is the way God relates to us. So, let me ask you. How many people did Jesus make blind, kill, make lame, hurt, or harm?"

"None," said Ella Mae, holding up some drapery material.

"Exactly," said Marcie. "So if Jesus is a picture of God, then he tells us God is not out to hurt us, but to heal us. And that changes everything."

"Even more," said Jay. "If the people of Jesus' day really believed the people Jesus healed had their suffering placed upon them by God, then Jesus was going against God's will when he healed them."

By this time Herbert was going to town. Click, click, click, click. Ella Mae glared at him some more. "Stop that, Herbert. What do you have to say about all this?"

Click. Click. "Well, I'll tell you . . . " Jay was shocked that he spoke. Click. Click. "Jay Hardy is right. God is a God of love. God didn't have anything to do with that boy's death at Fisher Lake. I also think God is a very patient and forbearing and enduring God to put up with our foolishness." He looked Ella Mae right in the eyes when he said that last line, picked up the *Home Life,* and went on with his reading.

"Well, I never!" exclaimed Ella Mae. She dipped into that sea of cloth to come up with another pattern.

"Anybody home?"

"Thank you, Lord," whispered Jay. It was his wife, Beth. She stuck her head in the door. "Hi, handsome, ready for some lunch? Oh, hello Ella Mae, Herbert, Marcie. My, we've got quite a group here. A meeting?"

"Nope," said Jay, as he got up. "Just a friendly discussion on theodicy: God's relationship to suffering and evil. Take care, Marcie. Let's talk some more . . . in my study. "Bye Ella Mae, Herbert." Click, click.

Jay and Beth went down the hall arm in arm. He had a good feeling. He had sown some good seed himself this day. It was going to be a great day all day. He remembered that line in the eighty-sixth psalm: "Thou, Lord, art God, compassionate and gracious, forbearing, ever constant and true" (86:15). Jay was sure his answers in the parlor were correct ones. Lunch would be good today. Very good.

# 18. The Principle of Substitution
## Glen Charles Knecht

Matthew 27:15–26

IN THESE DAYS before Easter, we are seeking to discover some of the aspects surrounding the cross of our Lord Jesus Christ in an attempt to gain a fresh grasp of its significance and of its power. The evangelists who record all of the accounts surrounding His death speak to us in minute detail of the things that took place. Their story is accurate and simple; it is told without emotion, even though it instills great feeling in us who read it. But not one of these details that the evangelists bring forth is without meaning to us. They all come by the power of the Holy Spirit. Each one is to be held up under the light of the Holy Spirit so that we can see how it displays more of the wonder and the glory of the Lord Jesus Christ.

One of these details here is the story of Barabbas. This notable man was a person guilty both of insurrection and of murder. Here was a man who had not only broken the fifth commandment, which has to do with respect for duly constituted authority, but he had gone on also to break the sixth commandment, "Thou shalt do no murder." He was a notorious man; and Pilate, finding himself caught in the tension between pleasing the Jews by the death of Jesus, and placating his own troubled conscience about the innocence of the man, sud-

*Glen Charles Knecht* was born in Ogdensburg, New York. He was educated at Maryville College, Fuller Theological Seminary and Princeton Theological Seminary, and was a contributor to the volume *The Preacher and Preaching.*

denly sees a way of escape in the annual amnesty which is given to one prisoner at the time of the Passover. When this prisoner is freed, he would become something of a hero to the people. His victory, his release, would be celebrated because it would remind them of Passover when they as a people were liberated from the prison-house of Egypt. And so this was an important element, and here Pilate saw his chance. Perhaps they would release Jesus, and he would be out of his quandary.

But the priests stirred them up to call out the name of Barabbas, so that the nefarious plan of seeking to bring the life of the Lord Jesus Christ to an end could be accomplished. So when Pilate put that terrible question to them, "Whom will you have me release?" (one of the most horrible questions ever issued on the face of the earth) they cried out, "Barabbas," and Jesus was cruelly scourged and sent on His way to Calvary.

Think about Barabbas as he went home that night, slept in his own bed, ate a home-cooked meal again, and began to feel some of the pleasure of being free. Could he not escape thinking of how the One, the Lord Jesus Christ, occupied his cross for him? Why, Christ was on that central cross between the thieves, and not I! Barabbas's mind had to be engaged with the idea that Christ had taken his place on the cross.

We do not know anything more about Barabbas, whether he had ever come to faith and repentance or not; but one thing is sure, that Barabbas in a certain sense stands for all people who believe in the Lord Jesus Christ, in the sense that Jesus Christ was a substitute for him on the cross. One of the most important aspects of understanding the dying of our Lord Jesus is to grasp this principle of substitution so that it is truly your own.

## I. The Principle of Substitution

What do we mean by the principle of substitution? It is based on the fact that God deals with a representative for a whole people. You remember how Adam was the representative of the whole creation, how his test was our test, and how when he fell, sin passed to us, and death by sin, for we all began to sin. Therefore his representation involved us in our fall. If that can be true of our spiritual demise, cannot that also be true of our spiritual resurrection? If there was a first Adam bringing us into ruin, can there not be a second Adam restoring us to grace? And that is the Lord Jesus Christ, the representative, not this time of all humanity, but the representative of those who believe.

Now the principle of substitution does not mean the transference of the moral character of the sinner to the sinless One. It does not mean there is any change in character—Barabbas was not a different man because Christ had taken his place. Nor does it mean that the innocent become guilty or the guilty become innocent in that inner sense. What it does mean is that the obligation of the sinner to pay the just punishment and penalty of the sin is cancelled, that the penalty can be paid by another, a representative of him, a substitute who is in his place. That is what the principle of substitution means.

This provides for us a key which opens the lock of understanding and mystery that surrounds all these passages about the death of Christ. They are inexplicable without this key. For example, there is the arrest of Christ. Why should the sinless Son of God be arrested in the midst of His night of praying? But He is! They put chains around Him and bound Him, the Son of God, and He does not protest. In fact, He says, "Let the others go." And when He says that, He is pointing to a great fact that He deserved the binding. "It is appropriate for me but not for them." Why is that? The reason is that He knows Himself consciously to be the sinless substitute. We are there in His bonds, there we are before the throne of God's justice. We deserve to be arrested, apprehended, and held before the judgment seat of a righteous God. He knows it; He is in our place. "Let them go"; He does not say, "Let me go."

Likewise at the trial before the Sanhedrin, the sentence of death is passed by the high priest upon the Lord Jesus Christ and the charge is blasphemy. Why is that done? Christ does not argue against that. He never tries to vindicate Himself; He is silent. The reason is He knows that the charge of blasphemy is just! Not upon Him as the sinless Savior, but upon Him as the substitute for sinners! You see, the revelation of God came forth from Him by His mighty power, and we have despised it and disregarded it, and therefore we have blasphemed the divine truths of God. So we are utterly subject and properly so to the charge of death on the basis of our blasphemy. So the Lord Jesus accepts that charge in the trial before the high priest as being utterly proper to Him as the substitute, the sin-bearer, for mankind who believe.

Follow Him now as He goes out for the trial before Pilate, the Roman governor. There Pilate tries to get Jesus to cooperate with him, that He might be freed. He does not want to put this man to death. He tries to give Him ways to get out of the situation, and the Lord does not cooperate. Finally, the name of Jesus is paired up with Barabbas, the criminal! At first it seems to us that Jesus is being maligned by being coupled with Barabbas, but in fact, it is the other way. It is Barabbas who is maligned, because Jesus Christ represents all the intensity and the demerit of human sin. It is all upon Him. And so Barabbas's violations of the law of God cannot compare with those of the sin-bearer, the substitute. Five times in that trial Pilate pronounces the Lord Jesus Christ innocent and calls Him a just man, a pure and holy man. At the same time he condemns Him to death. How can that be? The only reason is that the Lord Jesus Christ is both at once. He is the sinless Son of God; He is utterly innocent of the crimes laid against Him. At the same time He is the substitute for sinners and therefore utterly guilty in the eyes of God of all that is said about Him. He is innocent and at the same time found guilty. There is no other explanation for that paradox in the trial of the Lord Jesus Christ except the fact that when He stands there before the judicial bench of Pilate, He stands there in *our* place, substitute for sinners.

One of the ways we can get hold of this idea of substitution is to see that the mental anguish that the Lord Jesus Christ felt before the cross was far more severe than His physical pain on the cross. If Christ died simply to give us an example of how one ought to face suffering, or what a great hero ought to be like when he becomes a martyr, then we would expect Him to approach the cross with a certain confidence and composure. We would expect Him to come to it calmly and bravely. But what do we have? When you look at the Lord Jesus' approach to the cross, it is full of mental agony. He says on one occasion, "Now is my soul troubled, and what shall I say? Father, remove this cup." A great sense of foreboding comes upon Him, a dreadful anticipation, not of the physical pain, but of the fact that He will bear the burden of sinners. That is why the mental anguish was so great.

Other men have suffered tortures, some even worse than the cross. They did not have the agony that the Lord Jesus had. He agonized because He was substitute for sinners; no one else has ever done that. Take the occasion when He was in the garden praying over the cross, for example. The intense struggle of His soul was so deep, the horror of the cup He had to drink so bitter, that it seemed that the clockwork of His own life was brought to a halt by external pressures that would come upon Him. It seemed that humanity could sink no deeper than He had sunk in that awful wrestling, until blood oozed out from the pores of His skin, like sweat. No man has ever travailed like that. Our Lord Jesus Christ would not so travail over merely the physical agony of Calvary; it was because He would drink the cup of men's sin that He travailed in that degree. On the cross He cried that word of great desertion, "My God, my God, why hast Thou forsaken me?" He was not forsaken; He was the beloved Son of God. But He felt a tremendous abandonment. The vision of the Father's face was gone. He was cut off from the sense of the Father's love. Why? Not because He was the sinless Son of God, but because He stood in the place of sinners, and in that moment all the wrath of a righteous God who had been offended by His own creatures was visited upon Him. There is no other explanation for the spiritual agony and anguish of the Lord Jesus Christ in His dying hour than the fact that He was a substitute in our place.

As we begin to look at the experience itself, we realize more and more that the Lord Jesus would not have gone through any of this had it not been for His substitutionary character. For Christ was immune to disease and accident. The Lord never broke His arm or caught a common cold. He would not die as you and I die because He was utterly sinless and utterly the Son of God. Only because He voluntarily brought Himself into our sphere in order to be a substitute for us, could He suffer the mockery, the scourging, and finally the dying in our behalf. If we do not accept the principle of His substitution there is no way to explain the pain, the sorrow, and the dying of the Lord Jesus Christ.

Someone may say that in human life, we do not substitute people this way. No man goes to the electric chair for somebody else. It can't be done, and the reason is clear—no man has the right to give away His own life. My life is not mine to give in exchange for another. But Christ's life was His, and He could and did give it to be a substitute for others. No judge has the power to force repentance, to bring repentance upon a criminal. He has to use the pressures of the system to try to bring about repentance in that wicked heart. But God, through His Holy Spirit, had the power to produce repentance, and He does reproduce it. So He is the only One who can bring about the principle of substitution. No man can give his life for another because none of us can rise again from the dead. If a good man gives his life for a criminal, then society has been robbed and has lost a good man, and has a bad man in return. And when the Lord Jesus Christ substituted His life, He rose again from the dead and is alive forevermore. While the principle of substitution is not applicable in human life, perhaps only rarely and under extraordinary conditions where justice would otherwise be obstructed, is it ever done in human life. But when God does it, He has every right and He does it with the greatest of beauty and power.

## II. Christ Substituting Himself in the Perfect Obedience of the Law of God

I hope in this simple explanation of what is meant by the principle of substitution, you have been ready to see how that principle is applied in two clear lines of direction. The first is this: The principle of substitution is applied in Christ taking our place to fulfill the demands of the law of God. God the righteous Lawmaker has made His laws, and He has every right to expect perfect obedience to them. They are the laws of the Creator. But Adam broke them, and we break them, and none of us is able to keep the laws of God, not because the laws are too strict, but because our hearts are too wicked. Who will keep the law for us? The Lord Jesus Christ has no obligation to keep it on His own. He is exempt from the law, He is above the law, He made the law. But voluntarily He places Himself under the righteous law of God so that there as a substitute for us He may keep it fully, and that is just what He did throughout His beautiful life. He obeyed the law of God in every detail, interpreting it in the midst of very difficult situations, with great criticism all around Him. He never wavered from a perfect, active obedience in the law of God. He said, "I have come to do Thy will, O God," and He did it. In fact, His obedience increased; He learned more and more vigorous and energetic obedience. The more heavy his life became, the more complex, the more beautiful and vital was His obedience, so that the substitution of Christ was not simply upon the cross of Calvary, but it involved and engages all the years of His earthly existence. From His first days of consciousness back in Nazareth as a child, until when He expired on the cross, all those are encompassed together in the beautiful story of how He obeyed the law of God which we could not obey.

Do you see the wondrous fruits of that? Some day you will stand before God and He will say to you, "John, have you obeyed the law?" No use in bringing out those tattered scraps, those little efforts you have made to obey the law of God. Put those filthy rags away, those sporadic attempts. Point to your great Substitute. "No, I did not keep the law of God. I could not keep it because of my wicked heart, but One kept it for me. The shining Son of God who stood in my place—He obeyed it actively from beginning to end, glorifying and amazing the people with His utter obedience to your righteous law, He stood in my place, He is my substitute. The robe of His righteousness covers me." That then is the first line along which the substitutionary work of the Lord Jesus Christ prevails. He fulfilled the righteous demands of the law of God in the place of the believer.

## III. *Christ Substituting Himself in the Payment of Penalty for Sin*

Every life of obedience has to come to a great testing point, a crescendo, some great climax where it is seen whether this obedience can stand a kind of ultimate test or not. And Christ's obedience was tested in His dying. The command of His Father was, "The soul of the sinner shall die." The command of Christ, even from before the foundation of the world was, "My Son, in the place of my believing community, you will die as a substitute for them!" That was the command of God. And so all the lines of Jesus' beautiful obedience converge on the cross. There He consummates His obedience in one great act of dying love in which He stood there, not for any sins of His own, but for you and for me. O what a friend of sinners He is; He stood in our place and died there.

All the words of His that lead up to the cross, all point to this understanding. For example, He said, "Father, for their sakes I sanctify myself," meaning I give myself to the cross on behalf of those for whom I die. On another occasion, speaking about the work of the Holy Spirit, He said, "He will convict the world of righteousness because I go to the Father." What did He mean by that? He meant that righteousness would come upon believing people because He had used the doorway of suffering and dying to get to the Father. There were short-cuts to the Father. He had been tempted to take them, but He went through the doorway of suffering and death and because He did, righteousness met Him on the other side and was prepared to rest upon the heart and life of believing people. He said, "The Son of Man is come to seek and to save the lost and to give His life a ransom for many." So not only His words led up to it, but His actions accomplished it. He said, "No man takes my life from me; I lay it down and I take it again."

If Christ were mere man, He could not do that. Unless Jesus Christ is God He cannot be substitute. Because if He were a mortal, He would have obligations to the law of His own. He would have His own sin to contend with. But He is not mortal; He is God the Son, and therefore He can beautifully make His own provision as a substitute for sinners. If He were mortal and tried to die for the sins of the world, His death would have to stretch out forever. It would have to be eternal because the wrath of God upon sinners is eternal. But since He is the infinite God-man, He endures in the space of a few hours the agony and suffering to satisfy the righteous laws of God for all men and women of every age and every place, infinitely sufficient for the sin of men for ever and ever. So when He cries out, "It is finished," what does He mean but that the substitutionary work for which He came which was His calling and His cup, is full. He has done what the Father commanded Him to do. The penalty is paid in full!

When He says, "Father, into Thy hands I commit my Spirit," He is taking that lacerated body, that beautiful young body, strong in its manhood, covered now with bruises and brokenness, and He is Himself laying it down as a sacrifice for our sin. Nobody is taking it from Him. In a strong shout of victory, "Father, into Thy hands I commit my Spirit!" O what fruit there is in that for us who have tasted of the good things of the substitutionary death! O what love we have found at the cross! Has the last hymn been written about the Savior's dying? Has the last poem or painting been made?

Amazing life and can it be
That Thou my God shouldst die for me.

Death is no longer the same. The believer does not really die. He does not taste the sting of bitterness of death. Death for him has been transformed into a doorway. The pain is gone. There is no more punishment. The punishment was laid upon our surety, the Lord Jesus Christ. Death is just a transition for us now, a smooth and lovely passage into the face of our heavenly Father because our substitute has paid the penalty for our sin and purchased for us a place in heaven.

Do you see how the principle of substitution lights up the love and mercy of our God? He did not ask an angel to come and die; He did not ask another to come and die. He came, knowing distinctly the bitterness of the cup and the sorrow He would face. Feeling the intensity of human sin? If our sin required an action so momentous, so comprehensive, as the substitutionary work of the Lord Jesus Christ it cannot be trifled with. We cannot joke it away or act as if it does not exist. Sin becomes the great enemy of our souls, the thing for which Christ died. If the unextinguishable fury of divine wrath were so great as to cause this sorrow and this pain in the Lord Jesus Christ who had no guilty conscience, with what force shall those flames come upon the soul who disowns the substitute, who despises and disregards the provision that a righteous God has made? How will those flames be satisfied?

Suppose Barabbas, when the messenger came and said, "You are free," said "I don't believe that," and stayed in jail? "He is mad!" Suppose he had said, "I am not good enough. I have to get my character in order. I have to be reformed to get out of this jail. Who am I to walk down the street like this? I have to be a better man before I leave here"? We would call him mad. We would say, "Go out now and then let God change your character in gratitude." But there are men and women who won't come to Christ because they feel that they have to be reformed first. Come to Christ and let Him reform you! He is far better at it than you are.

Suppose he had said, "I like this prison; I have gotten used to it." We would say, "You are foolish, Barabbas. There is light and air and freedom out there. Do you like your sin? Do you like to live in it and wallow in it? Up there is abundant light, and Christ came to give it!"

# 19. What If We Find E.T.?
## Paul D. Simmons

Colossions 1:11–20

AMERICANS HAVE been treated to a plethora of sci-fi movies on the theme of extraterrestrial beings.

*Cocoon* is one of the latest dealing with the possibility that the lost city of Atlantis was actually a station for creatures from space. After a catastrophe struck Atlantis, many left for their outer space home in a hurry. They had to leave a number of their group in cocoons, which incubated them until friends could return and rescue them.

*E.T.* was one of the favorites with moviegoers. Steven Spielberg fascinated us with a child's-eye view of friendly and even beneficent visitors to planet earth. Before it was all over, most all of us had entered the world of fantasy and affection that brought strange but loveable E.T. into our hearts to stay. He wanted to go home, but we all felt that we had found a friend. We wanted him to stay—perhaps even bring others to join us.

*Aliens* was a space venture of a different sort. It explored some of our worst fears as we venture into space. A malevolent creature threatened to destroy all the people on the spaceship, and nearly succeeded.

*Paul D. Simmons* is a native of Troy, Tennessee. He is professor of Christian ethics at Southern Baptist Theological Seminary in Louisville, Kentucky. Dr. Simmons has spoken and written extensively on ethical issues, with a particular focus on bioethics.

The list could be extended. *Close Encounters of the Third Kind, 2001: A Space Odyssey,* and *Star Trek* all made their place on the hit movie list and made indelible impressions on the minds of all who saw them.

What interests me about these movies is the question they raise about the possibility of there being creatures in outer space. Suppose we should find that there are living beings who think, love, and hate on other planets in the universe?

A number of books have been written on this theme. There are even societies and organizations devoted to UFO watchings. Some persons claim actually to have been taken captive by such space aliens; some speculate that certain missing persons have been kidnapped and taken to outer space for investigation or out of curiosity (as *Close Encounters* implies).

A man in Germany claims he has had repeated contacts with visitors from the planet Pluto. We are, he says, their descendants, thus explaining the Old Testament reference to women having children by the sons of the Gods (Gen. 6:2, 4).

Erich von Däniken created a stir and considerable controversy with his book *Chariots of the Gods?,* which suggested that many of the strange things of the O.T. could be explained by a visitation from space beings who were far advanced over earthlings and thus able to dominate and determine many of the things done by ancient Hebrews.

The United States government has consistently denied that it knows more than it is telling about UFOs or that it knows anything at all about creatures on other planets in the cosmos. Even so, it has launched a space rocket designed to travel beyond the Milky Way and tell us a great deal more about the universe as it goes. *Explorer* is part of a venture called SETI (Search for Extra-Territorial Intelligence) and contains symbols of men and women that will hopefully communicate friendly intentions and something about who we are to any aliens that might get bumped in space.

All these things are part of the fascination with the question of whether there might be intelligent life elsewhere in the universe. In part it reflects the new ventures into space with astronauts and cosmonauts and satellites and space stations. It also reflects our own new self-awareness in the sense that we know we are also space creatures on a lonely and not very conspicuous planet on the edge of a not very impressive galaxy called the Milky Way. There are literally thousands of other galaxies if the scientists are to be believed. So our curiosity about ourselves prompts curiosity about the possibilities of other selves in the universe.

The question also has religious importance. Suppose there are other creatures somewhere "out there"; would Christian revelation be threatened or become outmoded?

## I. Might There Be Other Beings on Other Planets?

Might other creatures live in other galaxies thousands of light years away? And might there be some possibility of contacting them as portrayed in *Battlestar: Galactica* or *Close Encounters . . .*?

Based on mathematical probabilities as calculated by scientists, there probably are such creatures elsewhere in the universe. The filmmakers are dealing not only with fantasy and imagination, they are dealing imaginatively with scientific possibilities and attempting both to entertain and prepare us for such eventualities.

Scientists tell us that there are at least 10,000 billion trillion stars (or about as many stars as dollars in the national deficit!). Of these, there are at least a billion that are like our sun. That means that the conditions for the emergence or creation of intelligent life on other planets has likely been favorable, as in our own case. Harlow Shapley, astronomer at Harvard University, says that there are very strong possibilities of there being other worlds with intelligent life. He says that there are probably 100 million inhabited planets throughout the universe.

It is precisely the plausibility of such projections that make it necessary to reflect upon the importance of the question.

We can safely say that there probably are intelligent creatures elsewhere in the universe.

## II. Would E.T.s Bear the Image of God? Would the Christian Understanding of Human Nature Be Threatened?

First, it is entirely possible that *how we think about people* will have to be altered. Space creatures may look much more like E.T. or those in *Close Encounters* . . . than people of Earth. We think of people as beings who are more alike than they are different—we are Mongoloid, Negroid, or Caucasoid, but we are basically alike. Some of any group look almost exactly like persons in another group. Should we meet creatures from outer space, we may have to enlarge our understanding of what people look like.

Second, such a discovery would enlarge our notion of God. Too often God is considered the God of planet earth and not understood as the God who is Creator and Lord of the universe. All the planets are the creations of God and all creatures are the work of the divine power. God is not a local deity confined to this planet; nor are people of earth his only creatures.

Third, the fact that we are made in the "image of God" would in no way be altered. What we look like or how we are fashioned bodily has nothing to do with God's image. We do not *look* like God, nor does God look like people. The Sovereign of the universe is not a giant human being nor are people simply miniature gods. The *Image of God* in us is our capacity for reflective thought and our spiritual relation to transcendent Reality. It has nothing to do with physical appearances; it has everything to do with our ability to relate to God, to other beings and to ourselves. We are like God in our ability to know that we *are* and that God *is.* We are self-aware creatures who are agents of moral and religious reflection and awareness.

Theologically, we can know that wherever God has created beings that they have the *imago dei,* just as we do. In that sense, they will be *like us* no matter how much they may not *look* like us. We can also know, therefore, that God could have become incarnate in another place, and in another time, a distant galaxy or a faraway planet. We know by divine revelation that God is one who reveals Himself to his creatures. Just because we do not know the details of that revelation on a distant planet to other creatures does not mean that we do not know anything about the way in which God relates to those made in the divine image.

### III. The Final Question Concerns Redemption. Would Those in Other Worlds Be a Fallen Race? Would They Need the Salvation of God?

C. S. Lewis says that other races may not have sinned. He believes that the vast distances between earth and other inhabited planets may be God's way to quarantine them against the infection of our sinfulness and thus preserve them against the Fall. I believe he is wrong. Wherever there are creatures who are moral agents with religious capacities, there is also an awareness of sin and guilt. With Adam, we have all sinned; whether on Anterea or earth.

The Christian revelation makes it clear that sin is a universal reality. Paul may have been speaking only of Jews and Gentiles when he declared that "all that have sinned and come short of the glory of God" (Rom. 3:23), but it could be said for all creation. To be a creature made in the divine image means that one is aware of both dignity and fallenness. No creature is perfect; only God is absolutely good.

This truth is conveyed in stories like those of Darth Vader and the Alien. The dark side of creatureliness is part of reality. All intelligent creatures have the capacity for both good and evil; for doing good as well as for doing evil. We can be certain that those we meet in outer space will be like us in this respect; they will be capable of doing horrible things just as they will be able to do some wonderful things. Some will be more like

Darth Vader and Hitler; others will be more like E.T. and Gandhi, or St. Francis of Assisi. God's truth about the human race is the truth for all creation.

*Salvation* will also be a possibility. How we do not know exactly, but we can say for certain that God has made redemption possible for those who are fallen and aware of their sin. If we ever meet we will be able to discuss just how God acted on their behalf. We can compare our story to theirs. Our story centers on Jesus and the Cross and His resurrection as ways to understand that God made salvation possible for the human race. Their story might be significantly different or it might sound very much the same. In their own time and in that place, God may have come into their midst in the form of a Son to communicate the Divine Love in a remarkable and unforgettable way. On that planet far away from ours, what God has done for their redemption will have made all the difference.

The possibility of finding E.T. is exciting to the religious imagination. For myself, I just cannot wait to talk to these fellow creatures and learn more about the greatness of God and the variety of ways that have been used to communicate the Divine grace and love.

# 20. That God Will Be God

## *William H. Willimon*

"Say to the house of Israel, Thus says the Lord God: It is not for your
sake, O house of Israel, that I am about to act, but for the sake of my
holy name . . . "—Ezekiel 36:22–32

WE HAVE BEGUN today's service by chanting the Great Litany, an appropriate way to begin Lent. In those ancient cadences, we confess our manifold sins, all the ways that we fall
short. "Good Lord, deliver us."

And the Lord *will* deliver us; at least that is the testimony
of Scripture. Our God cares, hears, acts. God is a deliverer.
Today's scripture from Ezekiel speaks of this divine deliverance: God says, I will take you, I will gather, I will bring you, I
will give you . . . "

The prophet speaks these words to exiles, people who had
been cruelly deported from their land. These are words spok-
en to a people down and out, having hit bottom. "I will be
your God. I will deliver you . . . " This message of hope is not
original with Ezekiel. The prophets were unanimous in their
assertion that God delivers God's people from despair.

And as a pastor, I'm glad that I have that word to speak,
for (as the litany reminds us) there is always enough despair in

---

*William H. Willimon* is a graduate of Wofford College and Yale
Divinity School and received his doctorate at Emory University. Dr.
Willimon, a Methodist, is minister to the University and professor of
the practice of Christian ministry at Duke University in Durham,
North Carolina. He is the author of twenty-six books, including
*Sighing for Eden* and *What's Right with the Church*, and is an editor-at-
large for *The Christian Century.*

this life to be grateful that God is deliverer. I am grateful that the prophetic word is—when you are like Israel in exile, when you are down, utterly without possibility, there is hope—God will deliver. Every prayer by a believer, every cry for help is based upon that assertion: God delivers.

That hope is not being debated in today's text. There is another issue within today's text. "Thus says the Lord God: It is not for your sake, O house of Israel, that I am about to act, but for the sake of my holy name, which you have profaned among the nations . . . Through you I will vindicate the holiness of my great name. . . . It is not for your sake that I will act, says the Lord God."

It is not for your sake that I will act. The question is not about theodicy, a question about whether or not God will intervene and deliver. The question is *Why?* On what basis?

Well, we answer, God delivers because God cares. God loves us. But Ezekiel does not say that. Nowhere is it said that God's heart goes out to his suffering people. Jeremiah said that, and Isaiah. But Ezekiel says that God has come to such a low opinion of his people—"you have profaned, are unclean, you idolaters, your deeds are not good"—that, if there is to be deliverance, *Israel has nothing to contribute to that deliverance.* By its behavior, the nation now waits empty-handed to receive whatever God chooses to give.

"It is not for your sake, O House of Israel, that I am about to act, but for the sake of my holy name which you have profaned . . . I will vindicate the holiness of my great name . . . and the nations will know that I am the Lord . . . "

Walter Brueggemann says, "I regard this as one of the most dangerous and stunning texts in the Bible, for it sets God's free, unfettered sovereignty at a distance from Israel." God will act, but God's actions have nothing to do with God having pity, or mercy, or compassion for Israel or us. You can forget that motherly love business in Isaiah or Jeremiah; Ezekiel speaks nothing of it. Oh, I've preached about such a basis for God's intervention: "I have heard the cry of my people and I have come down to deliver them" (Exodus). "The Spirit of the Lord is upon me to preach good news to the poor, deliverance to the captives" (Isaiah, Luke).

A friend told of working at the penitentiary where, every week, parents would come to visit their imprisoned sons who would, every week, refuse to see them. Still they came back. He says, "God's love is even more like that with us."

But what happens, Ezekiel asks, what happens when even God's compassion goes dry? What happens when God has gone the second, third, fifth mile with his people and still they disobey? What then? Ezekiel says that God has had it with Israel. Took them back once, twice, twenty times. But now the mercy, compassion, of God have gone dry. What then?

Then (our text answers) there is holy God, in all of God's unaccommodating, prickly self-concern. God's reputation, God's good name, are important to God, even if they are unimportant to us. The nations have watched God's treatment of Israel. What will God do now that Israel has blown its fifteenth chance to straighten up? What will God do? God's reputation is on the line.

Brueggemann says this text portrays God like people in a restaurant watching parents with small children. The children are tired and they are not behaving well. The parents are also tired and embarrassed. Not much is at stake for the children; they are behaving just like children. But much is at stake for the parents; everybody is watching. They might like to swat the children, to let them have it. But they can't or the people in the restaurant will think that they are bad parents. How are they going to look when word gets around town that they can't cope with their kids? So they become the very models of parental patience. After all, people are looking.

Ezekiel says this same thing happened to God. Israel had thrown one long tantrum. God acted like the long-suffering, patient parent until God could take it no longer. All the nations were watching to see what God would do now that Israel had pushed God too far. Here, at the end of the rope, in desperation, there is no more mushy talk about compassion, mercy, the tolerance of God. Now there is nothing left but God.

Nothing Israel could repent of, or vow to do, could change things.

What now? Now God will look after God for a change. That may sound hard-nosed. We are obsessed with what God thinks about us. What do we need to do to get right with God, to get things straight? So at church on Sunday morning, we feel as if we ought to get our money back if the preacher expends too much time speaking about what God is doing and too little time telling us what we're suppose to do. That assumes God needs something we can do.

Ezekiel says it's too late for that. Now, the future rests solely upon the hope that God will take seriously being God. "I'm not going to deliver you because of you, but because of me and my holiness. That the nations will see that I am God." (They will watch and know that it takes a very great God to love a people like you.)

Hope, our text suggests, is a by-product of God's free, unfettered goodness. Our only hope, when the chips are down, is that God will be God.

We are unaccustomed to such thinking. There is hope for us, we think, because after all, down deep, we are very nice people, who are doing the best we can. We wish we didn't have to base our civilization upon nuclear weapons. We really don't mean to be self-centered, violent, cruel to one another. Hope lies in our attempts to straighten up and do better—better education, more brightly lit streets, tighter national security, a new administration in Washington. Christ has no hands but our hands. God just can't get along without good people like us.

The worst sin of all, says Augustine, is "the conceit of merit," the notion that somehow God's love is our entitlement. If we are honest about ourselves, our motives, our reasons, the way we live with one another, the secret, undisclosed desires of our hearts, we feel deep, deep guilt and are driven thereby to deep, deep despair. Today's text speaks to *that* despair—the despair of knowing that we are not worth saving, that we have cashed in our chips, that we have no markers left to call in. What then?

It is only the most honest of people who are drawn to that brand of despair. One reason that we are forever indebted to Israel is that Israel dared, in its scriptures, to be so utterly self-critical.

This text stands as a rebuke to those in Israel in Ezekiel's day who assumed that their restoration was based upon their merit. There were those who thought that God had to have a temple priesthood, or a royal dynasty, so God would, of course deliver them. We are a Christian, a democratic country; God needs us. I have tithed, gone to church, never knowingly sinned since graduation; God must deliver me. How would God save the freshman class without me? (God is my patron rather than my sovereign.)

Ezekiel puts forth the stunning assertion that our hope depends on God *not* having such commitments to us. We want to believe that God is dependent upon our goodness—our ability to get things together, the survival of democratic capitalism, the defeat of racism, the establishment of socialism—because then we can manage the future. It is in our hands. Conversely, if God is free to be God, God might surprise us.

The later possibility requires of us not goodness, but something much more difficult for us modern people even than goodness. It requires that we *trust*. It requires that we place the significance of our lives, our hope for the future solely in God's hands. Which of these views offers the surer hope? Of course, it all depends on whether or not God can be trusted or whether our hope is in ourselves and our systems.

We are notorious for our attempts to harness God for our schemes. Jesus told a story of two men who went to the temple to pray (Luke 18:9–14), a story told to those who "trusted in themselves, that they were righteous" (verse 9). The first man, a Pharisee, was a good religious liberal, the very embodiment of self-trust. He was the religiously confident, the psychologically assured, the politically bold. "I am not like the others, extortioners, unjust, adulterers. I fast twice a week. I give a tithe of all I get." God, I thank thee that I am not sexist, racist, materialist . . . God I thank thee for me.

But oh, how this posturing, pretentious prayer crumbles before today's text: "It is not for your sake . . . but for the sake of my holy name that I act."

Israel had hit bottom. Languishing in exile, some in Israel began to see that hope is possible, not because God has a preferential option for poor Israel, not because the old man has gotten soft on judgment, but because God wants to be true to himself. First we say, "Our Father who art in heaven, *holy* be your name . . . " then we say, "give us this day, . . . forgive us our trespasses, . . . deliver us. . . . " It is because God is holy, not us, that we dare to pray.

Ludwig Feuerbach argued that faith in God is a mere projection of our ideal images of ourselves. God has no real independent existence. When you pray to God, you are merely speaking to your highest ideal of who you wish to God you really were. Feuerbach's charge is difficult to refute today where many would make a virtue out of such projection. God is my father, mother, sister, brother, the justification for my particular ideology of the right or the left. God is on the side of the poor. God is for the Contras. I can't relate to God unless God is my gender, my class, my size. Narcissistic theology based on my inflated ego is the order of the day. Theology is no good unless it does something good for me and my minority. This God can be worshiped and prayed to only because God is like me.

God is drawn into and identified with our social commitments. Worship is a time for the preacher to identify which side God is on so that the congregation can get on with the business of rushing over to that side. Conservatives know that God is against homosexuality and communism. Liberals know that God is pro-busing and pro-choice.

It all sounds well and good that we should be about doing what God wants done, but ultimately this leads to despair. We stagger out of church under the burden of thinking that because we know what God wants and are able to do what God wants, we must be gods unto ourselves.

What a reprimanding word is this: not for your sake, but

for the sake of my name. And what a word of hope. All our feverish attempts to be right and do right are put in perspective. We don't have to brag in our prayer because finally, prayer is an act of yielding to holy God rather than justifying ourselves. In this society, paralyzed by its guilt, immobilized by its nuclear fear, beset with survival issues, in exile, hear again the hopeful word that tomorrow is in God's hands, something to be determined in God's own freedom. Our best hope, in life and death, is that God will be God. Which may sound ambiguous, threatening, or may cause us to fall back on a power other than our own, but the Bible teaches that that is the way to true hope.

Let us pray: *From our anxious attempts to know and be and do, good Lord deliver us, not for our sake, but for the sake of thy holy name.*

# 21. Creation and/or Evolution?
## John D. Suk

*Scripture:* Genesis 1:1–2:3

> In the beginning, God—
> Father, Word, and Spirit—
> called this world into being
> out of nothing,
> and gave it
> shape and order.[1]

ON THIS TABLE in front of me are just a few of my books about God's creation of the world. I brought these books along this morning to illustrate a problem. The problem is that these books fall into two sharply divided categories. This pile of books insists that the only possible interpretation of Genesis is that creation happened in six twenty-four-hour days a few thousand years ago. This pile of books suggests that there is no biblical reason for supposing that God didn't plan and execute his creation over the course of billions of years, as modern science suggests.

It should surprise no one that different people interpret the Bible differently, of course. In the Christian Reformed Church we have room for the "pre," the "post," and the "a" millennialists all. We had room for "infra" and "supra" lap-

---

*John D. Suk* is pastor of Redeemer Christian Reformed Church, Sarnia, Ontario, Canada. A graduate of Calvin College, he received the Master of Divinity from Calvin Theological Seminary in 1984. From 1979 to 1981 he taught English at a Christian secondary school in Ontario. Suk lives in Sarnia with his wife and two children.

sarianists (if you can remember what those were!). In the Christian Reformed Church we have room for people who think women ought to be office bearers, and for those who think not. We all believe the same infallible Bible, we all struggle to interpret it correctly, and we all disagree about this or that. We all agree that the Bible is about how God redeems us from our sins, but we sometimes don't agree on the details. After all, even if the Bible is an infallible book, we are not infallible interpreters of the book.

It should not be disturbing to anyone that we have to struggle with Genesis if we want to understand it correctly. What is disturbing is the rancor and anger; the fear and ignorance; the passion and ferocity of the arguments that are symbolized by the space between these two piles of books before me. That empty space is symbolic of a divide that threatens to split friends, families, and even the church, apart.

This morning I cannot bridge that space. But I will affirm the biblical doctrine of creation. The Contemporary Testimony, *Our World Belongs to God*, gets it right. "In the beginning, God—Father, Word, and Spirit—called this world into being out of nothing and gave it shape and order." This is true. This is biblical. This—in part—is what Genesis 1 is about. We believe it.

In line with this our confession, this morning we will explore what the Bible and our Reformed tradition of interpreting the Bible say about three things: first, about Genesis 1, second, about science and the Bible, and third, about evolution.

First, Genesis 1. Genesis 1 is a portrait of God the divine king. Genesis 1 is like Job 1, where God is pictured meeting with his royal counselors, including Satan. Genesis 1 is like Revelation 4, where the apostle John is given a vision of the heavenly throne room in all its magnificence and splendor.

That means Genesis 1 speaks of God's divine kingship. If you are a history buff, you will remember that after William the Conqueror came from France and conquered England, the language of the royal court in London became French.

That is one of the reasons why so many English words have French roots: words like pleasure, president, picket, and people. In any case, if you had walked around London nearly one thousand years ago, you would have been able to tell who was attached to the royal court on account of their speaking royal French rather than old English.

It is the same in Genesis 1. God's words here are spoken in the tones, style, and cadences of royalty. The heart of Genesis 1 is its language of royal decree—the six royal decrees of God, which he spoke from his throne room: "Let there be light," and "Let there be an expanse between the waters," and "Let the water teem with living creatures," and so on.

For the people of Israel, it made perfect sense that God would speak to them from Genesis using royal language, because Genesis is a royal document. God was Israel's king. God had a treaty, a covenant with Israel, to be their king if they would be his people. Like most treaties, the covenant between God and Israel had lots of fine print, lots of rules and regulations. We can find the fine print of the covenant treaty God made with Israel in the second half of Exodus, as well as all the laws of Leviticus, Numbers, and Deuteronomy.

In those ancient times, every covenant between a king and his people also included an introduction. The introduction named and described the king of the covenant for the benefit of the people he ruled. Covenant introductions made it plain to the people who was king and why. In Genesis 1, then, the sovereign God introduces himself to his people in Israel. Genesis 1 is God's business card.

When the Israelites read Genesis, their reaction was, "Look how special we are. Our king is not just any king, like Hammurabi or Nebuchadnezzar or Alexander the Great. Our king is the maker of heaven and earth!" Genesis 1 is not nearly so much about how creation happened as it is about the creator. Genesis is not about the physics or geology of creation. It is about the Lord who enacted the laws of physics and geology and made them work by his divine, royal edict. Genesis 1 introduces us to the God to whom we owe our allegiance—no, even more—to whom we owe every iota of our being and the surety of our redemption.

Secondly, even if Genesis 1 is not about science, does it say anything about how the world turns? Dr. Raymond Van Leeuwen, writing in the *Banner,* says that Genesis cannot be taken as a description of scientific facts.[2] If we read Genesis that way, we will become entangled in scientific confusion and contradictions. He is right.

For example, and this is just one of many, we read in Genesis 1:8 that "God made the expanse [the sky] and separated the water under the sky from the water above it." The ancient Hebrews, you see, had figured out that if you dug far enough down into earth, you came to water, and that rain always came from up high in the sky. Their conclusions were that the earth must be floating on water, that is was flat, and that God must have put water storage tanks above the sky. That, at least, is how Genesis 1:8 describes the world God created.

John Calvin read that and he knew that Genesis 1:8 made no scientific sense. Calvin trusted the science of his day enough to scoff at what he called "the ignorance" of Christians who continued to believe in waters above and below the earth on account of Genesis 1:8. Later on in his commentary on Genesis, Calvin made the point that in Genesis 1 Moses does not write like a philosopher or scientist about the secrets of nature. The same truth that applies to Genesis 1:8 ought also be considered today by everyone who wants to make Genesis 1 as a whole a scientific description of the how, when, and what order of creation and its six days.

Calvin followed here in the footsteps of his spiritual father, Saint Augustine. When some Christians gave Augustine a hard time because he did not believe Genesis 1 was a literal account of creation, Augustine answered that that if Christians had something to say about science or creation, they should not make hasty charges that one view or another was in conflict with scripture, unless they had engaged in serious study of nature. Augustine said that an ever-present danger for Christians is that they will make fools of themselves in the eyes of unbelieving scientists if they do not know their science, but simply make wild claims on the basis of how they interpret a portion of scripture.[3]

Genesis 1 does not make good scientific sense because it does not speak the language of science. God inspired people who were products of a scientifically primitive day and age to write scripture, and it shows in their scientifically limited grasp of how the world worked.

None of this makes Genesis wrong. It just means that when God inspired the writer of Genesis, God was inspiring him to write about how he, God, was the King of heaven and earth. God inspired the writer of Genesis to get out the good news of redemption. The writer of Genesis was inspired to shout from the rooftops that God made and holds the whole world in his hands, not how God did it.

Finally, I'd like to make the point that there is a world of difference between evolution and evolutionism. For example, we all know the words race and racism, and how closely they are related. A race is a certain kind of people. When we look around the world, we sing things like, "Red and yellow, black and white, all are precious in his sight." We accept that race is part of God's good plan for this world. We believe that every race is just as precious to God as the next.

You need add only three letters to the good word "race" though, to turn it into an ugly word, to turn it into racism. Racism is believing that "Red and yellow, black and white, but only one is precious in his sight." Racism is apartheid. Racism is snickers and catcalls when a Pakistani or a Jamaican walks down the street. Racism is 6 million dead Jews and the smoking ovens of Auschwitz and Treblinka.

Two words separated by three little letters: race and racism. A world of meaning separates those two words, though. Only three letters: i- s-m. But those letters add up to a horrible difference in meaning between race and racism. We celebrate God's gracious gift of race; we reject the godlessness of racism.

What about these theories that speak of Ice Ages and dinosaurs and development of animal species and billions of years?

What about evolution? How does a distinction between evolution and evolutionism help us with these books? What about the space between these two piles of books here?

Well, evolution is one of the many ways God works in the world. Evolution is just a scientific theory that we can evaluate on the basis of science. Abraham Kuyper once said of evolution something like, "If it pleased God not to create the species, but to have one species emerge from another, creation would still be no less miraculous."

But add three letters to evolution and suddenly you have evolutionism. Suddenly the word evolution becomes ugly, as ugly as the word "racism." Evolutionism is the belief that God had nothing to do with the way this world has changed over billions of years. Evolutionism is the belief that God is absent from the world. To study how God's royal decrees, how his laws in physics and in geology lead to change over the eons, lead to evolution, is one thing, and *amen* to that. But to say that God is not there is damnable. To say that God does not hold the whole world in his hands, watching it all the time; but rather, that the world hangs in there by itself, is wrong.

Paul says that "since the creation of the world God's invisible qualities—his eternal power and divine nature—have been seen." Right. We believe and confess the biblical truth that in the beginning God made the world out of nothing. He gave it being, shape, and order. And even now he holds it in his hands. The scientists will describe for us, in some small way, how God did, and does, that.

NOTES

1. Quoted from *Our World Belongs to God: A Contemporary Testimony*, stanza 8 (Grand Rapids, MI: Christian Reformed Church Board of Publications, 1987).

2. *Banner* (a publication of the Christian Reformed Church) (September 21, 1987):13.

3. Augustine, *Genesis*, I. 18–21.

# 22. Becoming One Christ's Way
## *Stephen Knox*

Ephesians 5:21–33

SEVERAL YEARS AGO, we were hearing sober arguments about the end of the marriage institution. It was declared to be an old, sick, and dying idea. Some prophesied that, just like the clumsy dinosaurs and dodo birds of old, marriage would soon become extinct.

Of course, this was nonsense. Marriage is "in." Tying the matrimonial knot is not only fashionable again, it's here to stay. Why? Because, for many of us, there is no better way to fulfill our deep human needs for security, intimacy, and companionship.

Christians have long considered marriage to be a gift from God. As the book of Genesis describes, the Creator provided this sacred union whereby "a man leaves his father and his mother and cleaves to his wife, and they become one flesh" (2:24). So even though it is the good gift of some to live the single life, there is no question that the marriage union is here to stay.

But there *is* a question as to *how* married Christians are to live out their oneness. In everyday life, how do the bride and

---

*Stephen Knox* is pastor of the First Christian Church (Disciples of Christ) of Waitsburg, Washington. He is a graduate of Northwest Christian College and of Fuller Theological Seminary, where he received the master of divinity in 1984. A native of Oklahoma, Knox has served churches in Oregon and California.

groom relate to each other? What is the husband's role, and what is the wife's role? Who is in charge here? And what makes a Christian marriage *Christian*?

I believe the answer to these questions is wrapped up in one very biblical concept: "mutual submission." I'd like to show you, from Scripture, that mutual submission is *the* guiding principle for the marriage relationship. In fact, it is the overriding principle for relationships among *all* believers in general. But we will here apply it to marriage.

Now, if you get a sneaking suspicion that this is a different viewpoint than the one often heard from pulpits, you're probably right. The "traditional" viewpoint is that there is a divinely ordained order for the family, and the hierarchy looks like this: God is the top authority, then husbands under God, then wives under their husbands. Wives submit to their husband's authority, and husbands submit to God's authority but rule their wives. This theory is sometimes called the "chain of command," and it is assumed that God intentionally created this hierarchy. Various biblical texts are used to support it. Most Christians over the centuries have accepted this traditional view, believing that it is both scriptural and natural, and of course male-dominated cultures have encouraged it.

But recently this view has been questioned and challenged, not just by "radical feminists," but also by other thoughtful students of the scriptures who are honestly searching for God's will in the matter. This is what we're finding: Those scriptures which seem to support the traditional view, such as "the women should keep silence in the churches," were pastoral instructions to correct abuses in the early churches. They are responses to particular problems in particular situations of that time. They cannot be used to support the traditional view at all.

In fact, a more thoughtful study of the whole of Scripture shows that the chain-of-command idea is not a Christian idea at all. It is pagan!

Let me show you how I can make so bold a statement . . . First, let's look at Genesis. Notice the pertinent passages within the accounts of creation. Genesis 1:27 tells us that "God created mankind in his own image, in the image of God he created him; *male and female* he created them." Then God blessed them *both,* and said to *both*: Be fruitful and multiply and have dominion. We see no male domination here, no hierarchy of human authority within this first marriage. They are addressed as equal persons, both created in God's image, both given dominion over the earth.

Then in the second chapter we find a more detailed creation story: In 2:18 we read, "Then the Lord God said, It is not good that the man should be alone; I will make a *helper fit* for him." The old King James version says "help meet," which is a poor translation of the Hebrew words: *ezer* and *neged. Ezer* means help, but never subordinate help. In Psalm 121, for instance: "I lift my eyes to the hills. From whence does my help come? My help comes from the Lord." In the Old Testament this word refers to a "helper" of greater or at least equal status and power. The Hebrew term *neged* means "appropriate, fitting." Eve was an appropriate, fitting partner for Adam. And he recognizes this with enthusiasm! "Ah, At last!" he shouts. "Bone of my bone, and flesh of my flesh!" (verse 23). Once again, there is no one superior, no hierarchy. Woman and man are depicted as wonderfully different, and yet wonderfully complementary to each other. They fit together, in a relationship of mutuality and equality.

But then, in the third chapter of Genesis, something happens which changes the whole picture: the Fall. The man and the woman eat the forbidden fruit and sin enters this Paradise and spoils it. The effects of sins are spelled out: shame, alienation from their Creator, alienation from each other. Notice the effects of the Fall in verse 16: "To the woman he said, 'I will greatly multiply your pain in childbearing; in pain you shall bring forth children, yet your desire shall be for your husband, and *he shall rule over you.*' "

Did you catch that last phrase? "He shall rule over you." Clearly, the domination of man over woman is a result of the Fall. Disobedience and sin created this hierarchy. Kari Malcolm comments that the oneness the couple had known in paradise was broken and replaced with a power struggle in which the man would try to rule over the woman.[1] And this has been the case throughout most of history. But, praise be to God, the story does not end with Genesis.

Consider secondly, *Jesus Christ.* Here is good news: The effects of sin *can* be overcome. What was lost in the Fall is restored through God's saving grace in Jesus. The old order is overcome, and we are made a new creation. We become more like Jesus as we seek not worldly power, but humble service. We become more like Jesus, who washed the disciples' feet as an example, and who declared in Mark 10: "You know that those who are supposed to rule over the Gentiles lord it over them, and their great men exercise authority over them. But it shall not be so among you; but whoever would be great among you must be your servant, and whoever would be first among you must be slave of all. For the Son of man also came not to be served but to serve, and to give his life as a ransom for many" (verses 42–45).

"Lording over others" is the Gentile way, the pagan way. It is not the Christ way. Mutual servanthood—that's the way Christ's followers are instructed to relate with each other.

This leads us, finally, to the apostle Paul and to our main text in Ephesians 5. Paul taught the "Christ way" of mutual servanthood as well. Yes, Paul—the one who has been long accused of encouraging male chauvinism. I think he's been falsely accused. Even Paul—whose whole upbringing and education gave him permission to regard women as inferior—even such a man as Paul understood the Christ way.

Ephesians 5 is a wonderful example. Some who teach the traditional, chain-of-command view might prefer to begin reading at verse 22, "Wives, submit to your husbands . . . " But that's not the beginning of the passage. The whole train of Paul's thought begins at verse 21, "Submit to one another out of reverence for Christ." *That's* the overriding principle: All Christians are to submit to each other. All brothers and sisters in Christ are called to relate in this new way. Rather than promoting ourselves, we are to lift up the other person. It is Christ's way of doing things, says Paul (Phil. 2).

"Mutual submission" is the principle for all times and all relationships in the church. In the verses that follow, Paul tells the first-century Ephesian Christians how they can apply this principle to their own marriages in their own cultural setting. In verses 22–24, he tells wives how to submit to their husbands. You may be thinking, "But he doesn't need to, women *already* had to submit to men in that day and age." True, but Paul knows there is a "pagan way" and there is a "Christian way" to submit to others. The pagan way was well known: A Greek wife had to obey her husband's every command. But she had subtle ways of gaining leverage over her husband. Patricia Gundry helps us understand: "It was so tempting to get back at an all-powerful husband for his neglect and mistreatment. A woman could waste and spoil her husband's goods, talk disparagingly about him, and be generally disrespectful and divisive . . . there were lots of things she could do to even the score. But the Christian woman was to stop all this destructive behavior."[2] The Christian wife is to submit to her husband "as to the Lord" (verse 22)—freely, willingly, lovingly. They would not treat Christ in destructive ways—they should not treat their husbands destructively either. The traditionalists might at this point say, "Yes, she must submit because the husband is the leader, the boss. After all, isn't that what Paul says in the next verse: 'the husband is the head of the wife'?"

Now I ask you: How can Paul lay out a general command for mutual submission in verse 21, then totally contradict himself when he applies the command to marriage in verse 23? Isn't it possible that we have misunderstood Paul when he says, "the husband is the 'head' of the wife"?

In our modern definition of the term, "head" means "leader" or "boss." But it can also mean many other things. It can mean "front"—(the "head of the line"), or it can refer to that thing that sits on our necks, or a certain number of cattle. Sometimes we use the word "head" to refer to "origin" or "source"—("head of the river").

What do you suppose Paul meant when he wrote these words so long ago to the Ephesians? Consider this: In the Greek language of Paul's day, the word "head" almost always referred to the "source" or "origin" of something. Paul probably has in mind Genesis 2, where woman is created from the rib of man. Paul uses this idea, that man is the "source" of woman, to encourage the Ephesian husbands to truly serve their marriage partners. These men were, by law and custom, in positions of power over their wives. So they are reminded that they, like Adam, can be a unique source of life for their wives. They can share their advantages with them. They can enable their wives to rise up to their levels of opportunity and effectiveness.

The pagan way for those Ephesian husbands to treat their wives was to oppress and degrade them. Paul says: Now that you are Christian, use the powers and privileges that society has given you to uplift and empower your wives. That requires sacrifice, and that's the way of Christ, who loved the church so much he gave himself up for her—as Paul says in verse 25.

So, let's put it all together . . . Paul lays out a principle which all Christians are to obey: "Submit to one another." Then he applies mutual submission to first-century marriages. Since the married women in that day were disadvantaged and often found ways to retaliate, Paul instructed these Christian wives to submit willingly and freely. And the husbands are reminded that they can use their advantages in a Christian way by being the source of their wives' growth, encouraging their wives to become the whole persons that God intended them to be. In this way, they can best serve and love their wives, just as Christ serves and loves the church.

Paul knew God's ideal will for his people: To be set free from the lust for power and the sins that accompany privilege. As he said in Galatians 3:28, for those that have been baptized into Christ, "There is neither Jew nor Greek, slave nor free, *male nor female*, for you are all *one* in Christ Jesus."

What, then, does all this mean for us today? First, it's time for all Christians to look this issue square in the face, and to repent of our love for power so that we can fully love and serve people. I once heard of a Christian speaker who was approached by a married couple. Said the husband, "I want to know *who* should be *in charge* in a Christian marriage?" The speaker looked at them and said, "But that's not a Christian question! The *Christian* question is: 'How can I serve my wife? How can I serve my husband?' "

Mutual servanthood requires personal sacrifice, and this is the second way the biblical teaching affects us. The willingness to sacrifice for each other, as Christ gave himself up for the church, is what makes a Christian marriage Christian. The bride should be saying to her new husband: "I'm going to do everything I can do to help you become all that God wills for you to be. I'm ready to sacrifice my own resources and time and plans for your sake." And then the husband should say, "Oh, no! I'm going to do everything *I* can do to help *you* become all that God wills for *you* to be. I'm ready to sacrifice my own resources and time and plans for *your* sake." And then she says, "Oh, no! It's the other way around . . . " and they have their first fight! It's the only kind of fight that a Christian couple is supposed to have: a fight to outdo the other in love.[3]

The third way mutual submission guides a Christian marriage is in the area of the practical, the everyday details and decisions. And this is where some couples begin to worry: "If the marriage is based on mutual submission, then who will make the big decisions? How can we resolve our differences when we are in conflict? Doesn't every home need a leader?"

Yes, clearly every home needs a leader, a Lord. I suggest Jesus Christ. As for making decisions together and resolving conflict, there are many options; negotiate, or take turns deciding, or let the one who is most effective in the area under discussion make the decision, or let the one most affected by the decision have the final say. As for dividing the work and responsibilities, why not encourage each other to do those things which each person is gifted to do? That's how the church functions—according to gifts. Why not the marriage? I noticed a cartoon recently in which a wife was tightly clutching the frying pan and yelling into her husband's face: "*My* doing the *cooking* and *your* doing the *eating* is *not* my idea of sharing chores!"[4] Mutual submission, it seems to me, means sharing the load—not that a couple needs to do the same tasks together, but trying to divide the work and responsibilities so that each person has an equal share, an equal amount of job satisfaction, and shared amount of those jobs that nobody wants to do but which have to be done. We can each submit to the other's leadership in their areas of strength. I submit gladly to my wife's leadership in financial matters. If I didn't, we would be doomed! And she submits to my leadership in other areas.

You see, the biblical model for Christian relationships looks very little like a military organization based on chain of command, but looks very much like a symphony orchestra, where each plays their different instrument in a unity of harmony. The Master Conductor is Jesus Christ.

If this were a more intimate setting, I might ask each married couple to take their spouse by the hand and look straight into his or her eyes. But right now, at least, you can picture your spouse in your mind's eye. Think of your beloved for a moment . . . uniquely created in God's image, with talents and strengths and incredible potential . . . Now picture him or her ten years from now, and imagine that he or she has blossomed into an even more radiant Christian person than ever before. More full of genuine love, joy, and kindness. More effective, doing excellently what God gave him or her the abilities to do. More fulfilled. A whole person.

And with that picture in your mind, I want to ask you *a very Christian question*: "How can you help your husband or wife become all that God wants them to be?"

NOTES

1. Kari Malcolm, *Women at the Crossroads* (Downers Grove, IL: InterVarsity Press, 1982), 157–158.

2. Patricia Gundry, *Heirs Together* (Grand Rapids, MI: Zondervan, 1980), 96.

3. Adapted from Anthony Campolo, *Who Switched the Price Tags?* (Waco, TX: Word Books, 1986), 158.

4. Reprinted from *Good Housekeeping* in Gundry, *Heirs Together,* 136.

# 23. Life's Single Constant

## Frank Pollard

Hebrews 13:8

OUR TEXT TODAY is Hebrews 13:8. One line almost disconnected from other lines of Holy Writ surrounding it, yet undeniably tied to every statement in all of God's Word: "Jesus Christ is the same yesterday, today, and forever."

We live in a changing world. It's always been changing. Adam probably said to Eve: "Honey, we're living in changing times." Can you think of anything in life that doesn't change? When we talk of "making change" in small money transactions, such as changing a dollar bill for four quarters, we are living out a parable of life. We are constantly changing one circumstance for another, one age for another. We change our childhood for adolescence. We change that for youth. We change youth for adulthood. One day we change this temporary life for eternal life. We link our life to someone and they change or they die and a massive change takes place in our lives. Every minister has heard it at one time or another: "I used to talk to him about everything. Now he's gone. What

---

*Frank Pollard* is pastor of the First Baptist Church in Jackson, Mississippi. Formerly president of the Golden Gate Baptist Theological Seminary, Pollard has also hosted the television show "At Home With the Bible." In 1979, *Time* magazine named him one of the "seven most outstanding Protestant preachers in America." He is the author of several books including *How to Know When You're a Success* and *Keeping Free.*

do I do?" *Life's deepest need* is for the unchanging, never-leaving friend. God's word that we need is: "Jesus Christ is the same yesterday, today and forever."

John the Baptist was beheaded at the orders of a drunken king titillated by the lustful dance of his wife's daughter. John's disciples tenderly took that headless body, buried it, and the Word says: "They came and told Jesus." They had left everything to follow John, had staked their lives on him. Instinctively, they knew that when you suffer loss like that, you can make a beeline to Jesus Christ. Always the same, always there.

In Matthew 17, Mark 9, and Luke 9, the Word pictures the transfiguration experience. Our Lord Christ was transformed. He was transfigured. He glowed with the very presence of God. To add to the frightening wondrousness of this moment, there appeared Moses and Elijah and, finally, the voice of God was a part of that experience. And when it was all over, the Bible says that Peter and James and John looked up and saw "Jesus only." Our Lord is certainly with us during life's spiritual highs. Indeed He is the center of the genuine experiences. But isn't it even greater to know that He's still there when the goosebumps are gone and it's time to walk into the valley?

Jesus Christ is the same yesterday, today, and forever. He is our need. He is the sum and substance of our theology.

One great old Christian said: "I used to seek the blessing, but I found victory in seeking the Lord."

He is the all in all. It is not the cross that saved us. It is the One on the cross. "I, if I be lifted up, will draw all people to me." The Apostle Paul went around his world saying: "One day I was walking down a road and something happened and that something was someone and His name is Jesus. Let me tell you about Him."

When we Christians think of that cataclysmic event "when the trumpet of the Lord shall sound and time will be no more," we don't think: "Something is going to happen." No, our message is: "Someone is coming again," "and every knee will bow and every tongue confess that Jesus Christ is Lord to the glory of God the Father."

It is not primarily a plan of salvation we preach. It is the person of salvation. "Jesus Christ is the same yesterday, today, and forever."

## He Is the Lord of Yesterday

We pragmatically talk of yesterday as past, bygone, former, expired.

There's nothing we can do about yesterday, we say. And that's sad because, in a real sense, we are products of our yesterdays. We are the sum total of decisions we have made. We are marked by what we did yesterday.

But Jesus Christ can walk backward. He can reenter our yesterdays. When we invite Him into the dark places in our past, He picks up and throws our sins into His sea of Forgetfulness and puts up a sign: "No fishing here."

Not once, but repeatedly does the psalmist declare: "He forgets our sins and remembers them no more."

With great delight we note that our Lord expressed His truth in the language of the marketplace. We put so much stained glass and organ music and pietistic preacher clichés around His truths that the world He loves has difficulty understanding them. But His word was contemporary, understandable. When we hear Him talking of forgiving sin, the word "forgive" is a word for paying a debt. Merchants had no business machines or computers or even paper in those days. Charge accounts were posted on the walls of their business. When you charged something at the store, your name was written on the wall along with the amount you owed. And one word indicated the thing done when the debt was forgiven or paid was that the merchant simply drew a line through the name of the debtor. I guess he wanted to keep a running record of how well people paid their debts. Another word described the merchant as simply taking a wet cloth and erasing the record of the debt. Biblical linguists say that without fail, each time our Lord's forgiveness is offered, it uses the word meaning "to wipe clean the record."

Do you catch the thrust of that? The Lord of yesterday walks into our past and cleanses us from our sins! He pulls up the record on Heaven's computer and punches the "delete" button. He throws our sins into the sea of His forgetfulness and puts up a sign: "No fishing here." "He forgets our sins and remembers them no more."

Some may say: "But I did such terrible things before I met Christ." Could it have been any worse than Paul's leading in the killing of Stephen, than his blaspheming the name of Christ, his avowal to destroy the churches of our Lord, to imprison women and children for being Christians? Yet our Lord walked into his yesterdays and cleansed Paul.

But you may say: "I have made mistakes since becoming a Christian." Is there anyone who hasn't? God's Word confronts us with that. In 1 John 1:8–9, the Bible says to Christians: "If we say we have no sin, we deceive ourselves and the truth is not in us. But if we confess our sins, He is faithful and just to forgive us our sins and cleanse us from all unrighteousness."

Simon Peter knew about that. He faced one bleak morning with a denial in his yesterday. Three times he had denied his Lord. When he confronted Christ that morning, they had fish for their meal and cleansing for dessert. Three times our Lord asked: "Do you love me?" and he walked back into that denial and erased it from His mind and the Heavenly record. Jesus Christ is the Lord of yesterday.

## And He Is the Lord of Today

It is so easy to forget that. Some of us want to. We say: "Lord, I can take care of today. Of course, I need you for yesterday. I sure want you tomorrow, but you can take today off. I can handle today." Yet most of yesterday's mistakes were made because of that attitude.

You may find it hard to realize He is Lord of today. Yet He

can reach back and touch yesterday, He can reach forward and touch tomorrow and still be the Lord of today. In today's stress and trials, He is here. You face the strain of making your way, of bills and taxes, but He is here and you need Him today.

In our relationships, we say: "Lord, I need you. I'm married to a woman. I need you."

"I'm married to a man. I need you."

"I have teenage children. I need you."

Teenagers may say: "I have middle-aged parents. I need you."

"I've lost my family. I've lost my job. I have to move. I need you."

"I'm sick and I'm afraid it may be serious. I need you."

"I'm sick and I know it's serious. I need you. I'm frightened. I need you."

"I don't know what we're going to do. I need you."

"Life is dull, unfulfilling, empty, without challenge—I need you!"

How well we may sing: "I need Thee, O, I need Thee, Every hour I need Thee; O bless me now, my Saviour, I come to Thee."

You have Him! Hear Him say: "I am with you always." Listen. The Lord of today is calling: "Come unto me, you who are tired and burdened. And I will give you rest."

He is the Lord of today. Genesis 28:15: "I am with you and will watch over you wherever you go."

## He Is the Lord of Tomorrow

In 1976, our bicentennial year, I was invited to speak to a Survival Conference in Boulder, Colorado. It was an annual meeting of a student honor society, a gathering of outstanding college students. Scientists from all over the world were brought in to talk about the prospects of this nation surviving for another one hundred years. I've never attended a more depressing meeting. One after another, these experts painted a bleak picture. One sociologist saw the day when boat people would be lined up on both coasts. And people from the starving and depressed nations of this world would come across Canadian and Mexican borders and would come upon us in such numbers that they would bring starvation over all the land. One said: "Our food supply can't last." Another declared: "The water will either be polluted or dry up." Nuclear experts described the holocaust if there is nuclear war.

My job was to speak about the survival of the Word, the Bible. How strange after all those hours of doom and gloom, it must have sounded to them when I read 1 Peter 2:25: "The Word of the Lord stands forever." That is true of the written Word, the Bible, because it is true of the Living Word: "Jesus Christ, the same yesterday, today, and forever."

Are you worried about tomorrow? Worried that the world will be destroyed if someone intoxicated by vodka or bourbon or power becomes unstable and pushes the button to involve us in nuclear war? Are you worried about economic depression? Young people, are you worried there'll be no jobs left for you? No income? Are you afraid you'll marry the wrong person, someone who looks like an angel and after the wedding turns into a devil? Are you afraid no one will marry you? He is the Lord of tomorrow.

Are you afraid to face eternity, the unknown on the other side of the grave? He is the Lord of tomorrow.

Jesus Christ is at work in your yesterdays and your todays and your tomorrows.

He is our friend. He is our Lord. He is our life. He is our purpose. We will find our strength as we find it in Him. As we make it our job to love Him and share Him and serve Him, then we will find life's constant and most reassuring purpose.

After His resurrection, our Lord specifically asked the people to whom He appeared to do three things. He met the women in the garden and said: "Go tell my disciples and Simon Peter." He said to an assembled group: "Go ye therefore and make disciples of all nations and baptize them in the name of the Father and the Son and the Holy Spirit."

He gave three commissions: "Go tell my disciples." Those disciples were of course disturbed and hurt and scattered. Our Lord is saying: "Go tell my hurting, disturbed church that I'm alive and I want to be with them."

"Go tell Simon Peter." Peter had denied Him, had slipped away from his commitment to our Lord. And Jesus' word to him was: "Go tell my backslidden, discouraged believer I'm alive and I want to be with him."

"Go tell the world." Tell the lost world, the world I love and died for, shamed by their yesterdays, stressed and strained by their todays, and frightened of tomorrow that Jesus Christ is the same—yesterday, today, and forever.

# 24. Advent Has Three Tenses

## Graham W. Hardy

In many and various ways God spoke of old to our fathers by the prophets, but in these last days He has spoken to us by a Son . . . heir of all things.—Hebrews 1:1–2

I am with you always, to the close of the age.—Matthew 28:20

The creation itself will be set free from its bondage to decay and obtain the glorious liberty of the children of God.—Romans 8:21

THE OLD STOCKMAN leaned against the fence, looking out over his parched "paddocks." We chatted till the stars shone with startling clarity. Sandy spoke of the isolation, of hard times when nature was cruel and unrelenting, and of better days when the drought broke for a good harvest and the stock thrived.

The awesome silence of that evening in the "red heart" of Australia prompted me to ask a very personal question: "Do you believe in God, Sandy?" He paused and then answered in a quiet voice: "Yes, I do." But something in the tone of his reply constrained me to ask a further question: "But what *kind* of a God do you believe in?" Again he paused, till words came

---

*Graham W. Hardy* is interim associate Pastor for the First Presbyterian Church in Sanford, Florida. He is a graduate of Edinburgh University; New College, Edinburgh; Union Theological Seminary in New York; and the London Royal Academy of Music. He was a member of the Order of Australia in the Queen of England's birthday honors in June 1988. Hardy has been a pastor of churches in Scotland and Australia, and he assisted James S. Stewart at North Morningside Church, Edinburgh.

with what seemed like a winsome sadness: "You ask me what kind of a God I believe in. I'll tell you. He's as far away and as silent as those stars."

We talked long into that balmy night. I hope I helped to introduce Sandy to another God, whose interaction with His creation was more constant and even closer than breathing. But I kept asking myself how many, like Sandy, believed in a God who was little more than a religious symbol, a detached deity who would not or could not communicate. Sometimes it seems that way. When we contemplate the saga of suffering, the wars and rumors of wars, hunger and violence, tragedy and heartbreak, and the doubts and fears that "rap and knock and enter in the soul," it may seem that God is either unable or unwilling to intervene or to answer the agonizing cries of those caught in whirlpools of despair and death.

Advent is the Christian answer to that dilemma. It tells of the God who could not endure the isolation even of His self-sufficient glory, who came not only as creator but as re-creator. Advent calls for a "Happy New Year" greeting, not from wistful optimism that things might improve, but because of the world-shaking news that God, despite all appearances to the contrary, does not reside in some distant galaxy, silent and unmoved at the tribulations of His creatures, but is God ever on the move, God who has arrived to become part of the whole complex of life in this world. His star has drawn so near that it has outshone all other stars. At Bethlehem God's creative Word became flesh and dwelt among us. Advent means quite simply, and yet profoundly, that God came. But it also means that God comes and that He will yet come. There are three tenses to Advent: past, present, and future.

Let us reach for a fresh grasp of *Advent past.* A Christian journalist, visiting Moscow, was in lively conversation with a Russian journalist who spoke fluent English. The Russian was trying to convince his Western colleague that the most significant event in the history of the world took place in Moscow in 1917, the year of the Marxist revolution. When the workers of the world began to unite to throw off the chains of capitalism, all history took a new direction. The journalist from the "decadent" West said nothing till the end of this passionate exposition of the blessings Lenin had brought to the world. Then with great restraint he asked a question: "You tell me that 1917 was the most important date in the history of the world; 1917 years after *what?*"

Not even the devotees of an atheistic political creed can deny that an event occurred at a specific date in history at a point on a map which, at a single stroke, divided history in two: B.C. from A.D. The world dates its letters from the birthday of a Child. "Nineteen centuries have come and gone and today He is the central figure of history. All the armies that ever marched, all the navies that ever sailed, all the parliaments that ever sat and all the kings that ever reigned, have not affected life on this earth as that one solitary life."

Napoleon, disillusioned in exile, confessed: "I am a failure. Jesus Christ is a world conqueror. . . . Alexander, Caesar, Charlemagne and I founded empire upon force. Christ founded His empire on love, and at this hour millions will die for Him."

We have heard "the old, old, story of Jesus and His love" so often that the astonishing reality of the historical Christ-event may become blurred. Every time I have been privileged to visit the "Shepherds' Fields" at Bethlehem, or have stood on the Mount of Olives overlooking the ancient walled city of Jerusalem over which Jesus once wept, or have walked in by-paths of Galilee or sailed across the waters of the Lake where fishermen were once called to be fishers of men, I am not concerned with the precise identification of holy sites, but I am faced with the inescapable fact of the historical Jesus. Faith is lifted out of the realm of metaphysical speculation or transcendental meditation and firmly rooted in events surrounding a real life with a date in history. Not through some cataclysmic upheaval, some primeval eruption or nuclear catastrophe that could have changed the contours of our physical environment, but through the most ordinary yet extraordinary birth of a child, God acted.

Only a stable and a starlit sky,
An infant crying in the night,
The sound of wings
Like the sighing of the wind at dawn,
And Christ was born.

In that life God showed His love to a world that had failed to respond to His prophetic messengers. Part of His own being became incarnate. Through Jesus of Nazareth as teacher and healer, through the mystery of His death and resurrection, as St. Athanasius expressed it far back in the fourth century, "God became like man that man might become like God." The blood and tears and sweat of humanity are now seen to flow through the very heart of God. A light of hope has shone that no darkness can diminish, a supernatural moral and spiritual dynamic has been released with power to turn the world upside down, casting the mighty from their seats and exalting those of low degree.

Advent not only takes us backward in time to a point in history, but brings us to an immediate encounter. The call is to awaken to *Advent present.*

Sydney Carter protests against a secondhand faith buried in the past:

Your holy hearsay is not evidence;
Give me the good news in the present tense . . .
The living truth is what I long to see;
I cannot lean upon what used to be . . .
Show me how the Christ you talk about is living now.

Attempts have always been made to bury Jesus Christ in the dust of the ages. In Russia many churches, like the Cathedral of St. Basil outside the Kremlin, have been turned into museums. The once greatest church in Christendom, the Church of Santa Sophia in Istanbul, became a mosque. It too is now a museum. One fears that some Western cathedrals, like Westminster Abbey, are in danger of becoming tourist attractions and mausoleums rather than centers of living worship.

But Christ cannot be locked up in the vaults of a vanished world. The story of His impact on human lives still continues with ever new recorded evidence. As Dr. A. C. Craig, a former Moderator of the Church of Scotland, expressed it: "Like an atom, from which a series of chain reactions is initiated, that short life has been explosive in its effect on the history of our race."

That explosive effect has come from more than the memory of a dynamic life. It has come from the continuing impact of a presence, the fulfillment of Jesus' last recorded words before His visible form was lost to human sight: "I shall be with you to the end of time." And He calls those "happy" who, though denied sight with their eyes, have yet believed and found insight, the more secure evidence of things unseen.

Real faith is born when Christ emerges from the dead chrysalis of formal religion to become a joyous and immediate source of power for living. C. F. Andrews, missionary to India, confessed: "I do not picture Jesus as I see Him in the Gospel story . . . for I have known the secret of His presence, here and now, as a daily reality."

Shortly before his death, American writer Theodore Dreiser made a wistful plea: "I wish it were true . . . that there was someone to whom man in his misery might turn for succor, or at least a kindly word; some definite universal heart of whom the declaration were true 'Come unto Me all ye that are weary and heavy-laden and I will give you rest.' " Andrews and a countless "cloud of witnesses" could have assured the Theodore Dreisers of this world that the offer of rest and renewal to the weary and the heavy-laden comes from a Christ who is alive now.

Suppose we were sitting alone, reading a biography of some great figure of the past. We looked up from our reading, and there, before us in real life, with new words to address to us, stands the very person of whom we have been reading. As we ponder the Gospel story this fantasy can become fact— such is the miracle of Advent present. Let us therefore awaken to Him who still offers healing and forgiveness, challenges mediocrity, judges dishonesty, calls us into action against principalities and powers of evil, and throws open to us the gates of new life.

Advent assures us that God came, God comes, and that God will yet come. What exactly does *Advent future* mean for us today? Here we enter a dimension that defies precise definition. The article, firmly embedded in our Creed: "I believe that He shall come again to judge both the living and the dead," is wide open for misinterpretation. It has become fair game for would-be prophets who presume to pinpoint the date and the location for the second coming of Christ.

Outside the Golden Gate of the old walled city of Jerusalem, a gate bricked up and only to be opened—tradition has it—on the day of Christ's majestic return, are three graveyards, Jewish, Christian, and Moslem, in morbid competition to be first on the scene for the general resurrection. All down the centuries, groups of zealous and expectant believers have gathered on hilltops or at designated sacred sites, waiting breathlessly for the midnight hour when the last trumpet would sound and sings in the heavens would herald the return of Christ in dazzling glory and fearful judgment. Biblical literalists have pored over the pages of Daniel and Revelation and deducted references to catastrophic events and historical figures, even identifying the site of the final Armageddon, if not at Megiddo in Israel. in some other place where an imminent nuclear holocaust will engulf the unwary.

One can only regret the presumption of those who claim to have received revelations concerning this final consummation that were denied even to Jesus Himself, who confessed that He did not know the times or the seasons of His return. We can perhaps be allowed a smile at the pious old Methodist couple who reached a point where they could no longer pray together because one of them believed that Christ would come as "a thief in the night," whereas the other believed that He would come with the sound of a trumpet on clouds of glory!

The danger is that, with so many misguided prophets, so

much uninformed biblical exegesis, so many firm forecasts of a second coming that never materialized, the whole message of a final vindication of the power and authority of Christ is dismissed or even mocked. But if we lose the real message of the Second Coming, we lose our ultimate hope. Paul, in his letter to the Romans, paints a picture of the whole of creation, groaning and travailing, struggling for rebirth, moving toward a final destiny that will resolve all unanswered questions. Instead of creation moving toward disintegration, to the scorched-earth wilderness of a post-nuclear catastrophe, all things are moving toward fulfillment, the completion of all that is incomplete, the consummation of the final V-day when the forces of darkness, still permitted to work their evil after the D-day of Christ's first coming, will be finally overcome.

Such a faith is essential to complete and vindicate the struggles and hopes of all who did not in their time enter into the promised inheritance. Here is the assurance that the pain and suffering of the saints of God down all the centuries has not been pointless and in vain. The final destiny of this world is not in the hands of the devil and his angels and of demonic people, but in the hands of the Almighty Father of all, whose Christ came to reveal His saving love. He will put all enemies under His feet, till "at the name of Jesus every knee shall bow and every tongue confess that He is Lord." This is the faith that compels us to rise to our feet when the Hallelujah Chorus is sung, for we know in our heart of hearts that He who came—who comes—and who will yet come in power and glory, shall indeed reign, King of Kings and Lord of Lords, Hallelujah! "Even so come, Lord Jesus!"

# IV. ETHICAL

# 25. Be Holy

## Frederick Buechner

And Moses went up unto God and the Lord called unto him out of
the mountain, saying, Thus shalt thou say to the house of Jacob and
tell the children of Israel: Ye have seen what I did unto the
Egyptians, and how I bare you on eagles' wings, and brought you
unto myself. Now therefore, if ye will obey my voice indeed, and
keep my covenant, then ye shall be a peculiar treasure unto me above
all people: for all the earth is mine: and ye shall be unto me a
kingdom of priests and an holy nation. These are the words which
thou shalt speak unto the children of Israel.—Exodus 19:3–6

So put away all malice and all guile and insincerity and envy and all
slander. Like newborn babes, long for the pure spiritual milk, that by
it you may grow up to salvation; for you have tasted the kindness of
the Lord. [But] you are a chosen race, a royal priesthood, a holy
nation, God's own people, that you may declare the wonderful deeds
of him who called you out of darkness into his marvelous light.—
1 Peter 2:1–2, 9

"RICH MAN, poor man, beggar man, thief, doctor, lawyer,
merchant chief" or "Indian chief" sometimes, if that's how
you happened to be feeling that day. That was how the rhyme
went in my time anyway, and you used it when you were

*Frederick Buechner* was born in New York City. He was educated at
Lawrenceville School, Princeton University, and Union Theological
Seminary in New York. He is a Presbyterian. Buechner taught English
at Lawrenceville School and creative writing at New York University.
At Phillips Exeter Academy he was chairman of the department of
religion and school minister. He is the author of novels, books of
sermons, autobiography, and books on religious themes. Buechner
delivered the Lyman Beecher Lectures at Yale University, published
as *Telling the Truth: The Gospel as Tragedy, Comedy, and Fairy Tale.* "Be
Holy" is a baccalaureate sermon preached at Lafayette College.

counting the cherry pits on your plate or the petals on a daisy or the buttons on your shirt or your blouse. The one you ended up counting was, of course, the one you ended up being. Rich, Poor. Standing on a street corner with a tin cup in your hand. Or maybe a career in organized crime. What in the world, what in heaven's name, were you going to be when you grew up? It was not just another question. It was the great question. Whether we remember to ask it or not, I strongly suspect that it may be the great question still. What are you going to be? What am I going to be? I'll turn fifty-eight this summer, and I've been in more or less the same trade for a long time, and I contemplate no immediate change, but I think of it still as a question that's wide open. For God's sake what do you suppose we're going to be, you and I? When we grow up.

Something in us rears back in indignation of course. At twenty-eight, fifty-eight, seventy-eight or whatever we are, surely we've got our growing up behind us. We've come many a long mile and thought many a long thought. We've taken on serious responsibilities, made mature decisions, weathered many a crisis. Surely the question is, rather, what are we now and how well are we doing at it. If not doctors, lawyers, merchant chiefs, we are whatever we are—computer analysts, businesswomen, schoolteachers, artists, ecologists, ministers even, or if the job isn't already in our pocket, it's well on its way to being. The letters of recommendation have all been written. The résumés have gone out. The interview on the whole went very well. We don't have to count cherry pits to find out what we're going to end up being, because for better or worse the die has already been cast. Now we simply get on with the game. That's what commencement is all about. That's what life is all about.

But then. Then maybe we have to listen—listen back farther than the rhymes of our childhood, thousands of years farther back than that. A thick cloud gathers on the mountain as the book of Exodus describes it. There are flickers of lighting, jagged and dangerous. A clap of thunder shakes the earth and sets the leaves of the trees trembling, sets even you and me trembling a little maybe, if we have our wits about us. Suddenly the great *shophar* sounds, the ram's horn—a long-drawn, pulsing note louder than thunder, more dangerous than lightning—and out of the darkness, out of the mystery, out of some cavernous part of who we are, a voice calls: "Now therefore, if ye will obey my voice indeed, and keep my covenant, then ye shall be a peculiar treasure unto me above all people"—my *segullah,* my precious ones, my darlings—"and ye shall be unto me a kingdom of priests and a holy nation." Then, thousands of years later but still thousands of years ago, there is another voice to listen to. It is the voice of an old man dictating a letter. There is reason to believe that he may actually have been the one who up till all but the end was the best friend that Jesus had, Peter himself. "So put away all malice and all guile and insincerity and envy and all slander," he says. "Like newborn babes, long for the pure spiritual milk that by it you may grow up to salvation; for you have tasted the kindness of the Lord." And then he echoes the great cry out of the thunderclouds with a cry of his own. "You are a chosen race, a royal priesthood, a holy nation, God's own people," he says, "that you may declare the wonderful deeds of him who called you out of darkness into his marvelous light."

What are we going to be when we grow up? Not what are we going to *do,* what profession are we going to follow what niche are we going to choose for ourselves. But what are we going to *be*—inside ourselves and among ourselves? That is the question that God answers with the Torah at Sinai. That is the question that the old saint answers in his letter from Rome. Holy. That is what we are going to be if God gets his way with us. It is wildly unreasonable because it makes a shambles of all our reasonable ambitions to be this or to be that. It's not really a human possibility at all because holiness is godness and only God makes holiness possible. But being holy is what growing up in the full sense means, Peter suggests. No matter how old we are or how much we've achieved or dream of achieving, we are not truly grown up till this extraordinary thing happens. Holiness is what is to happen. Out of darkness we are called into "his marvelous light," Peter writes, who knew more about darkness than most of us if you stop to think about it, and had looked into the very face itself of light. We are called to have faces like that—to be filled with light so that we can be bearers of light. I've seen a few such faces in my day, and so have you, unless I miss my guess. Are we going to be rich, poor, beggars, thieves, or in the case of most of us a little of each? Who knows? In the long run who even cares? Only one thing is really worth caring about, and it is this: "Ye shall be unto me a kingdom of priests and a holy nation."

Israel herself was never much good at it, God knows. That is what most of the Old Testament is mostly about. Israel didn't want to be a holy nation. Israel wanted to be a nation like all the other nations, a nation like Egypt, like Syria. She wanted clout. She wanted security. She wanted a place in the sun. It was her own way she wanted, not God's way, and when the prophets got after her for it, she got rid of the prophets, and when God's demands seemed too exorbitant, God's promises too remote, she took up with all the other gods who still get our votes and our money and our nine-to-five energies, because they couldn't care less whether we're holy or not and promise absolutely everything we really want and absolutely nothing we really need.

We can't very well blame Israel, because of course we are Israel. Who wants to be holy? The veryword has fallen into disrepute—holier-than-thou, holy Joe, holy mess. And "saint" comes to mean plaster saint, somebody of such stifling moral perfection that we'd run screaming in the other direction if our paths ever crossed. We are such children, you and I, the way we do such terrible things with such wonderful words. We are such babes in the woods the way we keep getting hopelessly lost.

And yet we have our moments. Every once in a while, I think, we actually long to be what out of darkness and mystery we are called to be; when we hunger for holiness even so, even if we'd never use the word. There come moments, I think, even in the midst of all our cynicism and worldliness and childishness, maybe especially then, when there's something about the saints of the earth that bowls us over a little. I mean real saints. I mean saints as men and women who are made not out of plaster and platitude and moral perfection but out of human flesh in all its richness and quirkiness for the simple reason that there's nothing else around except human flesh to make saints out of. I mean saints as human beings who have their rough edges and their blind spots like everybody else but whose lives are transparent to something so extraordinary that every once in a while it stops us dead in our tracks.

I remember going to see the movie *Gandhi* when it first came out, for instance. We were the usual kind of noisy, restless Saturday night crowd as we sat there waiting for the lights to dim with our popcorn and soda pop, girlfriends and boyfriends, our legs draped over the backs of empty seats; but by the time the movie came to a close with the flames of Gandhi's funeral pyre filling the entire screen, there wasn't a sound or a movement in that whole theater, and we filed out of there—teenagers and senior citizens, blacks and whites, swingers and squares—in as deep and telling a silence as I've ever been part of or has ever been part of me.

"Like newborn babes, long for the pure spiritual milk that by it you may grow up to salvation, for you have tasted of the kindness of the Lord," Peter wrote. We had tasted it. In the life of that little bandy-legged, bespectacled man with his spinning wheel and his bare feet and whatever he had in the way of selfless passion for peace, and passionate opposition to every form of violence, we had all of us tasted something that at least for a few moments that Saturday night made every other kind of life seem empty, something that at least for the moment I think every last one of us longed for the way in a far country you yearn for home.

"Ye shall be unto me a kingdom of priests, a holy nation." Can a nation be holy? It's hard to imagine it. Some element of a nation maybe, some remnant or root. "A shoot coming forth from the stump of Jesse," as Isaiah put it, "that with righteousness shall judge the poor and decide with equity for the meek of the earth." The eighteenth-century men and women who founded this nation dreamed just such a high and holy dream for us too and gave their first settlements over here names to match. New Haven, New Hope, they called them—names that almost bring tears to your eyes if you listen to what they are saying, or once said. Providence. Concord. Salem, which is *shalom*, the peace that passeth all understanding. Dreams like that die hard, and please God there's still some echo of them in the air around us. But the way things have turned out, the meek of the earth are scared stiff at the power we have to blow the earth to smithereens a hundred times over and at our failure year after year after year to work out with our enemies a way of limiting that ghastly power. In this richest of nations, the poor go to bed hungry, if they're lucky enough to have a bed, because after the staggering amounts we spend to defend ourselves, there isn't enough left over to feed the ones we're defending, to help give them decent roofs over their heads, decent schools for their kids, decent care when they're sick and old.

The nation that once dreamed of being a new hope, a new haven, for the world, has become instead one of the two great bullies of the world who blunder and bluster their way toward unspeakable horror. Maybe that's the way it inevitably is with all nations. They're so huge and complex. By definition they're so exclusively concerned with their own self-interest conceived in the narrowest terms that they have no eye for *holiness*, of all things, no ears to hear the great command to be saints, no heart to break at the thought of what this world could be—the friends we could be as nations, the common problems we could help each other solve, all the human anguish we could join together to heal.

You and I are the eyes and ears. You and I are the heart. It's to us that Peter's letter is addressed. "So put away all guile and insincerity and envy and all slander," he says. No *shophar* sounds or has to sound. It's as quiet as the scratching of a pen, as familiar as the sight of our own faces in the mirror. We've always known what was wrong with us. The malice in us even at our most civilized: the way we focus on the worst in the people we know and then rejoice when the disasters overtake them that we believe they so richly deserve. Our insincerity:

our phoniness, the masks we do our real business behind. The envy: the way other people's luck can sting like wasps. And all slander: all the ways we have of putting each other down, making such caricatures of each other that we treat each other like caricatures, even when we love each other. All this infantile nonsense and nastiness. Put it away! Peter says. Before nations can be holy, you must be holy. *Grow up* to salvation. For Christ's sake, grow up.

People at my stage of the game—fifty-eight come July? For us isn't it a little too late? People at your stage of the game? For you isn't it a little too early? No, I don't think so. Never too late, never too early, to grow up, to be holy. We've already tasted it—tasted the kindness of the Lord, Peter says. That's such a haunting thought. I think you can see it in our eyes sometimes. Just the way you can see something more than animal in animals' eyes. I think you can sometimes see something more than human in human eyes, even yours and mine. I think we belong to holiness even when we can't believe it exists anywhere, let alone in ourselves. That's why everybody left that crowded shopping-mall movie theater in such unearthly silence. It's why it's hard not to be haunted by that famous photograph of the only things that Gandhi owned at his death: his glasses and his watch, his sandals, a bowl and spoon, a book of songs. What do any of us own to match such riches as that?

Children that we are, even you and I, who have given up so little, know in our hearts not only that it's more blessed to give than to receive but that it's also more fun—the kind of holy fun that wells up like tears in the eyes of saints, the kind of blessed fun in which we lose ourselves and at the same time begin to find ourselves, to grow up into the selves we were created to become.

When Henry James, of all people, was saying good-bye once to his young nephew Billy, his brother William's son, he said something that the boy never forgot. And of all the labyrinthine and impenetrably subtle things that that most labyrinthine and impenetrable old romancer could have said, what he did say was this: "There are three things that are important in human life. The first is to be kind. The second is to be kind. The third is to be kind."

In the unlikely event that as the years go by anybody should ever happen to ask you what it was that the speaker said when he was telling you goodbye on this commencement day, I would be willing to settle for that. Be kind. That is what in his own labyrinthine way the speaker tried to say at least.

Be kind because though kindness isn't the same thing as holiness, kindness is next to holiness; because it's one of the doors that holiness enters the world through, enters us through—not just gently kind but sometimes fiercely kind.

Be kind enough to yourselves not just to play it safe with your lives for your own sakes but to spend at least part of your lives like drunken sailors for God's sake, if you believe in God, for the world's sake, if you believe in the world, and thus to come alive truly.

Be kind enough to others to listen, beneath the words they speak, for that usually unspoken hunger for holiness which I believe is part of even the unlikeliest of us and, by cherishing which, you can help bring to birth both in them and in yourselves.

Be kind to this nation of ours by remembering that New Haven, New Hope, Shalom, are the names not just of our oldest towns but of our holiest dreams, which most of the time are threatened by the madness of no enemy without as dangerously as they are threatened by our own madness.

"You have tasted of the kindness of the Lord," Peter wrote in his letter, and ultimately that, of course, is the kindness, the holiness, the sainthood and sanity we are all of us called to. So that by God's grace we may "grow up to salvation" at last.

The sounds of the birds. The way the light falls through the trees. The sense we have of each other's presence. The feeling in the air that one way or another we are all of us here—you who are graduating and we your well-wishers—to give each other our love. This kind moment itself is a door that holiness enters through. May it enter you. May it enter me. To the world's saving. Amen.

# 26. Hell Is Not to Love Anymore

*Walter J. Burghardt*

Jonah 3:1–5, 10; 1 Corinthians 7:29–31; and Mark 1:14–20

ONE WORD lights up today's liturgy. Christian though it is, Christians are not overly fond of it. From Jonah through John the Baptist to Jesus and Paul, the word echoes harshly to us: "Repent!" It sounds so negative: Activate those hidden guilt feelings, calculate your peccadillos on your personal computer, renounce Satan and all his works and pomps.

Now the negative is not necessarily a no-no. If you're guilty before God, a gram of guilt is not out of order. If sin plays a large role in your life, face up to it. If Satan is playing the devil with your Christlife, bid him (or her) goodbye. But this afternoon I want to accent the positive in repentance. To repent, as the Gospel Greek has it, is to change your mind, to convert, to turn. Not simply turning *from* but, more importantly, turning *to*. Better, turning from *by* turning to. Three turnings, all linked: (1) You turn to yourself. (2) You turn to Christ. (3) You turn to others. A word on each, with a real-life story for each.

---

*Walter J. Burghardt* was born in New York City. He was educated at Woodstock College and the Catholic University of America. Father Burghardt, a Jesuit priest, currently is theologian-in-residence at Georgetown University and is editor in chief of *Theological Studies*. He has received thirteen honorary degrees from American colleges and universities and is the author of a number of books, most recently *Preaching: The Art and the Craft.*

## I

First, to repent is to turn to yourself, to look inside. Here a fire-and-brimstone preacher would be tempted to paint graphically the rot and corruption in the human heart. I have no gift for that, no desire. Another might tear a page from the book of Revelation, repeat the risen Christ's threat to the bishop of Laodicea: "I know your works: You are neither cold nor hot. Would that you were cold or hot! So, because you are lukewarm, and neither cold nor hot, I will spew you out of my mouth" (Rev. 3:15–16). But only God has the right to speak such frightful language. I shall move away from the tepid, tell you of a red-hot Christian looking into himself. I mean that remarkable monk Thomas Merton.[1]

Aged forty, after thirteen years with the Trappists, Merton had to ask himself: Should I leave? Why ask? For one thing, the cloister in Kentucky had changed chokingly: it "is as crowded as a Paris street." His old dream, to live as a hermit, tempted him ever more seductively; he needed greater freedom for private prayer, for contemplation.

But superiors would have none of this. Merton "fans" would be scandalized: his students, his readers, other religious. Trappist vocations would plummet. Merton stayed; but after a year he was still depressed, sought help in analysis, lived on the brink of a breakdown. He realized that all through his life a crucial question confronts the monk with fresh meaning and urgency: What are you doing here?

Against all the odds, Merton's inner conflict turned him outward to a world's sin and suffering, released him to a universe outside Gethsemani's gates, immersed him in passionate protest: against Vietnam and violence, against pollution, against racial injustice and nuclear war.

At fifty, crisis flared up again. How live obedience when authority seems irrational? How deal with the perils and pressures of solitude? How harmonize his hermit side with his need for people and their need for him? The cost was high: stomach spasms, colitis, tensions that tied his "guts in knots of utter despair." No wonder he could write wittily to a troubled friend: "You think I got fun here? Man, you think more. You think I got no angst? Man, think again. I got angst up to the eyes."

Tempestuous years indeed. He did become confused, had to struggle with the life of a hermit, slipped in fidelity a while. But in that decade of looking within he had grown much, discovered much. Illusions about religious life had been stripped away. He had gone through the loneliness of the desert, lost his way, found a more profound self that pervaded his final years, till he died so tragically and so young—accidentally electrocuted in Bangkok at fifty-three—still looking for deeper and deeper identity.

And what of you? If you are not to stagnate, there are times—I cannot predict when—times when you must look within, ask yourself: What am I doing here? The problems are legion: God, work, people; church or family; desert or city. The problems will vary, depending on who you are, where you've been, where you're at. But turn inside you must, else you risk a living death, not even knowing you are dead. "Is this the way God wants me to live?" Oh, you may well answer: "Yes, by God yes! This *is* what God wants me to do, wants me to be." But you won't know that unless you look within, unless you risk discovering with Merton "I got angst up to the eyes."

## II

Second, to repent is to turn to Christ. Pious pap? No, a perennial paradox: You must turn once *and* you must turn each day. Too abstract? Let me put a face on it: The man who, almost sixteen centuries ago, changed the face of the Western world, laid the heritage of the old world at the feet of the new in a breathless synthesis. I mean St. Augustine.[2]

Till he was thirty-two, Augustine was just another bright young man in tortured quest of truth and love. Born to a

Christian mother but not baptized, with a superficial knowledge of Christ and Christianity, he confronted two major crises quite unprepared.

The moral crisis began at fifteen: "Arrived now at adolescence I . . . sank to the animal in a succession of dark lusts."[3] At sixteen he came to semipagan Carthage; there "a cauldron of illicit loves leaped and boiled about me. I was not yet in love, but I was in love with love. . . . "[4] At seventeen he took a mistress, lived with her for thirteen years, had a son by her, surrendered her with sorrow: "My heart . . . was broken and wounded and shed blood."[5] His prayer to God? " 'Grant me chastity and continence, but not yet.' For I was afraid that you would hear my prayer too soon, and too soon would heal me. . . . "[6]

The intellectual crisis began at eighteen. It started with Cicero, who triggered his thirst for wisdom, whose majestic language made the simple Bible distasteful. He moved to the Persian prophet Mani, mesmerized by a free philosophy without the bridle of faith, pleasing his pride by freeing him from moral fault. Skepticism tempted him lightly. Neoplatonism captivated him. Even when he discovered what Neoplatonism could not offer, the Savior Christ and his grace, it was Augustine's intellect that was captured; his will was not completely conquered—the pull of the flesh was still too powerful.

The drama reached its climax in Milan, in a little garden. "There I was, going mad on my way to sanity, dying on my way to life, aware how evil I was. . . . "[7] Pleasure plucked at his garment of flesh, murmuring softly: "Are you sending us away?" Torn by violent tears, he cried: "How long shall I go on saying 'tomorrow'?" Suddenly he heard a voice nearby, a sort of sing-song: "Take and read, take and read." He snatched up his Scripture, read the passage on which his eyes first fell, a passage from Paul to the Romans: "not in reveling and drunkenness, not in debauchery and licentiousness, not in quarreling and jealousy; but put on the Lord Jesus Christ, and make no provision for the flesh, to gratify its desires" (Rom. 13:13–14). Augustine tells us: "I had no wish to read further, and no need. For in that instant, with the very ending of the sentence, it was as though a light of utter confidence shone in all my heart, and all the darkness of uncertainty vanished away."[8] Almost nine months later, on the vigil of Easter 387, Augustine was baptized, the oil of confirmation completed his baptism, and he pillowed on his tongue the Christ he had fled "down the arches of the years."[9]

But baptism, at thirty-three or at birth, is only a beginning. For you as for Augustine, this radical, root turning to Christ makes a daily demand, a conversion to Christ that is constant. Ten years after his baptism Augustine had to confess that he was still wrestling with the lust of the flesh, the lust of the eyes, and the pride of life: with the memory of illicit love, the allurement of beauty sundered from Loveliness supreme, "the desire to be feared and loved by men for no other reason than the joy I get from it."[10]

Terribly true, but for you as for Augustine, turning to Christ each day is more than turning from temptation and sin. What was given you in baptism was life, a sharing in God's own life. From that moment, aware of it or not, you were a fresh creation, alive with the life of the risen Christ, empowered to know the living God and to love him, empowered to hope against hope for a life that will never end. The Christian can proclaim with Paul: "It is no longer I who live, but Christ who lives in me; and the life I now live in the flesh I live by faith in the Son of God, who loved me and gave himself for me" (Gal. 2:20).

But to stay alive in Christ, you must grow; for when you cease to grow, you begin to die. And how do you grow into Christ? Get to know him. Not a catechism Christ whom you memorize. Not simply the Christ of theology, revealed and concealed in concepts. Let him get inside of you. Listen to him thirstily as he speaks to you in his book and in his life, through his community and from his cross. Let him shake you and shiver you, tear you and strip you naked. Whatever you do, don't exile him to the edge of your existence, a shadow stalking your steps, the phantom of your opera.[11] Turn to Christ each day, if only to pray, with the father of the Gospel epileptic, "I do believe; help my unbelief" (Mark 9:24).

## III

A third and final point. You see, turning to yourself and turning to Christ is not the whole story; you haven't turned quite enough. Repentance in its positive sense is not a private party—you and Jesus. You and I are part of a people, of a world for which Christ was crucified. To repent fully, we must turn to others. But again, no abstractions; only a life, a saint of the homeless and hopeless, now seven years dead. I mean Dorothy Day.

Long a Communist, Dorothy moved from communism to Christ, from Union Square to Rome. A slow and painful journey, with strange turns in the road. She loved the Church, but "not for itself . . . it was so often a scandal" to her; she loved the Church because it made Christ visible.[12] And for Dorothy, Christ was crucifyingly visible in the poor and despised, the broken-down and the broken-hearted. For them she started houses of hospitality that spread across the country, breadlines in Depression days to feed the hungry, clothe the naked, shelter the homeless. She walked picket lines, struggled against segregation in Georgia, was jailed for supporting Mexican itinerant workers, squared off against a New York cardinal in defense of cemetery strikers. She argued passionately that "the poor do *not* have the Gospel preached to them."[13] To preach it to them, she lived with them, "with the criminal, the unbalanced, the drunken, the degraded . . . with rats, with vermin, bedbugs, roaches, lice. . . . Yes, the smell of sweat, blood, and tears spoken of so blithely by Mr. Churchill, so widely and bravely quoted by comfortable people."[14] Including me.

I am not suggesting that to repent you must mimic Dorothy Day, ape her actions—walk her picket lines, host her hospitality houses, bunk with the besotted, play the pacifist to the hilt. Here is where only Christ can summon with authority, can call with consummate conviction. But one charge I dare lay before all of you. It goes back to a spiritual reflection by Dorothy that has for title a declaration she derived from Dostoevsky: "Hell Is Not to Love Any More." It goes back to her autobiography, *The Long Loneliness,* and the note on which it closes: "We have all known the long loneliness and we have learned that the only solution is love and that *love comes with community.*"[15]

Love comes with community. Indeed with community already created: a husband and wife in love, a loving family, a church committed to love, a parish pervaded by love, a campus that cares. But within and around all these is a community still to be created. I mean a community where old fears and new, old hates and new, no longer keep us from reaching out to one another, reaching out hands and hearts: black and white, the haves and the have-nots, pacifists and the Pentagon, the hale and the frail, Catholic and agnostic, somehow even prolifers and prochoicers—and yes, the AIDS-afflicted and those who see in AIDS the judgment of an angry God. But for such miracles to happen, we not only need God's generous grace. We have to turn Dorothy Day's dictum on its head. If it is true (and it is) that love comes with community, it seems equally true that community comes only with love.

How begin? Go back to Dostoevsky, back to Dorothy Day. Sear your spirit and flesh with one imaginative insight: Hell is . . . not to love any more.

NOTES

1. For further details and the sources of my quotations, see Monica Furlong, *Merton: A Biography* (San Francisco: Harper & Row, 1980), esp. 202–340 *passim;* John Eudes Bamberger, "In Search of Thomas Merton," *America 147,* no. 9 (October 2, 1982): 165–69; and Walter J. Burghardt, *Seasons That Laugh or Weep: Musings on the Human Journey* (New York/Ramsey: Paulist, 1983), 78–82.

2. For greater detail, but still in homiletic form, see "St. Augustine: Sanctity and Conversion," in Walter J. Burghardt, *Saints and Sanctity* (Englewood Cliffs, NJ: Prentice-Hall, 1965), 37–47.

3. St. Augustine, *Confessions* 2, 1, in F. J. Sheed, translator *The Confessions of St. Augustine* (New York: Sheed & Ward, 1943), 27.

4. *Confessions* 3, 1, *Ibid.*, 41.

5. *Confessions* 6, 15, *Ibid.*, 126.

6. *Confessions* 8, 7, *Ibid.*, 170.

7. *Confessions* 8, 8, *Ibid.*, 171.

8. *Confessions* 8, 12, *Ibid.*, 178–79.

9. A phrase from the poem *The Hound of Heaven* by Francis Thompson.

10. *Confessions* 10, 36, in Sheed, *Confessions*, 249.

11. Reference to the famous film *The Phantom of the Opera*, recently staged in brilliant fashion as a musical by Andrew Lloyd Webber.

12. Dorothy Day, *The Long Loneliness: The Autobiography of Dorothy Day* (New York: Harper & Brothers, 1952), 149–50.

13. Quoted in William D. Miller, *Dorothy Day: A Biography* (San Francisco: Harper & Row, 1982), 341; emphasis mine.

14. *Ibid.*, 343–44.

15. Day, *The Long Loneliness*, 286; emphasis mine.

# 27. Christianity At Its Best
## Leonard Griffith

Text: Acts 27

TODAY I INVITE you to watch one of the most exciting dramas in the life of the early church. It is the story of the shipwreck in the twenty-seventh chapter of Acts, a gripping story, superbly written and so packed with vivid detail that it could only have come from the pen of an eyewitness whom we identify as Luke, the author of the Third Gospel and the Book of Acts.

Not only was Luke there, but we who read his account have a sense of being there also. You can almost smell the salt air of the Mediterranean Sea as you stand on the deck of the ship with the gathering gale howling in your ears. As the tempest reaches its fury, and the monstrous waves lash your body like a whip, you cling desperately to the rail to save yourself from being swept overboard. Blinded by the rain, drenched to the skin, numbed by the cold, you toss to and fro like a drunken man, certain that every lurch of the creaking timbers will plunge you to a watery grave. In terror you scream, as do the other passengers, but the sound of your voice is lost in the shrieking wind. This is the end, and you steel yourself to meet it as the shuddering ship grinds itself to splinters against a shoal.

*Leonard Griffith* was born in Lancashire, England. A member of the Anglican church of Canada, he has served as a minister of St. Paul's Church in Toronto and the City Temple in London. Dr. Griffith has written twenty-one books, most recently *From Sunday to Sunday: Fifty Years in the Pulpit.*

It is such an absorbing drama that we feel almost as though we were actors on the stage. Yet, looking at it from the audience, we can hear it speaking a timeless Word of God to the situation in our personal and corporate lives. Actually it proclaims several truths, one of which I lay upon your conscience today. It is the truth that Christianity is at its best when the world is at its worst. In fact, the whole drama puts flesh on these prophetic words written by a distinguished American preacher, Dr. Lynn Harold Hough. He said,

> Christianity is always at its best when the world
> is at its worst. It is at its best intellectually when
> the world is most confused in its thinking. It is
> at its best morally when men have lost the sense
> of good standards. It is at its best socially when
> men are leaping at each others' throats. It is at
> its best spiritually when men have lost the sense
> of the Presence of God. The crisis finds the
> Christian religion with the word of mastery.
> And if that word is heard and heeded, the crisis
> will be a crisis no longer.

## The Story

So now let us watch the drama of the shipwreck and see how it illustrates that truth. The central character is the Apostle Paul. When he arrived in Jerusalem at the end of his missionary career he was arrested and taken to Caeserea, where the Roman authorities put him in protective custody. At his trial before the Governor he invoked his right as a Roman citizen to be sent to Rome and tried before the Emperor. Along with other prisoners he was placed in the charge of a centurion who secured passage on a ship bound for Asia Minor. There he was transferred to a larger ship carrying grain and passengers bound for Italy. Swept off its course by a strong wind, the vessel had to put in at a harbor on the south shore of Crete.

Waiting for the wind to change, the officers held a ship's council to which, for some reason, they invited their distinguished prisoner. As an experienced traveler, Paul knew that the navigation season was over and that they could not complete the voyage to Italy before winter, so he advised them not even to attempt it. "I can see, gentlemen," he said, "that this voyage will be disastrous. It will mean grave loss, not only of ship and cargo but also of life." But they were not about to take the prisoner's advice. Instead, the officer in charge listened to the ship's owner and captain, who thought that they should make for a more commodious and protected harbor along the coast.

That proved to be a mistake, because no sooner did they leave than a typhoon, called a "northeaster," rushed upon them and drove them out to the open sea. At once they feared that they would be driven south to the quicksands off the coast of Africa. However, by throwing overboard the baggage and spare gear and eventually the cargo, they were able to lighten the vessel and therefore sail into the wind in a northeasterly direction. Yet they didn't really know where they were heading. The storm raged for days on end, blotting out the sky, so that they had neither sun by day nor stars by night to guide them. The ship was leaking badly and unless it reached land it would soon go down with all on board. Then the sailors did a cowardly thing. Hoping that they were getting close to land, they lowered the lifeboat, intending to make a getaway and save their own skins, leaving the passengers and ship to perish. They would have succeeded if Paul had not seen them and warned the centurion, who cut the ropes and let the boat fall away. A completely demoralized situation! A picture of unrelieved panic!

Yet Paul did not panic, and there were two reasons for that. First, he had faced death many times before and was inwardly prepared for it. Second, there came to him a vision in the night which revealed not only that he himself would survive to witness before the Emperor, but that the lives of all his shipmates would be spared. He was human enough to say, "I told you so" to the ship's council. What he actually said was,

"You should have taken my advice, gentlemen, not to sail for Crete; then you would have avoided this damage and loss." To the whole ship's company he declared, "I urge you not to lose heart. Not a single life will be lost, only the ship." To prove his confidence he, the prisoner, took command of the crisis. He had already foiled the sailors' plot to escape and now he persuaded the scared passengers to eat what turned out to be a sacred meal after their stomachs had been empty for fourteen days. What colossal nerve it took to say, "I urge you not to lose heart!"—like telling a man with a rope around his neck to sing Psalms. Paul said it nevertheless, as transcendent spirits have always done when things were at their worst. Such magnificent courage cannot be explained, it can only be wondered at.

Paul not only took command of the situation, he saved it. "Keep up your courage," he said, "I trust in God that it will turn out as I have been told; though we have to be cast ashore on some island." The island was Malta. On the fourteenth night the sound of breakers off a rocky coast gave warning of approaching land, and successive soundings confirmed it. The sailors dropped four anchors from the stern to secure the ship until daylight showed them where they were. In the morning they slipped anchor and ran the ship into a creek with a sandy beach. The creek had a mud bottom that became clay in which the front part of the ship got stuck while the stern, battered by the waves, began breaking up. At this point the soldiers would have killed the prisoners to stop them escaping, but the centurion prevented them because he wanted to keep Paul alive. The prisoners, soldiers, passengers, crew—276 persons in all—owed their deliverance to Paul, the man in chains. The centurion gave orders to abandon ship; and the whole company stormed ashore, some on rafts and some swimming. The story ends, "And thus it was that all came safely to land."

## Symptoms of Crisis

That is the story of the shipwreck, one of the thrilling dramas in the history of the early church, a living illustration of the truth that Christianity is at its best when the world is at its worst. You will surely agree that the world was at its worst on the ship bound for Rome. To begin with, it was a secular world that brought disaster upon itself because it listened to the voices of money and power and refused to heed the warning voice of God. In crisis the people of that world panicked, gave up hope, lost their nerve, and were paralyzed by their own despair. Some renounced their moral responsibilities, looking out only for themselves, trying to save their own skins and leaving everyone else to perish.

It would be stretching a point to regard the situation on that ship as an exact parallel to the human situation in our world today. We cannot totally agree with the little boy who was asked in school to tell the shape of the earth. He replied, "My father says it's in the worst shape it ever was." When the history books have been written they will probably show that there have been worse periods than the one through which we are passing at the close of the twentieth century. Yet we cannot miss the similarities between our world crisis today and that on the ill-fated ship.

There is the same secular spirit, a society that pays more attention to human voices than to the voice of God. Some years ago a religious journal in Canada conducted a nationwide opinion poll to discover the names of mass media communicators who then exercised the greatest influence on popular thinking. The fourteen people named were invited to answer questionnaires. Four described themselves as atheists, four as agnostics, and here is a sampling of their specific answers: "I define God as my conscience." "Jesus was a deluded Jewish youth." "The effect of religion on man has been to keep him in line through fear of the unknown." "The church is a nice little exercise in futility." "After death there is nothing." So say the spokesmen of our culture, the secular preachers who speak daily to hundreds of thousands of listeners and to whom people pay more attention than they do to all the spokesmen of God put together.

In our secular society there is also a mood of despair, hopelessness, pessimism, cynicism pervading the better elements of our culture. So much modern poetry, so many plays, novels, paintings, and motion pictures project that mood. Samuel Becket's play *Waiting for Godot* is an example. It has virtually no plot. Two disgusting, dirty tramps wait under a tree. They wait day after day, year after year, for what? For anything to relieve them of the intolerable burden of existence, the agony of making a decision. Age has withered and habit deadened that divine gift, the human will. They can no longer act, they can only wait, wait for someone else to do the work for them, to take the initiative, wait for a symbolic character who promises but never comes, named Godot. Cynically the playwright has dramatized his philosophy. What a pathetic creature is man—a clown who postures, apes, laughs, cries, and crawls, possessed of infinite loneliness, a helpless, gullible fool waiting for a small god to come to his rescue!

There is a loss of nerve in our secular society, comparable to that on the ship bound for Rome. Under the stress of world events life becomes burdensome, even terrifying, and people feel inadequate to its demands. They compensate by means that are self-destructive. Some become drug addicts, exploited by the pushers and peddlers who make fortunes out of human weakness. Others become alcoholics, drinking to excess, not because they enjoy the taste but because alcohol settles their nerves, bolsters their morale, and makes them equal to difficult situations. Still others commit suicide. World statistics reveal that every year a quarter-million people take this final route of escape from life and that three times that number attempt it without success.

There is also a breakdown of high moral standards which only the naive can ignore. The Royal Bank of Canada issues a monthly "Letter" which recently asked, "Whatever Happened to Morality?" It went on to say, "There are times these days when people brought up according to the traditional moral code of the Western world may wonder if our society has lost sight of the difference between right and wrong." We do wonder sometimes. Something has to explain the new permissiveness in male-female relationships that encourages the practice of sex before and outside marriage, the birth of babies to single mothers, the popularity of divorce, and the acceptance of abortion as a means of birth control. Something has to explain the widening gap between rich and poor, the almost obscene affluence in cities where thousands are homeless or living below the poverty level. Something has to explain a value system that spends millions to explore other worlds, while the great human problems of this world remain unsolved. Despair, loss of nerve, low moral standards—those are the symptoms of crisis, a human situation out of control because people will not listen to the warning voice of God.

## The Daring Claim

That is the world at its worst, and in such a time of crisis do we dare to claim that Christianity is at its best? Do life and history support such a claim?

Not always, of course. Christianity has a worse side too. Indeed, critics are quick to remind us that there have been periods in history when Christianity, as represented by the institutional church, lagged far behind the world in humanitarian ideals, times when it fed the fires of human passion and prejudice and actually became a stumbling-block in the way of social progress. The church supported slavery in the United States when enlightened politicians, journalists, and educators would have abolished it. The church in Europe persecuted the Jews when the rest of society would have welcomed and assimilated them. The church in South Africa sanctifies apartheid while public opinion all over the world protests against that inhuman system. The church in Northern Ireland divides people whom the common decencies would otherwise unite. There is less harmony, forbearance, and social conscience in some congregations than we find in a labor union or a jungle tribe which has never heard the Gospel. How shall we explain it except by quoting the old Latin proverb, "Corruptio optimi pessima," meaning, "The worst corruption is the corruption of the best."

On the other hand, how shall we explain Christianity at its best? How explain those occasions when the Christian religion had what Dr. Hough called "the word of mastery"? The most quoted example in recent history is the tribute that Albert Einstein paid early in the Second World War to the Protestant churches of Germany. He said,

> Being a lover of freedom, when the revolution
> came to Germany I looked to the universities to
> defend freedom, knowing that they had always
> boasted of their devotion to the cause of truth.
> But no. The universities were immediately
> silenced. Then I looked to the great
> newspapers whose flaming editorials in days
> gone by had proclaimed their love of freedom,
> but they, like the universities, were silenced in
> a few short weeks. Then I looked to the
> individual writers who, as literary guides of
> Germany had written much and often
> concerning the place of freedom in modern
> life, but they too were mute. Only the churches
> stood squarely across the path of Hitler's
> campaign for supporting truth.

Dr. Einstein went on to say, "I never had any special interest in the churches before but now I feel a great admiration and affection, because the church alone has had the courage and persistence to stand for intellectual truth and moral freedom."

Malcolm Muggeridge paid a similar tribute in his book *The End of Christendom*, which also supports the daring claim that Christianity is at its best when the world is at its worst. He says that one of the great miracles today, indeed the most extraordinary fact of the twentieth century, is the renewal of the Christian faith in its purest possible form in countries where it has been most fiercely persecuted. He says that if somebody had told him, when he was a young correspondent in Moscow, that after sixty years of atheistic communism in Russia there could emerge a figure like Alexander Solzhenitsyn, speaking the authentic language of the Christian, grasping such great truths as the Cross in a way that few people do in our time, he would have said, "No, it's impossible, it can't be!"

But it *is* possible, and it *can* be. Muggeridge says about Solzhenitsyn that, though now in compulsory exile, he could have chosen to remain in Russia as the most successful, favored, indulged, and honored writer, enjoying fame and travel abroad. Yet he didn't choose this because he learned in a prison camp that true freedom is the freedom of the soul, and in one of his books he thanks the prison camp for teaching him that truth. Also he thanks a fellow prisoner who every night, as he lay down on his bunk, would pull out pieces of paper on which he had scribbled verses copied from the Gospels. Those bits of paper in such grisly circumstances transformed the man from a broken, sour, bitter prisoner into a serene, cheerful, friendly human being. Says Muggeridge, "I suggest that this is a miracle of our time." Referring again to Solzhenitsyn, he adds, "Who would have believed in the days when I was in Moscow that a distinguished Soviet citizen would one day write these words: 'I myself see Christianity as the only living spiritual force capable of undertaking the spiritual healing of Russia.'?"

So, let us write indelibly on our minds the truth that Christianity is at its best when the world is at its worst. The church of Jesus Christ, which hobbles along rather feebly in untroubled days, has an amazing capacity to rise to its full stature and take command of the situation in a day of crisis. In the bleak atmosphere of despair the church speaks a word of hope, urging people not to lose heart but to trust the righteous, invincible, eternal purpose of Almighty God. To people who have lost their nerve the church speaks a word of courage as it reminds them of the competence of a God whose strength is made perfect in our weakness. To a generation lax in moral standards the church speaks a word of judgment, reminding people that God is not mocked and that whatsoever a man soweth that shall he also reap. All over the world today the light of religious faith still shines, in some places the one, brave, flickering candle that the darkness of tyranny and materialism has not extinguished. The church may appear woefully inept at times, yet we shall go on believing that, even should the storm of world conflict rage furiously, it will be the church that rises above the danger and sets people free.

## One Dedicated Life

We mustn't stop there. We must go further and ask what it means for each one of us that Christianity is at its best when the world is at its worst. What imperative does that truth lay upon our souls? Let's quote Dr. Hough again, this time changing a few words to describe the part that Paul played in the drama of the shipwreck:

> Paul was at his best when the world was at its
> worst. He was at his best intellectually when the
> world was most confused in its thinking. He was
> at his best morally when men had lost the sense
> of good standards. He was at his best socially
> when men were leaping at each other's throats.
> He was at his best spiritually when men had lost
> the sense of the Presence of God. The crisis
> found Paul with the word of mastery. And
> because that word was heard and heeded, the
> crisis was a crisis no longer.

The story of the shipwreck is telling us that Christianity at its best may consist of one person's obedience to God. One righteous man, or woman, can save a situation. Vitality is mightier than size. the world's salvation lies not in the hands of the many but in the hands of the few. Not quantity but quality will save the ship of our civilization. One dedicated life can be an effective instrument of God's redemptive power.

That truth is at once the source of our hope and of the imperative laid upon our souls. We all know the heart-in-throat feeling that paralyzed the company of Paul's ship because we can feel the ship of our civilization lurching crazily under the impact of elemental forces that rage out of control. We may abandon ourselves to those forces and to the panic all around us, or we may need the call of God to trust and obey him and become the lights of the world in our generation.

Albert Schweitzer showed the world a shining example of Christianity at its best. In his jungle hospital in Africa he was once summoned from a conference on nuclear warfare to attend a sick woman. As he rose to leave, Dr. Schweitzer said, "It is good to be reminded now and then that even in a world struggling with the momentous issues of war and peace the individual still has problems." We might add that it is good to be reminded also that the individual, if he is a person of faith, can still do something constructive about solving the world's problems. For, as this Man of our Century said on another occasion, "However much concerned I am with the problems of evil in the world, I never let myself get lost in brooding over it. I always hold firmly to the thought that each of us can do a little to bring some portion of it to an end. Because I have confidence in the power and truth of the Spirit, I believe in the future of mankind."

# 28. The Foundations of Fidelity
## William E. Hull

Exodus 20:14

WITH VICTORIAN RETICENCE, George Dana Boardman approached a discussion of adultery by remarking that
"this matter is too tremendously momentous to be passed over
in silence; at the same time, it is too delicate to admit of ampli-
fied discourse."[1] Most preachers feel compelled to begin a sermon on the seventh commandment by warning the
congregation that they must pierce the shroud of religious silence that has hung so long about this sensitive subject.

I, too, feel under pressure from the conflicting claims of
modesty and candor, but I find such tension more ironic than
ever before. For we live in a day when our culture is becoming
utterly explicit regarding sex. On every hand there are books,
magazines, motion pictures, and television programs that
leave nothing to the imagination. In the face of a ceaseless and
well-nigh inescapable barrage of outright obscenity, one wonders what secrets are left to be shielded, what modesty remains
to be protected? There may be some small comfort in the realization that I probably could not shock you even if I tried!

Needless to say, my purpose here is not to be provocative
but pastoral. If I must finally probe a sensitive agenda, it is not

*William E. Hull* is a native of Birmingham, Alabama. He received
graduate degrees from Southern Baptist Theological Seminary and,
after a number of years in both academic and pastoral positions,
currently is provost at Samford University. Dr. Hull has authored or
contributed to many publications.

out of some desire to be sensational, but out of an urgent need to do battle with fierce temptations bombarding not only youth and singles but the newly married and the "middle-married" as well. Frankly, this is no time to be squeamish or decorous when people are threatened with the loss of their happiness, their integrity, even their homes.

## I

Let us begin, then, by clarifying the divine ideal as summarized in the commandment, "You shall not commit adultery" (Exod. 20:14; Deut. 5.18), a prohibition designed to protect the institution of marriage by limiting sexual intimacy to husband and wife. This moral axiom emerged at a chaotic time when Moses was trying to forge twelve disorganized tribes into a stable society. History had already proved that this could not be done when marriage was by *capture*, the power of brute force; or by *contract*, the purchase of a mate as property; or even by *consent*, subject to fickleness and hardness of the human heart. Here, in a giant leap toward spiritual maturity, a fourth way was defined that has stood the test of time: marriage by *commitment*, absolute fidelity rooted in the will of a holy God.

At first it was sufficient to restrict the scope of this injunction to marital faithfulness, since the social custom in Israel was to arrange marriages in early childhood and to consummate them shortly after puberty. This approach avoided our prolonged period of late adolescence, during which a physical desire for sexual activity develops much sooner than the conventional timetable for its expression in marriage. But gradually the principle of sexual chastity was extended to premarital and postmarital relations as well. In such practical writings as Proverbs, for example, there are grave warnings against all forms of impure sexual indulgence, especially in the description of the seductive woman in chapters 5–7 (cf. 22:14; 23:26–28; 29:3; 30:20; 31:3).

The prophets of Israel were a transitional bridge to the

New Testament concern that the sin of adultery be seen in its religious as well as its domestic application. Out of his personal crisis with an unfaithful wife, Hosea came to realize that idolatry is a kind of religious adultery because it makes something tangible and therefore transient an end in itself, rather than worshiping the eternal Reality which lies beyond all limited symbols. Therefore he indicted his people for their love of other gods by describing it as a harlotry of the heart (Hos. 2:2–13; 3:1–5; 4:10–19; 7:4–7). To Jeremiah, the prevalence of overt adultery—which he minced no words in describing as "well-fed lusty stallions, each neighing for his neighbor's wife" (Jer. 5:8)—was rooted in Israel's lusting after Baal like a wild ass in heat (Jer. 2:23–25; cf. 3:6–10; 9:2; 13:27; 23:9–14). In two extended allegories, Ezekiel used the tragedy of destruction and exile to pass judgment on Jerusalem and Samaria for a long history of harlotry as the unfaithful wife of God (Ezek. 16:1–63; 23:1–49).

Jesus carried the prophetic insight that adultery is finally an affair of the heart to its ultimate expression in the Sermon on the Mount. There he tracked adultery to its lair in the lustful look and, in so doing, condemned any act or attitude, however private, that exploits sexuality for self-gratification (Matt. 5:27–28). By this teaching, Jesus laid equal responsibility on every person to purge the innermost being of any impulse that undermines the sanctity of sex as intended by God (cf. Mark 7:20–23; 10:2–12).

Now we see the deepest reason why the Bible forbids adultery: Because it corrupts sexuality into an instrument of possessive pleasure, whereas God meant it to be a channel for expressing an exclusive commitment. Some are shocked to find that the Old Testament took this perversion with such seriousness that it was punishable by death (Deut. 22:22–27; Ezek. 18:10–13; John 8:4–5). But in the New Testament we see the underlying reason why adultery was made a capital offense: It represents an approach to life utterly incompatible with the character of God and with His will for us as persons. That is why the New Testament does not soften the prohibition against adultery by permitting divorce, as is sometimes supposed (e.g., from Matt. 19:9; 1 Cor. 7:15), but actually intensifies it by insisting not that adulterers will be physically killed but that they will be eternally destroyed as unfit for the Kingdom of God (1 Cor. 6:9–10; cf. 1 Cor. 5:1–13; 1 Thess. 4:3–6; Heb. 13:4; 2 Peter 2:14).[2]

## II

Stepping back from this swift survey of the scriptural evidence, let us try to determine what is really at stake in the seriousness with which the Bible repudiates any form of adultery. Certainly far more than repressive prudery or a killjoy attitude toward life is involved. The Bible takes an uninhibited view of sex and unabashedly celebrates its delights (e.g., in the Song of Solomon). No, its uncompromising rejection of adultery is rooted in human nature, in the way God made us as both spirit and flesh. We are not just tangible bodies nor only intangible souls but a fusion of both; outwardly made in the image of man, inwardly made in the image of God (Gen. 1:27; 2:7). This unity means that the way in which we express our physical reality must be in harmony with the beliefs that constitute our spiritual reality or else we will tear our human nature asunder. Specifically, our sex life and our soul life must both express the same values or we become a contradiction in terms, a "walking civil war," a divided self, a split personality.

According to the Bible, because God made us "male and female" (Gen. 1:27) our creation is completed in the union of the two sexes, which is called marriage (Gen. 2:24). No other earthly relationship is more important for the fulfillment of the two partners, for the stability of society, or for the survival of the race. Therefore, the highest value attaches to the protection of the nuptial bond. If we truly believe in the sanctity of the home with the "soul side" of our lives, we have no choice but to express that conviction through complete commitment to one partner with the "sex side" of our lives. There is no way, short of a destructive dualism that shatters personal integrity, to affirm the necessity of fidelity with our hearts but exercise the option of promiscuity with our bodies.

Of course, we could be consistent by opting for infidelity in theory as well as in practice and so commit both spiritual and physical adultery, as did the worshipers of Baal in biblical times. But, according to the Scriptures, such a response violates the essential nature of both God and man. Just as there can be no true religion without *one* and only one God, by the very definition of what it means to be God, so there can be no true marriage without *one* and only one partner, by the very definition of what it means to be male and female. Just as God cannot be Lord *at all* unless He is Lord *in all* things, so a male and a female cannot "become one" *at all* unless they truly "become one" *in all* things, sexuality included. To be sure, anyone may flout the nature of marriage by committing adultery, just as anyone may flout the nature of the stomach by swallowing a nail; but in the end reality itself will expose the folly of such experiments.[3]

Centuries of experience have confirmed the wisdom of the seventh commandment. Without such costly devotion, individuals can never find the sense of self-worth and personal security which comes from knowing that they will always matter most regardless of what competitor may appear upon the scene. Without such exclusive attachment, families can never be sure which children are their own, thus confusing those continuities of birthright and inheritance by which noble traditions of conduct are built. Without such undivided allegiance, communities can never be free from simmering suspicions and jealousies that erupt into outraged vendettas when honor has been offended. In short, we are dealing here not with a puritanical stricture of ancient Israel but with an essential foundation of civilized life which is crucial to our very existence.[4]

## III

Then why has this imperative been so blithely ignored and even contemptuously rejected by our contemporary society?

We seem to be inching forward in our resolve not to kill (VI) or steal (VIII), but to be racing backward in our disregard of the commandment between these two (VII). I need not describe the Sexual Revolution, which has made adultery a commonplace in premarital, extramarital, and postmarital relations. Statistics are slippery, but apparently a decisive majority of Americans actually engage in sexual intercourse outside of wedlock.[5] In a culture where the principle of "majority rule" can assume tyrannical force, this means that each person in the shrinking minority (which may have recently begun to stabilize) is under intense pressure to conform.

The standard Christian strategy since the sexual revolution began to accelerate in the 1960s has been to decry each new outbreak of permissiveness as another layer of slime sinking America into debauchery and shame. While I have no question about the depravity of much that has been passing as "The New Morality," I have come to question the wisdom of responding to all of this obscenity with pious outrage. My hunch is that the uncommitted seeker in desperate need of moral guidance hears our chagrined breast-beating as a frustrated lament over losing the power to regulate public conduct rather than as a reasoned answer to the siren song being whispered in the other ear. If I am not mistaken, the time has come to meet what John Drakeford aptly calls "The Great Sex Swindle"[6] on its own ground with a hard-nosed critique of its inflated claims.

The basis for my contention is a growing suspicion that in this particular revolution the enemy has changed its tactics. There have been periods of promiscuousness throughout history—the first century, in New Testament time, was one such era—in which carnality dressed itself out in the lurid garb of a harlot, flaunting its lasciviousness in orgies of dissipation. But this time adultery has cleaned up its act, taken on a new sophistication, and come dressed in the grey flannels of respectability. What better strategy to outsmart red-faced preachers fulminating against indecency than to appear thoughtful, restrained, almost—dare I say it?—*self-righteous* by contrast? In short, I suggest that adultery has hidden in the Trojan Horse of enlightened emancipation and so been invited into the camp of the faithful by many who would be horrified if it knocked at the door dressed as a slut!

To document this charge, I propose to show how old-fashioned sensuality has achieved a new-found decency by seeming to more beyond rather than to fall short of the traditional sanctions against adultery. Take first the elemental constraint of fear—fear of discovery, fear of venereal disease, fear of pregnancy. "Nonsense," replies our cool advocate of hot passion. "No need for furtive back-seat escapades on deserted country roads or out-of-town trips to second-class motels. Now you are free to bring your friends to your own dormitory room or apartment complex, no questions asked. Medical science has long since solved the problem of syphilis and gonorrhea, while foolproof contraceptives to prevent pregnancy are readily available at the corner drug." In other words, any lingering fears of sexual misadventure are interpreted purely as a problem of technique which may be easily remedied by reading such manuals as "A Gourmet Guide to Love Making"[7] that answers all your questions.

Move a step deeper to the argument from antiquity: Adultery must be bad since society has condemned it for thousands of years. "True," our open-minded opponent concedes, "but that taboo roots in a primitive culture when husbands wanted to keep their wives subjugated for life so that they might have exclusive possession of them whenever they pleased. Surely you don't cling to that outdated restriction which would deny a woman the freedom to shop around for herself in deciding with whom to share her affections. Times have changed, nowhere more so than in the relations between the sexes." Thus does fornication flourish under such noble banners as "sexual equality" and "the right to decide" and "time marches on."

But there is one final bulwark against infidelity, its explicit condemnation in Holy Writ. Surely these new libertines will not try to contradict divine authority! On the contrary, our apostles of adultery are here at their condescending best.

"The Bible taught us a valuable, even essential lesson about sexuality, that it is corrupted by exploitation. This is why all sensible moderns now base their sex lives on mutual agreements, freely entered into by both parties, which ask only for respect in the present rather than for binding commitments in the future. Unfortunately, the church has forgotten this fine principle in its eagerness to judge and condemn, having become an agent of guilt and repression rather than of joy and openness." Anyone who follows closely the "Playboy Philosophy" in which Hugh Hefner espouses his enlightened hedonism will find unmistakable insinuations that those of his ilk really understand and practice the ethical maturity of the Bible better than the host of "true believers" running around sewing scarlet letters on everyone unfortunate enough to be caught in bed with the wrong person.

## *IV*

Not for one moment do I find these arguments convincing, but I would contend that they have shifted the ground on which our ancient mandate is to be commended. No longer is it sufficient simply to point a finger toward the gutter in derision, for what was once the gutter view of sex has now occupied higher ground. I would even argue that the traditional sanctions still have merit. For example, a frightfully high percentage of "novices" in training to become "gourmet" lovers still stumble into venereal disease or illegitimate pregnancies along the way. But for those too full of modernity to heed ancient wisdom, we must carry our case to the enemy's own ground. I would therefore propose that we take the glamorized new view of adultery at face value and ask whether its claims, in fact, are actually true.

There are four basic components in the view of sex underlying our contemporary licentiousness. We have watched the scenario unfold *ad nauseam* in the popular media: (1) The initial appeal of sex is seductive. That is, in an endless variety of ways, one's masculinity or femininity is to be used as a magnet attracting those of opposite gender to explore fascinating mysteries made all the more fascinating because they were hitherto forbidden. (2) For those who succeed in this delicious game of hide-and-seek, there waits the prize of the body beautiful, like luscious fruit hidden behind a concealing leaf. (3) Copulation with this body beautiful confers instant gratification, an immediate ecstasy that flows from a bite of the forbidden fruit. (4) Because this sudden gush of euphoria is the *summum bonum* of life, the pinnacle of pleasure, it should be avidly sought now as an end in itself rather than being postponed until it can become the means to a more distant goal. Now let us critique this alluring fantasy that has been etched so vividly in the modern imagination.

(1) *The myth of the irresistible mystery, or "Will curiosity kill the cat?"* We live in an era of exciting discoveries when humankind is penetrating barriers never before breached. There is a certain allure to the unknown, which the sexual revolution has exploited with half-buttoned shirts, plunging necklines, and swirling skirts. The tantalizing glimpses which such daring styles afford add to the intrigue and thus whet a desire to peer behind the facade, to discover the buried secret, to unveil the hidden mystery.

But only fool's gold lies at the end of this rainbow. As one frustrated youth who had built his whole approach to women on a quest for the inner sanctum of sex complained, there are just so many square inches of flesh on the human body and this ground is quickly covered by the eager explorer. Even with the help of imaginative sex manuals, there are precious few surprises after the initial thrill of discovery wears off. In the 1950s, Marilyn Monroe and Joe DiMaggio united the world's most shapely feminine figure with the world's most graceful masculine physique in a relationship that was supposed to "have everything," but after nine months they were headed for the divorce court because "there was nothing to say."[8] The point is that sex alone, however seductive, is insufficient to unite two lives unless it expresses a growing fund of meanings and values and purposes that are more than skin deep.

(2) *The myth of the body beautiful, or "What if I have a wart?"* As magazines, movies, and TV screens vividly portray, the Sexual Revolution comes packaged for men in exaggerated curves, pure complexion, silken hair, and youthful vitality. Now for women a similar male stereotype is available with rippling muscles, jutting jaw, bronzed skin, and barrel chest. The assumption apparently is that emancipation somehow confers allurement, permitting the sexual revolutionist to associate only with beautiful people.

But this premise is patently false, as a quick glance around will show. Not 10 percent of us, even in our biological prime, have the anatomy to qualify for a centerfold spread. But even those who do, such as the Hollywood stars, fall into a trap when they equate sex with desirability. For in this approach everything is lost when someone more desirable comes along. Which always happens, even to the most glamorous, either because novelty appears more alluring than familiarity or because the aging process has taken its inexorable toll. A sexual attachment to the outward surface of the body as an object has crested as soon as it begins and has no way to go but down, whereas a sexual attachment to the inward essence of the person as a subject leads to a lifetime of unfolding adventure together and has no way to go but up.

(3) *The myth of instant gratification, or "What if I don't hear bells?"* A sacred dogma of the sexual revolution is that ecstasy is automatic. All of the arts of acting and the rhetoric of writing are exhausted to portray this doctrine of irresistible bliss. As the lights fade or the chapter closes, two casual acquaintances who have never had a serious conversation nevertheless experience the ultimate in rapture simply by "doing what comes naturally."

Unfortunately, as every physician and marriage counselor knows, sexual fulfillment is neither that easy nor automatic to achieve. A surprisingly high percentage of couples who have been trying to adjust to each other for years report persistent problems that hinder the realization of true harmony. Why? Because intercourse is so intimate an act of the total being that it requires the most candid communication, the most sensitive awareness, the most profound rapport, the most patient understanding, in order to succeed. If that be true, then why do so many contemporary descriptions of sex falsify reality by ignoring the price to be paid for true ecstasy? These popular fantasies exploit widespread frustration by providing a momentary escape from the costly obligation of forging a truly mature relationship in which sex will be meaningful because it has something of substance to convey.

(4) *The myth of the ultimate moment, or "What will I do for an encore?"* To hear the sexual liberationists tell it, the instant gratification that comes with copulation is not the beginning but the end of the journey, the pinnacle of the relationship, the highest note on the scale, the final color in the rainbow. To even think beyond that fleeting moment is to become captive to future expectations rather than to live in the freedom of the present. The problem with old-fashioned marital commitments is that they impose upon today the weight of too many tomorrows.

But if that be true, if sex does indeed "stop the clock," then what shall we do when it starts ticking again? Is life to become an endless succession of "moments," each no more ultimate than the one before? Once nothing is held "in reserve," as it were, for marriage, then marriage no longer holds out a fulfillment all its own. Which is but a way of saying that when sex becomes entirely imprisoned in the present moment, then, quite literally, it no longer has a "future."

"But," our emancipated sexualist responds, "why worry about the future if you can have everything in the present?" I would answer: Because you are right in the claim that one cannot go deeper or higher or farther in relating to another person than through sex. Here our emotions and affections and intimacies do reach a climax. Body, mind, and heart all testify that this is indeed the summit of relational experience. There simply does not exist a more ultimate way to say in body language, "I love you, I give myself to you, I belong to you without reservation." But if we squander this unique experience on a casual liaison merely to achieve fleeting pleasure, then how will we ever express an absolute commitment? To be sure, we could vow in words that "this time things will be different," but it is precisely in this area more than anywhere else that "actions speak louder than words." The dilemma of adultery is that the very act itself communicates a desire for self-satisfaction and pleasure so profoundly that no greater act is available by which to communicate the desire for an exclusive and permanent commitment to another.

In summary, the exercise of *restraint* is the key to discovering the deepest meaning of our sexuality. Proper restraint enables one to say of sex: "By this deed I affirm you as the one and only love of my life. To demonstrate the depth of that commitment, I have paid the price to invest our physical intimacy with unique meaning. Temptation is real, desire is strong, weakness is present. But I have resisted a thousand enticing compromises to save the best for you." By contrast, without restraint one can only claim of the marital union: "In all honesty, what we are about to do is no different from what I have done with other persons in the past. I have no faith strong enough to limit my sexual expression to this one relationship. Since I did not prove, either to myself or to you, the capacity for an exclusive loyalty before marriage, I am not sure that it is possible or even desirable to demonstrate an exclusive loyalty within marriage. I can only hope that our marriage will somehow survive despite the fact that it is not based on tangible evidence of a unique relationship."

In all of this we have discovered that our sexual practices are but an outward test of whether we have our inward values straight. To renounce adultery is not to become a prude. Rather, it is to confess a faith that shapes the very core of being: that there is no true pleasure without responsibility, no true intimacy without understanding, no true privilege without commitment, no true desire without discipline.

NOTES

1. George Dana Boardman, *The Ten Commandments* (Philadelphia: Judson Press, 1952 reprint), 234.

2. F. Hauck, *Theological Dictionary of the New Testament*, edited by Gerhard Kittel (Grand Rapids, MI: Eerdmans, 1967), vol. IV, 734.

3. The comparison is developed by John R. Claypool, "Irresponsible Love," *Crescent Hill Sermons* (Louisville: Crescent Hill Baptist Church, July 11, 1965), vol. I, no. 11: 5.

4. This paragraph is indebted to Harold A. Bosley, "You Shall Not Commit Adultery," *The Reader's Digest,* (October 1967): 140.

5. A 1976 survey of actual practice indicated that at least 85 percent of males and 55 percent of females had engaged in sexual intercourse by age nineteen. However, such percentages need adjustment for wide variation between subcultures. For example, Catholics tend to be more permissive than Protestants, the Northeast and the Far West than the South and the Midwest, the young than the old. cf. "The New Morality," *Time* (November 21, 1977): 114.

6. John W. Drakeford, *The Great Sex Swindle* (Nashville: Broadman Press, 1966).

7. The subtitle of a sex manual by Alex Comfort, *The Joy of Sex* (New York: Simon and Schuster, 1972). Perhaps the most significant characteristic of this bestseller is its effort to legitimate unrestrained eroticism by linking it to such virtues as "professionalism" and "honesty." The preface makes clear that, for the author, any sexual activity is justified if only it is performed with sophisticated technique (i.e., as a gourmet would approach a meal).

8. "To Aristophanes & Back," *Time* (May 14, 1956): 76, 81. The divorce was announced on October 4, 1954 after marriage on January 14, 1954.

# 29. Jesus' Messiahship and Our Discipleship

## *Allan M. Parrent*

*Texts:* Mark 8:31–38 and Romans 8:31–39

SPEAKING TO A graduating class a few years ago, Woody Allen said to the graduates: "More than any other time in its history humankind faces a crossroads. One path leads to despair and utter hopelessness. The other to total extinction. Let us pray that we have the wisdom to choose correctly." Perhaps things are not quite that bad, and our choices not quite that limited. But there is an inescapable tragic element in human history that some of the more utopian accounts of Christian faith tend to ignore or even deny.

The gospel lesson for today is a case in point. It speaks first of a suffering Messiah, of his rejection by the religious leadership, and of his being killed and rising again. The passage reflects the perennial and tragic conflict between God and his people, between the kind of God he is and the kind of God we find acceptable. There is more than a little truth in the saying that God created us in his own image, and we have been trying to return the compliment ever since. The gospel lesson also speaks about denial of self, about taking up crosses, and about

---

*Allan M. Parrent* was born in Frankfort, Kentucky. He received his doctorate from Duke University and currently serves as professor of Christian ethics, associate dean for academic affairs, and vice-president at Episcopal Theological Seminary in Virginia. He writes and speaks frequently on ethical issues.

the possibility of losing one's life for the sake of the gospel. This reflects the perennial and tragic conflict within us as God's people, between what we know we are called to do and what we in fact do. We all experience with Paul that constant conflict between the law in our members and the law in our minds.

This kind of language is far removed from the upbeat ad I saw recently in the *Post*. Ostensibly advertising a book on business ethics, the ad said: "You can do what's right and still be a winner." On the book's jacket cover were the words: "Integrity pays. You don't have to cheat to win." The fact is that "integrity" and "doing what is right" are as likely to cause one to be a loser as a winner. Christian faith is no guarantor of success and happiness in this world, at least as the world understands those terms, and it can be costly. The rain, as we know, falls equally on the just and the unjust, and always will.

## I

The gospel lesson tells us something about both Jesus' Messiahship and our discipleship. Peter has just made his electrifying confession, "You are the Messiah." But Jesus then begins to tell his disciples what that means. Jesus tells them he must suffer, be rejected, and be killed. But what the disciples wanted was one who would come in triumph, one who would victoriously liberate them from their foreign oppressors. Peter rebukes Jesus for espousing such a radically different and seemingly defeatist scenario.

But Jesus rebukes Peter in return. Recalling his temptations in the wilderness to be a different kind of Messiah, Jesus says harshly to Peter: "Get behind me, Satan. For you are not on the side of God but of man." You are trying to substitute your human agenda—religion as a success story, a way of winning, a means to victory—for God's agenda. You want a political messiah, one who will make everything come out right, i.e., the way you want it, one who will establish a pure and just human society within history, according to your view of justice, a utopian society free of human conflict and sin.

Jesus clearly rejects that role and the human agenda behind it. His own understanding of a suffering and atoning Messiah was central to that rejection. But he also knew that every human messianic expectation is tilted in favor of the particular perspective of the group that has the expectation. Such perspectives will always be limited and partial, culturally conditioned and self-serving. They will be easily adaptable to ideological use. When such messianic expectations are taken up into political ideologies, as for example in Marxism with its vision of a secularized Kingdom of God on earth, they can become the basis for large-scale evil. Any and all actions can be justified in the name of bringing to full fruition an idealized vision of the perfect human society.

The gospel lesson also addresses the question of what it means to be a disciple. "If anyone would come after me, let him deny himself, and take up his cross and follow me. For whoever would save his life will lose it; and whoever would lose his life for my sake and the gospel's will save it." Here again, Jesus' words go against the grain of human expectation and desire. We want to follow winners, not losers. We want to satisfy our desires and needs, not deny ourselves. We want if possible to dispense with our crosses, not take them up. But to be a disciple of Jesus, we are told, means reversing those very natural and human inclinations. That is a far cry from the gospel of self-fulfillment and self-realization heard in many quarters.

Similarly, our natural and very human inclination is to preserve our lives. But we are told that that very desire may be the cause of losing them when it becomes our primary motivation. Jesus clearly understood the religious temptation to engage in subtle calculations about losing our lives (at least figuratively) in order to save them, or putting ourselves last in order eventually to be first. But those who go through the motions of losing in order to gain, or denying themselves and taking up crosses in order to win divine brownie points, clearly never intended to lose anything for the sake of the gospel, but only for the sake of themselves. In short, we in our self-centered condition can no more legitimately set our own agenda for what it means to be a disciple of Christ than we can set our own criteria for what kind of Messiah he is to be.

## II

Here we have, then, two rich biblical themes—messiahship and discipleship. Here we have also two illustrations of the human tendency to try to redefine the meaning of biblical teachings to make them more palatable, thereby distorting or corrupting them. But something else is also illustrated here. We can see at work here two fundamental moral impulses that are part of our essential God-given human nature. They are innate human moral impulses that our more self-regarding tendencies may distort, but which they cannot entirely obliterate.

The first of these impulses is our human desire to achieve a good end or purpose, to bring about a final victory of the righteous over the unrighteous, to resolve the contradictions of life by realizing some perfect state of things, some version of the Kingdom of God. Hence Peter's negative response to the idea of a suffering Messiah, one who would only take sin onto himself but not finally resolve the contradictions and tragedies of human history. The second impulse is the human need to live in accord with some understanding of human obligation, to be faithful to that to which we have given allegiance, to do what is right. Hence our desire to water down the demands of discipleship to the level of the humanly possible, so that we can have the satisfaction of being obedient, but without excessive cost. The first impulse is to achieve some state of affairs we acknowledge to be good—peace, a just society, the Kingdom of God. The second is to act rightly in obedience to what we acknowledge to be our highest law—the Constitution, social expectations, the great commandment. The first asks, "What goal am I to seek?"; the second asks, "What is it my obligation to do?"

Those were in fact the underlying questions in the encounter between Jesus and his disciples. They are also the underlying questions for us in our Christian pilgrimage. We cannot help but try to answer those two basic human questions about our goals and our obligations. But our answers are seldom free from moral ambiguity and seldom capable of being fully realized. They will always be both imperfect and subject to misuse.

### III

First, we know ourselves to be called to achieve goals or ends that are in keeping with our understanding of God's purpose for human life. In our more optimistic times we even speak of building the Kingdom of God. But we often find that there are conflicts among the goals themselves, e.g., freedom and equality for all God's children. When we try to translate these into policies and actions we find that they are to some degree in conflict. When pushed to their extremes they result in either anarchy or tyranny. We also find ourselves tempted to identify some particular political program, social or economic arrangement, or public policy with the Kingdom of God, and to make that into a kind of idol. It then becomes a litmus test of ultimate religious commitment, requiring absolute devotion to what is at best a relative political or social end (and all political or social ends are relative). Those who question it are therefore considered to be not only wrong but also morally defective.

In his book, *The Ayatollah in the Cathedral,* former Iranian hostage and Episcopalian Morehead Kennedy describes the months he spent as Director of the Peace Institute at the Cathedral of St. John the Divine in New York. This was just after his 1981 release from Teheran. When he took a less than wholehearted and unquestioning position on the nuclear freeze issue, which was high on the agenda of the peace movement at the time, he was summarily removed from the Cathedral post. His efforts at objectivity and balance were unacceptable. In his book he is quite critical of those who, he says, "seek the equivalent of religious certainty in the causes they advocate. By this transference they become true believers who insist that the Freeze is the only approach, who claim far too much for it, who regard any questioning as heresy and, particularly from colleagues, as betrayal." Kennedy later commented that in some Christian groups, "I would have a much easier time denying the Resurrection than I would have questioning the nuclear freeze." The same tendency can be found at both ends of the political spectrum.

Second, we also know ourselves as Christians to be under obligation to be obedient to the command to love our neighbors, to be faithful to Jesus' command not to neglect the weightier matters of the law, which includes justice. But in order to do the work God has given us to do, in order to translate love into justice, we need the necessary power to act effectively. Using power to seek justice, to protect liberty, or to discover new knowledge for improving the human condition is a way of giving concrete expression to love.

Yet one of the most obvious facts of human history is that any extension of human power, individually or collectively, is open equally to good or evil uses. Its creative and destructive possibilities are inextricably intertwined. Neither the power of greater knowledge, nor the power of greater control over nature, nor the power of military might, nor the power of greater technical competence is guaranteed to bring self- centered human nature under control. A case in point is the discovery and development of nuclear energy, with its almost infinite capacity for good and evil. The movement from a partial to a total war capability occurred at precisely the same time that a naively optimistic Western culture was talking of the real possibility of the abolition of war as a result of human moral progress. There is no direct relation between the new power given to us by scientific and technological advances on the one hand, and growth in human virtue on the other. Only time will tell whether developments such as those we are now seeing in genetic engineering can be matched by the prudence and virtue necessary to control their use.

So we are caught in the potentially tragic conflicts and contradictions of human existence. Our aspirations to achieve that which we consider good in human terms may put us, as it did Peter, in the role of Satan, working at cross-purposes with the will of God. Yet we are called to seek the Kingdom of God, and without a vision toward which to work we will perish as a people. Similarly, our efforts to fulfill what we consider to be our obligations and duties may lead us to misuse our power, or to develop human powers over which we lose human control. Yet powerlessness cannot maintain itself against the self-assertion of others. It is only by the responsible use of power that we can minimize the exploitation of the powerless and maintain systems of justice that can enable a fairer balance between competing human wills and interests, including our own.

These contradictions are inescapable. They cannot be overcome by human actions because those very actions will be less than morally pure. For example, the monastic life may be a more pure witness to the principles of the Sermon on the Mount, but at the same time it abdicates responsibility for establishing the relative standards of justice without which human community cannot exist. History, in short, cannot solve its own problems, not by increased knowledge, or wisdom, or virtue, or power.

## IV

But what human action cannot do, divine action can do. God's action in Jesus Christ is God's ultimate response to the contradictions and tragedies of human life. It does not do away with them, and could not without violating human freedom. But it does reveal their significance and give us a perspective from which to view them.

The cross of Christ, which stands at the center of the Christian worldview, reveals both our violation of God's will, even in our highest moral and spiritual strivings, and God's absorption of that evil. In the words of Luther's great hymn, "Did we in our own strength confide, our striving would be losing, were not the right man on our side, the man of God's own choosing." The cross of Christ reveals both the hope of reconciliation, from God's side, and the continuing possibility of repentance and service as agents of reconciliation from the human side. The cross of Christ reveals both that the ultimate norm of human life is selfless agape love and that that norm must be translated into systems of justice which are necessary precisely because human life never fully achieves that norm.

Finally, the cross of Christ gives us a vantage point from which we may survey the relative harmony or discord of any historical moment without being led astray by either. Without the cross we may be led astray by what is good in human life into the faithlessness of putting our trust solely in human possibilities and achievements. Without the cross we may also be led astray by what is tragic in human life into the faithlessness of cynicism and despair. The kind of faith inspired by the cross of Christ, even in the midst of the inescapable contradictions of human life and history, is perhaps best expressed by the Apostle Paul in today's epistle, which was also the text for the anthem:

> Who shall separate us from the love of Christ?
> Shall tribulation, or distress, or persecution, or
> famine, or nakedness, or peril, or sword? . . .
> No, in all things we are more than conquerors
> through him who loved us. For I am sure that
> neither death, nor life, nor angels, nor
> principalities, nor things present, nor things to
> come, nor powers, nor height, nor depth, nor
> anything else in all creation, will be able to
> separate us from the love of God in Christ Jesus
> our Lord.

# *30.* Being a Christian in America
## *Thomas D. Campbell*

Romans 13:1–7 and Revelation 13:1–10

DO YOU KNOW what is the most tense and anxious moment at a baseball game? It's not in the ninth inning with the bases loaded and the score tied and two strikes on the batter. And it's not when one of the pitchers has a perfect game through eight innings, with only three more outs to go. No, the most tense and anxious moment at a baseball game is before the game starts, with the singing of the national anthem. Two aspects of this moment are downright frightening. One is the fear that the singer will forget the words. The other is the anxiety over whether or not the vocalist will be able to handle the high notes of "and the rockets' red glare . . . "

On a recent summer day I settled down to watch some baseball on television. Of course I *really* didn't settle down until after it was obvious the guest soloist had a good memory and a suitable range. But as I shifted in my reclining chair to achieve maximum comfort, as I prepared body and mind and soul to watch Chicago and Montreal fight for fourth place, I

*Thomas D. Campbell* is senior pastor of the Beaver Creek Cumberland Presbyterian Church in Knoxville, Tennessee. A graduate of Bethel College and of Memphis Theological Seminary, he attended Brite Divinity School, where he received the Master of Theology and Doctor of Ministry degrees. Campbell was the organizing pastor of Cumberland Presbyterian churches in Batesville, Arkansas, Fort Worth, Texas, and Burleson, Texas, and he is the author of *One Family Under God.*

was startled by an unfamiliar sound. It was another song being sung. I heard some unfamiliar words and an unfamiliar tune as somebody else was singing "O Canada," or some such melody. I was upset, to say the least. Besides breaking the train of thought whose pattern had been the same for years, this unfamiliar musical rendition was creating anger and surprise and no little frustration. What's going on? What is *this* song? And why? Then it came to me that one of the teams was from Canada, and it was appropriate to the game officials that the national anthem of that country also should be rendered. I'll have to admit it was not easy to make the mental adjustment. It took more than a couple of innings to get comfortable again.

In fact, I did not pay as much attention to the game as I usually did, for going through my mind were thoughts about patriotism and America and other nations. It was a bit sobering to be reminded that other nations have their national anthems, too, just as they have their legendary heroes, their traditions, and even their own stories of revolutions, victorious battles, and historic documents and writings. The more I thought about all of that, the more I began to consider our own land and the patriotism and traditions we enjoy. Thoughts of movements and crises in American history emerged, reminding me that the struggle to become a nation involved the struggle to know what we wanted to be and with what attitude conscientious citizens should be involved.

This train of thought led to the question of what is the place of the Christian in relation to America. In recent years our land has experienced at least two extremes of loyalty and support: the unflagging, unquestioning, flag-waving "super-patriots" at one end, and the at the other the questioning, critical, often skeptical groups who have never hesitated to express anger and impatience. A couple of decades ago the first element's favorite bumper sticker was: "America—Love It or Leave It." And the second element's was: "Make Love, Not War." As the 1970s and 1980s have come and gone, these two contrasting viewpoints, poles apart from each other, have continued to represent the convictions of many different Christians in America.

I hardly noticed the game now, as more and more thoughts and questions competed with the procession of batters and innings. Confused more than content now with my patriotism, I thought it was appropriate to turn to the Bible. Surely, the scriptures would clear up once and for all the issues of national loyalty for Christians. Just how should we relate to our country? What does the Bible say? "Turn to the New Testament," wisdom seemed to say. "To Paul first," it continued. And there, from Romans, I thought I remembered something from Paul about the Christians and government. Sure enough, in Romans 13 these words stepped forth:

> Let every person be subject to the governing
> authorities. For there is no authority except
> from God, and those that exist have been
> instituted by God. Therefore he who resists the
> authorities resists what God has appointed. . . .

Paul was telling Christians to be submissive to the government in Rome, to be thankful for it, in essence to be unquestioning and supportive with taxes, trusting the authorities to do rightly but not protesting if the government failed to be fair and just with the people. Many Christians have found comfort and strength in Paul's admonition, as many did in A.D. 56 or 57 when the words in Romans were written. The apostle felt constrained to call on followers of Christ to obey the Roman empire, which had not inflicted any unbearable hardships on the Christians. This call to obey the laws of the land, to be submissive to the government, and to give unquestioning loyalty to the authorities has been echoed many times since then. It has been an instrument of correction and often a weapon of discipline with some Christians in America who have feared rapid change and a radical reordering of national priorities as they have understood them. Thus, when some of the faithful would express concern about the wisdom of American involvement in Vietnam, someone could cry, "Romans thirteen! Romans thirteen!" and hold any rebellions in check. Indeed, even hazy memories of the 1960s reveal that if someone advocated visible protest, someone else would reply, "But that's against the law!" When black people were sitting down in whites-only restaurants and in the front sections of buses, some Christian leaders said, "They're breaking the law." The bedrock of Romans 13 loomed large for many.

It still does. The Sanctuary movement, which has seen pastors and laypeople provide safe haven from persecution in Central America, has been criticized by many other Christians because the movement seems to be a violation of United States law. "Romans thirteen! Romans thirteen!" The antinuclear movements of the 1980s often have been characterized by acts of civil disobedience, such as physically blocking the movement of a train loaded with questionable nuclear contents by sitting on the railroad tracks, or by cutting through a fence surrounding a nuclear plant to go and render the plant inoperable. It has meant for some standing in front of the South African embassy in Washington in protest of apartheid in that land, only to be arrested and taken to jail for at least a brief period. "Lawbreakers," comes one cry. "America's conscience," comes another. "Romans thirteen!" echoes as people in all communities and in church debates try, with the argument of scripture, to thwart the decisions and actions of concerned people.

Some believe Paul had a good leg to stand on. But somewhere else in the New Testament, I vaguely remembered, there was another "leg" that some people had stood on. It can be found in the book of Revelation, also in chapter thirteen. Now it is thirty years later. Nero has come along. Rome has ceased to be the reasonably benevolent and tolerant government. So far as the author of Revelation is concerned, Rome has become the beast. He does not paint a pretty picture:

> And I saw a beast rising out of the sea, with ten
> horns and seven heads, with the diadems upon
> its horns and a blasphemous name upon its
> heads. . . . it was allowed to exercise authority.
> . . . it was allowed to make war on the saints and

to conquer them. And authority was given it
over every tribe and people and tongue and
nation. . . . Here is a call for the endurance and
faith of the saints.

Here is another view of Christian and government, one entirely different from that of Romans 13. Implicit in the passage from Revelation is the belief that sometimes God and government are not in agreement, and occasionally Christians are entitled to view authorities with hostility instead of peaceful submission. The protestors of the 1960s certainly looked upon government with suspicion, regarding the police and military more as guardians of the status quo than as protectors of the rights of all people. They called for free speech, and exercised it, as national policy collided with their Christian consciences. While some were holding up the "Stop" sign by repeating, "Romans thirteen! Romans thirteen!" others were holding up the "Go" sign and chanting, "Revelation thirteen! Revelation thirteen!" They still are today.

What is a Christian to do? Here it was hoped that a fervent look into the scriptures would bring clear help, yet the tug-of-war still continues. I have practiced one form of decision making in the past and am just now beginning to recognize what criteria I have been using. In effect, whenever the government of this country has done what I feel it should be doing, I have advocated Romans 13. Anytime it has violated what I felt to be important principles, I have advocated Revelation 13.

Looking back, I see that this has been very convenient and easy. Should America be in Vietnam? "Revelation thirteen!" What about those people who protest in front of abortion clinics, and even bomb these establishments? My answer: "Romans thirteen!" What about the Sanctuary movement and its differences with United States policy? "Revelation thirteen!" And how should we handle the school prayer issue? It's easy: "Romans thirteen!"

Over the years I have conveniently and neatly categorized the many conflicts and issues that have arisen in our society.

But I am slowly learning that I have been using the scriptures for my own advantage, cozying up to whichever one pleased me at the moment, refusing to let these scriptures and others render the judgment they are intended to render. I cannot be totally comfortable with either extreme. Isn't it possible for a believer to love country while also feeling free to be its critic? Are we being inconsistent if we waver back and forth from one extreme view to the other, depending upon our own prejudices and passions?

Turning to the Bible in this debate with myself has helped, but it has also told me that the struggle continues, as Christians live their lives as citizens of a land. Committed to fairness and justice, we find ourselves also choking up, holding back a tear in a patriotic moment. Passionate about equality, we still sing with gusto the national hymns, knowing that administrations that come and go sometimes will be weaker than we want them to be, and sometimes rather acceptable, concerning social justice. We walk on both "legs"—Romans 13 and Revelation 13—clearly aware that each one alone is a cripple but that both of them together will continue to clash within each of us, clamoring for attention and support.

# 31. A Nicaraguan Pilgrimage
## David Sammons

THIS PAST SUMMER I journeyed to a village in the jungles of Nicaragua that had just recently been attacked by the Contras. I went impressed by Oliver North's testimony that he was justified in taking the profits from secret arms sales, telling lies, breaking laws—doing anything—to help "freedom fighters" stem the spread of "Marxist-Leninism" in Central America. I came back heartsick at what the "freedom fighters" were actually doing. They were not "stemming the tide of communism." They were using tactics meant to terrorize, impoverish, and kill innocent civilians.

I saw the results of our support for the Contras in Kusuli, a tiny village without running water, sanitation, or other conveniences, hours away from the nearest telephone or electricity. A group of Contras had attacked late one night in July. They had murdered three men, destroyed the home of the village's leader, ruined the roofs and walls of several other houses, and

*David Sammons* is senior minister of the Mt. Diablo Unitarian Universalist Church in Walnut Creek, California. He has previously been minister of Unitarian churches in Illinois, Ohio, and New York. He holds degrees from Dartmouth College, Starr King School for the Ministry, and Pacific School of Religion. He is currently the chair of the Unitarian Universalist General Assembly's Commission on Appraisal, and he has served on the boards of Beacon Press and Starr King School for the Ministry. Sammons is the author of *The Marriage Option* and several articles.

shot holes in the families' cooking pots. Then they stole the people's money, took the clothes out of their houses and burned them, and slaughtered cattle. That's what our government is providing for when it aids the "freedom fighters." The Contras are not fighting a war with a Communist army. They are attempting to destroy Nicaragua's economy and to terrorize its civilians in hopes that this will so undermine support for the government it will have to relinquish its power.

What we are supporting is an inhumane policy, one based on exactly the kind of terrorism our government claims to oppose—and it's also a policy that, although it's adding untold misery to the lives of people in an already poor country, isn't working. The men defending the village we visited weren't outsiders holding unwilling peasants under their control. They were poor farmers who had been forced to leave land farther off in the mountains to bring their families together in a place they could protect—and it was *they* who were protecting it, not Marxist-Leninists. The notion that the people of Nicaragua feel oppressed by their government—and are ready to rise up against it—is refuted by the fact that the government is willing to give almost anyone who wants one a gun to protect themselves from attack.

The fact is, in spite of the enormous hardships caused by our funding of the Contras and our economic embargo of Nicaragua, most Nicaraguans oppose what our government is doing to them. And why not? How could they possibly be supportive of a policy based on murder, terror, and economic ruin?

Even some of those recruited by the Contras feel this way. Before leaving for Nicaragua I had the chance to speak with Edgar Chamorro, a Nicaraguan businessman who belonged to one of the country's most prominent families. He had left Nicaragua, by his own confession, because "it would be easier to maintain his lifestyle" in Miami. After arriving in the United States he was recruited by the CIA to be member of the Contra directorate. His job was to bring together all the others chosen by the CIA whenever the Reagan Administration thought it was important to have a word from what it called the "Nicaraguan opposition." For a while Chamorro took the CIA's money to do this. He said, "It was a way to make a living." But he couldn't keep it up. He became disgusted with being a "hired hand" for a group of puppets that had no program of its own and no ties with the legitimate Nicaraguan opposition. He said the directorate had no reason to exist other than to put a good face on a brutal war being waged against civilians. In Managua, Bayardo Guzman, a leader of the Liberal Independent Party, though he was hardly a supporter of the current government in his country, said that he agreed with Chamorro that the United States should take its hands off Nicaragua. He said that continued aid to the Contras would only justify further abuses by the government.

The conversations I had with Chamorro and Guzman, as well as the visit to the village that had been attacked by the Contras, were arranged by Witness for Peace, an ecumenical organization working in Nicaragua at the invitation of the country's equivalent of our National Council of Churches.

Witness for Peace is committed to maintaining a nonviolent presence in the war zones of Nicaragua. Its staff spend much of their time in the countryside reporting on Contra attacks, building rapport with the civilians amongst whom they are living, and introducing to them people willing to share in the risks and deprivations they are experiencing.

I've seen poverty before, and there have been times in my life when I haven't had much money, but I've never experienced anything like I did in Nicaragua. The family I stayed with in Kusuli had virtually no possessions except the clothes on their backs. The rest had been burned by the Contras. Their house, though it was new, was tiny and crawling with bugs. For sleeping there was only a hammock for the two babies and a platform for the adults. For furniture there was a rough-hewn table and a stool. Like the rest of the people in the village the family with which I stayed had nothing to eat except corn. They had used up all their rice and beans.

The situation for people in Managua wasn't much better.

Food was in short supply, as was gasoline and most other things and the center of the city lay in ruins. Seventy percent of Managua was destroyed by an earthquake in 1972 and has never been rebuilt. Samoza had stolen most of the relief money and under the current circumstances the government couldn't even think about reconstruction. In what had been downtown the cathedral lies in ruins. The only large buildings still standing are the Intercontinental Hotel, from which visiting American dignitaries seldom stray, and the former Bank of America, a stark reminder of non-absent American money. The government would like to be able to help the people who have flocked into Managua from the war zones, but about the best it can do is give out small plots of land on which people can erect shacks for housing. If it weren't for the remarkable spirit of Nicaraguans a visit to their country would be terribly depressing.

Years ago when I had first thought of going to Nicaragua—a time before the earthquake and Sandanista uprising—I was advised not to go because Nicaraguans were "dirty and lived in hovels." The implication was that this was the result of a fault in their characters. Nicaragua has long been a poor country and there is a lot about poverty that's not attractive. But this doesn't mean that the people of Nicaragua have wanted to live in poverty. In fact, when finally given the chance, they rose up against their oppressors. And now, in spite of the hardships being caused by the American embargo and our funding of the Contras, children who would have never had the chance to do so before are going to school and adults who were illiterate are learning to read and write. The government is also training people to go out into the countryside to give inoculations and dispense medications in an effort to fight diseases for which people had never before been given any help. The people of Nicaragua want to improve their lives and, Marxist-Leninist or not, their government wants to help them.

In spite of the Reagan Administration's claims to the contrary, religion in Nicaragua is also being allowed to flourish. This is important, because Nicaraguans are an extremely religious people. In fact, the religiousness of the people of Nicaragua is one of the things which prompted its revolution. While the Sandanista government isn't pleased with the opposition to its policies on the part of some religionists—and has, at times, censored religious organizations or asked dissidents to leave the country—it has within its leadership many whose religious faith was the basis of their coming to believe that a revolution would be necessary if oppression was to be ended in their country. They are joined by thousands and thousands of religiously motivated people meeting in small groups throughout the country. In these groups, in reading the Bible, people come across words like those of the God who says in Isaiah:

> Is not this [what] I choose: to loose the bonds of
> wickedness, to undo the thongs of the yoke, to
> let the oppressed go free, and to break every
> yoke. Is it not to share your bread with the
> hungry and bring the homeless poor into your
> house. . . .

And they read the words of Jesus who, when asked in the Temple to describe his calling, quotes Isaiah as saying:

> The Spirit of the Lord is upon me, because he
> has anointed me to preach good news to the
> poor. He has sent me to proclaim release to the
> captives and recovering of sight to the blind, to
> set at liberty those who are oppressed.

While not everyone who reads the New Testament may choose to pay attention to what Jesus was saying in the Temple, the thrust of his message is clear: We should love our neighbors and life just as much as we do ourselves. In saying this Jesus was proclaiming a radical gospel, one whose implications are revolutionary. That's why in Nicaragua those who were serious about trying to respond to the prophetic thrust of the Bible felt they had to challenge the control of an elite who wanted to keep the country's wealth to themselves.

I've come home from Nicaragua affected by both my experience with a brave people and my experience with their radical gospel. It's a gospel whose social message should be as important to us as it is to the people of that country.

I knew when I decided to go to Nicaragua that I'd be changed by the experience. I knew that it would create a tension in me—a tension related to my desire to keep my life as comfortable as it can be and a knowledge of how doing that contributes to the violence and misery of the people of Nicaragua. I went knowing that such a tension would disturb my comfort because I believe such a discomfort is essential to an authentic religiousness. Being responsive to the prophetic thrust of the Bible requires that we go beyond a compliant faith centered on some sort of egoistic salvation.

One of the reasons I appreciated the experience I had in Nicaragua was because it put me in a situation in which I couldn't escape from the demands of a prophetic faith. I couldn't ignore the words of Isaiah or Jesus anymore than could the Nicaraguan peasants when they met to read their Bibles. But one doesn't have to go to Nicaragua to experience such a call. After all, even in relationship to what's happening in Nicaragua, the real battle to be fought isn't in some far-off place. It's here in the United States. As they've admitted themselves, the Contras could not survive without the material aid, the logistical support, the training and advice of our government. They've been unable to gain any substantial support in the country they claim they want to liberate.

If our government continues to aid the Contras the agony of Nicaragua will go on. The presidents of the five major countries of Central America have proposed a peace plan which would require an end to such support. In exchange, the governments of the region have agreed to send home foreign military advisors, to withdraw the states of emergency they may have declared in the face of violence, to end censorship, to reaffirm the freedom of their political parties, and to hold free and open elections. Since it's a plan devised by the leaders of Central America themselves—and has won for the President of Costa Rica who first proposed it the Nobel Prize for Peace—it deserves a chance to succeed. It's up to us both as citizens and as people of faith to insist that our government give it such a chance.

Understanding what is happening in Nicaragua and the other countries should create tension within us, tension between what is and what ought to be—and it should create in us an urge to do something to make the "ought to be" come true. If we are to be real in our religion we must be responsive to the words of faith, such as those of Micah, who said: "What does the Lord require of us but to love mercy, to seek justice and to walk humbly with our God."

If we do this we'll see that the central issue in Central America—the central issue in our world—is not a battle between what our current government defines as "freedom" and "Marxist-Leninism." It's a struggle between those who have and want to protect it and those who would like to be able to better their lives.

If we are all God's children, as the Bible puts it—if we are all entitled to the same "life, liberty, and the pursuit of happiness," promised to us by the Declaration of Independence—then what we must do is clear. We must be outspoken and forceful in opposition to our government's policy of trying to strangle and bleed the people of Nicaragua. We must do what's necessary to help bring into being for them and all others the world of peace and justice sought by both Jesus and the prophets.

# 32. Be Angry, But Sin Not!
*Paul Boecler*

Ephesians 4:26

MANY OF YOU graduates were in diapers at most when some of us were experiencing that decade of our nation's history called the 1960s. Those were years of angry protest. And many of the protestors were students. Evils in church and nation were identified and attacked. The rape of our environment, which is what air and water pollution were called, needed to be corrected. When the war in Vietnam heated up, some went into the streets with their massive demonstrations. Peter, Paul, and Mary made hits out of their peace songs. Social injustices were attacked and people rallied for civil rights. The rhetoric of radical revolution was in the air: bombs were thrown, buildings were burnt. You name the evil, and there were always some ready for protest, angry protest.

That was then. This is now. And here we are approaching the end of the 1980s. Whatever in all the world happened to the angry protests of the 1960s? The hippies have become yuppies, patriotism is in vogue, the street demonstrations are down to a trickle. Well and good, some would say, perhaps.

---

*Paul Boecler* is associate professor of religion at Concordia College in Bronxville, New York. Affiliated with the Lutheran Church—Missouri Synod, he is a graduate of Concordia Theological Seminary, St. Louis, and Washington University. He has been a pastor of a Lutheran church in Ohio and associate professor of theology at Concordia Senior College, Fort Wayne, Indiana, and he was chaplain for the Pan-Lutheran Teachers' Conference in 1984.

But some observers have labeled the early years of this decade the "me generation," with its "go for it" mentality of materialism and its charge after the big bucks. We have turned inward, some say, not outward; and the question has become not, What about social injustices? but instead, What's in it for me? A certain numbness has infiltrated our thinking which leaves us blind to the evils of our day. That is a generalization, of course, but there is probably at least a kernel of truth in it, applicable in various degrees to any one of us.

Now, believe you me, this is not a call to a return to the excesses of the 1960s, God forbid, a decade which a friend of mine has called a decade exactly ten years too long. Those protests of the 1960s were often immature, empty-headed, and misdirected. But if Lance Morrow in a recent essay in *Time* magazine is correct, people are now ready for a "new period of activism and social change.[1] Presidential candidates are talking more and more about compassion and more active approaches to deep-rooted social problems." Our own church leaders have gone on record saying that more people are hurting mentally, morally, and psychologically than ever before and that we need to turn with some new vigor to the ills of our fellow men.

You graduates may well be at the cutting edge of that new mood. Not the violent mood of the 1960s. But the enthusiasm of the 1960s for serious causes.

Whether or not that new mood arrives in society, and at the risk of being misunderstood, I hope that if you get good and angry when you become alert in a new and fresh way, to the evils of our day, then good for you. Get angry. Don't sweep the dirt under the rug. There is nothing loving about such a head-in-the-sand approach to any form of evil. Get angry. Get good and angry. And when you do, I can assure you that there is such a thing as Christian anger, and that that book which we call the Bible contains many a story of God's People who were angry, yes furiously angry, at the evil confronting them.

Take some examples. Here is Moses descending from the

mountain after forty-some days in communion with the Lord, and with the will of the Lord in his hands. It is the gracious will of a Lord for His people who have been graciously delivered by him from slavery under a mad Egyptian tyrant. Now what does Moses see? He sees that ungrateful people dancing around the image of a pagan god. So what does Moses do? Does he tip-toe up to the people, arrange to dialogue with them to explore the possible philosophical causes for their infidelity, and volunteer to remove that offensive golden calf to a more inconspicuous place? He does nothing of the kind. Instead he shatters the tablets of the law on the ground, strides angrily up to that golden calf, reduces it to powder, and throws it on the drinking water of the Israelites. Take that! What was that in Moses? Was it the temper tantrum of an indulged youth? Not at all. It was righteous indignation, holy wrath, red-blooded anger. And there isn't a syllable in the inspired record which criticizes Moses for what he did.

Take another example. There was a day when they were bringing children, even infants, to Jesus that He might bless them. What sentimental silliness, the disciples felt. What a waste of the Master's time. But Jesus felt otherwise. He became not peeved and not annoyed. He was indignant, St. Mark tells us, and stung the disciples with a word I'm sure they never forgot. That's how Jesus felt then. How do you think he feels now at the sight of child abuse, child neglect, child prostitution?

Or think of Jesus' attitude toward sickness and death. Some ghastly disease has taken his friend Lazarus to the grave. Jesus did not brush that human tragedy aside as though it were somehow the will of God. Jesus burst into tears, we are told. But we are told more than that. Twice St. John frames Jesus' tears with the statement that He, Jesus, was deeply moved in spirit and troubled. Tears running down Jesus' face, but those were tears of frustrated anger. Anger over that calamity we call death, angry as He always was, at any misfortune that devastates the lives of God's creatures. That's how Jesus felt then. How do you think He feels now when famine and Alzheimer's disease and the drug traffic waste the lives of people created in the image of God?

Or better yet, think of this. I would not like to have been one of those merchants or moneychangers in the temple area when Jesus came to Jerusalem for the Passover. Those men were profaning the temple with their selling of animals and making a cool profit out of religion. "You den of robbers," Jesus called them. So, right there on the spot, He made a whip and put it into His hand and snapped it at the behinds of the animals and merchants till they were driven out. He grabbed hold of the end of one table after another and flipped them over and all the coins stacked neatly on those tables went flying through the air. I chuckle at the sight of grown men falling over each other in their wild dash to escape the fire blazing in the eyes of this lone Galilean reformer. But I wouldn't want to be caught laughing now if I were guilty of commercializing the Christian church or making a big business out of the Gospel of Jesus Christ.

There is such a thing as righteous indignation. And if some fire is ignited in your belly at the presence of unvarnished wrongs in church and world, don't douse that fire out with complacent indifference. Some healthy anger may go a long way to correct evils under which people suffer and which corrupt the word and will of a gracious God.

Having said all that, remember however, that Christian anger is a special kind of anger. Be angry, but sin not, wrote the apostle Paul. We can get angry for the silliest and most self-centered of reasons. And we usually do: angry at some clumsy oaf who accidently steps on our toes, angry at the malicious tongue which has slandered our name. That anger is triggered by some personal slight or injury.

Moreover, anybody can rant and rave without attempting to correct the wrong. We curse the darkness, as the saying goes, without ever thinking to light a candle. My dog is like that. He barks and snarls at everyone. But it's all noise, and I'll wager not even a midnight intruder will the fool thing attack.

And then too there is anger which is irrationally destructive. People who bomb abortion clinics are angry. But what folly that is!

Christian anger is entirely different. It is anger in the service of some high and holy cause. It is anger at work for some righteous purpose which transcends our personal whims and welfare. And it is anger resulting in saving, redemptive activity for others. I hope you get the idea. It's not any kind of anger I'm advocating. Rather it is anger stimulated by the sight of some evil which thwarts God's loving will for people and which resolves to do what it can to remedy the wrong.

And most important, this anger is motivated by an experience. It is the personal experience of being delivered from God's own wrath for human sin.

It works, I believe, like this.

Once there was a triple execution on a hill outside Jerusalem. From the center cross was heard such a cry of dereliction that must have caused God Himself to cringe in pain: "My God, my God, why have you forsaken me." All the wrath of God for human sin came crashing down on Christ Himself. Then and there and once and for all, God dealt radically with human sin. And when Christ had finished the last drop in God's cup of wrath, what an act of deliverance that was for us! What a heroic rescue from God's wrath for the human race!

And what that tells us is that God does not ignore, or condone, or excuse our human wrongdoing. He dealt with it seriously and radically. He paid for it with His own life. But it tells us this also: that when He dealt with it, He dealt with it mercifully; and not for His sake, but for our sakes, wrote St. Paul, for our sake God made Him who knew no sin, Jesus, share our sin that in union with Him we might share the goodness of God himself.

"Who shall deliver me from this body of death?" Paul once asked. And Paul's immediate answer was, "Thanks be to God who gives us the victory through our Lord Jesus Christ!"

If that can be your answer, then you can say to yourself what Paul said, Be angry, but sin not. Call it love in action if you prefer. But make it sometimes indignant love determined to rectify some Satanic blight which besets the lives of other people.

So it was with Candy Lightner, whose daughter was killed by a drunken driver. She got angry, and all the more so when the offender was released from prison only to commit the same crime a second time. Candy Lightner not only got angry. She got mad, if I may play with words for a moment. She founded Mothers Against Drunk Driving. And who knows now much that organization has helped to spare the lives of other potential victims and raised the level of our nation's awareness of that disease and that crime. First the tears and heartache and bereavement. And then the anger turned unselfishly in the direction of saving activity on behalf of others.

So too it was with Moses. He wasn't the only one angry at Israel's infidelity. So was the Lord. So angry, in fact, that the Lord threatened to do away with this people entirely and start all over again with a new nation founded on Moses and his descendants. What an opportunity for Moses to make a name for himself and to justify it in the name of the Lord. How many of us church workers would resist a similar opportunity to make a big name for ourselves and all in the cause of Christ supposedly? Not so with Moses, however. Twenty-four hours after he smashes the tablets to pieces, he is interceding for the people. "Don't blot them out. Forgive them. And if not forgive, then blot me out. Not them. Not them. But me." Moral indignation yes, but then on his knees pleading for the people he loved.

Before he became president, Abraham Lincoln, thinking of slavery, is reported to have said, "If ever I get a chance, I shall hit that thing and hit it hard."

Now I realize that much of our Christian activity is not aroused by anger. That includes changing dirty diapers and paying our taxes, though some may disagree with me on that score.

I know also that a great many evils fall somewhere in a grey area, not all white, not all black, the solutions for which are exceedingly complicated, leaving sensitive Christians in a quandary as to which corrective remedy is best.

But there are enough bare, naked evils around which are crying out for correction: In society, everything from adult illiteracy to our nation's veterans languishing forgotten on their hospital beds. In church, a message which encourages pompous self-righteousness, and a mission which degenerates into superficial trivialities. If we cannot lead some movement that will change the course of history, we can at least make a generous charitable contribution or say a simple prayer. What we dare not do is pass by those evils on the other side. Be angry then, but sin not. As God gives you the opportunity, hit that thing and hit it hard. He who delivered us from the wrath of God, Jesus the Christ, asks of His followers nothing less than that.

NOTES

1. Lance Morrow. *Time*, March 30, 1987, 28–29.

# 33. Lovers
## *Hal Missourie Warheim*

Friends, let us love one another; for love is of God, and anyone who loves is born of God and knows God. Anyone who does not love does not know God; for God is love.—1 John 4:7–8

> Since my conception by Love,
> I have been birthed,
>     buttered-up and bartered,
>     belittled and betrayed.
> And now at the end of my life
> I am bewildered
> Because I still believe in Love.

### *"Teach Us About Love!"*

Once upon a time, as I entered the pulpit prepared to preach a five-star, three-point sermon on "Stewardship, Spirituality, and Clown Ministries," the congregation rose up as a mighty host and began to chant: "Teach us about Love! Teach us about Love!"

"As you can see from the bulletin," I replied, "the topic for today's sermon is 'Stewardship, Spirituality, and Clown Ministries.' These are matters modern Christians need to

---

*Hal Missourie Warheim* is professor of Christianity and society at Louisville Presbyterian Theological Seminary in Louisville, Kentucky. An ordained minister of the United Church of Christ, and a member of the Kentucky Bar, Warheim is a graduate of Elmhurst College, Eden Theological Seminary, and the University of Louisville.

know about. Moreover, these subjects are suggested by the lectionary texts for today."

"We've had it up to our keesters with Stewardship, Spirituality, and Clown Ministries, not to speak of lectionaries," they protested. "We want to learn about Love. Love is important to us. Love is supposed to be what life, Christianity, and church membership are all about. But, mostly, we are just hungry for Love. None of us gets enough loving here at St. Valentine's or any other place in the world. Teach us to be lovers so we can at least try it out and decide for ourselves if Love is everything preachers, poets, psychiatrists, and other love-propagandists say it is."

"Why don't you write to Miss Manners about Love?" I resisted. "My professional opinion is that this is mostly a concern about the etiquette of mundane social relations."

Just then I heard the organist behind me whisper with prayerlike passion, "O, Reverend, won't you please teach us to be Lovers!"

I started to yield. "Why not?" I mused to myself. "This probably has interesting homiletical possibilities: a biblical text for authority, a few deft exegetical moves, some choice quotes from Eric Fromm and Barry Manilow, and a closing illustration from the life of Mother Teresa."

"Okay," I said, "next week's sermon will be about Love and I'll build it around a comparison of Karl Barth's and Leo Buscaglia's ideas on the subject, even though I know that only the strong among you will be able to stand the excitement."

"Hold it!" shouted the people. "We want your ideas about Love and we want them now."

"But, why me?" I whined. "Why do you want me to teach you about Love?"

"Because we're paying your salary," growled a deacon from the front pew. "And because you are supposed to care about how and where we are hurting."

I became ashamed of my reluctance. Also, I was afraid of what the deacon might be able to do to my salary. I began quickly to call up everything I had ever read or heard about

Love and I was prepared as well to invent things about Love which nobody ever thought of. "O God . . ?" I prayed desperately as I motioned the congregation to be seated, clutched the solid sides of the pulpit, and tried to begin at the beginning.

## Genesis

"In the beginning," I began, "there was Love; a mysterious spiritual hunger to be in relationship.

"In the beginning, there was Love; a powerful passion to be with an other.

"In the beginning, there was Love; an infinite urge toward intimate belonging.

"In the beginning, there was Love; an ultimate need to care and to be cared for.

"In the beginning, there was Love; and there was nothing but this Love.

"And Love created Chaos and Cosmos and designed them with such intense desire for one another that they united into a single reality and now these two are always found inseparably together.

"Love also created Night and Light each with a deep loneliness for the other which destines them forever to follow one another for the bliss of embracing briefly in the twilights of dawn and evening.

"Love too created the Sea and the Soil each with precious gifts needed by the other which are exchanged through caresses and collisions wherever the surf encounters the shore.

"Then Love created human beings: Created us out of the very being of Love itself. Created us with the same passionate need to live in relationship. Created us with the ultimate desire to belong with others. Created us with an aching loveliness which can be assuaged only through the giving and accepting of urgently needed gifts in intimate, caring encounters.

"Each one of us is a wonderful, contemporary creature of the infinite and eternal reality of Love. We were conceived in

Love. We were born for Love. We were nurtured by Love. And, to the extent that there is fulfillment in our lives, it is the consequence of appropriately expressing the unique and universal potentials of Love with which we are created."

"That's wonderful," sighed the organist.

"Metaphysical speculation," muttered the deacon.

"But it's a start," chimed the choir. "So, tell us why is there so little Love is our lives today?"

It was now time to get down to business, since descriptions of evil have always been my strong suit.

## East of Eden

"Yes," I said, "we were created by Love and created to Love. What a bitter irony it is then that we human beings have a history of starvation for Love. Certainly, Love is the most powerful and persistent reality in the world and, yet, paradoxically, Love is a fragile thing with many obstacles and enemies. It is frequently under siege by selfishness, competition, inequality, carelessness, fatigue, insensitivity, and, especially, fear of Love itself. Love is easily broken and, when Love is broken, those who did the loving get hurt with the most awful agony the human heart can know. Our modern society is a junkyard of demolished love relationships which is haunted by wounded lovers who are searching for scrap pieces of Love to salvage.

"Indeed, from the past to the present, Love in our human family has been prevented and perverted by suspicion, hostility, discrimination, subordination, persecution, and oppression. These pathologies of Love have made all of us weak and sick and deprived us of the abundant benefits of human solidarity.

"Consequently, nobody gets enough Love in this world where so much of our national, psychic, and social resources are wasted on paranoid protection of the narrow self-interests of nations, classes, races, religions, sexes, and other divisions into which we get sifted.

"We are presently in need of liberation from the spirit of enmity which is embodied in the many divisive traditions which set us against each other."

At this point, the well of my mind went dry except for a little poem by Langston Hughes which I felt belonged somewhere in this sermon on Love but I wasn't sure where. So, I just pitched it into the hole and hoped that it would help:

> Folks, I'm telling you
> birthing is hard
> and dying is mean—
> so get yourselves
> a little loving
> in between.

"I love poetry," murmured the organist.

"I'd rather hear some more about evil," I heard the deacon say.

Just then, a voice from somewhere in the midst of the congregation called out, "What about the future of Love? Reverend. Are there any ways by which we can hope to become real lovers someday?"

"Amen!" shouted the congregation. "Get practical!"

"Now they want prophecy!" I moaned to myself. "Why can't Christians be satisfied with 'Stewardship, Spirituality, and Clown Ministries'? " I wondered.

So, anxiously, I went back to the well, dropped the bucket as far down as it would go into the waters of my own experiences of Love, and pulled up a futuristic parable as the most meaningful resource I had to give to these Love-thirsty people.

## The City of Lovers

"A thousand years from now," I told them, "there will be a city here where the experience of Love will be known mainly by rumor. There will be lots of talk about Love and plenty of polite associations among the people here. But throughout the entire population, from one end of the city to the other, there will be a famine for participation in intimate relationships where the partners respect, trust, enjoy, and sincerely care for the welfare of one another. In these hungry hearts there will be the awful hurt of Love's absence, an urgent need for Love's presence, and a prayer-like hope that Love might soon become powerful and prevalent in their community.

"The City Council will become concerned about this situation eventually, because Love-starved people engage in socially explosive behaviors and the Mayor of the city will authorize a program to promote Love in the lives and relationships of the citizens. Typically, no one in the city government will know how to carry out the program so they will employ four expert Lovers from other cities to begin the task. Each Lover will use a somewhat different strategy to promote love relationships and they will divide the city into four quadrants where each Lover will put his/her strategy to the test."

## The Model

"The first Lover will be an accomplished and attractive Model who over the years developed her personality and maximized her potentials and who, consequently, became a very desirable and cherished friend and companion for a great number of people. By inheriting a pleasant appearance and acquiring a number of socially esteemed attributes and skills, she had become supremely lovable to other people and always had more Love in her life than she really needed.

"Her assumption about Love will be that it is like a shy gypsy who has to be lured out of the dark forest by the inviting sight and sounds of a dancing campfire and soul-stirring music; that most people, even people hungry for Love, must be tempted out of their loneliness and seduced into intimate caring relationships by partners with qualities which they need, appreciate, and admire.

"This Lover's strategy will involve helping the people of her quadrant to become lovable to one another. She will teach them to discern what potential Love partners find attractive and desirable. She will encourage them to improve their physical appearances, public images, and social graces. She will prompt them to develop their interests and latent abilities in order to become the best and most beautiful persons they can be.

"Under this woman's program many of the city's loveless population will become lovable human beings who will arouse Love in other people and who, finally, will have a real opportunity to experience Love in their own lives."

### The Little Girl

"The Lover who will come to the city's second quadrant will be a charming Little Girl. She will be able to articulate no philosophy about Love and her simple strategy will be just to give and demand Love from everyone she meets. As a child she will be unaware of the lack of Love in the city and innocent to the dangers of Loving. Thus, she will trustingly lavish her kitten-like affections of anyone, without fear or discrimination. Also she will expect people to Love her and to care for her welfare. She will assume that to be Loved is her birthright and, if such Loving is not given, she will cry or cajole or cuddle up to the people from whom she wants it until she gets it.

"This little Lover will invade the empty hearts of many of her people and fill their lives with an experience of Love which they never knew could exist. In loving her and in being loved by her, these citizens will learn the fundamentals for loving one another."

### The Gardener

"The third quadrant's Lover will be a Gardener with an understanding of how things grow. He will know that Love, like a flower, is ultimately a miracle which cannot be manufactured, but that miracles of Love and flowers alike are extremely dependent upon the condition and care of the gardens in which they are expected to bloom. This man will build his strategy upon the knowledge that Love relationships, like roses and periwinkles, need good soil, healthy seeds, and lots of intelligent cultivation as well as the help of the sun and the rain. Love relations among people are extremely dependent upon conducive cultural conditions and supportive social structures. For Love to bud and blossom in the lives of these Love-starved citizens, they will need to create the kind of customs, policies, laws, values, programs, and institutions which motivate, train, provide incentives and opportunities, and even put pressure on people to love one another.

"This Lover will organize his people to revolutionize the culture of their quadrant which has produced the famine of Love in their lives. Together they will redefine their sex roles, rearrange their power structures, reform their tax policies, reformulate their religious doctrines, reorganize their school's curricula, and revise their economic goals into a social system which will cultivate Love, honor Lovers, and protect Love relationships. In their new society, there will be greater equality, fairness, courage, honest communication, security, trust, and all the other nutrients necessary for the growth of Love. In a word, the Gardener will redeem his people from Lovelessness by leading them through a cultural revolution to a new social order which maximizes their changes of experiencing the miracles of Love."

### The Scientist

"The fourth Lover will be an old man full of memories about Love and with many scars on his heart from participating in a lot of love relationships during his lengthy life. He will be a sort of Love-scientist and, from all of his experiments with Love, his trial and error experiences of Love, he will have distilled two clear drops of wisdom which he will give as medicine to the people of his district who are sick for lack of Love.

"The first is his conclusion that, of all the experiences in life, Love is the most precious—the pearl of supreme value—and the most necessary to becoming an authentic human being. Without Love, people are worthless, weak, incomplete, poor, and prone to doing themselves and others evil. But with Love, they are strong, rich, fulfilled, priceless, and motivated to do good to others and themselves.

"Therefore, as this old Lover mingles with his people, he will persuade them to pride Love above every other value and to seek Love first, last, and always in everything they do. 'Go for Love!' he will counsel them, 'and the rest of what you want in life—security, success, self-actualization—will come to you as spin-offs of Love. Go all out for Love!'

"This old Lover's second drop of wisdom is his studied observation that everyone who goes after Love gets wounded and needs healing before she or he can go after Love again. Love may be supremely important and necessary to people, but so many adverse things can happen in a Love relationship which hurt the Lovers deeply and bleed their courage to try Love once more. Misunderstanding. Conflict. Disillusionment. Rejection. Alienation. Betrayal. Loss. Sooner or later all would-be Lovers as well as the world's great Lovers get lanced and suffer the sores of confusion, anger, guilt, doubt, and fear. These wounds must be skillfully treated or they will fester or callous the lover's soul and make it too weary or too wary to fully love ever again.

"Therefore, as this old Lover moves among his people, he will be sensitive to the pains which deter them from participating in Love relationships and treat them with the healing balms of acceptance, forgiveness, peace, confidence, and encourage them to try loving some more. He will heal them of their Love-hurts and teach them to heal the Love-hurts of one another. Actually, he will be able to heal only a few of them himself, and he will trust and depend on them to heal the rest.

## Outcome

"When these four Lovers will have completed their work, there will be a significant increase in Love relationships among the people of the city. Then the Mayor and the City Council will debate which Lover's strategy was the most productive of Love and which if any or all of the Lovers should be retained to continue their efforts with the population. And this debate will go on for at least another thousand years into the future."

## Questions

"This parable is now finished," I said at the end, "but its meaning for our lives and the future of Love must yet be puzzled out because it raises questions for us to wrestle with. And upon your answers to these questions hang the future of the world, the mission of the Christian Church, and the quality of life which we have with one another: In which of these quadrants of this city would you like to live? Which of these strategies or others do you think will produce the most Love in the lives of people? Do you really want to be a Lover? What kind of Love-strategy will you use to promote and participate in Love relationships with other human beings?

"These are fundamental questions of human existence and Christian faith, and wrestling with them is the prerequisite for an authentic, abundant life, for understanding God, and for participating in God's redemption of this Love-starved world."

Then I stopped preaching and we started wrestling and, in the process, the God who is Love became known to us and, miraculously, we began to Love one another better than before.

# V. PASTORAL

# *34.* Not Many People Want to Go to Heaven Anymore

## *Daniel Aleshire*

Revelation 21; Numbers 13:17–14:3; and John 14:1–7

YOU CAN ALMOST see it, off in the distance, just on the other side of time. The heavenly city. Look at it: Walls made of jasper are sitting on foundations that dazzle with jewels. Sapphire. Emerald. Topaz. Amethyst. The sight makes Tiffany's look like a K-Mart blue-light special! Look at the gates. Solid pearl, one huge pearl forming each gate. And through the gates, you can see the city and its street of solid gold. There's gold everywhere; there's more gold in a storage closet than in Fort Knox and Sammy Davis Jr.'s dresser put together!

The whole place glows in the glory of God—so bright it makes your eyes hurt. Through your squinting gaze, you can see a river that flows through the middle of the city. It dazzles like crystal when it catches the light. So much light there is no night. By the river, there's a huge tree, and every month it bears a different fruit.

As you look, it's hard to realize how big the place is. There

---

*Daniel Aleshire* was born in Columbus, Ohio. He was educated at Belmont College, Southern Baptist Theological Seminary, and George Peabody College, from which he received his doctorate. Dr. Aleshire has been a research scientist and a pastor and is now professor of psychology and Christian education at Southern Baptist Theological Seminary. He is the author of *Faithcare* and of *Understanding Today's Youth*.

is no scale for comparison. It's a cube, 1,500 miles in each dimension. New York City *is* about the size of a big apple beside this place. It would take 5,000 World Trade Center buildings, all stacked on top of each other, to reach the top of this city.

You and I get to go to this heavenly city. Aren't you excited? See the pearl, touch the gold, hear the choir, smell the fruit, taste the feast. The Lord God will be your light, for ever and ever. People shall praise the Lord God and the Lamb, forever. These streets, these stones, these songs . . . forever. This house, this fruit, these companions . . . forever.

Won't that be wonderful? *Or will it?* Does it sound beautiful—*or a bit gaudy?* Does it sound exciting—*or a bit boring?* Maybe I am wrong, but I don't think "many people want to go to heaven anymore."

## I

My hunch is that when most twentieth-century people look at the picture of the future painted in Revelation 21 they react like the Israelites when they looked toward the promised land.

### The Old Testament Reaction to the Promised Land

Remember the story? The spies returned from their trip into the land of promise and reported their findings to the children of Israel. It *was* a land that flowed with milk and honey, where a grape branch was so laden with clusters that it had to be carried on a pole by two men. But they also heard something on the grapevine. There were people in the land bigger than the grapes. The men were strong, the cities well fortified and, no doubt, all the children were above average. They went looking for a land that would yield milk and honey for people to devour, and returned with the report that the land could devour people.

They saw the promised land, and suddenly the desert didn't look so bad anymore. They looked into the land of promise, saw its size, its fruit, and its threat, and the whole congregation cried out: "Why does the Lord bring us into this land, to fall by the sword? Our wives and our little ones will fall prey; would it not be better for us to go back to Egypt?" (Num. 14:3).

They didn't go back to Egypt, but they did spend a lifetime in the desert. There would be manna, but no honey. There would be water, but precious little milk. There would be a cloud to show the guidance of God, but no wine to celebrate the presence of God.

## Twentieth-Century Reactions to Heaven

American Christians of this century, it seems, are not unlike the ancient children of Israel. We have looked toward the Bible's land of promise for us; we believe that heaven exists; but we do not let its existence touch our lives or settle into our souls.

We are not sure about heaven. We have seen its fruit, but are not sure how hungry we are for such food. We have seen its rooms, but are suspicious that a move there will be to a slightly lower-class neighborhood. We have seen its jewels, but secretly wonder if they are not out-of-date costume jewelry—the kind you give to children when they want to play dress-up.

Some Christians greet heaven like a congregation of Scrooges. Bah, humbug! They see the spirit of Christian future, roll over, and go back to sleep.

Maybe I am just imagining things. Maybe it's not so. But as I look at the religion on television, as I listen to the groans of people struggling with the traumas of life, as I read the survey results of those people on the street who believe in God and Jesus and heaven and hell—but have no heart for the Gospel—I don't think many people long to go to heaven anymore. They will go there when they have to, but would much prefer heaven come to earth. They find the hope of heaven a comfort at death, but would much prefer there be no death at all. Heaven does not touch our imagination or stir our souls much these days. It has not always been this way.

For centuries, the vision of a promised land—a land of milk and honey, of gold and jewels, of glory and praise—has stretched from the future into the present. It has caught the imagination of Christian people. Just last century, people stood on Jordan's stormy banks, "and cast a wistful eye, to Canaan's fair and happy land, where their possessions lie." They were convinced there was "a land that is fairer than day, and by faith they could see it afar, where the Father waits over the way, to prepare a dwelling place there— in the sweet bye and bye." There was power in the image of God's future creation that gave a peace and purpose in the midst of this creation.

## II

But it seems very different in this day. People of this century look at the longing for heaven as a symptom of some human problem or weakness. They think heaven is more a wish born of human need than a reality invented by a creative God. We suspect that the people who sang those nineteenth-century hymns wanted a religion that would give them "pie in the sky—in the sweet bye and bye." Perhaps they wanted something in the future because the present gave them so little. Disease came, and people died for lack of penicillin. Rains came, and people died for lack of a dam. Drought came, and people starved for lack of irrigation. The baby came, and a mother died for lack of a high-tech birthing room. Life was rough; people died young; there was too little justice and too much violence. Christians longed for heaven as a coping device for the tragedy of life.

### The Problem with This Analysis

But this analysis is not fair to Christians whose lives have been shaped by a heavenly hope, and it deprives us of a truth, a reality, that we desperately need. Our lack of passion for heaven reveals our own problem more than it corrects the problem of someone else's fixation on heaven. If the nineteenth-century error was "bye and bye, pie in the sky," the error of this century has to be: "Here is how I want it now."

Our prayers betray us: "Because you love me, and want your children to have the best, Lord, would you grant me this?" "Lord, I do believe, bless thou my seed faith." Some of our pleading is more sophisticated and intellectually acceptable, but it all wants to squeeze the doings of God into our time, compress the integrity of God into our dimensions, and force the future of God into the present of our lives. "Here is how I want it now," we tell God.

If other generations of Christians have not taken this world seriously enough, we have taken it too seriously. If they had their noses stuck in the world to come, we have our heads stuck in the sands of this time. We are obsessed with *this* week. We want to know exactly what our religion has done for us— by the end of this quarter. We want our lives made whole by Friday and our enemies made into friends before next Sunday.

We have a vision of what we want, but have no vision of the future in which it will come. Our refusal to take seriously God's creative future locks us into the present, and temporary problems look like they need permanent solutions.

We have been given tents for a journey, and feel cheated we did not get land for a homestead. We have been given provisions to set sail, but are terrified because we fear God's future is flat, and the ship will surely fall off the edge.

We have convinced ourselves that thinking of heaven is a sentimental escape, a denial of the horror of a century of two world wars, one worldwide depression, the holocaust that came to European Jews, and the holocaust we fear might come to us all. As a result, we live with too narrow a focus. We see the horror in the absence of the hope.

The Need for a Heavenly Vision

We need to relearn the longing for heaven. We need the power of its vision. Living in the hope of heaven can help us see this world more accurately, more perceptively. We need to learn to live in this world in light of the reality of the next. Perhaps my earlier statement was too strong. Christian people still want to go to heaven when they die. What seems to be missing is the longing for a life that can be qualitatively better than this one. We lack patience for the work the God of creation yet has to do. Longing for heaven need not be an escapism or coping device. It can be the acceptance of a reality.

Maybe biblical images of heaven do not help us much these days. When we think of beauty, we may not think of gold and jewels. When we think of a feast, we may not think of milk and honey. Perhaps we need to re-image heaven, so the power of the future can once again invade the present. The hymns we have sung this morning have linked texts with tunes we have not typically used together. Maybe that is what we need to do with our images of heaven. Remember the truth and refashion the image. Sing the words to a new tune.

We need to imagine anew the hope and dream, feel the reality of heaven once again. Religious imagination is no hallucination—it helps us trace the contours of reality. What vision would convey heaven's reality to you?

## III

Imagine the best there can be, and it is better. Imagine the most beautiful there is, and it is better. If imagination is hard for you, how about math?

Take the best day you ever had, add to it your tenderest moment ever, multiply that by the best thing you ever did, then add the greatest joy you have ever experienced and the most noble desire you ever had. Now multiply that by 1,500, taken to the power of a cube, and you will have some of the dimension of heaven. If math is hard for you, how about a picture?

Picture a world where each person makes a difference, each makes a contribution, and everybody knows life is better because of the gifts each brings. Picture a world where every unblessed child has a beaming parent telling people on the street, "This child is mine, and I am so proud with her." Picture a world where every abused spouse experiences only gentle touches and kind words and knows the joy of fearless love. Picture a world where every poor soul who craved the addictive and was slave to the destructive has been set free, and never feels those death-dealing compulsions again.

Imagine a world where there is more than enough food for everybody, and none of it ever goes to waste. Imagine a world where everybody has a room, and everyone is perfectly content with the place that was made just for them.

Picture a world where Russian and American have both forgotten which they were, where Ku Klux Klanner and neo-Nazi cry in joy while they sing with people they used to hate, "Free at last, free at last, thank God almighty, we're free at least."

Imagine—*you*. You get up in the morning, wanting to do what is right. And that's exactly what you do! As you do the good and perfect, you never get bored by it. You get a kick out of it. It feels right . . . fits like an old shoe. It's so much fun doing good, some days you sneak off by yourself late at night, when nobody is looking, and do some more. It's more fun than getting that last bowl of Frusen Gladje. It no longer seems so strange for you to do what is right and loving and just. It is just what comes naturally to you. You go to bed at night with no regrets, no remorse, no second thoughts. No one is upset with you. No one has misunderstood you, no one has offended by you. You go to sleep thinking to yourself, "Life just can't get any better than this." And in the morning when you wake up, it does. Imagine that.

Heaven can have a power in our lives. We can borrow from its vision to put our hurts into perspective.

Heaven can tutor our hopes. Our legitimate longing for the world yet to be teaches us about God's intimate longing for the world that is. We can long for heaven and still love earth.

We can long for heaven and not assume we have a problem. Longing for God's Heavenly Kingdom is no grown-up version of a child's longing to go to Disney's Magic Kingdom.

For some reason or the other our four-year-old son, Jonathan, began asking his mother some questions a few months ago. The conversation went like this: Jonathan asked: "Mommy, when do we go to live with Jesus?" Jo responded: "When we die." Jonathan then asked: "Will Jesus have any food?" And Jo, responding this time with a smile, said, "Yes." Jonathan pushed the issue: "Will Jesus have food *I* like?" Jo, smiling wider, said, "Yes." Jonathan had one more question in him: "Will Jesus have macaroni and cheese?" And, Jo, responding like God no doubt will, said, "Yes." Jonathan then jumped, clapped his hands, and said, "Goodie, goodie."

Whatever heaven is: There is a room, a food, a hope, a healing, a future, with your name, if you want it.

# 35. God's Secret of Renewed Self-Esteem

*Elam Davies*

John 3:1–17

SELF-ESTEEM APPEARS to be the "in" topic of the day, and in most circles. It was not always a priority subject for pulpit concern. Other matters bothered us. Peace of mind, for instance, or success or social relevance, or war and peace, to name a few.

There is nothing strange in this shift of emphasis. In our more conservative frame of mind we may deplore the "topicality" of much preaching, but if we were better students of the New Testament we would discover the constant shifts of subject matter in proclamation and writing. The church was always up-to-date in its message, whether it spoke about the religious differences between Christian and Jew, the philosophical conflicts of Christian and Greek, the esoteric struggle with the teaching of the cults, or the moral issue of the "laissez-faire" lifestyle of the pagans.

One big difference, however, arises between the topicality

*Elam Davies* was born in Grovesend, Swansea, Wales. He was educated at the University of Wales and the University of Cambridge, England. From 1961 until his retirement he was minister of the Fourth Presbyterian Church, Chicago and was more recently interim minister at the Fifth Avenue Presbyterian Church, New York City. In 1980, he was cited by *Time* as one of seven outstanding American preachers. He is author of *This Side of Eden,* a volume of sermons.

of much of our modern preaching and the teaching of the New Testament. The latter was *always* rooted in the stupendous wonder of God's saving Grace in Jesus Christ. Take the *equality of sexes:* not just a fact of human dignity, but "there is neither male nor female [in the order of importance]: for you are all one in Christ Jesus."

Or take the issue of *self-assertion,* the modern day "being me" at all costs, often irrespective of what others feel or think. Would you imagine, for instance, that the beautiful passage from Philippians set to music by Mrs. Beach and sung so magnificently by our soprano and baritone soloists today, dealt with this very modern phenomenon, but against the background of a large canvas, "Let this mind be in you which was also in Christ Jesus, who humbled himself."

The New Testament never trivializes the issues. It doesn't deal with our problems as if they were pieces of tinsel on a string. It doesn't send you off searching desperately and introspectively into your own being, as if the answer were only to be found within. It is found, within, of course, but if I may put it this way, it offers us an answer to the *answer* that comes from without.

Let me be more explicit. When we are dealing with the complicated question of self-esteem, there are more ways than one that we try to answer.

One way is to attempt to encase our personalities in the protection of *vanity.* I am always amused by the explicit vanity of the young woman with beautiful hair who, after flouncing her L'Oreal tresses, talks in superlative terms about her own attractiveness and concludes, "Frankly . . . I'm worth it." Of course she may be. No one wants to deny that, but the inference that her self-esteem depends on her looks is a shabby substitute for the real thing.

Others of us try to bolster our self-esteem by our *pride.* Let me say immediately that there is a legitimate place for self-pride—the satisfaction in achievement, realization of goals, attainment of merit. I am also aware of the fact that Pride is considered the deadliest of the Deadly Sins, but there is a world of difference between what the Greeks called Hubris, which is always self-destructive in the end, and the kind of delight we take in something which is well-conceived or well-done.

The remarkable fact about Pride with a capital P is that it creeps insidiously into our confessions as well as our claims. Perhaps you have heard this piece of doggerel.

> Once in a saintly passion
> I cried with bitter grief,
> "O, Lord, my heart is black with sin;
> Of sinners I'm the chief."
> Then stooped my guardian angel
> And whispered from behind,
> "Vanity, my dear one;
> You're nothing of the kind!"

Of course we laugh! It touches us at a delicate point, a sensitive spot deep within our psyche. We need to be on our guard against those confessions which are promotions of our ego-love, those boastings of depravity or even delinquency which we wish to use as religious adornments. When the Apostle Paul claimed that "Christ Jesus came into the world to save sinners, of whom I am chief," he was not bragging about his excesses. He was saying in different words what many members say at AA meetings "My name is . . . and I am an alcoholic." Not I *was,* but I am! And only the grace of God keeps me together, and the love of God keeps me functioning, and the power of God enables me to triumph. Do you understand what I am saying, now? The confession which conquers pride is the confession of One who is Greater than Ourselves, who is Savior.

Well, then, if self-esteem doesn't come from vanity or pride or any of the other ego-serving indulgences of which we are capable, what is it? I'll answer the question immediately, and then come back to it later on. Self- esteem is *confidence in our personal worth* irrespective of the forces that would rob us of it.

God knows that there are such forces in our day. Take those who manipulate us, treat us as "*things.*" Some time ago I came across an article with the subtle title, *The Thingification of the Self.* Who of us doesn't know what this is? You become an "it," an object, a mere surd or cipher.

And what about the *stereotypes,* the putting of the stamp on you whether or not you deserve it, and the franking of that stamp by the fickle assent of public opinion? It may have something to do with your color, or accent, or race or religion. It may have something to do with the clothes you wear, or the job you have, or the area you live in. We all become "one of *them*" to some other group different from us. How depersonalizing! How demeaning! The Master didn't escape it. The religious of his day couldn't stand the fact that he consorted with people of a questionable kind, "tax-gatherers," "wine bibbers," "sinners," "Sabbath breakers," and so on. They whispered behind his back, "He's one of them, don't you know. He's their kind, their ilk!" And so, the stereotypes compounded which would have robbed him of his self-esteem had it not been rooted in a magnificent self-awareness of personal worth.

Think again of the way the *process* robs us of our self-esteem. The machine-like way we are dealt with. British National Health, as socialized medicine is called in the United Kingdom, has a standard joke of the delivery man who brings a package to a hospital and momentarily parks his van outside to find which door to enter. He finds himself before a desk where a clerk with bent head and pen in hand mechanically intones, "Name? Address? Age? Disease?" Too flabbergasted to do anything but answer routinely, except to say "None" for disease, he is X-rayed, blood-tested, and put through all the machine-like system and finally asked, "What are you doing here in such good health?" Answer, "Delivering a package!"

Life often does this to us. It robs us of our self-esteem by "thingification" or stereotype or process. But there is more to it than that. What we do to ourselves frequently depersonalizes us.

Let me speak about that as we think together about *renew-*

*al*. Keep in mind our subject, "God's secret of renewed self-esteem." Wordsworth, in one of his sonnets, says that, "trailing clouds of glory do we come from God, who is our home," but soon "shades of the prison-house" begin to close upon us. Poetically he was speaking about what we do to ourselves. Not only literally do we "get into trouble" with society's rules, but we are far more deeply imprisoned by our habits, guilts, and relationships. You know what that means, and so do I. Before we know it we are trapped in the very situation which seemed so promising, or by the habit that looked so socially attractive, or the relationship which appeared to offer security. All this to say nothing of the way we become victim to our guilts, our fears, our frustrations, and our recurring anxieties.

This is why we are so interested in the issue of personal renewal. We would like to start all over again, begin again, or to use the New Testament idiom, be *born again*.

Why is it, though, that when we think about being born again we fall figuratively into the Nicodemus syndrome? Let me explain. This obviously intelligent seeker, a ruler among religious people, came surreptitiously by night to inquire and to learn. He was told almost abruptly, according to the narrative, that "unless a (person) is born again" he or she cannot enter the Kingdom of God. This threw the man completely, as it throws so many religious people in our own day. He immediately became literal, "How can a man be born again when he is old? Can he enter into his mother's womb and be born?" Unwittingly he expressed what modern psychologists have discovered in all of us, a primeval desire to return to the womb of being. But much more. A longing for the securities and promises and hopes we once knew, the conversion experience that offers a clean slate and a brand new start.

Personally, I think that this is what accounts for both the impact and the attraction of much of the teaching about "born-again" Christians. It is sad how this religious expression has been debased by being attached to all sorts of personal changes. In the old days, it was attached only to the profound change that came into a person's life when repentance and commitment to Jesus Christ were professed. In many parts of the country and in many religious traditions this terminology is still being used. There is something startling, compelling, and challenging about testimonies which describe a complete and dramatic turnabout: "O happy day that fixed my choice when Jesus washed my sins away."

Many of us within the more traditional and formal church settings may wonder wistfully about all this, and some of us, let it be confessed, are a little "put off" because the tendency in the born-again testimony is to speak subjectively. The first-person-singular pronoun (which Gibbon called the most indecent in the English language) plays a dominant role, and the Nicodemus syndrome reappears. There is no such thing as being born again with new genes, new personality traits. A well-known evangelist was once asked, "What's the difference in a curmudgeon after he is born again?" Flashing a quick and knowing smile, the evangelist replied, "He becomes a *Christian* curmudgeon!" What he was saying was that the difference doesn't appear immediately in the person. It is his recognition and response to the need for a power beyond himself to change the direction of his life and enable him to grow in the grace which can change a Saul into a Paul.

That's why the New Testament meaning is "born from *above*," rather than "born again." Nicodemus had to understand that, and so must we if we are to avoid the dangers of subjectivity and pride. Jesus went on to describe the work as akin to the blowing of the wind—"The wind bloweth yet thou canst not tell whence it cometh, or whither it goeth: so is *everyone born of the Spirit*." It's a process which begins with the action of God. We are all "born again in Jesus Christ." This is an indisputable New Testament emphasis. Hear it in its own strange idiom. "As in Adam all die, so in Christ we shall all be made alive." Or, "Praise be to the God and Father of our Lord Jesus Christ! [Notice now where the emphasis is. . .] In His great mercy He has given us *new birth* into a living hope, *through the resurrection* of Jesus Christ from the dead." His glorious resurrection is the new birth, and the power of that stupendous action of God "blows" hither and thither in the lives of those who experience it.

As we look out over Central Park and observe the effects of the winds which whistle promise in the cold days of winter, which spread reproduction with the gentle breezes of spring, which salute fulfillment in the splendor of summer, which scatter myriad colors in the demise of fall, we see *renewal in action.* You can't tell how this wind comes. You can't analyze its mystery. You can't even prove it if you don't want to see its effects. But there it is, taking place before our very eyes, something dynamic not static, something ever-changing not once-for-all as the Nicodemus syndrome wants to make it. "You *can't* tell . . . " said Jesus. Indeed you can't. If you could, you would kill the power in the very act of discovering it.

An untutored Christian who was experiencing this "born again" power in her life, was being heckled. What had taken place? How had she known? How could she prove it? To all these questions she answered disarmingly, "I don't know! All I'm saying is that I give as much as I know of myself to as much as I know of God!" Again, no finished product.

Now I come to the most important truth. We are thinking about *God's secret* of renewed self-esteem. You will recall that earlier we said "self-esteem is *confidence in our personal worth, irrespective of the forces that would rob us of it.*" I want to talk about that now.

What is the secret of that confidence? We've seen how vanity and pride will never support it. We've also discovered how easily we can be robbed of it. So, what can guarantee and sustain it?

We're familiar with the transactional analysis formula—"I'm o.k. . . . you're o.k." But we know that this tit-for-tat affirmation won't stand the test. Supposing we think the other person *isn't* o.k.? You see what I mean, don't you? You can never discover the ultimate secret of self-esteem through disguised double-talk. Do you, perhaps, remember a time when you didn't think much of yourself and a well-meaning friend tried to jostle you along by saying, "You've got to build up your self-confidence!" Didn't you suppress the retort, "You're telling me!"

But self-esteem fundamentally can only be built up when—listen carefully now men and women—it is *conferred* on us. Someone has got to think you are wonderful! Will you permit me very reverently to say that *that someone is God.* The whole meaning of the Gospel is that. God, the heart of this vast and mysterious universe, has come, comes now, to you in Jesus Christ and says, "You matter to me more than anything else!"

That's why this Communion table is prepared for us today. That's why we shall hear again the ancient words of the institution, "my body broken for *you*—my blood shed for *you!*" The message of the Cross of Calvary is:

> God loves *you* unconditionally;
> God esteems *you* unqualifiedly;
> God affirms *you* irrevocably.

And He has spared no limits to show all this to you and me in Jesus Christ. Did you know you counted that much?

I was preaching at a Hundredth Anniversary Lutheran service not long ago, a special reunion of past and present members and friends. There was a Communion service following in which the Pastor gave the elements to those of us kneeling in the chancel. I shall never forget the experience! Quietly he gave me the bread and wine, each time addressing me personally, "Elam! Receive the body of Christ broken for *you!* Receive the blood of Christ shed for *you!*" Do you wonder why I was deeply, deeply moved. Suddenly "the heart of the universe" knew my name and declared that I was worth it! I knew as never before something of what the Apostle Paul meant when he said, "The Son of God who loved *me* and gave himself for *me.*" Are you with me now? This is the most humbling and exalting of experiences. The most searching and affirming of moments. When God tells you that you count without measure to Him. You can get up again forgiven, renewed, confident, "standing tall" in spite of what life or others (or we ourselves) have done to us. That's the Divine Secret of renewed self-esteem which happens not only on Communion Sunday, *but every single day.*

Recently Christopher Nolan was given the prestigious British Whitbread Award for his autobiographical "novel," *Under the Eye of the Clock.* There is nothing spectacular about this latest recognition for this author/poet until you remember that he was born with severe brain damage and from infancy could only communicate with his eyes. His "I can't make my bedamned body do anything" is his verdict, and that body imprisons a brilliant mind. The only way he can type is by means of a pen-like stick attached to his forehead. Each page takes twelve hours of slow, concentrated hard work. But what accounts for the triumph? At three years of age he said he faced the only spark within himself. He knew he was *alive, wanted,* and *loved.* "Accept me for what I am, and I'll accept you for what you are accepted as."

That's what Jesus Christ does. He accepts us for what we are in spite of our limitations and sends us out to "love our neighbor as ourselves." Have we sensed that lately? Do we know that we are spectacularly wanted and loved by the One "in whom we live and move and have our being?"

# 36. The Unseen Benefactors
## John Killinger

Mark 11:1–10

I DON'T SUPPOSE I have ever read this passage (Mark 11:1–10) without wondering about the nameless owners of the colt. Who were they? And what was their connection to Jesus? Were they Jesus' friends Mary, Martha, and Lazarus, who lived in Bethany? Were they friends and neighbors of Mary, Martha, and Lazarus, whom Jesus had come to know on one of his visits? Had Jesus once done some great favor for them, restoring sight to a blind child or making a crippled aunt to walk? The Bible is extremely reticent about them, almost carelessly so.

Jesus merely pointed the disciples to a village and told them they would find the colt tied at the edge of the town. They were to untie it and bring it to him. If anyone asked what they were doing, they were to say, "The Lord has need of it."

There is a sermon in that, isn't there? "The Lord has need of it." What do you suppose we have that the Lord has need of? Do some of us have houses he needs for the homeless? Do some have cars he needs for visiting the lonely? Do some have money he needs for Third World food and medicine, or for

*John Killinger* received his education at Baylor University, the University of Kentucky, Harvard Divinity School, and Princeton Theological Seminary. Dr. Killinger currently is senior minister of the First Congregational Church in Los Angeles, California. He is the author of many books, including *Bread for the Wilderness, Wine for the Journey,* and *The Fundamentals of Preaching.*

wells and agriculture? Do some have brains he needs for organizing new services for the poor in our community, or for teaching us how to make government more responsive to the demands of the gospel? "The Lord has need of it," and who can withhold it, knowing that?

The disciples walked over to the village, and there, just as Jesus had said, they found the colt tied. Wagging their heads together at his strange powers, they started untying the long rope that tethered the colt. And then, also as he said, a woman came out of a nearby house and asked what they were up to. "The Lord has need of it," they said.

"Oh fine," she said, "take it away."

Just like that. No "Let me see your credentials" or "How do I know the Lord sent you?" It was as simple as if it were something she did every day, letting some strange men lead the colt away.

We assume the owners got the colt back. Jesus said they would, though there is no record of the return. Just this quick, unembellished reference to the event itself. And no mention of the owners' names.

Perhaps the owners were the sort of people who never get their names in the paper and never get publicly mentioned for anything. There are people like that, you know. They appear to have an almost genetic aptitude for being overlooked when credits are handed out. Like the poor woman who slaves over the stove in the kitchen preparing a church dinner. The master of ceremonies thanks the people who set up all the tables, and the people who laid on the silverware, and the people who were responsible for decorations, and the people who sold tickets, and then completely fails to mention her. You know there are such people who are naturally overlooked all the time, because some of you are this way yourselves, aren't you? You almost have to wear a sign to get noticed.

Yet how important these unseen, nameless benefactors are! Think of them for a moment: The teacher who inspired Shakespeare to write. The campaign manager who enabled Lincoln to get to the White House. The congressman who helped Dwight Eisenhower get into West Point. The man who hired Mozart to write a requiem Mass. The woman who gave Lloyd Douglas the idea for his novel *The Robe.*

Did you ever hear that story? She was not really nameless, though few people today have heard of her. Her name was Hazel McCann, and she lived in Canton, Ohio. One day she wrote Lloyd Douglas a note inquiring about the Roman soldier who won the seamless robe of Jesus when Jesus was crucified. Was there any legend, she wondered, about the man and what happened to him after he acquired the robe? The idea took hold in Douglas, first as a short story appropriate for the Easter season, and eventually as a novel. When *The Robe* finally appeared, it carried a dedication to Hazel McCann, and Douglas traveled to Canton, Ohio, to present a copy to her and be photographed with her for the local papers.

Life is a web of people and circumstances, and we should love it all, not just part of it. Behind every great or famous person, there is a network of smaller people, often anonymous people, without whose efforts he or she would not have become great or famous.

I sometimes watch the teams making movies here in our church. The stars are there, and they're the ones the people want to see. But there are always dozens of other persons arranging lights, setting the scenes, doing the makeup, directing the picture, making sure everything is right. Without them, the stars would be nothing. And I'm happy to say, the stars usually know this. They don't behave like prima donnas, they behave like ordinary people, because they realize they need the little people, the unknown people.

Jesus was wonderful with little people. He knew he was important, for he understood his mission as being the most significant mission ever entrusted to a human being. Yet he never let this put him off from the anonymous folk around him. He dealt with each one on a personal basis, granting favors of healing, forgiveness, and friendship. We tend to see only him when he enters a scene. After all, he was the star. But he saw and honored everybody else. He knew that life is filled with unseen benefactors, unsung heroes, unrecognized donors.

Part of what the gospel has to give us is a new ability to spot these people, to see them without somebody's putting a neon sign over their heads that says, "This is somebody important; notice him or notice her!" We're clearly bad about this, aren't we? We're so apt to miss the beauty or grace of a person until somebody else notices it and points it out to us.

Bishop Gerald Kennedy told a wonderful story on himself in his autobiography *While I'm on My Feet.* He said he was in Australia on a speaking tour and his hosts were working him hard. He had to spend every spare minute between speaking engagements going over his thoughts for the next presentation. One morning when the hotel maid came to clean his room he took his chair and went into the hall and sat there, continuing to work, so that he wouldn't fall behind in his schedule. As he was trying to concentrate, someone in an adjoining room began to play the violin. "This is all I need!" he complained to himself, and picked up his chair and went back to his room. "Oh," said the maid, "did you hear Mr. Menuhin?" "Who?" asked Kennedy. "Yehudi Menuhin. He's your neighbor down the hall. He's getting ready for a big concert." Ashamed of himself, Kennedy took his chair back out into the hall and listened to the great artist rehearsing. It was a wonderful concert, he said—once he realized who was doing the playing!

Aren't we all like that? In Kennedy's place, we would have done the same thing, and failed to appreciate the music until we learned who the player was. But the music wouldn't have been a whit less wonderful if it had been produced by an unknown teenager from Beirut or a little old lady from Texarkana.

We should pray for the ability to see the richness and beauty in people regardless of who they are and what their station in life is.

I think of another illustration of this that was provided by my friend David Burhans, the chaplain of the University of Richmond in Virginia. David's brother Rollin Jr. was graduating from Harvard, and their father had gone to Harvard to pick him up and take him home. For some reason I have probably forgotten, they did not have time to stay for the commencement services, and were walking around Harvard Yard to their car at the very hour when the degrees were being granted. As they rounded the wall at Massachusetts Avenue, the father spotted a long, black limousine standing by the curb near an entrance to the Yard. He stopped his son and said, "Look, son. I'll bet that car is waiting for Konrad Adenauer, the chancellor of West Germany, who was to receive an honorary degree today. Let's stand here a moment and see him when he comes out." They waited a few minutes. Two elderly women came through the gate and headed toward the car. A driver quickly leapt out and opened the door for them. Disappointed, the two men proceeded to their car and began the long trip home to Kentucky. Some days later, said David, they picked up a newspaper back in Louisville and read about the commencement at Harvard, and suddenly realized who the two ladies were: Helen Keller and her companion Anne Sullivan had been awarded honorary doctorates by the university. It was a lesson neither of the men has forgotten!

But what if they had not been Helen Keller and Anne Sullivan? What if they had been merely two frail women who had gone to Harvard University that day to see a favorite grandson graduate? God would have looked on the mystery of their lives with the same tenderness and love he felt for the women of fame and glory, for they too would have played an important part in the makeup and history of the world. Everyone plays an important part; there are no secondary roles in life.

Once we realize this, and know that all people are sacramental, capable of revealing God to us, then we see that the anonymous person who loaned Jesus a colt is as important in the gospel story as the disciples themselves, or even—is it a heresy to say it?—as important as Jesus himself. Maybe that's the message God was trying to get across by sending his only Son to die on the cross for the sins of the world—that *every* person is as important in God's eyes as his Son, and that therefore we ought to treat every person as important.

It hurts me to see one human being mistreating another. Not just because I am sentimental and tenderhearted, but because it is religiously and theologically wrong, because God himself doesn't like it. Jesus said, "Whoever causes one of these little ones to stumble and fall, it were better if a millstone were tied around his neck and he were drowned in the sea." That's strong language; it says how God feels about mistreating people. And it especially hurts me to see anyone mistreating anyone else in the church. In the *church*, of all places! For the church is Jesus' family, the church is the institution of Christ, the church is the lengthened shadow of the Son of God. And when I see someone who is naturally cantankerous or proud or thoughtless turn on someone in the church, maybe someone who is simpleminded, or of a different color, or with a different accent, and say something harsh or cutting or unkind to that person, it races through me like the sudden blast from a smelter's furnace. I want to say, "Shame on you! How can you behave that way toward one of God's children?!"

Then I'm caught in a bind. That person is one of God's children too, and I'm sorry for him or her that he doesn't know any better, or can't control his temper any more suitably. For I remember that Jesus loved even poor Judas, the disciple who betrayed him, who sold him for money, and that Jesus loved the fickle crowds that disowned him on the day he was crucified, and that Jesus prayed for his persecutors, "Father, forgive them, for they know not what they do."

Jesus, you see, had a mature understanding of life and the world. He was able to love everyone, to see the special gifts and beauty in all human beings, regardless of what they did to him. Maturity. Do you know what it is? Maturity is when we can accept every gift as personal and no injury as personal, when we can forgive others from a cross as Jesus did, and bless a thief in the hour of our injury, and be satisfied with God even when we are hurting more than we have ever hurt in our lives. That's maturity. That's the way Jesus was. That's what Jesus had.

"Go, and take the colt, and, if anyone asks you, say, 'The Lord has need of it.' " The world is a tapestry, and everybody is part of the fabric. Life is a mosaic, and even the colts and owners of colts are important in it. Thank God, we're *all* important!

# 37. A Hope That Will Not Disappoint

*Bill Kynes*

Luke 24: 13–35

WE THOUGHT we could trust the *military,*
    but then came *Vietnam;*
We thought we could trust the *politicians,*
    but then came *Watergate;*
We thought we could trust the *engineers,*
    but then came the *Challenger disaster;*
We thought we could trust our *broker,*
    but then came *Black Monday;*
We thought we could trust the *preachers,*
    but then came *PTL and Jimmy Swaggart.*

So, who can I trust? Who dare I trust?
    It seems there are only three left—me, myself, and I.

This would-be confession of an American Baby-Boomer
    expresses a sentiment widespread in our society—
Hardened by disappointment and disillusionment,
    many have grown cynical about notions of faith and trust.

---

*Bill Kynes* was born in Ocala, Florida. He was educated at the University of Florida; the University of Oxford, England; Trinity Evangelical Divinity School; and the University of Cambridge, England, where he received his doctorate. He was a Rhodes Scholar while at Cambridge. Since 1986, he has served as pastor of the National Evangelical Free Church, Annandale, Virginia. This sermon was preached on Easter Sunday.

They've been let down once too often, and that's enough—
    They withdraw into a protective shell,
        insulating themselves from the trauma of betrayal.

I'm sure we've all at least felt the temptation to do that at some point.
Why take the chance?
    Trusting someone only makes you vulnerable.
        You can't let down your guard these days—
            You'll just get yourself slapped in the face!

This was a temptation, no doubt, that was felt strongly by the two people of our gospel story, walking down the road from Jerusalem to the small village of Emmaus on the afternoon of that first Easter Day.

Only a few days had passed since Cleopas and his companion
    had joined the throngs of pilgrims going up to the capital
        for the Passover Festival.[1]
Never had they gone with such enthusiasm and excitement—
    For it was rumored that Jesus would be there—

Jesus of Nazareth—a prophet, powerful in word and deed
                before God and all the people—
Perhaps this was the time that he would assert himself,
    and bring about the mighty deliverance of Israel—
        a deliverance for which they had so long prayed.

Perhaps at long last
    he would lead an uprising against the tyranny of the Romans;
Jesus would bring peace and justice to our land, they thought.
    If anyone could do it—he was the one.

Just a few days ago . . . now it seems as if an eternity had passed!

We had hoped that Jesus was the one who was going to redeem Israel—
    but now this disaster—this total wreck of hope,

this awful disappointment.

These two could very well have been eyewitnesses
of that procession of death moving out from the city to
Calvary.
They had seen the crown of thorns, the jeering and hooting of
the crowds—
the nails in his hands and feet.
They had seen him crucified,
and all their hopes and dreams crucified with him—
Dead, buried and hidden forever in a tomb.

It was all over—it would never happen now.

They thought they could trust in Jesus,
but then came *the cross.*


Of all the disappointments of life, this has to be the most
shattering.
—To be disappointed in Christ.
To feel that perhaps God Himself can't be counted on to make
sense of life.
—To make things right again.
"To see the Kingdom of heaven sabotaged by the strategies
of Satan."[2]

We hear much about the scientific, humanistic thinking
that permeates our modern world,
But I'm convinced that much skepticism and agnosticism
today
has its root in *cynicism*, cynicism pure and simple—
Many simply *fear* that even God cannot be trusted.

A tragedy strikes—
the death of a loved one, the birth of a malformed child—
"God how could you let this happen to me!"

You pray and pray and nothing changes;
Your marriage problem won't go away;
a marriage partner never appears—

"God aren't you there? God, don't you care?"

The Bible assures us of the sovereign control of God
    over all the affairs of our lives—
He arranges, he orders, all things according to his will.
"In his heart a man plans his course,
    but the Lord determines his steps," we read in the Book
    of Proverbs.

Or as Thomas À Kempis paraphrased that truth—
    "Man proposes, but God disposes."

But for many the version given by Cervantes in his story of
Don Quixote
    seems more to the point:
        "Man appoints, but God disappoints."


Even Christians are subject to this pressure—

In John Bunyan's *Pilgrim's Progress,*
    Atheist mocks Christian about his journey to the Celestial
    City—
He roars with laughter when told that Christian is heading for
Mount Zion.

Christian seems shaken by it—
"What is the meaning of your laughter?" he asks.
Atheist replies, "I laugh to see what an ignorant person you
are, to take upon you so tedious a journey and yet [you] are
like to have nothing but *travel* for your pains."

"Why man?" Christian queries, "Do you think we shall not be
received?"
"Received!" Atheist scoffs,
    "There is no such place as you dream of in all the world."

Is there no such place?
Will we be disappointed in the end?
    We all have an inner voice that begs an answer to these
    questions.

Will we find ourselves like these two on the road to Emmaus, wondering if it will all end tragically on the cross?

But these two travelers of Luke's Gospel
      had heard some bewildering rumors—

*"Some of our women amazed us.*
*They went to the tomb early this morning*
   *but didn't find his body*
*They came and told us that they had seen a vision of angels,*
   *who said he was alive.*
*Then some of our companions went to the tomb*
   *and found it just as the women had said,*
      *but him they did not see."* (verses 21–24)

Perhaps you've heard some rumors, too—
You've heard people talk about some strange things—
   You've heard them talk as if God were real
     and as if he could be known and loved personally.
   Maybe you've heard rumors
     of people who pray and are sure that God hears them.
   Maybe you've heard them talk of something they call eternal life,
which begins here and now, and goes on forever in the presence of God.

There are such rumors going around—
   Would that they were true, you may say—
     but you dare not believe them.
You refuse to be disappointed yet again.

That's perhaps how these two felt
   as they were trudging dejectedly along the seven-mile road back home.
When quite unexpectedly they were joined on their journey by a Stranger—

"What are you discussing?" he asks them.
   The question is almost as shocking as the answer—
"Haven't you heard?

"Are you the only one living in Jerusalem
>who doesn't know the things that have happened there in
>these days?"

"What things?" the stranger asks—.
"Why, the things about Jesus of Nazareth!— .
>Jesus the powerful prophet who was to redeem our
>nation—
Have you not heard what happened to him two days ago?
Have you not heard of Calvary?"

Imagine asking *that* Stranger such a question!
The irony of these words is almost ludicrous—
>This is the stuff situation comedies are made of—

"They were kept from recognizing him," Luke tells us.
>But we the readers know the truth—this is *Jesus* they're
>talking to!

There is humor here in the absurd discrepancy
>between perception and reality.

If only they knew who they were talking to!
>They would realize that everything they were saying was
>ridiculous!

How does the stranger respond to all this?
We might have expected him
>to commiserate with these two in their sad state
>to cheer them up with soft words of comfort and
>hope.

Instead he delivers what can only be described as a stinging
rebuke—
>" 'How foolish you are,
and how slow of heart to believe
>all that the prophets have spoken!
Did not the Christ have to suffer these things
>and then enter his glory?'
And beginning with Moses and all the Prophets, he explained to them

*what was said in all the Scriptures concerning himself."*

You think God has disappointed you, but you're wrong—
Just *search the Scriptures,* he says to them—
And you'll find that Jesus spoke the truth,
    the truth of his heavenly Father,
        the truth of the Scriptures—Why won't you believe
        it?

The cross—
  it was the greatest injustice ever perpetrated in the history
  of the world.
Yet the cross, with all its agony, was a part of God's perfect
plan—
    his plan to redeem his people, to bring glory to himself.

Search the Scriptures and you will see that God was there on
the cross—
    bearing the sin of the world.
Search the Scriptures and you will see
        that evil will never gain the final victory—
    God is always and forever in control—He reigns
    supreme.

Search the Scriptures, Jesus the stranger says to them,
    and you would know that no grave could ever hold me
    prisoner.

And what Jesus said to those two on the road, he says to us
also—
Search the Scriptures—for God's truth,
    and you will know that he is worthy of your trust—
        you will know the reality of his risen Son Jesus.

But *how* can we know that these things are true?
I could present you with the rational arguments for the truth
of the Bible—
particularly, I could give the historical evidence for the resurrection of Jesus.

There are plenty good reasons

for believing the things that are written in this
book—
And Jesus, it seems, *reasoned* with these men from the Word of
God.

But notice what they say in verse 32, looking back on this
conversation—
*"Were not our hearts burning within us*
*while he talked with us on the road*
*and opened up the Scriptures to us?"*

If you're looking for sure *proofs* of the truth of the Scriptures
I offer *none,*
except that which is offered here—
the *"burning of our hearts within us"*—
the work of the Holy Spirit of God
confirming in our hearts the truth of the Word of
God.

Do you feel that God has disappointed you?
*Search the Scriptures for the truth of God*—
allow God's Spirit to touch your heart with its truth—
and you may find that you hadn't got the whole story.

These two travelers hadn't—
for Jesus *hadn't* let them down—
God's Word testified that Christ's path to *glory*
had to be by way of a *cross.*

So you wonder if God can be trusted?
Search the Scriptures—
Go home and take that Bible off the shelf,
dust it off—
and begin reading one of the Gospels—
By God's grace you may find your heart burning within
you
as you discover the kind of God who is revealed in those
pages.

But there's another way that we may discover God's

trustworthiness—
Not only should we search the Scriptures for God's truth,
  but also we should *open our eyes to Christ's presence.*

Verse 30—"*When he was at the table with them, he took bread,
    gave thanks, broke it and began to give it to them.
Then their eyes were opened and they recognized him . . . "*

There are many of us who are like the Apostle Thomas—
"Unless I see the nail marks in his hands, . . .
    and put my hand into his side,
        I will not believe it." (John 20:27)

Or there's Woody Allen's view—
    "If only God would give me a clear sign!
        Like making a large deposit in my name at a Swiss
        bank."

"God, if you're there, just give me a sign," we plead.

His reply to us?
    I'm already here. Just open your eyes and you will see.

The Scriptures *testify* to it—
    but this is the *proof* of the resurrection of Christ—
        when we meet him ourselves.

There was an empty tomb,
    but only a personal encounter with the risen Christ
        makes that empty tomb a symbol of the victory of
        God.

The Scriptures tell us this morning that Jesus was raised from
the dead—
    that he ascended to his Father's throne in heaven.
If he is, indeed, *risen* as it says,
        then he is *here* in our midst today.

Are your eyes opened to see him?
Can you see him in the lives of people in this room—
    lives that have been profoundly affected by his presence
    and power.

Can you hear his voice in the preaching of his word—
  through the music, in our prayers,
    is he speaking to your heart this morning.
      "Is he saying to you, 'Listen, I've got something to tell
      you.' "

Open your eyes to Christ's presence—
How often has God in Christ been right there in front of us,
  in the events of our lives, but we have failed to recognize
  him.

Perhaps you've just come through a hard time—
    Don't just thank your lucky stars—
    It may have been the Savior of your Soul,
      traveling there beside you all the time, unrecognized.

I feel certain that the angels in heaven
      are tempted to laugh at us, if not pity us, from time to
      time—
There is something of the comedic, something of the ridiculous, in our lives
    when, like those two travelers,
      the One we so desire to see is closer to us than we can
      imagine.

Is he still just a stranger to you?
He needn't be—
    Open your eyes—and let him reveal himself to you.


But perhaps you're saying to yourself—
    I just can't—I can't see him—as much as I would like, I
feel blind to him.

I can sympathize with your condition—
      and in fact our passage supports it—
For it doesn't say that these two *opened* their eyes,
      but that their eyes *were opened*.

This spiritual sight was an act of God's Spirit,
      as an evidence of God's grace in their lives—

If you can't see, but want to—
I have one piece of advice and one promise for you this
morning—

> Seek and you shall find;
> Knock and the door shall be opened to you;
> Ask and you shall receive.

It is only to open *hearts* that God grants the privilege of open
*eyes.*
> As an act of faith, ask him to heal your blindness.

These two travelers had seen him—
> They got up, Luke tells us,
> and at once returned the seven miles to Jerusalem to tell the
> others.
> "It is true! The Lord has risen."

We thought we *couldn't* trust in God,
> but then came the resurrection.

Suddenly the cross did not appear as the tragic end,
> but as a new beginning—
> the true meaning of the cross suddenly became clear—
> it was a death *for us,* for *our* sin.

"They had hoped that Jesus would have been the deliverer of
Israel;
> They knew now He was the conqueror of the world."[3]

The Lord has demonstrated once and for all that he can be
trusted.
> That's what the resurrection is all about.

The resurrection of Jesus is the sign and seal
> of God's loving purpose as we look *back* on the cross.
It is God's promise for the *future*—he has conquered death
forever.
And it is the nearness of God in the *present*—
> He is risen—he is here with us.

Let me ask you—

What's your conception of Christianity this morning?
Is it merely a vague sort of theism—
   like that printed on our dollar bill—"In God we trust"?
Is it a series of articles in a creed—
   doctrines which you would agree with
      if asked in a public opinion poll?
Does it consist of a list of ethical principles—
      sort of like the Boy Scout Pledge?

Let me tell you,
   Christianity is the *resurrection* or it is nothing.

It is trusting the *crucified* Christ, that's true—
   Jesus is the lamb of God who takes away the sin of the
   world
—but that trust in the Christ of *the cross*
   comes only through knowing the Christ of the *empty tomb*—
   the risen Christ, who is alive forever.

The rumors are true!—
   We can know him and enjoy his love!

We live in a world that is distrustful of trust;
   It seems to have little faith in faith.

It's easy to become cynical.
   So many people have let us down—

But Jesus won't—
   I assure you, Jesus won't.
   The *Scriptures* assure you, Jesus won't.
   The *resurrection* assures you, Jesus won't let you down.

No one who puts his trust in him will ever be disappointed.

## NOTES

1. On the disappointment of the disciples, I am indebted to James S. Stewart, "The Christ of the Emmaus Road," in *King Forever* (London: Hodder and Stoughton, 1974), 50–52.
   2. *Ibid.*, 51.
   3. *Ibid.*, 56.

# 38. The Day Doug Came to Church

*Roger Lovette*

Ephesians 2:11–17

ABOUT ONCE A YEAR, after the service had already started, you could count on it. Down the aisle, right down to the
front seat, in the center, Doug would come. He wore overalls,
before overalls were in vogue. He always wore a cap, which he
never removed, and he carried his shoe-shine box. And there
he would sit, to the mortification of everybody in the well-
dressed room, until the Benediction finally sounded.

When he walked in the children would huddle closer to
their parents. A tension would grip the whole congregation in
that little mill church.

Doug, in his late forties, was the village character. Low
mentally, shoe-shine box always under his arm, he made his
living on the corner of 48th Street and Second Avenue on the
nickels and dimes people paid him for shining their shoes. He
had a terrible speech impediment and was scary looking, He
was the central character in a hundred children's nightmares.

When Doug would saunter into church, teenagers would
giggle. The adults would just sit there stone-faced in their

*Roger Lovette* is a native of Columbus, Georgia. He received his
doctorate from Lexington Theological Seminary and is currently
senior minister at Second Baptist Church in Memphis, Tennessee. Dr.
Lovette has written four books and numerous articles for a variety of
publications.

Sunday finery and act as if Doug wasn't even there. The little kids would roll their eyes around at Doug if they thought he wasn't looking at them and their mamas would gently nudge them back into line with an elbow. And the preacher would try to keep things moving until, finally, thank God, the service was over. And to the relief of everyone, Doug would beat the preacher to the door and be setting up for business on the corner. The poor fool didn't know you didn't break the Sabbath by shining shoes on Sunday in the Bible belt in the 1940s.

I have often wondered why Doug came to church. I am pretty sure that this lonely, strange man died as he lived with his deep needs largely unfulfilled.

Doug's difficulty is an age-old problem. In the New Testament, the people of Ephesus certainly faced this issue of not fitting in. So did all the churches in Asia Minor. The unity of the church was the most pressing pastoral problem of that time. Perhaps it has always been. The mood of disconnection was there. Not quite fitting in. Distant. Apart. Feeling a little strange. Not at home. The disconnections were everywhere: Gentiles and Jews, women and men, old and young, rich and poor, the enslaved and the free.

When Paul wrote to Ephesus he called them Gentiles. He used the term "uncircumcised." They did not bear the mark. And this is how he categorized them: "Remember that you were at that time separated from Christ, alienated from the commonwealth of Israel, and strangers to the covenants of promise, having no hope and without God in the world" (Eph. 2:12).

We have all felt it sometimes, this alienation, this feeling of being a stranger. I felt it most keenly two summers ago in Belgium. My son and I were on a ferry boat that would take us from Dover, England, to the coast of Belgium where we would then board a bus for Amsterdam. And my son, leaving his ferry seat, hit his head on a plastic light fixture and cut his scalp. I discovered that head wounds bleed terribly. It looked as if he had been mortally wounded. And the bus driver took a look at him and said he would have to get off the bus and go to a hospital. And so, at four o'clock in the morning in a cab, driven by a driver who could not speak English, I looked out the window and saw billboards in a foreign language. And then we got to a hospital where all the doctors and nurses wore clogs, spoke in broken English, and could not understand us. They put eleven stitches in his head, admitted him to the hospital, spoke of a concussion and even brain damage, and said we might have to be there five days or longer. I had no Belgian francs. I only had Dutch gilders and English pounds and American dollars. We had missed our bus. I did not know how sick he was. And there was no one familiar to turn to. We left the hospital six hours later, but it was a scary time.

But we don't have to be in a foreign country to feel alienation. Sometimes we feel this distance sitting around the table with the people we have known all our lives. And sometimes, like Doug, we feel the big chill on Sunday morning. Some of us have felt it when the doctor calls and says: "Could you and your husband be in my office at eleven?" Paul describes the mood well. Separated. Alienated. Strangers. Hopeless. Wondering where God is, if there is a God at all. This is the mood of disconnection. Like Paul and Ephesus and Doug, we have all faced this dilemma from time to time.

Sometimes sin brings on the feeling. Our own or somebody else's. It cuts us off. That's the worst thing sin does. It isolates us. We have all known it. But sometimes it is simply the mood we are in. Or the roller-coaster of body chemistry or moving to another place or a terrible business deal or a stretch of insomnia or worrying about someone we love. Sometimes the disconnection comes from pressure, pressure, pressure. Many things bring on this mood: being gay in a straight world, black in South Africa, nonathletic in a jock society. Sometimes it is being old, with varicose veins, in a mini-skirted world. Walking down the hall of a nursing home recently a little lady scarcely five feet tall looked up at me as we walked and confessed: "Sometimes I feel like I am a thousand years old." This is the mood of disconnection.

One of the ways that many of us try to deal with this mood

is to do what Paul recommended and Doug tried. We go to church. James Dittes has said that any time any of us decide to get up and go to church we are reaching out beyond ourselves to something greater. We are trying to make connections, to close the gap, to find something we didn't have before.

Paul paints a beautiful word picture of what ought to happen in church. "But now in Christ Jesus you who once were far off have been brought near in the blood of Christ. For he is our peace, who has made us both one, and has broken down the dividing wall of hostility, by abolishing in his flesh the law of commandments and ordinances, that he might create in himself one new man in place of the two, so making peace, and might reconcile us both to God in one body through the cross, thereby bringing the hostility to an end" (Eph. 2:13–16).

Paul says that Jesus Christ closes the gap. In Jesus Christ we who once were far off are now brought near. I wonder if Paul was not thinking of that time in his own life when he had been struck blind by God. And there in the dark he did not know what to do and Ananias came and whispered, "Brother Saul." And the scales fell off and he had a whole new family, the church. And I wonder if, as he wrote those lines, he did not remember what happened after his long absence in the Arabian desert. There he tried to sort it all out and wondered what he was supposed to do with his life. He had given up so much to follow Jesus and nobody seemed to care and everybody seemed suspicious and the church was not sure of him at all. Did he not remember as he wrote those words, the day that Barnabas came and took a chance and put his own reputation on the line, twisting the church's arm all the time as he said: "This is our new brother, Paul, aren't we glad to have him?" That's how it happened, Paul said. *In Christ.* But Paul knew, deep in his heart, that God had used Ananias and Barnabas and how many more to close the gap.

What was the result of all of this? *Peace.* Not the absence of war, Paul knew his audience far too well. He knew that peace never was the absence of conflict. But, despite the difficulties, he makes us both one, brothers and sisters. He tears down all the walls and brings the hostility to an end. And, in his very body, the Lord Jesus created one new person in place of two.

Paul follows the term, peace, with a strong word, *katalla-gete*. The Father reconciles us. He brings us together. He makes a friend out of an enemy, even ourselves, especially ourselves.

And then the old Apostle returned to the word he had used earlier: *peace*. For this gospel is not doctrine or even theory. There is nothing to learn or do or even be. For the end result of real faith is a connection that brings, at the heart of it all, peace.

An amazing thing happens. Through him we both, friend and enemy, liberal and conservative, Republican and Democrat, have access to one father. The father makes brothers and sisters of us all.

And so the symphony continues. We are no longer strangers and sojourners. This word, stranger, means visitor. Not a very good word to use in church. For in the church of Jesus Christ there are no visitor's cards. We will all be the same and we are to open our arms and accept and love one another despite our differences.

Dag Hammarskjöld tells us of going to church one Sunday in New York where they recognized him as a visitor. They made a big to-do about his being Secretary-General of the United Nations and taking time from his busy schedule to come to church. He wrote of that experience: "I never went back!"

Paul says in the church of Jesus Christ we will all be members of the household of God. We are now part of the family, the clan, *oikos*. The word means house—no, it goes deeper than that. This is our home. We find that amazing place that, "When you have to go there, They have to take you in."[1] Home.

Do you remember the play *The Elephant Man?* He was ugly and misshapen and everybody made fun of him. He was the brunt of a thousand jokes and so miserable he wanted to die. But a surgeon from a London hospital saw more. The physician took this pathetic human being in and loved him and gave him a chance to be who he was. And on stage, before our eyes, this misshapen creature began to change. Love and acceptance transformed his life. And the most wonderful moment in the play comes when the Elephant Man, John Merrick, says: "This is my home. This is my home!" He had, at long last, found a place of acceptance where being ugly did not matter and being strange was inconsequential. Why did this story of the Elephant Man strike such a chord? Because we see in him something of ourselves. For there is, at the bottom of the well of every heart, that deep, deep need to be connected, to be part of something big and special and enduring.

To say, from the depths of our being, this is my home. To discover finally, the connection. This is what Sunday is all about. This is what church is all about. And this is what faith is all about.

> Therefore remember that at one time you
> Gentiles in the flesh, called the uncircumcision
> by what is called the circumcision, which is
> made in the flesh by hands—remember that
> you were at that time separated from Christ,
> alienated from the commonwealth of Israel,
> and strangers to the covenants of promise,
> having no hope and without God in the world.
> But now in Christ Jesus you who once were far
> off have been brought near in the blood of
> Christ. For he is our peace, who has made us
> both one, and has broken down the dividing
> wall of hostility, by abolishing in his flesh the
> law of commandments and ordinances, that he
> might create in himself one new man in place
> of the two so making peace, and might
> reconcile us both to God in one body through
> the cross, thereby bringing the hostility to an
> end. And he came and preached peace to you
> who were far off and peace to those who were
> near; for through him we both have access in

one Spirit to the Father. So then you are no
longer strangers and sojourners, but you are
fellow citizens with the saints and members of
the household of God.
(Eph. 2:11–19)

NOTES

1. Robert Frost, from "The Death of the Hired Man," in *Complete Poems of Robert Frost* (New York: Rinehart and Winston, 1965), 53.

# 39. The Final Giants
## Calvin Miller

2 Samuel 21:14–22

## Introduction

Near the beginning of David's life stands a giant! At the end of his life there are four. But David fights the final giants differently than Goliath. All of our lives, it seems, we struggle against the odds while the giants multiply. And every wise man must mature in the art of giant-fighting. For life hurries past the stamina it needs. The frame is too soon bent, the effort spent, and the fire sleeps cold upon the flint. If, in the salad days of life, the giants keep on coming, we must learn to fight with brains when the brawn is gone.

Defeating these final giants is possible, but only to the degree that we can change the way we fight. Those who cannot change the direction and mode of their struggle will die of inflexibility. And even if they're not dead enough to bury, they will be far too dead to make a difference in their world.

---

*Calvin Miller* was born in Oklahoma. He was educated at Oklahoma Baptist University and Midwestern Baptist Theological Seminary, from which he received his Doctor of Ministry degree. Since 1966 he has served as pastor of the Westside Church in Omaha, Nebraska, a Baptist congregation that has grown from 10 members to more than 2,500 during his pastorate. Dr. Miller is the author of nineteen books of popular theology and inspiration.

## I. Burying Yesterday (2 Samuel 21:14)

Yesterday is too much with us and keeps us from challenging tomorrow. So it is most significant that as David faces the future he buries the bones of Saul. Saul was king in the glorious days of David's early battles. Now, at long last, in the later years of his reign he buries the bones of his old conquests. We can only guess why they were not buried earlier. Yet these restless skeletons, like old Halloween doorhangers, were oddly representative of old victories. Saul had hated and pursued David. He had sought to kill him. Now he is only bones and the visible trophy of David's survival. But old trophies must be buried, for only then is David ready to look to the future. Old trophies do not prepare us for tomorrow's giants. We cannot walk into meaning or significance through fondling yesterday's victories.

Change is always hard work, but its salary is life. To change our outer world means we have already altered our inner perceptions: and that's the hardest work of change. For Goliath, in his most fearsome form, is inward. Giants are always bigger in conception than reality. The real Goliath, therefore, is the terror of idea—the denizen of hatred unmet; the phantom of decisions unmade. Such inner giants stand and shout their rallying words of ostracism or acceptance: words like "liberal" and "conservative."

The words "liberal" and "conservative" forever puzzle me. There are instances where people call me a liberal and instances where I wear the conservative label. Facing the need to define my enemies, I constantly reevaluate what those words mean. The word "liberal" comes from the Latin word *liber*, to be free, unbound by anything, especially the past. The word "conservative" (from the Latin, *con* and *servo*) means "to save" or "to keep" what's best from the past.

There are always great values that come packaged in the studied traditions of yesteryear. Consider the longevity of family life in 1870 before it eroded so disastrously. Near the end of the nineteenth century, there was only one divorce for every thirty-four marriages in America. By 1900 there was one divorce for every twelve marriages. By 1940 there was one divorce for every five marriages. This last year, there was one divorce for every two marriages.[1] We do not want to abandon those values of the past. In allegiance to those values we are conservative, and unashamedly so.

But remember, the word "liberal" implies that somehow the world is changing, and we must not strap ourselves to the outmoded and unusable past. When we barnacle our value system to the past, we stumble blindly into the future. We sit backward in the trenches facing away from the future with its fickle and fluctuating transitions. It is said that when Adam and Eve left Eden together, Adam turned to Eve and said, "My dear, we are living in a time of transition." All time is in transition, ever on the move. Still, God never sits backwise, fondling old victories. He rather stands facing into the winds, beckoning us to the future, which is the ultimate address for either God or ourselves.

Malcolm Muggeridge confesses with some shame and humility in his autobiography that in 1933 he thought communism was the last best hope of man. He left England with *The Manchester Guardian* to go serve in Moscow as a correspondent. He said he went there believing that he would never in his life go back to England again. He believed he would die in Russia, the golden new state. But as he began to suspect and later to be sure of the atrocities of Stalinization, he sent his articles back home to *The Manchester Guardian*, which never published them. It was impossible, he said, for English liberals to come to believe that communism was not the golden dream they wanted so to believe. They wanted to believe Stalin the legitimate messiah for a golden age and not the ideological butcher of millions and millions of his own countrymen. Disillusionment is an unwelcome friend, but never honest. Gradually Muggeridge had to admit that he was more of a conservative than he thought. He changed the way he fought the giants and even the way he identified who they were.

Generally I'm a conservative, and I prefer the title. I (having been called so many things in life) can even tolerate being called a fundamentalist. But I always have to realize that Jesus was even in trouble with the real conservatives of his day. Thus Christ teaches me that it is hard to be so far right that there is not someone still "righter" who will call me a leftist. Honestly, Jesus was a liberal. All you had to do to prove it is ask the Pharisees.

The Pharisees were holding onto yesterday's values so tightly they were insecure with new ideas. The right-wingers demonstrate my dichotomy: I always like saying that I'm a conservative, especially when compared to major newspaper editors or Supreme Court justices. But I try to listen to the most avant-garde understanding that God himself is avant-garde. Faith itself is venture and no person of faith holds to the bones of God, crying, "See here, God! Here is what I once did!"

I do believe there was only one great idea to come out of the first century: *Grace!* The conservatives made no place for it in Jesus' day. The Pharisees were too legalistic to give *grace* room. This dynamic, liberal grace cast off old skeletons and cried with Isaiah 55:1, "Ho, everyone that thirsteth, come ye to the waters." Now, of course, grace is a conservative idea. But back then it was brand-new. Brand-new ideas are resisted by people who just don't want to change.

Ah, but change . . . How good it is when we remain open to it. How we grow as we change. Change makes us less harsh, more human. Change makes us more compassionate, less cocksure of ourselves. But David teaches us that yesterday's trophies cannot make us certain that we will conquer tomorrow's calamities. The bones of Saul are piteous witness to the needs of today.

I don't like tobacco (particularly in my car or house). My anti-smoking view isn't particularly biblical. But I confess now to my shame that one of my very first sermons dealt with the issue of smoking. Steeped in the fundamentalist hangups of the 1950s, it seemed to me then that my no-nonsense, down-with-all-appearance-of-evil sermon was right. I once thundered rebuke over all nicotine. "If God had wanted us to smoke he would have vented our sinuses with a chimney." So I decided I would stamp out the sin of smoking in our congregation. Admittedly, the sin was not widespread in our little country church. To my knowledge, nobody in the church smoked except for Harry C., who did not have a chimney. Poor Harry! I can't believe that I would deliver a whole sermon to one man out of fifty, but I did. After church that Sunday, Harry, who didn't deserve my open rebuke, walked around me quietly at the door of the church. Everyone who didn't smoke told me it was a wonderful sermon. I insinuated in that sermon that Harry and his ilk would all die young from nicotine indulgence. Harry C. is now eighty years old and still smoking. My feelings would have been hurt when I was twenty if you had told me that Harry C., lung-cankered as he was, could possibly have lived to that ripe old age. Since Harry outlived my speech, I have now trashed the old sermon in embarrassment, while Roy, brisk of stride and firm of hand, smokes on into the future. Yes, I have changed my way of fighting sin. I'm better at identifying the real giants now. And, as I said, changing is the key to survival in life (and certainly in the ministry).

What was the sin of my sermon? Just this! The world has a lot of big issues. Most people who come into my congregation are hurting. David has, in the course of life, learned some things. Oh, there was a day when in youthful confidence, he picked up five smooth stones and put those stones in his sling and threw them with pride. The reporters were all there. The *Jerusalem Gazette* put his picture on the front page: David! Heady! Triumphant! Photogenic! David, Eagle Scout, standing there with the head of Goliath in his hand. David was young and, of course, a leading teenage authority on giant-killing.

All of this glory had a trophy: the bones of Saul. At last David frees himself from yesterday and buries his egotistic youth. Old giant-slaying holds little interest when we have over-told the stories. David buries his youth and faces the real facts. He is old now. He must not face the future flagging old conquests in the face of new terrors.

## *II. Overcoming Exhaustion (and Age) (2 Samuel 21:15)*

Here is the proof that David has really changed. He looks at the old press clippings and smiled that he was once so young—so naive. His sling now is rotting under old yellow newsprint. He is tired in the mornings. He pushes back his hot Mexican omelette and dives into his stewed prunes. He must ride today and do battle. But his horse is getting higher every year and his sword heavier with every battle. His cellulite bulges under his mail. It is spring! Drat it! The Philistine giants are back! Like Hell's Angels at a motorcross! If David is going to win against these latter giants, he's going to have to change the way he fights.

For change is the essence of life, but hardest in the tired years. David can only defeat giants now by fighting smarter, not harder. He is "exhausted," this scripture says. The "exhaust," in case you've forgotten, is that little place in your car where the residual fuel comes out after the best has all been burned. Nothing much ever comes out of an exhaust, in fact, having been "exhausted" before it gets there.

David really would like to have defeated these latter giants. He remembers Goliath! There's a wonderful little song still ringing in his mind, "Saul has slain his thousands, and David his ten thousands" (1 Sam. 18:7). It was, after all, David's favorite song, a salute to his Schwarzenegger years. But now David's arthritis keeps him from snapping his fingers to yesteryear's music. The joy of fighting the big boys is tougher than it ever had been, and as the Bible says, David frankly is "exhausted"—burned out at the tailpipe end of life.

Hans Selye wrote:

> Among all my autopsies (and I have performed well over a thousand), I have never seen a person who died of old age. In fact, *I do not think anyone has died of old age yet.* To permit this would be the ideal accomplishment of medical

> research. . . . To die of old age would mean
> that all the organs of the body had worn out
> proportionately, merely by having been used
> too long. This is never the case. We invariably
> die because one vital part has worn out too
> early in proportion to the rest of the body. . . .
> The lesson seems to be that, as far as man can
> regulate his life by voluntary actions, he should
> seek to equalize stress throughout his being! . . .
> The human body—like the tires of a car, or the
> rug on a floor—wears longest when it wears
> evenly.[2]

I often lament the energy it takes to do the same little things I did with gusto two decades ago when I first came to my current pastorate. I try to imagine what it must have felt like when I had the stamina to do it right. I would like to suggest to you to conjure a little picture of what you're going to be like as you get closer and closer to the tailpipe end of life. What will exhaustion look like when it is *your* customary uniform of the day?

I've hired a young staff because I am hoping to keep a little stamina at the church. But my bifocals have a certain *noblesse oblige* about them. Wiser if not better—old eyes are less optic but more discerning. So David has to have the giants closer to read their rage and threat. Still, the giants must go and David must not lie at ease while terror stalks his kingdom. Fear can spawn laziness and laziness can become an excuse for quitting early in life. David did not stop fighting giants. He did change how he went about it. He assigns the fearsome work: "Abishai, you go over and skin this big one out. I fought my last one seventeen or eighteen years ago." David, older and wiser now, delegates the giants.

Still, none can say David is not in charge of giant-killing, nor can we charge David with laziness.

Scott Peck says diligence and laziness are polar concepts: Ultimately there is only the one impediment, and that is laziness.

> If we overcome laziness, all the other
> impediments will be overcome. If we do not
> overcome laziness, none of the others will be
> hurdled. . . . In examining discipline we were
> considering the laziness of attempting to avoid
> necessary suffering, or taking the easy way out.
> In examining love we were also examining the
> fact that nonlove is the unwillingness to extend
> one's self. Laziness is love's opposite.[3]

If you love, you're disciplined. Undisciplined living is what makes you act old. Letting the giants live and bully the world is insane. They're so unreasonable and voracious. But the worst thing is that we grow accustomed to living on the lazy end of life. Discipline requires us to keep fighting giants all our lives. We need to decide at each stage of life how we are going to fight: hard or smart!

## III. Changing by Allowing Others to Rescue You (2 Samuel 21:17)

Ishni-Benob was the new Goliath and as he charges down on David, "Abishai son of Zeruiah came to David's rescue." David wouldn't have let anybody rescue him in the old days. But age and wisdom leave us more content to be rescued.

Being rescued is good. It leaves us dependent and sires humility. Self-defense is, after all, the worst kind of defense. Could David have handled Ishni-Benob? Maybe. But it would have been a huffing and puffing affair. And even if he beats this particular giant, somewhere, some other giant will get him.

Abishai kills four giants. actually! The show-off!

But David is aware that old litanies die: "Saul has slain his thousands, and David his ten thousands," will be heard no longer in the land. After Abishai gets through, he will be writing his own egotistic jingle: "David has slain his thousands, and Abishai his ten thousands." And *People* magazine will have a new cover article: *"Abishai Eclipses David!"* The sports page will read in the World-Series-size headlines: "Abishai-Four, David-One!"

## IV. Changing by Realizing There Is Always a New Crop of Giants (2 Samuel 21:15–20)

When I read of these giants, I'm amazed at who they all are. Verse 16 mentions Ishni-Benob, but another one is called Saph (it's just "sap" with an "h" on it). Another is Goliath, or the brother of Goliath. And then in verse 20 there's a big Philistine wookie they don't even name; he is just a circus runaway with six toes on each foot and six fingers on each hand. Against such freaky foes, David has one primary life goal: He would like to be a survivor. Life never runs out of giants!

One woman in our church even struggled with cancer, a great giant, which was claiming her life. "My struggle," she said, "seems so hopeless. I just cannot lick this thing. Each night I go to bed promising myself I'll be stronger tomorrow. And each tomorrow, in spite of my resolve, I wake up weaker." And the giant of carcinoma won on a rainy morning when weakness could no longer reach for pulse and the valiant heart gave way to let the grinning giant reign over hissing tubes and murky bags on chrome hooks and flowers that didn't care.

My mother once lost her job, and yet she was brave before old Ishni-Benob, the uncaring Gentile. I saw her come home from the battle broken. And I could tell the giant had won. I rarely saw my mother cry. But with nine children and no other means of support, the tears came as she said, "Somehow, I can't lick this one. We have to change the way we attack life. There's got to be another way." There was. Her nine children went out and learned to survive in the fearsome field of giants. We could all work. We could all contribute income to the family survival.

Shame was the giant who bested the reputation of a great

friend of mine. He had lived all his life in perfect control with lots of pride. Enter calamity! Suddenly there were pictures in the newspaper. There were circumstances he didn't plan and could not wrap in dignity and self-esteem. There were black headlines unfriendly to his picture. His pride was torn apart and ripped in two by gossip. The giant of shame had conquered; integrity and virtue lost. But not my friend . . . he lived. He walked again in the world. He *changed* to a self-image that could live without the affirmation of the press.

Rejection itself is a giant.

Some years ago, a presidential candidate lost after millions of dollars and tireless campaigning: Losing! He always knew that somebody had to lose, but not him! Lying on the political field of standing giants, he said, "I am too old to cry and it hurts too much to laugh." Giant! Yes, but now that giant is gone, and the candidate is alive, changed in his goal and powerful in his self-respect.

## Conclusion

I have always wondered what would have happened that day in the valley of Elah if David had thrown his five smooth stones and missed. If, while he had tried to reload his sluggish sling, Goliath had cut the teenager down in cold blood. There is not much to celebrate in killing little boys, so the story would not have gotten much press back in Phylistia. Goliath, had he not been killed by David, would have died of old age. I must confess that there are a couple of giants I have never managed to outfight. But I did at least outlive them.

Giants have a life span and are subject to some ordinary killing faults. They, too, get flabby with age and are buried quite dead in big, powerless graves—buried, they are underneath the daisies they were once too macho to acknowledge. Giants die as we do! My motto is never fight with a giant who I can see is getting older and soon will be too weak for war. A sick giant is not much of a victory anyway, and I'd just as soon let gravity and arthritis do my giant-killing for me when I can.

Still, even such simple wisdom means that I must change—change from a fighting mentality to a waiting mentality. Why storm a wooden Trojan horse when you can hear the termites nibbling inside it?

Death is perhaps the last giant. He taunts us that he lives and makes us aware that our own dying cannot stop the grieving war. It's safe to say that when David finally dies in 2 Kings 2, he doesn't have all the giants killed. We die leaving the mocking monsters young and quite alive.

If you look at Jesus' life as he would have looked in A.D. 27, he looks like a failure. Only if you read his life in terms of his relationship with his Father and his desire to be faithful unto death can his glory be measured. Faithfulness in struggle is all that matters. God's competency will always be our adequacy. In the ultimate course of life the giants usually show themselves to be dwarves and grace has the towering, final word. Goliath cannot speak terror in any world where God is sovereign and the warriors are willing to be flexible! In such a world the giants may multiply, but commitment holds the sling and stones.

NOTES

1. "To Illustrate," *Preaching* (January, February 1986), 54.

2. Hans Selye, *The Stress of Life* cited in Archibald D. Hart, *Adrenalin & Stress* (Waco, TX: Word Books, 1986), 65.

3. M. Scott Peck, *The Road Less Traveled* (New York: Simon and Schuster, 1978), 271.

# 40. Taking a New Way
## K. H. Ting

You have not passed this way before.—Joshua 3:4
Be imitators of me, as I am of Christ.—1 Corinthians 11:1

THE CHURCH IS the household of believers. Today, in our household, we are celebrating a big event: the consecration of our beloved Sun Yan-li and Shen I-fan as bishops in the church of God. This is the first time in thirty-three years that bishops have been consecrated. This church became full long before the beginning of the service. Hundreds of late arrivers are standing outside. This shows that Christians are recognizing this to be an event of their own.

In recent years Christians all over China are heartened and thankful over the fact that the voice of "building up our church well" is growing louder and louder. The church is not anything to be destroyed, but the Body of Christ, something to be built up, and built up well—this is a point that has gone deeper and deeper into our hearts and minds. In the 1950s,

K. H. Ting (Ding Guangxun) was born in Shanghai, China. He was educated at St. John's University, Shanghai, and Columbia University. An Anglican, he was consecrated Bishop of Chekiang in 1955. Since 1953 he has served as principal of Nanking Theological College. Among many other recent positions held, he has been professor and director of the Centre for Religious Studies, Nanking University. This sermon was preached on the occasion of the consecration of two bishops by the laying on of hands by seven persons: four Anglican bishops, one Presbyterian minister, one Methodist minister, and one Baptist minister. The service took place in Shanghai on June 26, 1988, the first time bishops had been consecrated in thirty-three years.

1960s, and 1970s, there were not a few persons both within and outside our church who assumed that the fate of the church was extinction. Some thought it was a good thing; others thought it was bad. But they were agreed that the church did not have much of a chance to last in China and that what was awaiting it was its demise. Today, many have given up this view; others are not talking about it even if they do not want to give it up. We are now talking about the building up of the life and work of our church. Even many of our friends outside the church are supportive of our efforts. We feel excited and encouraged.

To build up our church is not only a voice or slogan. It shows itself in many actions:

In the last eight years, in Shanghai, Fuzhou, and Nanjing, we printed and published nearly 3 million Chinese Bibles and New Testaments with Psalms. We now have the Amity Printing Press, a gift from many national Bible societies through the United Bible Societies, which gives first priority to fulfilling the orders of church bodies for printing and binding Bibles. In 1988 Amity is to produce 900,000 Bibles, including reference Bibles and Bibles in simplified script.

We now have twelve theological schools with some 650 full-time students under training for church work.

There are now over 4,000 renovated and newly built church buildings used for public worship. There are tens of thousands of groups of Christians meeting in homes, mostly providing them with good, normal church life.

The number of Protestant Christians has increased to several million.

We are publishing *Tian Feng* and other journals. In recent months the contents of our *Syllabus* are turning themselves to rural readership. Several friends abroad have told us that our *Nanjing Theological Review* is probably the theological journal which enjoys the largest circulation in the world with 19,000 copies for each issue, including 4,000 copies in old script for the benefit of readers overseas.

Thus the church in China is building itself up. Christians

welcome our work to govern ourselves well, to support ourselves well, and to do the work of propagation well.

Yet, the work of building up our church is far from completion. There are in the church things that are not good, that should not have happened, that cause Christians sorrow. As long as such things exist, Christians do not feel at ease when worshiping. As is said in a hymn, "I often shed tears out of my love for the church." We need to see this state of affairs.

In some places relationship between colleagues is not good.

In some places relationship between religious believers and government cadres is not normal.

In some places there is poverty of spiritual ministration.

In some places, if Christians of a particular denominational background are a minority, their special characteristics in faith and worship are not given respect or are not given sufficient respect. This is not conducive to unity.

In some places, the emphasis is not on evangelism and nurturing but on endeavors to seek fame and money.

In some places Christians are meeting out in the open air in summer and in winter, holding umbrellas while it is raining or snowing. Some feel sad upon hearing this. Others say, "They deserve it. Who asked them to meet anyway?" Here are two diametrically opposed attitudes to the people and to the church.

All these tell us the building up of our church involves a tremendous degree of dedication and a tremendous amount of work. It is understandable our Christian people worry and weep for the church in face of difficulties.

In 1937, in Oxford, England, there was held the Conference on the Life and Work of the Church from which came the cry: "Let the church be the church." This is the cry of the Christians throughout the ages. The church is not to be made into a bureaucracy, an office, a recreational center, an economic enterprise, a mouthpiece of anything not the church. First of all, the church has to be the church.

Today, our society in general takes a much more favorable attitude toward our church. More and more people think that

Christianity and socialism are compatible. We welcome this point of view. In so far as our faith permits, I like to see greater compatibility between our church and socialism. But, what the church does must first of all be compatible with God's loving purpose, with the teachings of the Bible, with the nature of the church as church, and with the rightful wishes of the masses of our Christians. Only then the church is the church.

The church in China is a part of the Universal Church. Which part of it? The part of it that is composed of the younger churches, and that part of the younger churches, which is situated in a country with a civilization of thousands of years and now having entered the period of socialist reconstruction. Joshua's words, "You have not passed this way before," are an apt description of our situation. We are poorly qualified to be explorers of the new path. But God has not asked what in our sight is a better-qualified church to do this. Then let us gladly explore. In bearing witness to Christ in this new situation, we want to be independent, but we also like to feel we are carrying on our work with the prayer and the blessing of the Universal Church.

The ordination of the two new bishops also needs to be looked at from the point of view of building up our church.

Some tried to understand the step we are taking as a restoration of denominationalism, particularly the restoration of the Anglican denomination. No, this is not the case. We practice the breaking of bread, but this is not the restoration of the Little Flock. We honor the Sabbath Day and practice the humility rite, but this is not the restoration of Seventh Day Adventism. These are all ways for implementing our principle of mutual respect in matters of faith and worship, so as to insure our unity.

The episcopal system is followed not only by the Anglican Church, but also by Roman Catholicism, Orthodoxy, the Eastern Churches (actually Churches in West Asia and North Africa), Lutheran Churches in Scandinavia and North America, and the United Methodist Church.

What is more is that we, the church in China, are just *hav-*

*ing* bishops and not adopting the episcopal system of church government. The church in New Testament days also *had* bishops.

By having bishops, the ministry of our church becomes complete, or more complete. It is an important step we are taking.

What are the roles of bishops in the church in China? It is hard to enumerate systematically. We will have to let the Holy Spirit lead us and enable us to see more clearly. Practice and see the whole meaning of our practice later on as we look back—this has been an experience many times. When Peter came down from the house top and started for where Cornelius was, he also could not see clearly what was going to happen and could see still less clearly the whole repercussion of his action. Again, "You have not passed this way before."

This much is clear: We will have bishops, but we are not choosing the episcopal system of church government. Our bishops are not diocesan and not administrative: They have their authority, but their authority does not base itself on any written constitutional stipulation or on any executive position, but on their spiritual, moral, theological, and pastoral ministration, on their service to others. Bishops are servants of servants. The better they serve, the greater their authority and the people's readiness to listen. The more democratic they are, the more powerful are their appeals.

I especially hope that our two new bishops can serve our church and our country in four respects: (1) theological enrichment; (2) renewal and improvement of the quality of our worship; (3) upholding religious freedom and proper relation between church and state; and (4) strengthening the unity of our colleagues, including the proper implementation of the principle of mutual respect in matters of faith and worship.

All our clergy and bishops are to depend on the power of love and of example, and not on the power of position.

In 1 Corinthians 11:1 Paul admonished the Christians: "Be imitators of me, as I am Christ."

Paul dared to say this because he strived hard to imitate

Christ. I do not dare to ask people to imitate me, because I know I lag behind in imitating Christ. Many of us feel painful when we realize how high is the demand this biblical passage puts on us and how far short of the demand we are. The distance between the demand and the reality is too great. But, since God has entrusted us with the task of building up the church in China, he cannot make the demand any lower.

Let us therefore ask the Holy Spirit to strengthen us, help us once again to resolve to imitate Christ, so that we also dare to say, "Be imitators of me."

We are on a new path, untrodden before. Let the Holy Spirit guide us. Let us support each other on the way as we build together the edifice which is the church in China.

# *41.* Near Your House
## *Joanna Adams*

Nehemiah 3: Selected Verses

I WANT TO tell you first today the story of Nehemiah. He was the cupbearer to the King of Persia—the Persians who defeated the Babylonians. He lived in about the fifth century B.C. To tell you the truth, Nehemiah was basically a butler. He was not a man who made big decisions affecting the national interests. Mainly, he did things like helping the King decide what to wear to the palace. He recommended the wine for royal dinner parties. He was in a position of honor, which carried a certain amount of prestige, but it wasn't the same thing as being an Archduke or the Ambassador to Czechoslovakia, or something like that.

Still, it was obvious that Nehemiah was well thought of by the King. When some visitors from Judah came to town telling of what had happened to the wall in Jerusalem, and how the Babylonians had let it crumble, Nehemiah asked for and got permission to return to Jerusalem, which was where he and his people were from originally. He wanted to go home and supervise the rebuilding of the walls of Jerusalem. The King said that would be fine and, in fact, the King sent with Nehemiah Persian soldiers, the calvary, and a lot of letters of endorsement. He even gave Nehemiah permission to stop along the

*Joanna Adams* was born in Atlanta, Georgia, and was raised in Meridian, Mississippi. She is pastor of the North Decatur Presbyterian Church in Decatur, Georgia, and is active in several social ministries, particularly in efforts for the homeless.

way and chop trees in the royal forest, which Nehemiah did. Unless Nehemiah gave himself a promotion while writing his own autobiography, it looks as if the King decided that his cupbearer simply had more potential than he had been able to live up to at the royal wine tastings because, before he left, the King decided to just go ahead and let Nehemiah be the Governor of the whole province of Judah when he got there.

We are taking Nehemiah's word for it, of course, but it does seem as if the King's confidence was well placed. Nehemiah had no sooner hit town than he set out on a secret inspection of the wall, after which (in spite of the grief he was given by the enemies of the Jews, who were not only all around the town but also inside the town) he organized work teams. He put the priests to work first, obviously having fallen victim to the erroneous notion that priest-types only work one day of the week and that they need something constructive to do the rest of the week besides playing bingo and going to potluck suppers.

The priests were not the only ones into whose hands Nehemiah put hammer and nail and into whose wheelbarrows he put bricks and cement, because the outside of the wall was restored within fifty-two days. The man had, shall we say, rather extraordinary organizational skills. I've never heard of a similar sort of phenomenon in the modern age! In fact, when I thought of how well Nehemiah organized his construction team, I was reminded of the woman who was visited by an evangelism team by a church in her neighborhood. She said, "I'll tell you, I've never had much for organized religion." One of the folks from the church said, "Well, you'd like our church a lot. We've been trying for thirty years, and we haven't gotten things organized yet!"

The truth is that, while Nehemiah knew how to organize work crews for getting the wall up, cleaning up things *inside* the wall took him a long time—twelve years, in fact. The Jews in Jerusalem had themselves gotten in the habit of not taking the Torah very seriously, and having Nehemiah around was sort of like having your high school principal decide that he would accompany the senior class on their hay ride.

It took him twelve years, but at last he did it. When he had things pretty well shaped up, he decided to go back to Persia for a visit. He stayed a short time and when he returned to Jerusalem, he found out, much to his dismay, that things were worse than they had been when he had arrived the first time! Once again, Nehemiah got everybody shaped up, even up to the point of locking the city gates on the Sabbath, so that nobody could get out, even to go to the mall to a movie.

One of the things that got Nehemiah in a snit was the subject of mixed marriages—Jews should not marry outside the faith for any reason, he believed, and so he made all the fellows take an oath not to do so. To say Nehemiah felt strongly on the subject is an understatement. Here is what he himself wrote: "In those days also I saw the Jews who had married women of Ashdod, Ammon, and Moab; and half of their children spoke the language of Ashdod, and they could not speak the language of Judah, but the language of each people. And I contended with them and cursed them and beat some of them and pulled out their hair." (Nehemiah 13:23–25).

Herein lies my problem with Nehemiah. Probably the people deserved to have their hair yanked out; I'm not debating that. Certainly in the mind of Nehemiah, that was just what they deserved. But the mind can play funny tricks, especially on a cupbearer-turned-governor, who carries around the weight of the province on his shoulders and might sometimes take things a little more seriously than he should. My concern is that Nehemiah took much more pleasure, it seems, in citing the shortcomings of the people and letting them have it in the bad times, than he did in celebrating their contributions to the kingdom and thanking God for them in the good times.

The second story I want to tell you today is not Nehemiah's story at all. It is the story, in fact, that Nehemiah brushes by on his way looking for all the sinners who he knows are sitting on every Jerusalem street corner. The story I want to tell you now is the story of the people whose names you no doubt have never heard before and will no doubt never hear again. These people, whose names appear in the third chapter of Nehemiah, do not get books in the Bible named after them. In fact, they have been content throughout history to let Nehemiah get all the credit for rebuilding the walls of Jerusalem. They have been content to be his construction crew, but to me their story is at least as important as his, if not more important to us, because we are more like them than we are like him. We are ordinary people who try to do our part. We are not people like Nehemiah or Martin Luther or Martin Luther King or Jeremiah or Mother Teresa—people who have been famous for their contributions to the faith. We are not like them. We are like Hasshub and Zadok and Uzziel. We are the Uzziels of our time, because we are just regular people participating in our own way in our own backyards, if you will, and the coming of the kingdom and in the restoration of the righteousness of God which is God's will for all of creation.

The most amazing part of their story is that what they did not only sounds like no big deal, but *is*, in fact, no big deal. What they did was work on the wall that was near their house. Brick by brick, day by day, they did their part where they were. I'm sure it didn't look like this, but I love the picture that comes into my mind's eye of everybody going out his or her back door, past the clothesline and the swing set and the vegetable garden, and doing some work each day on that portion of the broken-down wall that their property backed up to. Then the day came that Zadok's work and Hasshub's work came together, neighbor's labor met neighbor's labor, and the holy city was secure again.

I like to think that when it was all done, they had a big barbecue, and gave the kids pony rides or something. I also like to think that this is somewhat similar to the way the reign comes among us. If it is so, and I believe it is so, it is surely encouragingly so for people of faith like us who care so much and are concerned that we can do so little. Maybe it is through the dogged, everyday faithfulness of modern-day, down-to-earth Christians, where we live, that we too participate in the restoration of the community of God. As the wall was rebuilt person by person, family by family, one beam, one brick, one door, one step at a time, so God's love surely is similarly manifested among us deed by deed, day by day. This is as gracious a story as we can hear, for who among us has not felt overwhelmed by the tasks at hand and by the enormity of the faithlessness of our age, by its injustice, by its sheer heartlessness, by its hunger, by its poverty, inexcusable things. How many of us have asked ourselves, "Who am I to make a difference? What can I do against these global giants? Who am I to fight the global giants who seem to have the run of the earth?"

I got a letter last week at the church. In the left-hand corner of the envelope were these words: "A Message for Peace and Justice Christians." It was addressed to Joanna Decatur. It was a good and gracious reminder that what I am called to do is the same thing that you are called to do—to work where we are, to do what we can. As Gandhi said, "Whatever you do will never be enough; all that matters is that you do it." Isn't it so?

You will never know what God can do with your little bit, how God can take your witness and her witness and put them together to create a stronger, more durable witness than you could ever have made on your own. It never looks like much. You might be standing in your kitchen chopping fruit for a fruit salad at the night shelter; you might be writing a letter to Washington to a person in power you are sure never opens the mail—it never looks like much, but that is how God's reign comes. God takes what we do and puts it in the mix, and our little efforts all together become the brick and the mortar of God's tomorrow.

The last story I'll tell is one about what happened one day where we live in Decatur. A year or so ago, I was sitting in our den at home watching the evening news. I was by myself. Everyone else was away except for Sam, our teenage son, and me. Sam and I had earlier had one of those arguments only a teenager and a teenager's mother can have. It was a bell-ringer over one of the burning issues of our age: when the dirty clothes basket was going to be taken upstairs. We had, shall we say, not resolved our differences, and Sam had disappeared and the cat and I had the den all to ourselves. "CBS News" was doing a series that week on World War II, and that particular night the focus was on the Soviet Union. The statistics of the deaths, the losses that the Soviet Union experienced during World War II were mindboggling—20 million people killed.

The cameras first panned the stark, mammoth war monuments that the Soviets seemed to love so. Then they focused in on a young, bright-faced bride and groom who were laying a bouquet of red tulips at the foot of a soldier's tomb. It has become the custom there for couples as they begin their lives together. The bride and groom didn't look much different from American couples on their wedding day—same hopes, same dreams. Just as I was getting misty-eyed about it and thinking about the next Peacemaking Task Force meeting I could attend, I remembered our world's love affair with war. As I remembered, I got deeply frightened, and just as I remembered, Sam walked into the den and sat down. All of a sudden it seemed the most important thing in the world for us to talk and to make our peace. We turned off the television set and we made our peace.

Shalom at home, to compassion for your neighbor, forgiveness for your friend, respect for your spouse, service to your community, stewardship to your church, a little gentleness here and there—where you live. In just such ways our story is told, the story that was also the story of Nehemiah, the King's cupbearer who decided to change occupations and go into the construction business over in Jerusalem.

# *42.* Will You Give Them Stones?
## *Al Hill*

Matthew 7:7–11 and Joshua 4:1–9

WHEN JESUS SAYS to His mostly male audience (Matt. 7:7–11), "Which of you, if his sons asks for bread, will give him a stone?" the answer appears obvious. Any decent parent would be quick to respond: "I love my child; I wouldn't give him a stone!" Only a cruel, twisted mind would think of giving a child a useless piece of rock when his little stomach is empty. The point of the question is clear: You and I can depend on our Heavenly Father to meet our needs.

But what if a stone represented more than just a useless piece of rock? What if a stone was a timeless, visible reminder of a people's life-changing encounter with Almighty God? For Joshua and the children of Israel (Josh. 4:1–9), this was the case twelve times over as they crossed the Jordan River to take possession of the Promised Land. Twelve strong men shouldered the weight of twelve great stones as this new nation

*Al Hill* is Protestant Chaplain at the Cathedral of the Air, Naval Air Engineering Center, Lakehurst, New Jersey. A lieutenant commander, chaplain corps, United States Navy, Hill has also been a Navy chaplain in North Carolina, Maine, and Virginia. He attended the United States Naval Academy, Jacksonville State University, and Southern Baptist Theological Seminary, where he received the Master of Divinity. Hill is a recipient of the National Defense Medal and Sea Service Deployment Ribbon. A Southern Baptist, from 1977 to 1980 he was a civilian pastor in Kentucky and Virginia. "Will You Give Them Stones?" is a Fathers' Day sermon.

walked through a miracle. And when that special moment in time was over, the stones remained as witness to the day when a people walked with God between the waters—and lived!

If we could speak symbolically of a stone as the "souvenir" of God's divine involvement in our human experience—if we could use the word "stone" with the meaning Joshua found in it—perhaps Jesus would not mind if we took another look at His apparently rhetorical question.

You see, this is a question of greatest importance for us today: Bread, or stones? Our children ask for bread. That is, they have physical needs like adults, but they aren't yet able to meet these needs by themselves. They depend on you and me—they trust you and me—to provide what they need. Jesus expects that, as parents, we will provide.

But as we read in the book of Joshua, children also ask about stones. Their hunger for food and physical nourishment is often equalled, and occasionally surpassed, by their curiosity and hunger for spiritual understanding. And again they depend on, and trust, you and me to provide.

Now parents must meet the physical needs of their children. Boys and girls must be fed and clothed and housed. Nothing is so disgusting as a mother or father who will not fulfill this obligation, who abuses this sacred trust. Nothing is so pitiful as the despair of a mother or father who does not have the means to feed his or her children, or treat their illnesses, or give them a home. And the world has far too many parents in both categories.

Some of you are of that generation which provided the needed bread to your children during the Great Depression, when many could not even feed themselves. Others of you watched parents work long and hard to provide the barest of necessities. A still newer generation has grown up with parents whose attitudes and values were shaped by those years of uncertainty and sacrifice. For most of us, then, there is a strong commitment to giving our children what we couldn't have— to giving them "bread": meeting their material requirements—and their wants. We also pay a lot of attention to their social needs, and their educational needs, and their psychological and emotional needs. We bend over backward and go the second (and third) mile to insure that our sons and daughters experience the best of everything our efforts and our incomes can provide.

And yet, the words of Jesus seem to echo faintly in the recesses of our minds: "Man does not live by bread alone."

"But bread is important!" Yes it is, but not *all*-important. Remember the setting of these words of Jesus? Our Lord had gone into the Wilderness, not eating for many days. Then he faced a battle of wills with Satan who said, "Why don't you turn these stones into bread?" Stones aren't important, are they? They're just rocks. Ignore them. Do away with them. Direct all your attention and energy to making bread.

Now the land of Israel is not a very big place; maybe the size of New Hampshire. And as Jesus went up into its mountainous wilderness, struggling with Satan's great temptations, He could look out over the miles to the Jordan River, just as some of us have scanned the distant horizon from a Mount Washington, or a Lookout Mountain, or a Pike's Peak. He could have looked out over the Jordan River that flowed along to the south past a little village called Gilgal. And perhaps (being a Jew and well versed in the sacred scriptures) Jesus remembered at that moment the times when he asked His father, Joseph, or read in the family Bible as we have done today: "What do these stones mean?" And Jesus said to Satan, "Bread isn't everything!"

While you and I work to meet the material needs and wants of our children, are we ignoring or neglecting or shortchanging their spiritual needs? God had Joshua erect that monument of stones, not for the people who crossed the Jordan that day, but for their children, and for the children who would follow after them, generation by generation. And if the stones at Gilgal were a timeless symbol of God's presence and help in the lives of His people, *where are our stones—our* timeless evidence of God's hand in the affairs of *our* lives.

The question you and I must ask ourselves as parents this

morning is not, "If my child asks for bread, will I give her a rock?" but rather, "If my child asks for a stone—a symbol of my encounter with God—will I try to distract her with bread?" When your child is asking questions of spiritual importance to him or her—whether openly, or silently in that active little mind—will you address your child's spiritual need honestly and effectively, or will you try to avoid it with more attention to supplying goods and services? So many of us try to give our children everything they want, and can't understand why they are neither happy nor satisfied.

The reason is that "bread" is perishable while "stone" endures. Bread meets the need of the moment while the kind of stone we are talking about meets the needs of eternity. "Stone" suggests substance and solidity, strength and security. We sing the hymn, "On Christ the Solid Rock I Stand." There are some things that money just can't buy, and some hungers that no bread can satisfy.

In those critical and important moments of your life and mine when God sends His Holy Spirit to take an active part, there ought to be some marker to show that God was at that experience. There ought to be a reminder to which our youngsters can point and say, "What does that mean?"

"Why do you pray, Daddy?"

"Why do you read the Bible every day, Mommy?"

"Why do we (have to) go to church?"

"Why do we put all that money in the offering plate?" (Remember, of course, that little children also think a nickel is worth more than a dime because it's bigger!)

"Why don't you get nervous and upset and say ugly words when things don't go the way we want them to?"

"What do these stones mean?"

Sometimes Navy chaplains like myself are assigned to Marine Corps units. On my daughter's second birthday, I was "deposited" on a beach in Oman (a small country in Arabia) with my Marine battalion. We were not allowed to take pictures, for security reasons, and there were no shops or markets in this deserted region of the coastline from which to buy souvenirs. The only reminder—the only evidence—I could bring home of my experience there was a collection of uniquely shaped rocks I gathered along the shore. I want you to know that I carried those rocks halfway around the world for my daughter to see. Those rocks showed her where I had been and what it had been like for me there. Now the stones of Joshua we read about in the Bible were not little rocks gracefully plucked from the dry riverbed in passing, but great stones carried with supreme physical effort and spiritual dedication. They were carried to tell of deliverance from danger and despair.

What about those times when *you* faced situations that threatened to overwhelm you like a raging flood, and instead God seemed to part the waters and bring you through? Yes, you may wear the wrinkles or bear the scars from it, but these may be the very symbolic stones to which a boy or girl can point and say, "What does that mean?" And if the symbols— the monuments—are there, can we tell our children what they mean about God and our relationship with Him?

You know, in the fourth chapter of the book of Joshua there are actually two accounts of setting up these stones. In the second account the children are to ask, "What do these stones mean?" But at the beginning of the chapter the question is worded a little differently: "What do these stones mean *to you*?" That's really what our children want to know. They aren't interested in *theology;* they want *testimony!* They want to look at you and me and see "a beacon to God, to faith, and loyalty."

A class of seminary students was confronted one day by this simple question: "What do you know about God that you haven't read or heard from someone else?" That's what every child is asking every father and mother. They're looking into your heart and mine, looking for the God Who lives and reigns there, wanting to discover Him from the spiritual monuments you have erected to Him: your faith, your character, your lifestyle. Our children are on a great spiritual quest of discovery. You and I, more than anyone else, must provide the markers and the milestones along their way. If your children ask you for bread, give them bread. But if they ask for stones . . .

# 43. Why Remember?

## Gary L. Ziccardi

1 Samuel 31:1–6; 2 Samuel 1:2–4, 11–12, 17–27; and 1 Corinthians
15:51–58

"HOW ARE the mighty fallen. They were swifter than eagles.
They were stronger than lions. How are the mighty fallen in
the midst of battle."

Though young children don't usually remember many of
the landmark events and details of their childhood, some experiences inevitably make an indelible impression and are never forgotten. One such experience for me came in the annual
pilgrimage my mother and I would make each Memorial Day
to the Lakeview cemetery in East Cleveland, Ohio.

The cemetery I found to be a strange place. Row upon row
of meticulously manicured lawn around myriads of smooth
stone slabs and distinguished monuments. Birds singing in the
shelter of a quiet, grassy, and tree-filled area. People and cars
moving painfully slowly up and down the narrow cemetery
lanes. All so quiet and peaceful. But the people always seemed
out of character with the beautiful cemetery grounds. Steps
were heavy. Eyes were clouded and noses were weepy and I
remember that people were very sad.

*Gary L. Ziccardi* is associate pastor of the First Presbyterian Church
of Newark, California. A graduate of Wheaton College, he received
the Master of Divinity from Princeton Theological Seminary in 1987.
Ziccardi was named one of the Outstanding Young Men of America in
1983 and he has served as a surface line officer in the United States
Navy.

Though the understanding of the significance of the finality of death came to me gradually over the years of my youth, the understanding of my part in the annual Memorial Day pilgrimage came quickly. I learned to tend the stone and plot of my father, washing clean the speckled granite slab, trimming the grass carefully, digging out the permanent flower pot and arranging fresh flowers while my mother or sister or other relatives would weep. Reading and rereading the inscription in view of the myriad miniature United States flags placed on the graves of all veterans, "Joe J. Ziccardi, Ohio, Tec 5 Company A 517, Port Battalion Transportation Corps, WWII, February 5, 1925—January 12, 1964," and though no one ever told me to do it, just before leaving, rendering a salute of honor to my father.

"O how are the mighty and beloved fallen." The words belong to ancient Israel's David who has just received the news of the death in battle of King Saul, who out of jealous envy and blind rage had sought to kill David on several different occasions, and Saul's son Jonathan, David's intimate friend. The words come from the lips of one who lived thousands of years ago, and yet they could be our own today. The pain and sorrow in our imperfect world from the bearing of and usage of arms in war and other circumstances is with humanity perennially throughout our history. And we also do sometimes have periods of lament to express our feelings.

The tragedy of the Iraqi-fired cruise missile killing thirty-seven Navy crew members of the USS *Stark* this past week is a disaster over which we lament and pray for the survivors. Just as I have wondered how David could possibly lament the death of Saul, who had tried to kill him on numerous occasions, I marvel at the attitude of Barbara Kiser, the widow of Chief Petty Officer Stephen Greg Kiser from the *Stark*, who wrote a letter of peace accompanied by a New Testament to the Iraqi pilot who fired the missile. The media description of Chief Kiser's five-year-old son John at one of the brief ceremonies in honor of the dead veterans draws our compassion: "huddled in his mother's skirt during the twenty-minute ceremony. He sometimes put his hand over his heart at his mother's bidding but did not seem to realize his father was among those being honored." Together Barbara and John and the friends and relatives of those killed will go on with the lives that have been extended to them under the hand of God's providence, and together they will try to understand.

But as the time passes and the grief begins to ease, doesn't it make more sense to leave the past in the past, to leave the painful memories behind, and to think only of today and of the future? Why do we have such things as Memorial Day and flowers offered "in loving memory of" those whom we have loved and are gone? Why do we subject ourselves to remembering and feeling some of the old aches? Why do we remember at all? It hurts so much at times.

Perhaps one reason why we risk remembering is because we have the hope in Christ of seeing them again, as Paul says, "Lo, I tell you a mystery. We shall not all sleep, but we shall all be changed, in a moment, in the twinkling of an eye, at the last trumpet. For the trumpet will sound, and the dead will be raised imperishable, and we shall be changed." Without this hope based on Christ's resurrection, our faith is futile or vain. We risk remembering because of the hope we have of seeing them again.

Yes, the pain is real, but I believe that it is necessary to let the feelings be felt and recognized. During a long period in the 1970s, the nation indulged in a remarkable exercise of recoil and denial and amnesia about the Vietnam war. Americans did not want to hear about it or to think about it. That denial was part of the special ordeal of the Vietnam veterans, an ordeal that began when they arrived back in the United States and found that even many of their family members were not interested in talking about what they had just been through, or were embarrassed about it.

Perhaps that is why the Vietnam War Veterans Memorial in Washington has meant so much to Vietnam veterans who have not been able to remember and experience some healing. The two skinny black granite triangles wedged onto a mound of Washington sod with the names of all 58,022 Americans who gave their lives has become a sort of sanctum, beautiful and terrible. For veterans, the memorial was a touchstone from the beginning, and the 1982 dedication ceremony a delayed national embrace. As John Wheeler, the chairman of the veteran's group that raised the money and built the memorial has described it, "The actual act of being at the memorial is healing for the man or woman who went to Vietnam. It has to do with the *felt presence of comrades*."

Is this not one reason why we dare to remember? We desire to feel the presence of ones that we have loved. We desire to draw close in memory to ones who have been precious to us. We hope to feel their support as we venture forth with the trials and difficulties of our day. Do the pains and loneliness and the great expenditure of our energy and emotions which accompany our memories make the remembering worth it at all?

Lt. Tom Reilly from my Naval Reserve unit certainly believes that the effort to remember is worth it. Last weekend he was a part of the Vietnam veterans group which completed a march from Washington, D.C., to Philadelphia to remember and recognize and together be strengthened as they carried the names of ones who had been lost or missing in action in Vietnam. In a poor neighborhood of Philadelphia an old woman walked out into the street and asked Tom why the group was dressed in parts of military uniforms and why they were marching. It turned out that one of the names which they were carrying to remember was the name of her son who had been killed in Vietnam. Because of some lost paperwork, she had never known what military decorations or honors had been his. Because of a chance meeting of this group of veterans who were trying to recognize and remember those who had died and a mother who had lost her son, the records finally made it to the next of kin, many tears were shed, and part of an old wound was healed.

The apostle Paul puts the fundamental question of remembering to us in the New Testament lesson, "O death, where is thy victory? O death, where is thy sting?" It is certain that we're well acquainted with the sting of death. We see evidence of death or decay every day of our lives in one form or another, whether through the media or personal circumstance or the simple biological clock inside all mortals which keeps on ticking and tells us what the time is periodically with knee injuries or backaches or the fitting appointment for dentures or the birth of great-grandchildren. Yes, we know of the sting. The Scripture tells us that the root of the sting is sin and the law.

But friends, listen to the good news, in this sixth week of the season of Easter we are reminded that Christ conquered sin by his death and he conquered death itself by his resurrection. We may rejoice that our risen savior takes the lasting sting out of death for us.

Why should we risk remembering? Because we are children of the covenant who are on a journey together headed for the same destination. Because God has made us promises in Christ, that we shall all be changed, that the perishable will put on the imperishable, that the mortal nature will put on the immortal. These promises are for us and for those who have died in Christ. The significance of our baptism is that we have died with Christ to sin in the past tense and we shall surely be raised with Christ in the future sense. Yes, we feel the sting of death here and now, but we also know the promise of the future which is sure in Christ.

In the upper room Christ taught his disciples that the key to the future would be to remember the past with him through the institution of his holy supper. Christ left them with bread and wine, simple elements to serve as an ongoing memorial to his life together with and sacrifice for them. In the remembrance of Christ's death and resurrection for us, we receive grace and strength to carry on, yes, and even to remember with thankfulness for what was with loved ones and hope for what will be in the eternal joyous presence of our Lord.

"O how the mighty are fallen."

"O death, where is thy victory? O death, where is thy sting? ... Thanks be to God, who gives us the victory through our Lord Jesus Christ. Therefore, my beloved brethren, be steadfast, immovable, always abounding in the work of the Lord, knowing that in the Lord your labor is not in vain." To the glory of Christ. Amen.

# 44. The Life That Maketh All Things New

*Gary Kowalski*

I THINK THAT my grandfather was puzzled when I decided to become a minister. He had eight uncles who were Baptist preachers, and spoke as if he had narrowly escaped a similar fate. His attitudes about religion were probably shaped by the small town of Shannon, Texas, where he grew up. There were only two churches in town, the Baptist and the Methodist, and most folks belonged to one or the other, without too much rivalry or competition. At least until the Holy Rollers came to town and stirred things up, people would go to the Baptist church when the Baptist minister was in town, and then worship with the Methodists when the Methodist circuit rider came through. It was an ecumenically minded community. There was one man who lived on the outskirts of town who claimed to be something called a Presbyterian, and another who called himself a Republican, but these aberrations were tolerated in Shannon. People were pretty much free to do their own thinking, and my grandfather always tried to keep an open mind.

---

*Gary Kowalski* is minister of the First Unitarian Universalist Church of Seattle, Washington. A graduate of Harvard College, he received the Master of Divinity from Harvard Divinity School in 1982. Kowalski won the Harvard Billings Prize for Excellence in Preaching in 1979 and the Clarence Skinner Sermon Award of the Unitarian Universalist Association in 1985.

My grandfather would have made a good preacher. He loved to talk and tell stories. He had a hundred of them, and many of them could even be repeated in church. He had the instincts of a moralist with the saving grace of humor that preserves the preacher from his own pomposity. There were stories about Aunt Tidy and Uncle Mood and the early pioneer days from the era when his family moved to Oklahoma in the last Land Lottery in 1901. He liked to recall the "good old days," but never pretended that the "good old days" were always easy, or that he would trade the present for the past. He was an artist by training and profession, and in his art as in life he was always a realist. He was a keen observer of nature and human nature; he could paint the shadows as well as the light. He was tough-minded, but had an eye for those flashes of brilliance and beauty that are the artwork of a higher creativity.

He was the sort of person who liked to read and think and ponder about the "big picture" of what life means and how we came to be. He was born in 1894—before the discoveries of Freud or Einstein, before the Wright brothers' first plane or Henry Ford's tin lizzie—but he was up-to-date as the morning's headlines. There were books by Lewis Thomas, Carl Sagan, and Jacob Bronowski on his shelf, for he had a keen interest in the world of nature and the investigations of science. He had a sense of wonder before the spiral chamber of a nautilus, at the joining of mathematical perfection and eye-pleasing curves within a single natural form. His curiosity was coupled with a sense of reverence that could be called mystical. He wrote—

> Me a mystic? God only knows.
> If I am one I'm glad it shows.
> For folks who think their way secure
> Their path is plain and heaven sure
> Adventure not, nor dream, nor hope
> In Mystery of Heaven's scope.

He was a doggerel poet, and some of his poems were fairly doggy, but he knew many of the classics by heart. I was fortunate that I happened to be visiting him a few days before he died, and we had a chance to spend an evening talking poetry, arguing, and misquoting passages from the "Rubaiyat" and "Tintern Abbey." I think he was at home with the poets even more than with the scientists, for the poets fed his inwardness and touched the springs of faith.

His was a faith that included doubt and wondering and skepticism. He loved to quote from Edward Fitzgerald:

> Oh, come with old Khayyam, and leave the Wise
> To talk; one thing is certain, that Life flies;
>     One thing is certain, that the Rest is Lies;
> The Flower that once has blown for ever dies;
> Myself when young did eagerly frequent
> Doctor and Saint, and heard great Argument
>     About it and about: but evermore
> Came out by the same Door as in I went.
> With them the Seed of Wisdom did I sow,
> And with my own hand labour'd it to grow:
>     And this was all the Harvest that I reap'd—
> "I came like Water, and Wind I go."

He was not religious in any dogmatic sense. He felt the impermanence, uncertainty, and effervescence that belongs to mortal existence. He realized the finitude of his own mind and body within the trackless millenia of time. But this realization was never reason for despair. For in his own way, he was a person of faith and deeply spiritual.

Several years ago, my grandfather gave me a brown paper folder full of ruminations and jottings that he accumulated at odd moments of musing in his life. The thoughts were on diverse subjects—time, eternity, evolution, life and death—and most are fragmentary at best. He called them "Birdseed": not to be taken too seriously. I'd like to share one or two of these thoughts with you now.

> Most all high moments in life, whether of
> sorrow or happiness are generally embroidered

with tears. Moments of high emotional impact are the punctuation marks in the story of human experience that would otherwise be a tale of drab and dull existence.

A sense of humor, when we view the frustrations of human experience from a distance, makes us laugh. But when we move in close and identify with these same frustrations it makes us want to cry.

I am not hung up on death, but it is the one and only absolute reality in my future. In eighty-four years, I have not seen one shred of evidence of the existence of a soul or spirit that is separate from the physical being of man. I believe the seat of consciousness is the brain and that there is no conscious entity apart from the physical workings of the brain. When the brain dies there is no more consciousness.

How does a man of eighty years face the life before him? On what does his spirit feed? What does he expect from the daily round of duties that never cease to crowd in upon him? As we grow older the burdens of others accumulate on us also—more and more of the people we have known seem to acquire greater loads of grief, loneliness, and physical handicap.

The highest moment in human experience comes, and in most of our lives all too seldom, when someone close to you, either young or old, takes your hand or puts an arm around you and in a quivering voice says, "I love you so much." In that moment you suddenly know what life is all about, and you also know that it is definitely worth living.

To hear again the birds sing in early morn and to see the flowers kissed with dew. To see a smile on a face that loves you. These things

keep alive the forces that prevail in one's life
and fill the heart with gratitude for being
allowed to live another day.

I am not an atheist, nor am I an agnostic
even though the whole conception of God
remains an unanswerable question to me. I am
somehow plagued with a faith that persists in
spite of all reason and speculation. If God is
only a myth I will die and never know the
difference. If he is my creator who has
endowed me with a mysterious relevance to
him, in due time I shall know.

It's been over two years now since my grandfather died.
The way that I feel about death has changed since then. I can't
say that I'm no longer afraid of it. Illness and infirmity will
never be pleasant to contemplate, and there may be an irreducible core of anxiety in all of us when we face this dark unknown. I no longer think of death as the enemy of life,
however. I no longer look on it as out of place or as an intruder in the ultimate scheme of things. Losing my grandfather
brought me a sharp stab of grief but also helped me come to a
point of acceptance. It made me feel that the most important
life is the life which is ongoing: the life which passes on from
grandfathers and grandmothers to fathers and mothers to
daughters and sons, and which renews itself in every generation. I've come to feel that my own individual life is part of a
much grander and richer life which flows through me and
through every living creature. I've come to believe that there
is some primordial aliveness within our universe itself, in the
wind and sea and even in the stones. In the words of William
Wordsworth, in lines that my grandfather might have been
able to quote from memory:

> I have felt
> A presence that disturbs me with the joy
> Of elevated thoughts; a sense sublime
> Of something far more deeply interfused,

Whose dwelling is the light of setting suns,
And the round ocean and the living air,
And the blue sky, and in the mind of man:
A motion and a spirit, that impels
All thinking things, all objects of all thought,
And rolls through all things . . .

In this season of resurgent life when flowers blossom and the entire earth is roused to a bustle of activity, the divinity which courses through things is almost palpably present. Now is the time when it becomes most meaningful to celebrate Easter. Just as we commemorate the birth of Jesus in the wintertime as a reminder that life exists in the midst of seeming death, so we memorialize the death of Jesus with this holiday in the spring, reminding us that death exists in the very midst of life. Birth and death cannot be separated from each other. Together they form one integrated whole. To die and to be born are not so different as they seem. They are aspects of a single, interpenetrating Reality.

The affirmation of Easter is that this Reality is ultimately trustworthy. Its essential character is dependable and gracious and good. Although the people that we love and we ourselves will one day die, this Reality which brings all creation into being and which pours through all things in ceaseless transformation need not be feared. We can respond to it with gratitude and joy. In gladness and in sorrow, in loving and in letting go, in the world which is dying and the world which is always coming into birth, we can pronounce a blessing upon life.

I invite you to pray with me now:

Life that maketh all things new,
Flow within us to give us strength for the experiencing of our
days,
For the enrichment of our relationships,
For the building of loving community.
Flow within us as the courage to bear grief and
disappointment,

As the courage to accept death without fear,
And as the faith to believe that in spite of death, life still has
    meaning.
Life that maketh all things new,
Flow within us as friendship and human feeling;
Flow within us as the search for wisdom and the quest for
    truth;
Flow within us as the compassion which makes itself of service;
Flow within us as laughter and dance and song.
Life that maketh all things new,
Lure us to more abundant living;
Enchant us once again with myth and story;
Bewitch us with the beauty which lies everywhere at hand;
Tease us with your playful spirit.
Life that maketh all things new,
Creator of earth and its creatures,
Soul of the universe,
Conspiracy of change,
May we be open to your enlivening presence. Amen.

# 45. The Days of Our Years
## *Joseph A. Hill*

> So teach us to number our days that we may get a heart of wisdom.
> —Psalm 90:12

THREESCORE AND TEN YEARS—perhaps fourscore—that is our life span, in round numbers, according to the ancient psalmist. To a boy or girl in the prime of life, seventy or eighty years seem to stretch out in an endless succession of days. But in fact, life has its limits; our days are numbered.

A seventy-year life span equals exactly 25,567 days, counting the extra days in leap years. We have no way of knowing how many days are allotted to us—that is true. But even if we did know, a mere numerical count of so many days would give us neither wisdom nor virtue. Surely, then, the psalmist meant something more than numeration when he prayed, "Teach us to number our days . . . "

When we make the psalmist's brief prayer our own, we ask for wisdom rightly to contemplate our mortality; but also we seek wisdom to live well all the remaining days of our life.

---

*Joseph A. Hill* is a parish associate for the North Branch Presbyterian Church in Monaca, Pennsylvania. He has been associate professor of biblical studies and Greek at Geneva College. A graduate of Pittsburgh Theological Seminary, he has been a pastor of Presbyterian churches in Colorado, New York, and Pennsylvania. Hill was an adviser for the translation of the New International Version of the Bible and he has written for *Christianity Today.*

*I*

Some years ago, Karl Barth frequently left his study and the lecture hall to worship with the inmates of the prison at Basel, Switzerland. He led the convicts in prayer and preached in words that offered them deliverance from sin and hope for the future. Using this text from the Ninetieth Psalm on one occasion, he emphasized the brevity of life and admonished his captive audience to consider their own mortality. To make the matter vivid, he drew their attention to a painting which portrays a great Catholic saint holding a skull in his hand. The saint is obviously meditating on his own death.[1]

Contemplation of death and dying need not be so macabre as the image of a skull in one's hand. But it will always be sobering, as it was for me one memorable autumn afternoon. Strolling through the cemetery that flanks a stately old church in New England, I paused respectfully at the grave of Robert Frost. The burnished gold of Vermont's venerable sugar maples betokened the passing of yet another summer. But the date chiseled into the granite slab covering the poet's grave was a more solemn reminder of death's measured steps. The death of Robert Frost occurred on the 29th of January, which happens to be my own birthday. That coincidence has no significance in itself, to be sure. But as I mused upon it, suddenly to my mind it became a sinister prophecy of my own death in due time.

A merely human contemplation of our mortality, needless to say, is wholly inadequate; by our own wisdom we cannot comprehend either the meaning of life or the mystery of death. We must have God's revelation to enlighten and hearten us. That is why the psalmist's words are a prayer, a request for divine instruction: *Teach us* to number our days. Remind us that we are mortal. Instruct us how to approach our death hopefully, and meanwhile how to live wisely all our remaining days.

If tradition is correct in designating Moses as the author of

Psalm 90, such a prayer would seem to have been unnecessary, for Moses needed no divine revelation to warn him that life is precarious. Death and dying were all around him. Several plagues had already devastated the Israelite community, and Moses' words reflect strong pathos for his sorrowing people. Resigned to the swiftness of life's passage, he laments,

> Seventy years is the span of our life,
>    eighty if our strength holds;
> the hurrying years are labor and sorrow,
> so quickly they pass and are forgotten.
> (Psalm 90:10, NEB)

The brevity of life is too evident to require confirmation; but the right way to contemplate it does need to be learned. And so we must pray: Teach us, Lord, to number our days aright.

## II

Happily, God answers this simple request in the New Testament. God answers it fundamentally in the death of Jesus. God teaches us that we remember rightly that we must die when we remember that Jesus died, that he died for us.

That lesson is made plain in the painting of the old praying saint. He is holding a skull in his hand, but he is facing a cross on which is nailed the figure of the dying Savior. The saint's eyes look beyond the skull; they are focused on the crucified Jesus. The artist knew that we have the right perspective on our own death when we view it in relation to the death of Jesus.[2].

What then is the death of Jesus? Is it the saddest tragedy in the world's history? The extinguishing of the world's brightest light? The most hideous miscarriage of justice? Yes, of course it is all of these. But it is something more. The death of Jesus is, above all else, God's judgment of sin, God's condemnation of sin.

The death of Jesus, therefore, is our death. "Our old self

was crucified with him"; we have died with Christ (Rom. 6:6,8). Our days lived in darkness and doubt now lie in the past, for Jesus' death on the cross has destroyed the power of sin. At the same time, the death of Jesus has opened the future for us to live in harmony with God's purpose and calling. Once we are "in Christ" by a true and living faith, our separation from God (the worst death of all) is a thing of the past and we have, in communion with Christ, a new and eternal life.

If God gives us the wisdom always to look beyond our dying self to the crucified Savior and to live by the virtue of his death and in the power of his resurrection, then we need not fear our own death in due time but accept it joyfully as God's final summons to eternal life.

## III

In the meantime, because our life now is "in Christ," all our remaining days, whether many or few, are precious and therefore deserve to be spent wisely. If you knew that you had only a few days to live, you would want to make each day count. Do you know the value of a single day of your life?

No one can perceive the value of time quite so keenly as a condemned man; the Russian author Dostoyevsky reveals this most compellingly in one of his incomparable novels. His central character, a prince named Myshkin, dwells on the experience of an acquaintance who was under a death sentence for a political offense. This man had been led out of his prison cell to the scaffold where he was to be shot. But at the last moment his sentence was commuted. During what he imagined were the last minutes of his life he kept thinking: "What if I were not to die! What if I could go back to life—what an eternity! And it would all be mine! I would turn every minute into a whole age; I would not let anything be lost. I would count every minute as it passed, I would not waste one!"[3]

Life is a precious treasure to us no less than to Myshkin's unfortunate friend. This is because our days are given—and numbered—by God, and our life is in God's benevolent hands from day to day. When, therefore, we ask for wisdom to live according to God's intention, we must be ready to offer our life to God with unreserved dedication.

John Calvin's dedication to God is uniquely represented in a well-known pictorial symbol. An extended hand is holding a human heart, and around it in a circle is a Latin inscription: *COR MEUM TIBI OFFERO DOMINE PROMPTE ET SINCERE*—"I offer my heart to Thee, Lord, promptly and sincerely." That is the fitting response of every man or woman who has obtained a heart of wisdom. A wise heart is one that is aflame with daily devotion to God. A wise heart is the humble heart of one who, in life and in death, depends on God's grace alone and knows that he or she belongs to our faithful Savior, Jesus Christ. A wise heart is the heart of one who resolves to live faithfully every day that he or she may yet be permitted to live.

Coupled with Calvin's wholehearted devotion to God was his lifelong motto: *Seize the day before the face of God.* No other rule of life expresses more aptly the wisdom of the heart that loves God. Let us make it *our* rule for everyday life. Let us seize every day with its varied opportunities and make the most of them. Let us learn to number our days aright by making every day count.

Emerson once remarked, "We ask for long life, but 'tis deep life or grand moments that signify. Let the measure of time be spiritual, not mechanical." That is wise counsel for us all, for life cannot be measured by clock and calendar. It is the spiritual quality of life that is bound to give meaning and value to the days of our years. What finally matters is not how long or comfortable our life has been, but whether we have found the wisdom to live every day as if it were to be our last.

NOTES

1. Karl Barth, *Deliverance to The Captives* (New York: Harper & Brothers, 1961), 118 ff.

2. *Ibid.*, 121.

3. Fyodor Dostoyevsky, *The Idiot*, part 1, chapter 5.

# VI.  DEVOTIONAL

# 46. Together

*Elizabeth Achtemeier*

Genesis 22:1–19 and Mark 15:6–39

THE SCRIPTURE PASSAGE that we heard for our Old Testament lesson may seem like a monstrous story to us—that command from God to Abraham: "Take your son, your only son Isaac, whom you love, and go to the land of Moriah, and offer him there as a burnt offering upon one of the mountains of which I shall tell you." That seems like an awful and simply unbelievable command for any God of love to give.

And so down through the years, Sunday School lessons and preachers and we ourselves have tried to soften the story. Abraham came from a pagan background in Mesopotamia, goes the reasoning, and so he just mistakenly believed that God wanted him to sacrifice Isaac. The great Danish theologian, Kierkegaard, even made up a series of fanciful endings to the story. Abraham tried to kill himself instead of Isaac, imagined Kierkegaard. Or Abraham pretended that his actions were the result of temporary insanity. Indeed, even the wife of Luther once objected to the Genesis account. "Mar-

---

*Elizabeth Achtemeier* was born in Bartlesville, Oklahoma. She was educated at Stanford University, Union Theological Seminary in New York, and Columbia University, where she received her doctorate. A Presbyterian, Dr. Achtemeier has served as adjunct professor of Bible and homiletics at Union Theological Seminary in Virginia since 1973. She is the author of several books on preaching, including *Creative Preaching, Preaching as Theology and Art,* and, most recently, *Preaching About Family Relationships.*

tin," she said to her husband, "I don't believe God would ask anyone to sacrifice his only son."

But for all of our objections to the Bible's words, the story means for us to take it literally. "God tested Abraham, and said to him, 'Take your son, your only son Isaac whom you love, and sacrifice him in the land of Moriah.' "

Now why? Why would God demand such a thing? After all, Isaac had been a gift from God Himself just a few years earlier. Abraham and his wife Sarah were old and past the age of childbearing, and yet in utter mercy, out of His love for us all, God had given them a promise. "I will make of your descendants a great nation," God told the aged couple, "and through those descendants, I will bring my blessing on all the families of the earth."

So Isaac had been born, to start the line, and now God was saying here, *kill him*. Why, for heaven's sake, why? Abraham must have asked himself that a hundred times. And surely the answer is that sometimes God works through human faith. And so you see, the question in the story is, does Abraham have that faith, does he believe God's promise? Does he totally trust that God knows what He is doing? Abraham has been given the gift of Isaac, to begin the fulfillment of the promise. But having been given Isaac, does Abraham now trust the gift or the Giver?

That test put to Abraham is crucial for us, too, is it not? For starting with Abraham, God begins a history through which He intends to bring blessings on you and me and all people. And certainly this earth of ours needs its cursed ways turned into blessing.

I doubt that I need to spell it out in detail for you. You can read the morning headlines. In our attempts to run our own lives and be our own masters, we daily try to shake off our dependence on God and to be our own gods and goddesses instead, with power over our own affairs, our own futures, our own relationships. The results have been that we have corrupted God's world and despoiled its goodness, disrupting all the beauty of nature and all the loveliness of human community. Death now stalks our streets, which were intended to be full of life. Hatreds, suspicions, envies, greed now poison our commerce and loves. Blood flows, polluting the ground. Loneliness sits in our living rooms. The scarred earth gives back thorns and thistles; and we walk in some awful twilight, where our feet stumble and the goal is uncertain and there is no meaning at all.

Yes, you and I live on a cursed earth, corrupted by our sin, and we dearly need for God to turn it all into blessing. And so through Abraham's faith, God wants to start a history in which He can bless and save us all, in which the final chapter will be not evil but good, not death but life abundant. Oh yes, you and I have a stake in the test put to Father Abraham.

And Abraham, man of faith that he is, goes as he is commanded, to take his son, his only son Isaac whom he loves, to the land of Moriah, to offer him as a burnt offering upon one of the mountains that God will show him.

There is not a word said in this Genesis story about how Abraham feels or how much the mother Sarah knows. Apparently the son and the father journey three days in silence, sharing the stillness of love. For what do you say to a son when you know he has to die?

During the Second World War, I had two brothers stationed in the Pacific, and both of them were assigned to be among the first wave of troops to invade the Japanese Islands. We had no idea at the time, of course, that the atomic bomb was being readied, and it was estimated that it could cost the lives of 1 million men to take and hold Japan. Both brothers had a short leave on the West Coast before they shipped out to battle, and mother flew out to tell them both goodbye. I have often wondered what she said to them. What do you say to a son when you know he has to die?

Certainly the son Isaac, in Genesis, has the most innocent trust in his father. "Father, here are the fire and the wood," he says, "but where is the lamb for the burnt offering?" And certainly, the father has the most tender concern for his son. He himself carries the fire and the knife, lest the boy cut or burn himself with them. And so it is father with son, and son with father, and they go both of them together.

I wonder if you can sense and feel in that Genesis story at the beginning of the sacred history a foreshadowing of the climax of the Bible's history, part of which we read for our Gospel lesson from Mark. For surely there too we have the picture of a Father and a Son, a Son and a Father, going both of them together to Moriah. Later legend even has it that the place of Moriah became the site of the City of Jerusalem. But whether that is true or not, the Father and His beloved Son go up to Jerusalem together. "My Father and I are one," Jesus said. He makes His last journey in the company of God His Father. Father and Son, Son and Father—they go both of them together.

The Son Jesus trusts His Father with His life, just as Isaac trusted Abraham. But there is no record of anything they said to one another on the journey—only that brief conversation in the garden, a little way from the hill of sacrifice: "My Father, if it be possible, let this cup pass from me" (Matthew). Apparently the answer Jesus received was the same one Abraham implied to Isaac: "The sacrifice must be carried out, my son."

Like Isaac, Jesus begins to carry the wood up the hill to the place of offering, until He is relieved of the burden by Simon of Cyrene. Like Isaac, Jesus is laid out upon the wood. And as the knife was raised over Isaac's breast, so the hammers are raised over the nails for Jesus.

But here our stories become very different, do they not? There is no rescue for Jesus—no last-minute voice from heaven to save Him from the awful death—no substitutionary ram, no rescuing Elijah to take away the pain. No, the hammers descend, the nails pierce flesh, the cross is reared up against the sky. And Jesus cries out with the voice of a Son who has been abandoned by His Father: "My God, my God, why have You forsaken me?" He might have cried, "Father, Father, why have you so cursed me?" For you see, to be forsaken by God is indeed to be cursed—to be separated from the one source of all life, all goodness, all love. And Jesus, feeling Himself to be forsaken by His Father, feels Himself accursed.

I wonder what it cost God as He heard Jesus cry out to Him. Someone once said, "If you wish to know how God the Almighty One feels . . . listen to the beating of your own heart, and then add to it infinity." Listen to the beating of a mother's heart, telling her sons goodbye. Listen to the sound of Abraham's sobs as he raises the knife above Isaac. God stands off to the side of the cross, and hears His Son cry out to Him. And God weeps, "Oh Jesu, Jesu, my Son, my Son: O Jesu!"

Here once again, our Scripture confronts us with a monstrous *why?* Why would God do such a thing to His only begotten Son? Why would He condemn Him to a criminal's cross, with its pain, and thirst, and shame? Why would He abandon Him to be accursed in His hour of need? Luther's wife said, "I don't believe God would ask anyone to sacrifice His only son." But God the father sacrificed His Son, and that raises the question, why?

Could it be that the Son of God had to be so cursed by His Father for a little while, because God really meant that promise to Abraham? Could it be that God really wants to take our broken lives and heal them? Could it be that He really wants to bring blessing on us through Jesus, the descendant of Abraham? And that therefore He had to forsake His Son for a while to find all us lost, wandering children? Tell me, how far are we away from our Father's house, do you think? Three long days' journey? Lost somewhere in our own private lands of darkness and death, in our own desolate Moriahs?

We are such a violent people, riding roughshod over one another's feelings. In anger and impatience, we snap at one another until a wife becomes afraid even to admit an error to her husband, or a husband gives up trying to reveal his inmost feelings to his wife. And our homes turn into silent battlegrounds, where gentleness and forgiveness are gone, and God's loving will for marriage is made a total impossibility.

We make friends on the basis of how important they are, and the dull, the incompetent, the shy are glibly dismissed or ignored, because they cannot perform or produce in this performance-oriented society. Thus we ignore the will of that One who made the lowly and forgotten His friends, and we forget the God who promised that the meek shall inherit the earth.

Oh, we did not mean to get lost out here in Moriah. We meant to be kind. We mean always to be good people, to be religious people, to be unselfish—to claim somehow our place among those who truly love God and neighbor. But most of the time we love ourselves and our status and our comfort much more instead. And so we abandon God and wander off into the night. And then we wonder why our world is chaotic and full of death and evil. And we cannot quite shake the feeling that we are very, very lonely—inhabiting a dark and ruthless universe that could not care less about us.

Yes, we are lost and wandering—cursed—you and I, not because God has forsaken us, but because we have forsaken God and His will for our lives. In the words of the prophet, "Your iniquities have made a separation between you and your God, and your sins have hid His face from you."

And so, you see, God sends His Son, His only Son Jesus, whom He loves, into our darkness and death, out here into the land of Moriah, where you and I are lost. And the price is that the Son must be abandoned by the Father. "When the sixth hour had come, there was darkness over the whole land until the ninth hour. And at the ninth hour, Jesus cried with a loud voice, 'My God, my God, why have You forsaken me?' " The price is that the Father weeps as He watches His only Son die. But that was the only way He could find you and me, lost out here in the darkness. Only by journeying into our deathly Moriahs could Jesus come to where we are. And so now He has joined us in our cursed state, and it is Jesus and we, we and Jesus, who are all of us together.

But that of course is not the end of the story, for God did not finally forsake Jesus any more than He forsook Abraham and Isaac. The cross is reared up on Golgotha, yes. The Son of God hangs there, dead, against the sky. But beyond the blackness, at the end of this Passion Week, there are the first rays of light in the eastern sky. And on Easter morn, God will take our death, our evil, our cursed ways, and turn them all into blessing—the blessing of abundant life, both now and eternally.

God sent His Son into our death that we might share His victory over death. God allowed His Son to be cursed with our curse that we might share His everlasting blessing. God forsook His Son for a while that Jesus might find us and return us to the Father.

And so if we will, dear friends—if you will—if we will take the crucified Christ's hand here this morning, and trust Him with our lives, and obey His directions given us in the Scriptures, every step along the way, He will lead us, surely, steadfastly, out of our deadly Moriahs, back to the Father's house, where there is indeed love overflowing. And then it will be, as it was always meant to be, God the Father and all of us together—and life and joy, and blessing abundant, both now and eternally. Amen.

# 47. In the House of the Lord Forever
## Earl G. Hunt

Psalm 23, RSV

> THE LORD IS my shepherd, I shall not want;
>    he makes me lie down in green pastures.
> He leads me beside still waters;
>    he restores my soul.
> He leads me in paths of righteousness
>    for his name's sake.
> Even though I walk through the valley of
>    the shadow of death,
> I fear no evil; for thou art with me;
>    thy rod and thy staff, they comfort me.
> Thou preparest a table before me
>    in the presence of my enemies;
> thou anointest my head with oil,
>    my cup overflows.
> Surely goodness and mercy shall follow me
>    all the days of my life;
> and I shall dwell in the house of the Lord
>    forever.

---

*Earl G. Hunt* is a native of Johnson City, Tennessee. He has served in a number of pastorates and is a visiting professor of Evangelical Christianity at Emory University in 1989. Bishop Hunt recently has been president of the Council of Bishops of the United Methodist Church and in 1988 received the chair of honor from the World Methodist Council. This sermon was delivered at the opening worship service of the United Methodist Church's General Conference in St. Louis, Missouri, on April 26, 1988.

Henry Ward Beecher called this the "nightingale" of the Psalms. Its musical cadences translated into seventeenth-century English have been a part of the lives of millions of educated men and women since childhood. The charm and power of these simple sentences haunt our hearts. They easily suggest a blending of the *memorial* and *communion* themes. The Psalm portrays the pilgrimage of a man or woman of faith and climaxes with a ringing affirmation that such a person, at the end of life's earthly journey, will "dwell in the house of the Lord forever." It also speaks about a table which is prepared, a Host who presides over that table with unfailing care for His guests, and ample food for the famished pilgrim. Implicit in these lovely verses is the idea of love undivided, the kind of love that produces, beyond earthly differences, the priceless treasure of *unity* among God's people.

Let us, then, attempt to bring together the concepts of memorial moments and holy communion against the backdrop of a great phrase from the final verse of the Shepherd Psalm, "In the house of the Lord forever."

## I. Memorial Moments

It is appropriate to begin this General Conference by remembering those Bishops, episcopal spouses, a Judicial Council Member, and General Conference delegates who have completed their journey into Christian immortality. We do this reverently and with heartfelt gratitude for their lives, remembering that all of God's leaders, ourselves included, are sinners saved by grace before they are anything else. Because the gospel is forever true, God gives us, in spite of our human frailty, the privilege of telling its wonder and power. We pay our affectionate tribute of Christian love to all those memorialized today, into whose mighty labors we have entered.

Basic to all other Christian doctrines is the biblical faith in life beyond death. The great Russian novelist Dostoevsky, filled always with the Resurrection certainty of his Eastern

Orthodox church, declared that without confidence in immortality one actually believes nothing. Often in recent decades this particular Christian tenet has seemed to be the "lost chord" of theology.

Somewhere, long ago, I heard Bishop Edwin Holt Hughes, the unforgettable sage of an earlier episcopacy, tell about an evening stroll he took on an ocean beach and a casual encounter with a man who complained that he hadn't heard a sermon on Heaven since childhood. Walking on, gazing into the lovely tints of a sunset sky, Bishop Hughes pondered the man's statement and recalled his own predictable preoccupation with the valid claims of the social gospel across the years. Then, remembering the Savior's perfect blending of time and eternity, he resolved to provide at least a partial answer to that man's problem. Returning to his hotel, he sat down and wrote a sermon on Heaven, giving this story as his introduction.

We correctly deplored the use of the old "pie in the sky" emphasis to sanctify the idea of religion as an escape from the brutal realities of this world. We struggled to make our United Methodism one of God's viable vehicles for applying the Gospel to the open, bleeding wounds of suffering society. But somewhere in the process, unintentionally I think, we came close to abandoning Christianity's historic use of the *eternal dimension* to complete its portrait of human life. The price we have paid for this omission is startling, complex, and devastating. It amounts to neglect of the Resurrection itself, although the first Christians never saw the Resurrection primarily as the means of Jesus' escape from the grave, but rather as the living God in omnipotent action. As we remember today our beloved Christian dead, it is appropriate, to borrow the title of a great sermon by Michael Ramsey, that we should be "thinking about Heaven"—and, more importantly, about the power of the Resurrection. Otherwise, those of us gathered here in St. Louis, to paraphrase Thomas Carlyle's words about Coleridge, will be addressing our massive tasks with looks "of anxious impotence" in our eyes.

Because of the awful heaviness of decisions to be made

here, we would do well to remember that, in Wesleyan religion, social conscience and courage must spring from a saving awareness of God in Jesus Christ, otherwise they are impermanent and dangerous. Our passion to help the poor, the oppressed, and the wronged results from the revolutionary liberation which has come to us through personal encounter with the Resurrection God. Not to recognize this is to invite *missional disaster:* we cannot, we dare not erect a constantly expanding superstructure of social activism upon a steadily diminishing foundation of religious faith. Great enterprises for God grow in the rich soil of vital belief, intentional spiritual discipline, and steadily renewed exposure to the whole treasury of Christian doctrine, especially the Resurrection.

The Shepherd Psalm closes with the statement, "I will dwell in the house of the Lord forever." The foundation of the Christian's confidence that life continues beyond the grave is his or her unshakable faith in the *supernatural power of God,* the same power which was at work dramatically in the lives of those whom we remember in this hour, and which has prepared for them places in another and better world where, beyond these shadows, there are new tasks, new dreams, new goals.

Celebrating their fidelity, we must take candid inventory of our own faithfulness as this General Conference begins. If, indeed, the Lord is truly our Shepherd, it should matter to us most that God's own will be done here. Not what we seek, but *what God wishes* should be the guidelines for each day's work. Our motivation and our toil must please the heart of the Eternal One. Through this simple commitment, in a way quite beyond our knowing, the great, inexplicable energies of Creation will be released both in and through this General Conference. Because there are spiritual laws quite as operative as physical laws, United Methodism can never reclaim its historic power in our day until it affirms again that the eager discovery of Almighty God's will is the one diapason note of real religion. There is no purer way to remember those who have died in Christ and who dwell now in the house of the Lord forever than to think, speak, and act in such a manner that the Holy Spirit may find it easy to dwell in this place during these sessions. When such occurs, this vast headquarters for General Conference will become, indeed, the house of the Lord!

## II. Holy Communion

"Thou preparest a table before me in the presence of my enemies; thou anointest my head with oil, my cup overflows." In this beautiful poem we encounter the hospitality of a gracious and generous host along with a quaint, curious characteristic of ancient Eastern culture. Those of vastly different convictions could eat at the same table without prejudice or danger, for the place of eating had all the privileges of a city of refuge. In these beloved verses, a faithful shepherd has brought his flock safely home. Allowing here for the picture of the flock to shift abruptly to one of people, the image of home is made alluring by mention of a lavishly spread table and a watchful, kind host ready to meet his guest's every need. Nestled in the midst of the Old Testament, this passage lends itself gracefully to Christian application. What a portrait of the meaning of Holy Communion! Surely there are here today hundreds of strong, independent, committed Christian thinkers and leaders, representing vastly different opinions and judgments on vital matters, but belonging gratefully to one Lord, the Lord whose love and concern have prepared the supper. We have come from our many places and lands with our personal needs, our doubts and fears, our weariness, our resentment of wrongs, our anxieties and uncertainties. Yet we are one in our devotion to what we understand to be our church's best interests. Our Lord Jesus knows all of this, and hovers near to bring us renewal and restored faith, and to share with us His own mind if we will allow it. Too, in a dear and intimate way, the very ones whom we have sought to memorialize in these solemn moments are also with us. It is a time for the communion of saints. We are about to enter into the greatest privilege a child of God has on earth, that of taking for ourselves the symbols of the broken body and the shed blood of our Lord.

The Lord's table represents always *unity of spirit* even when there is disagreement in viewpoint. Unity is never achieved easily, and not at all until those who go in its quest have it as their magnificent obsession. Even then it is hard to come by. Many years ago Mr. Justice Holmes said that he would not give a fig for the simplicity *this* side of complexity, but that he would give his very life for the simplicity on *the other* side of complexity. I speak of the unity of our church which lies on the other side of complexity; and I exalt it in these opening moments of General Conference as a precious treasure which must be sought relentlessly, even painfully by all of us.

The Lord's table also symbolizes a common faith and, for us, the historic content of the Wesleyan tradition. We are both liberated and restrained by this realization, liberated to experience new insights of truth within the rich repertoire of our special heritage, restrained lest we violate the time-honored parameters of our knowledge of the gospel. By our commitment to the clear, historic interpretation of the Scriptures left to us by the little Oxford don, we avoid the tempting *privatization* of religious beliefs and practices which has become such a deadly peril in our time. Thank God, we are never free to design our own understanding of Jesus' message, except within those guidelines which generations of devout scholars have developed for us. This was never intended to stifle creativity or to discourage new and valid insights. It was meant to lend necessary spiritual and historical discipline to our contemporary ventures across fresh frontiers. We are the church, not a sect or a cult, and there *are* standards that must always apply.

We take Holy Communion in gratitude for those whom we memorialize, and in humble hope that their mantles of effectiveness may fall upon us as we seek wisdom and sound judgment for the labors ahead. We know we must have this if we are to discharge well our responsibility here in St. Louis.

I sat as a delegate to the General Conference of 1964 in

Pittsburgh and listened to Bishop Herbert Welch, age 102, preach the sermon at the beginning of the great conclave. I can still hear his vibrant voice as it rang out with these words:

> There is no room here for self assertion, or
> suspicion, for contempt or hatred. There is no
> room for bitterness, for parties and slogans. . . .
> For here, in the house of the Lord, belong
> peace and good will, understanding, and
> patience, humility and compassion. . . . We
> shall be united in the confidence that "our
> times are in His hand"; that He will fight our
> battles for us, and the peace of God will keep
> our minds and hearts.

Ah, Herbert Welch, prince of the church, prophet of the faith, may we hear your voice again here in St. Louis as it was heard nearly a quarter of a century ago in Pittsburgh!

Memorial moments and Holy Communion *do* go together: They unite the church triumphant and the church militant in a common effort to know the mind of Christ and to do the will of God. Because love is one and undivided, the Christian's hope for Heaven is never far from his or her hope that the Kingdom will come here on earth. So it is that we have invoked this *nightingale* of the Psalms to build a bridge for our minds and hearts between the memory of heroic disciples and the memory of a suffering Savior. The haunting beauty of this ancient poem thrills each of us. It pleads for the unity of the people of God, living and dead, and more importantly the unity of The United Methodist Church, whose very life is in our hands during these sessions. Our challenge is to respond that we may dwell in the house of the Lord forever.

Nels Ferré once told about a missionary to a leper colony visiting the Vanderbilt Chapel and saying to the students and faculty, "I have come to the seminary here to learn how to pray." Then Professor Ferré wrote: "Deep in the pew I felt very small, knowing that we seminary professors could teach other things far better than we could teach that."

Members of this General Conference, some have feared, may be able to do other things far better than to lead United Methodism toward the fuller implementation of God's will and the discovery of a stronger unity in Christ. They may be right. God grant that they are not. So it is that we come now *in the house of the Lord* to His table, remembering His own prayer in a long-ago garden, *"that they all may be one."*

Amen.

# 48. I Adore You
## Gwyn Walters

Mark 14:3–9; Luke 7:37b–38; and John 12:3

"I ADORE YOU!" Do you deeply desire to say this to some-one? Do you express it in words? Or in symbolic action? Or in neither? In the romantic sphere, we agonize to embrace warm-ly the one we adore, though we may sometimes draw back and idealize or idolize at a distance. In hero worship, we may wish to rush forward for the autograph of that statuesque athlete or that ravishingly beautiful performer; but we're rooted to the seat. In Britain, there are those who feel such adoration for Queen Elizabeth, the Queen Mother, that they would wish to hug her, but protocol forbids. When we are faced with the night sky and span its awesomeness, we sometimes desire to reach out and grasp those scintillating stars, but our finitude inhibits. We spy a powerful red Porsche and pulsate to get our foot on its accelerator—but the speed limit deters us, and any-way it's not ours! We itch to get our hands on the Gothic four-manual organ, but wonder if the vaulted roof will remain intact. Lured by a galaxy of dials in a power plant, we pocket our hands lest we cause an explosion.

*Gwyn Walters* was born in Llanelli, Wales, He was educated at the University of Wales and the University of Edinburgh, where he received his doctorate. A Presbyterian, Dr. Walters has served as professor of ministry at Gordon-Conwell Theological Seminary since 1962. He has been president of the Academy of Homiletics and is the author of *Towards Healthy Preaching*.

What we meet in these instances are faint analogies of adoration in which there is a coming together of two disparate elements. There is the endearing and the endangering; the fascinating and the forbidding—akin to Otto's *mysterium tremendum et fascinans.* There is that which draws us close and that which keeps us at bay. We have a sense of being in the presence of Asian, C. S. Lewis's mighty, majestic lion, who is not safe, but is very good. As we are lifted up in the direction and into the presence of him who is triune God, Father, Son, and Holy Spirit, we feel an entwining of the affection for the intimate and awe at the ultimate. This is how it should be: due reticence and reverence, though there is a magnetism, an attraction that cannot be escaped.

It is right to feel this toward God, who reveals himself in Jesus Christ as the Lover of our soul. It is right not merely to cogitate it, to reflect upon it cerebrally, but to feel it deeply by the Spirit of God. The beloved says to her lover in Song of Songs, "How right they are to adore you!" It is wrong to give adoration to sticks and stones or to satanic beings, but it is right to give it to God because it is his right to be adored. He deserves, desires, and designs each of us who are his, through Christ, to adore him; to know that sense of spontaneous outpouring towards him; to know intense devotion; to have utmost love; to be subjugated marvelously by him and to reach up, and out, and in to him.

It is right that we adore him—that we learn to adore him; in the secret solitude, the silence of our own hearts; as a kind of private act in the presence of others; or concertedly as a group brought together and integrated by the Spirit of God. Our adoration may be expressed variously and grow from the less to the more articulate.

Three somewhat similar vignettes in Scripture—in Mark 14:3–9, Luke 7:36–50, and John 12:1–8—give us glimpses of true adoration. Here are two (or three?) women who are so different. One is unnamed, one a repentant sinner; the other is the lovable sister of Lazarus and Martha, Mary of Bethany. Each of them, in her way, engages in an act of adoration. The adorer utters not a word, but the adoration is eloquent, beyond words, and elicits the commendation of the Lord Jesus.

The Savior commends their *posture*—a posture different from that of most of us who sit with bowed head and clasped hand or kneel or stand with arms uplifted. This posture goes beyond prostration. It vibrates in humility with the Incarnation in its down-to-earthness. It is an anointing of the head and feet of the Lord of Glory—a washing of his feet with tears, a wiping with hair let down not in libertinism, but in emancipated adoration of the King of Kings. That's adoration, and what a posture!

And what a *passion* the Lord Jesus commends here! What a vibrant, vivacious outflow of love aptly tempered by the right degree of reticence. It is utterly reverent and devoid of undue familiarity.

The lavish Lover of our souls, prodigal and prodigious in self-giving, conditions our approach. The Lord commends the *preciousness* of true giving. We come to God at great expense—first his, then ours. One woman's gift, appraised by the undiscerning, is prosaically noted as if it were in dollar and cents. The priceless is priced, forgetting that "High heaven rejects the lore of nicely calculated less or more."

When we come in privacy to adore, we should not be clock-watchers. And when we are called to public worship, we do well not to allow the experiences of life—our studies or work, our domestic concerns or leisure, our societal relationships or anything else to impede us in adoration. Admittedly, adoration seems to be rather unpragmatic, unproductive. It does not appear to get us anywhere. In fact, when we engage in prayer we often want to get beyond it quickly—if we spend any time at all adoring. We prefer the particularities of thanksgiving which we can list a, b, c . . . or confession of sin for which we can provide ample documentation—1,2,3,4 . . . *ad infinitum*. We are tempted to bypass adoration or just skim, skimp, and skip it or speed-read it. We hasten on to petition and intercession which we can concretize more specifically. Adoration is in danger of being at best an adumbration and at worst an aberration.

Are the other elements of prayer and worship, however, as worshipful without adoration? Are they even worshipful at all without it? Here we face the suspicion that there is something unduly pietistic and quietistic about adoration. We are urged to advance not only to the particularities, but to the practicalities of dealing with the issues of society, since true worship issues in (if not consists of) action. Let us not spend time in adoring; let us get on with something more expedient and prudentially profitable! But is there no echo of "seek first the kingdom" in adoration so that the other aspects of worship and the "other things" may be added on in proper order? And will not authentic adoration impel to ingenuous and ingenious action?

The Lord Jesus Christ encourages these women in their adoring actions, not only for their posture, their passion, and preciousness, but for their *perceptiveness*. There are here theological alertness and astuteness; a knowledge of faith, forgiveness, and love. Theology construes and constrains what the Holy Spirit produces. Who knows what insight and spiritual premonition Mary had as she anointed him who is Prophet, Priest, and King and helped prepare Messiah for redemptive burial. In Mark 14, the Lord commends the woman who bows before him for her knowledge and action as worth recalling wherever the Gospel is preached.

Such theologically focused adoration is not appreciated by everyone. There's many a Simon the Pharisee and a Judas Iscariot around. Is there a Simon (or a Simone!) and a Judas (or a Judy!) present? Beware him, beware her! They are sometimes active in church, on campus, in society. They cast doubt upon the Lord and his knowledge because someone has given extravagant expression to adoration. They give priority to economic expediency and rationalized compassion and care for the poor.

The public setting then, when such as Simon and Judas are present, may be a hindrance to adoration. But more often (when such are not present) it can be a great help by the very sense of occasion that coming together can provide. This can happen when bells peal out the welcome "Come to adore" and we imagine the response in concentric circles—in the community, the county, the country, and in the cosmic reaches—because God is adored as Lord of all.

Sometimes it is the palpable silence of a congregation that helps; sometimes it is speech—the simple testimony of someone who knows the Lord intimately. We feel palpitation of heart and say, "Oh, she loves the Lord, doesn't she!" It may be the sermon that lifts up the Lord of Glory, and we feel the anointing of the Holy One upon the preacher. Inhibitions are inhibited and a "Hallelujah" uncircumspectedly erupts! This happened when a spiritually effervescent African student, attending a rather formal Bible study, could not contain himself any longer. With courteous urgency, he interrupted the leader, "Excuse me, Mr. Davies, Hallelujah!"

The sound of music—not on the Swiss mountains but on the hill where we have ascended to adore—is sometimes what helps: music ancient and modern rising into the heart of God. The sacrament or ordinance gives us the sense not so much of the host reserved in a receptacle, but the Lord of hosts for whom all adoration is reserved. And not least, our help to adore may come through prayer—spontaneous or set.

The opening cadences of the Lord's "set" prayer also provide a marvelous formula for adoration. They combine the elements we need. *Our Father.* Here is endearment, embracing, closeness, and intimacy; here is love, here is adoration. But lest we become unduly familiar: *which art in heaven:* here is distance, difference, deference. I am on earth, finite, creaturely. He is in heaven, *Hallowed be thy name.* I recognize Him as separated and sanctified, and my needs as sinful to be made holy. *Thy kingdom come.* As King of love he is to hold sway over me. *Thy will be done on earth as it is in heaven.* Celestial beings may have an edge on us mere earthlings, but their expertise is a stimulus for us to adore:

> My God, how wonderful thou art,
> Thy majesty how bright!

How beautiful thy mercy seat
　In depths of burning light!
How dread are Thine eternal years,
　O everlasting Lord,
By prostrate spirits day and night
　Incessantly adored!
Oh, how I fear thee, Living God,
　With deepest, tenderest fears,
And worship thee with trembling hope
　And penitential tears!
Yet I may love thee too, O Lord,
　Almighty as thou art,
For thou hast stooped to ask of me
　The love of my poor heart.
—Frederick William Faber, 1814–1863

In the love marriage of adoration, I willingly submit in obedience. And heaven and earth are wed in the healthy tension of holy love.

# 49. Between a Lion and a Bear
## *Timothy L. Carson*

Amos 5:18–24

THERE ARE MANY descriptions of God in the Bible. Throughout the scriptures, we have word after word, phrase after phrase, which do not easily express the weight of their subject matter. The words themselves are the problem, of course, for they simply are not adequate to their descriptive task. It is no wonder that Jesus, upon speaking of God, so often spoke in parables which hinted at the reality to which he pointed, teasing his listeners.

More than anything else, the Bible is a book full of metaphors. It says, "the Kingdom of God is like this . . . like this . . . like that . . . like that." The hope is that inadequate words will somehow make a connection with our experience so that we cry out, "Aha! That is it!" Some mysterious naming of the unnameable followed by a nod.

In the text before us, we have another of these grand descriptions. It is strange, but extremely compelling. It, too, tries to answer the question, "So how do you describe the indescribable?" It comes from the prophet Amos.

---

*Timothy L. Carson* is pastor of Community Christian Church (Disciples of Christ) in Camdenton, Missouri. A graduate of Drury College, he received the Master of Divinity from Brite Divinity School in 1980. Carson has been a public schoolteacher, has published articles in *The Disciple*, and has completed a course in ecumenics at the Ecumenical Institute, Bossey, Switzerland.

Already you might be bracing yourself, and for good reason. If you know anything about Amos, you know him to be one who does not mince words. He was not known for diplomacy. Before he speaks you lean back and set your feet.

His words came at a time when Israel was wayward, a nation and a people turning away from their God. And his call is a stern and alarming warning about their future destiny. Their fate is already sealed, he says. The consequences of their behavior have already been earned. But then he tells them to repent. It's too late, and it's not too late.

And sure enough, some do repent. You might think that a good start, and perhaps it was. But Amos just draws the noose tighter. He says, "Woe to you who desire the day of the Lord." In other words, just because you have gone through the motions of repentance, of change, don't imagine yourself to be so safe that you can stand before God without shaking in your boots. Don't imagine yourself safe enough to seek the day of the Lord, that day when everything is seen for what it is, leaving only the naked truth. Don't think you are ready for that day. Don't flatter yourself. Who can stand such a test? You are not as ready as you supposed.

It is at the point of this severe warning, this shocking confrontation, that we hear another naming of the unnameable, this hinting at what an encounter with this One who is fire and smoke might be like. He says: "As if a man fled from a lion, only to run into a bear."

What can this mean? It is walking through a house of mirrors in an amusement park, only to keep colliding with the same image that seems to be everywhere. The exit is hidden. It is a fleeing, running away, and escape on the one hand, and a surprising reencounter on the other.

So it was with Israel. The more they ran from God, the jealous God who sought them like dogs on the hunt, the more they paradoxically ran into God. And of course it is true for us as well. To run *from* is to run *to* at the same time.

As T. S. Eliot writes, "And the end of all our exploring will be to arrive where we started and know the place for the first time."[1] Now that is an extremely uncomfortable prospect. To think that we are dealing with an inescapable Presence. As the Psalmist asks, "Where shall I go from thy Spirit? Or where shall I go from thy Presence?" (Psalm 139).

The answer is all too obvious: nowhere. No escape. God's domain includes me, especially the center of me, and wherever I go, God goes—or rather, I go into God. Fleeing from a Lion, only to run into a Bear.

Why is that so uncomfortable? For one, because we all, for the most part, hate to be really known by anyone, especially ourselves.

The philosopher Friedrich Nietzsche, in *Thus Spake Zarathustra*, told a symbolic story about how Zarathustra, the prophet of a higher humanity, says to the Ugliest Man, the murderer of God, "You could not bear him to see you, always to see you through and through . . . you took revenge on the witness . . . you are the murderer of God." The Ugliest Man agrees with Zarathustra and replies, "He *had* to die." Here in this most secular of books the shadow of the cross quietly falls across the page.

All of us relish that certain masquerade by which we appear as something that we really are not. Or we can say one thing, do another. Or we cling to the props we have treasured for so long—the selfishness, greed, insecurities of the years, the pride that hurts others. But all this the Lion threatens to undo. And this is troubling. At least when we begin to get the feeling that we are being cornered.

This is what is at the heart of Christian conversion, and our Christian reconversions: It has to do with feeling cornered, and bumping into God whatever way we may turn, whatever wrong paths we have taken, however we might have been distracted.

It is as though no matter how much we think we are finished with God, we discover that God is not finished with us.

But it makes sense that God is not finished with us. Think of it: Each one of us is a walking civil war. The unfinished issues in our lives just keep coming around and around, striking us between the eyes until we finally take notice.

Frederick Buechner wrote about a strange compulsion to make a certain pilgrimage to a monastery in his autobiography, *The Sacred Journey*. In it he wrote, "I felt I needed to be cleansed of the too-muchness and too-littleness of my life, to be cleansed as much as anything, I suppose, of myself."

It is the bankruptcy of our lives and the poverty of our spirits that finally catches up with us. And there, standing behind it all, is a Lion. And we turn away only to see a Bear. And suddenly it hits us: "I am going to have to come to terms with this."

No wonder Amos issued his stern warning. Your words about the day of the Lord are nothing, he says. You don't know about the Lion and the Bear, he shouts. And that is uncomfortable to be sure.

But it is also extremely comforting. Would it not be the most tremendous disappointment, the greatest possible disaster, if during our running from God we were *not* caught? Sometimes we are confused, even frightened by this kind of pursuing God, but how could a God who loves, as we know our God does love, do otherwise?

In Martin Luther's delightful collection *Tabletalk*, he spoke of one experience as a young student in Magedeburg, singing in the streets with another student in the hopes of receiving some small contribution of food or money.

A huge man suddenly came running toward them from a house, waving his arms and shouting, "What are you boys up to with such a racket?" What he waved in his hands were sausages, but in fear they ran away from him as fast as they could. What they did not notice was the wide grin on the man's face.

And so we are offered an extremely uncomfortable word as we stand here trembling between the Lion and Bear. That word is: God is not yet finished with us. There is no escape except one. And that is to throw ourselves into the mad clutches of the One who waves sausages at our ridiculous singing.

Luther continued to say that like the man frantically waving the sausages, God holds out Jesus Christ to us, seeking not to frighten us but to draw us to himself.

It is only in an act of surrender that our eyes will fall upon another surprising character, for there is another face of the Lion and the Bear: It is the face of a Lamb—the Lamb of God who takes away the sins of the world.

To fall prey to a Lion and a Bear, only to be loved by the Lamb. Now that is grace. And it's the only thing that makes any difference, whatever way you turn.

NOTES

1. T. S. Eliot, *Four Quartets,* V, line 240.

# 50. Peter Finds the Warmth: A Sermon in Verse

*Dwyn M. Mounger*

THE YEAR IS A.D. 64. The place, imperial Rome. Mad Emperor Nero is killing the Christians. Crucifying them. Throwing them to wild animals. Burning them as torches in his gardens.

Come with me now to the horrible Mamertine Prison, near the entrance to the Roman Forum. An old man there awaits his death. His name? Simon Peter, the apostle.

> How cold it is in this dark Roman cell!
> The moisture covers all the prison's stones;
> It surely seems an icy form of hell,
> That pains and chills a weary, old man's bones.
>
> I'll die tomorrow—so my guard just spoke—
> For Nero's fury rages unrestrained

---

*Dwyn M. Mounger* is senior minister of the First Presbyterian Church of Valdosta, Georgia. Mounger holds a Ph.D. from Union Theological Seminary in New York and is a graduate of Princeton Theological Seminary, Mississippi State University, and Belhaven College. He has been published in magazines such as *Presbyterian Survey* and *Presbyterian Outlook,* among others. Mounger is also the author, narrator, and occasional actor of a series of plays and vignettes and uses his acting skills in many of his sermons.

Against God's own, us peaceful, Christian folk;
The emperor's hands with our red blood are strained.

I'm freezing now! This filthy blanket's thin;
I'll try to think of Galilee's warm air—
So long ago, the sun beamed on our skin;
We fished; the lake was calm, the sky was fair.

Can I recall it?—Yes! Barebacked we stood
Aboard the boat and, laughing, cast the net;
With Andrew, James, and John I thought I would
Stay warm forever, relishing the sweat.

But one bright afternoon the Master came;
He said, "I'll show you greater fish than these."
We dropped our nets, for fishing now seemed tame,
And dreamed he'd give us lives of fun and ease.

Would I have followed had I known the truth?
I hate to say it now, but surely not;
Like Andrew, James, and John, I was a youth;
We thought the sun would stay so nice and hot.

How wrong we were! But I would follow still—
A thousand times through cold and shadows grim;
Though now I face hard death and painful chill,
Christ's call that day transformed me, gave me him.

To think, the Savior chose someone like me—
A fisherman, so stubborn, rough, profane!
Amazing, yes; and still I cannot see
What made him view me more than with disdain.

But Andrew, James, and John and I obeyed;
We warmed to Jesus' every deed and word;
With patient love he saw our lives remade;
Our hearts began to burn with all we heard.

"Peter," he called me: "Stony"—my new name;
He dubbed me that when I cried, "You're God's Son."
I thought I'd always share his pow'r and fame;

How could I know the cold had just begun?

That very day Christ, frowning, said, "Now hear:
My days in sunny Galilee are by;
My time of mocking, suffering is near;
I journey to Jerusalem to die."

"You're wrong!" I cried, "Oh Lord, please don't talk so!"
The Master's eyes flashed fire; he turned to me:
"You're Satan, Peter!—Not my friend but foe."
His words cut deeply; still I couldn't see.

How quickly I forgot his hot tirade,
For soon the light shone brighter than before;
The Galilean sun had never made
A beam that caused our spirits so to soar.

It happened on the mount that awesome day:
With James and John I followed to the height;
The Savior's face itself became a ray;
His very garments glowed in brilliant light.

And Moses and Elijah did appear;
I cried, "Let's never leave this place, good Lord!
Let's build three shining tabernacles here,
And bask in all this warm sunlight!" I roared.

But gently Jesus led us down the hill,
Back to the tablelands and valleys dim;
On further we descended in the chill,
Until we reached dread, dark Jerusalem.

That final week yet seems a harsh nightmare;
Its bitter anguish sears my memory still;
The Passover was set, the table fair;
But how the darkness lingered and the chill!

"Tonight you all will fall away," Christ spoke;
In horror, I could not believe it true;
"Oh, no!" I cried, "though all these other folk
Deny you, I will fight and die for you!"

He answered, "Peter, you're as weak as they;
Before the rooster crows for dawn this night
Your boastful words will vanish all away;
You'll swear you never knew me, much less fight."

Gethsemane seemed haunted, and no star
Appeared to cheer, with gleam to reassure;
The air was cold, unseasonable, far
More like the winter than springtime's allure.

"Please watch with me," he begged, and strode away;
We huddled close; we thought we'd nearly freeze;
And even as, in grief, he bowed to pray,
We fell asleep, with Jesus on his knees.

The long hours passed, and when I woke, I felt
The Master's robe now covering my arm;
For in the night, I knew, the Lord had knelt
And tucked it round me—yes, to keep me warm.

The darkness and the cold still made us quake,
But soon we saw bright torches through the trees
And Judas, with a mob, come there to take
The Savior by the high priest's own decrees.

"Oh no you don't!" I cried, and with my blade
I struck the high priest's slave, who screamed in pain;
"Put up your sword!" yelled Christ; his eyes, they made
Us cower with their blaze of pure disdain.

Then quietly Jesus let himself be led
Straight to the home of Caiaphas, high priest;
I followed at a distance in my dread;
Yet in my heart still raged a furious beast.

The cold seemed worse; I shivered through and through,
But in the high priest's courtyard glowed a flame;
I said, "They'll think me just another Jew;
I'll go inside; no one will know my name."

The charcoal fire felt wonderful; the guard

Had kindled it; I thought of Jesus' fate:
Would they berate him, censure him? How hard!
I prayed they'd simply cast him out the gate.

But then I turned, and through the window saw
The Master standing there in misery;
The priests screamed, "Blasphemy!" and slapped his jaw;
The guards struck, spat upon him in their glee.

I stared into the flaming charcoal blaze
And hope no one would see my boiling tears;
The cold came back—the worst of all my days;
I shivered with the chill and with my fears.

A saucy servant girl came up and cried,
"You're one of Jesus' followers, I know."
I gasped, and blinked my tears away, and sighed:
"Why you're mistaken, lass, to think me so."

Another girl approached and, pointing, jeered,
"This man was surely with the Nazarene!"
"Be gone, accursed Jerusalem wench!" I sneered,
"Why, damn it, Jesus I have never seen!"

The courtyard mob then laughed at me, declared:
"You Galilean bumpkin! Don't you know
Your northern accent means you lie?—You're scared!
You fear that Caiaphas will treat you so!"

"May I be damned to hell," I heard me shriek,
"May I forever burn in Sheol's fire,
If I have ever met of whom you speak!
I swear to you the truth; I am no liar!"

Just then I heard a sound that pierced me through;
Indeed, I hear it yet—through all these years:
The rooster crowed for dawn to start anew;
I turned and looked at Jesus through my tears.

With eyes of pity he returned my gaze;
Upon his face was blood and spit and pain;

My anguish was the worst of all my days;
I fled. I wept. It dawned. I wept again.

Or did the sun come up that day at all?
So long ago; how dark it was and cold:
The taunts, the nails, the blood, the crosses tall;
I, trembling, stood afar, no longer bold.

You fault me—and you should; I sank so low;
In frozen fear I did my Lord deny;
Would you have done the same?—You cry, "Oh no!"
Don't boast so loudly, friend, for so did I.

Besides, don't you your Lord deny each day?
Be honest now, and tell me what is true:
When you your needy neighbor turn away,
You spit upon the Savior's face anew.

And when you ridicule a child of God
Because of foreign tongue or different hue,
Don't you, like Caiaphas, take up the rod,
And beat and crucify the Lord anew?

How cold it is in this dark Roman pen!
The dawn comes soon, and then I go to die;
Oh, will I feel a moment on my skin
The warm sunlight once more, and see the sky?

For even cold and darkness have to end;
If otherwise, I couldn't persevere;
And God forgave my guilt and shame, my friend;
His brilliant light bedazzled all my fear.

Yes, with these very eyes, now old and weak,
I saw the risen Christ, resplendent, bright!
No longer was I scared to act or speak;
All death and darkness fell before his might.

I feel it now: On Galilee we fished;
Barebacked, we stood aboard the boat and cast
Our net into the heaving sea, and wished;

By dawn we still had naught to break our fast.

We didn't mind; the early sun beamed down
And warmed us with its comforting new ray;
A man approached—had he come from the town?
And on the shadowed beach he stopped that day.

"Hey, children, any luck?" the stranger cried.
"Oh no," I answered, "though we've fished all night."
"Well, cast your net upon the other side."
We shrugged and said, "Why not? The net is light."

We cast, but when we tried to pull it in,
The net, now filled with fish, refused to move;
We strained; the sweat popped out upon our skin;
I knew then what the swollen net did prove.

"It is the Lord!" cried John—and I cried too,
Threw on my robe, jumped in the chilly sea;
Straight to the beach I swam, for now I knew
The risen Lord stood there; he'd come for me.

"Say, Simon, son of John, do you love me?"
He asked with probing, penetrating gaze;
"Oh, Christ, you know all things so wondrously,"
I said, "You know I'll love you all my days."

"Then feed my lambs!" he cried, "then tend my sheep.
Then follow me through death and dark and cold!"
I nodded silently; I couldn't keep
The tears from flowing down my cheeks, once bold.

So all these years, my friend, Christ's sheep I've sought,
And found them, fed them, tended them with care;
I've shared with them his light and warmth, and fought
To save them from chill death and Satan's snare.

Though far I've traveled from bright Galilee,
And though my path through chasms dark has led,
Yet Christ has gone before me, made me see;
And stooped to warm me, cure my fear and dread.

But still it's cold in this dark Roman jail,
And Nero's fury reigns without restraint;
Now, facing death, will I again Christ fail?
O God, forbid it! Do not let me faint.

Ah, what's that sound—The guard is coming now?
So soon? I can't believe it. Dawn's at hand?
But I'm not ready! God, to you I bow;
And courage, strength, and light humbly demand.

Yes, guard, I'll come with you—just let me pull
This blanket better round me; I'm so cold;
And please don't think me stubborn, daft, or dull,
If I move slowly, for my legs are old.

Here on the stairs the stones are not as damp;
So I won't fall, I'll climb them carefully;
What's that I see up at the top—a lamp?
Why no, the beam's too brilliant—can it be . . . ?

It is! Oh God, you've sent the dawn at last!
Forever let its light wash over me:
I do not fear the sword, the cross, death's blast,
For always you will warm me, make me see.

Here, guard, please take this blanket all away;
No longer are my heart and body numb;
I stand here in the light of God's full day;
Oh Christ, receive me now. I come! I come!

# 51. Waiting Room
## *Brian K. Bauknight*

*Text:* Our soul waits for the Lord. . . .—Psalm 33:20

IMAGES OF VARIOUS "waiting rooms" in our lives are mostly negative.

For example, there is the small, intimate waiting room of a physician or dentist. You walk in: The sign on the door reads, "Doctor is in. Please be seated." Then you wait—endlessly, it seems—wondering whether anyone is really on the other side of the door.

Or, the larger waiting room of the multiple-team medical practice. When you enter, ten or twelve persons are already waiting. You wonder just how long your wait will be. More people arrive, and then you begin to doubt the capabilities of the receptionist to keep track in proper order of who has entered. Meanwhile, you browse through the outdated copies of *People* magazine or *Business Week.*

Then there is the small examination room to which the nurse leads you when your turn is finally announced. Here you wait—again—this time, shivering half naked on a piece of noisy white paper until the doctor finally enters, clipboard in hand.

---

*Brian K. Bauknight* is senior minister of Christ United Methodist Church in Bethel Park, Pennsylvania. A graduate of Lehigh University and the Theological School at Drew University, he received the D. Min. degree from Pittsburgh Theological Seminary. Bauknight is a founding member of the Make-A-Wish Foundation of Western Pennsylvania, and he has been minister of two other Methodist churches in Pennsylvania. "Waiting Room" is a sermon for Advent.

Or, what about the doctor's own private office? Occasionally, the nurse will say, "The doctor wants to see you in his office before you leave." So, you wait, in more comfortable surroundings, expecting some kind of verdict to be rendered about your future. (I recall one doctor's personal office which has a sign on the desk which reads, "Please take off all your clothes and have a seat. I will be with you in a minute.")

There are also the hospital waiting rooms. One type is located outside critical or coronary care. In this area, you wait the seemingly endless hours until you are allowed to visit the patient a few minutes at designated times each day.

Another is the waiting room for those who have a family member in surgery. After an interminable period of time, you are convinced that something has gone wrong. No one seems to know anything. Why hasn't the doctor come in yet? Why doesn't someone call in with a report?

And there are the airport waiting rooms, sometimes relatively quiet, but more often, noisy, smoke-filled, littered areas, packed with people. Some people are traveling, some are waiting for incoming loved ones to arrive, or some are waiting to give friends and family members a send-off.

The "waiting room" is not a positive image. Frankly, it is very hard to create a positive mental image of any waiting space!

Yet this is what is asked of us during Advent. To do just that! We are waiting in positive expectation. Advent is about creating a waiting room in our hearts!

In fact, waiting is one of the paradoxes of Christian living. It is one of the great positive images of the Bible. The Psalmist writes, "For God alone my soul waits in silence" (Psalm 62). Or, again: "Take courage, wait for the Lord" (Psalm 27). Or, as Isaiah 40 reminds us so beautifully: "They that wait upon the Lord shall renew their strength."

Luke begins his Gospel narrative by telling us of at least six persons who are waiting! Do you remember who they are? The first two are Zechariah and Elizabeth, the parents of John. The second two are Mary and Joseph. Another is Simeon, the old man who faithfully waits in the Temple each day for the coming of God's Messiah. Finally, there is the aged prophetess, Anna. Luke tells us she was married for seven years and widowed for eighty-five years. Anna spent a portion of each day fasting and praying in the temple.

At the very outset, then, Luke tells us of six remarkable people who have opened a waiting room in their hearts. He begins his Gospel with their stories. We could well use the Advent season simply to meditate upon these six waiting souls.

Our text provides another focal point of Advent meditation: "Our soul waits for the Lord." It is a text for building a marvelous waiting room in the human heart. Here is a major component of the Advent pilgrimage. Here is specific instruction and discipline for the days before Christmas.

Yet, we make Advent about so much else. We make it a season of parties, shopping, breakfasts with Santa, sending cards, decorating the home, and baking dozens and dozens of cookies. If we would not normally spend time shopping on a Sunday during the other portions of the year, we do find ourselves at the malls and shopping centers during December. It is probably true that most of us have tighter schedules during December than during any of the other eleven months of the year.

Advent calls us to a waiting room. Yet it is precisely during this season when we have so little time for waiting. Some of the most nurturing portions of our daily walk are suspended or crowded out.

If we have a holy habit of daily devotions, we are less faithful during December. If we are part of a Covenant Group, or a Home Bible Study, or a Sunday School class, we tend to be irregular in our attendance during December. Ironically, many churches suspend some of the most spiritually helpful events during the Advent season.

The weeks of December move so fast. One of the parcel package services had a slogan a few years ago which read, "We WHISH you a Merry Christmas." How apt! Indeed, sometimes the preparation for the Christ Event is little more than a "whish." We spend so much time with the urgent that we have little time for the important.

Instead of a season of waiting, Advent becomes a season of doing. There is a fundamental difference between "being" and "doing." I know that difference all too well, for I am a "doer" by nature. Only in recent years have I started to learn the beauty of the discipline of "being"—of "waiting."

Advent calls us into "being" before God. And we respond with more "doing" than at any other time of the year. We are called by God to be. Yet the secularization of the world compels us to do. We are called by God to listen. Yet the world propels us toward action and activity.

Is it any wonder that our text can seem more of a plaintive cry than an affirmation of faith?

## *My Soul Waits for the Lord!*

Simone Weil, the Jewish writer, once wrote, "Waiting patiently in expectation is the foundation of the spiritual life." That's quite a challenge and a promise for us.

For what, then, do we wait? Essentially, we wait for the same experience as Zechariah and Elizabeth, Mary and Joseph, Simeon and Anna. We wait for the promise of God to be fulfilled once again. We wait for the renewed reality of the Presence of God.

We do not actually wait for Jesus. He has already come. We do not wait for the Nativity. That is already an accomplished fact of history. We wait in fervent hope for the further manifestation of the promises of God.

Most of us gathered here in worship this day have come because we have experienced something of the Advent of God in our lives. Surely, we would not be here if that were not so. We have had some precious moments on our own journey.

Advent, then, is the season of renewing the hope and expectation that God will break gloriously into our lives once more. It is a season of expectant waiting for the God who is always among us, beside us, around us, and within us.

Advent calls us to open a waiting room within and to expect new and confirming moments with God. It is an active experience. In the training of lay pastors in my congregation, we stress the discipline of "active listening." Listening with care and sensitivity is not a passive exercise. Nor is waiting. Waiting is an active event.

We await new promptings, new inspiration, new direction. If life is going reasonably well, we await new challenges and responsibilities. If life is broken—or breaking apart—we await the healing and wholeness that God promises.

This is the season to cultivate the power of the waiting spirit of the Bible alive in us.

We wait in community. The text is plural: *our* soul waits for the Lord. It is in community that much of the richness of God's promise is revealed. The Bible is a community book. We are a community gathered around a promise. We are promised the gift of a beautiful, nurturing waiting room.

The promise is characterized by joy! The message is clear; "Behold, I bring you good tidings of great joy" (Luke 2).

During the days of early December, I will crawl out onto the ornamental balcony of our home and put up the lighted letters of the word "JOY." This single word has been the only exterior decoration of our home for the past fifteen years. Joy is the fundamental character of the promise which greets us in the waiting room of the heart.

When we allow a waiting room to be a positive component of Advent, there is unbounded joy. When we wait expectantly for God's promises to unfold once again, there is unbounded joy.

Surely, there is no greater stability for the struggling, searching soul than the open, prepared, expectant waiting room of the human heart.

Thanks be to God.

# 52. The Parable of the Wise Old Woman

*Nancy Ore*

Matthew 21:28–32

ONCE UPON A TIME on a Friday morning in late September, a pastor, serving a two-point charge in the northeast portion of an upper Midwest state whose thumb sticks up into Lake Michigan, woke up.

The first thing the pastor thought of was the dream she had just been having. It was about a waitress named Spiceina. The pastor had just given Spiceina a five dollar tip for a cup of coffee and, in the dream, the hostess of the restaurant was chasing the pastor with the five dollars trying to give it back to her. The pastor was saying to the hostess, "Waitressing is hard work with low pay. Spiceina has four children to feed . . ."

The pastor woke up as the hostess was heading toward the kitchen waving the five dollars and hollering, "Spicy . . . Spicy . . ."

The second thing the pastor thought of was the sermon for Sunday. It wasn't even started. She'd thought about the scripture all week, but still didn't have any words down. She tried

---

*Nancy Ore* is pastor of Oconto and Abrams United Methodist Church in Oconto, Wisconsin. A graduate of the University of Wisconsin at Oshkosh, she received the Master of Divinity from Garrett-Evangelical Theological Seminary in 1986. Her articles and poems have been published in several journals, and she has won awards for both her poetry and music.

to go back to sleep and couldn't. She decided that this morning was one of those times she'd have to go ask the wise old woman for advice.

Seventeen minutes later, the pastor found herself in the back corner of the French Town Custard Restaurant where the outrageous wise old woman hangs out drinking coffee, painting her long fingernails neon colors, and polishing her rings.

"So," said the Wise Old Woman, talking loudly to be heard over the speaker tuned in to WIXX which was blaring out a song about the NFL strike called "Picket Line Shuffle."

"So, you're stuck again."

"Yes," said the pastor dejectedly and explained, "I'm not stuck over what to say to the folks on Sunday morning so much as I am stuck *how* to say it. You see, the scripture is a parable. It is one of Jesus' *stories.* The Bible is full of a wide variety of writing: geneologies, battle accounts, laws, histories, poetry, measurements of arks! All of the writing, of course, is meant to point to God, but parables are unique. Jesus took a common, everyday situation, wove a story around it which got folks to think and ask questions about God, and then in conversation maybe discover an answer or two."

"What's the matter, pastor?" asked the Wise Old Woman. "Can't you think of any examples? Sermon illustrations? Common stuff of the everyday life of your congregations?

"On the contrary, Wise Old Woman. Jesus used a *very* common example easily applied to our lives. He tells about two men who are asked to make a decision to go to work. One man says, 'No, I won't go,'—and then changes his mind and goes. The other man says the opposite: 'Sure, I'll go,'—and then he doesn't.

"That behavior happens all the time," continued the pastor. "Sometimes I do it myself. I've got *lots* of examples. All week I've dealt with people saying 'Yes' or 'No' to invitations or responsibilities:

'No, I don't want to be on that committee.'

'Yes, I'll be at that meeting.'

'No, I'm not coming to Confirmation.'

"*Today,* Linda, Joe, Pearl, Norma, Shirley, and I are trying to get folks to go to our District Fall Celebration next week. Who knows by next Sunday *who* will actually get on the bus? Some people come. Some don't. *That's* not the problem."

The Wise Old Woman looks impatient. The pastor thinks maybe she wants to get back to painting her nails. The Wise Old Woman plays with one of her rings and says,

"Well, what *is* your problem, then?"

"Well, my problem isn't who shows up next Sunday. Whoever shows up represents the Body of Christ gathered and God's presence is there. And my problem isn't with folks keeping their word. Most people, when they say they'll be somewhere, are there. And, if they can't make it, they call. I mean . . . things change in people's lives . . . folks get sick . . . some get tired."

"Some folks get sick and tired," quipped the Wise Old Woman. The pastor wondered if the Wise Old Woman was getting sick and tired of *her.*

"So," the Wise Old Woman asked again not trying to disguise her impatience, "The *problem?*"

The pastor stated her case.

"Well, Wise Old Woman, Jesus used this common situation story to point to God. *How* can I use the story to do the same? My job is to tell Good News in such a way that folks' relationship with God is made stronger. *How* can I do that?"

"Oh," said the Wise Old Woman, sitting up a little straighter and becoming a little more interested now that the problem was clearly defined. "Where *is* the Good News in this parable?"

"That's where it gets tricky to explain," answered the pastor.

"Jesus told the story to all sorts of Jewish people. Some were outcasts, some sinners, some stiff-necked self-righteous religious officials. Some were sick, some were tired . . . some were sick and tired.

"In this story, Jesus points to the ministry of John the Baptist and seems to be saying that the folks listening to John are getting into the Kingdom of God before the religious establishment people."

The Wise Old Woman continues the flow of conversation.

"And John? What was his ministry?"

The pastor answers directly out of New Testament 101.

"Well, John was saying, 'Repent.' That meant 'just turn around.' Turn from participating in destructive things and turn back toward God. That implies that the folks didn't have to be a church member or official. That implies that folks didn't have to live out a bunch of rules to be in God's Kingdom."

The Wise Old Woman shrugged her shoulders, stretched out her hands in a gesture which indicated the problem was solved, and said,

"So, there it is. Say to the people: *'Turn toward God. Go to the vineyard.'*"

"Sure," said the pastor who liked complexity and good dialogue. "It still isn't that simple. Matthew (who wrote this story) wrote it *after* Jesus had died and *after* the amazing claim that Jesus was resurrected. Matthew wasn't writing it to Jewish folks only. He was writing to Gentiles as well."

"Oh, I see," said the Wise Old Woman. And, she quickly demonstrated her wisdom with a remark that proved she *did*, indeed, see:

"You're saying the same story said to different people may have a different meaning to the hearers. Depending upon their situation, folks may look at the same story in different ways."

"Yes," replied the pastor. "Matthew took many of Christ's stories and arranged them in such a way that certain points were made. In this case, Matthew put the story with a couple of other parables which have the intention of proving Jesus' authority. By Matthew's time, the story of Christ's death and resurrection was spreading throughout the area: to Jews, Gentiles, everyone. The question for folks to decide was, 'Who *is* this man, Jesus? God's son? The Messiah?' The question for folks was, 'Is what Jesus said about God *true?* If so, what does that mean for *my* life?'

"Oh, Wise Old Woman," continued the pastor, "My problem is the folks I preach to are baptized. They *already* say they believe in Christ as the Son of God and have turned toward God. With regard to the Kingdom of God, they are folks like the second son in the parable. Each one, by being baptized, has already said, 'Yes, I'll go. Yes, I'll work in God's vineyard world.' "

Now the light dawns on the face of the Wise Old Woman. She knows this pastor very well.

"I see your problem, honey. You're afraid of the second part of the equation of the second son. The conclusion. The son in the parable says, 'Yes, I'll go,' and he doesn't. You're worried because you wonder if that means that conclusion is also the one to be drawn on Sunday morning. You're afraid to put that question before the folks. You're afraid the scripture is requiring you to say, 'Look folks—you've promised to work in God's world. How are you doing?' And you're afraid the folks will infer that you don't think they're doing very well. And you are very uncomfortable calling folks to be accountable to their promises."

The Wise Old Woman takes a deep sigh and, as her chest expands, the pastor notices for the first time, the Wise Old Woman has on an outrageous purple sweatshirt decorated with sequins, rhinestones, and sparkling beads. With astonishment, the pastor notices the glitter spells out the wise old woman's initials: W.O.W. WOW!

Across the front of the Wise Old Woman, the *word* WOW!

As the pastor is contemplating this amazing connection, the Wise Old Woman speaks.

"In reality, honey, even the parables don't contain the *whole* truth. There are at least two other options not even mentioned in this story. There are two sons, right? The son who says he'll go and doesn't and the son who says he won't and does??

"What about the other two options which immediately come to mind? A son who says, 'No, I won't go' and doesn't, and a son who says, 'Yes, I will go'—and, *does.*

"What's the bottom line in this parable, honey? What does Jesus want to communicate above all else? That God wants folks in the vineyard kingdom. God wants all people to love God and each other and creation. That is a truth for *all* time for *all* people."

The Wise Old Woman, having made her point, looks at the pastor and asks, "Who are the folks you'll be preaching to Sunday morning?"

Faces of the folks in the two congregations flash in front of the pastor's face. She watches with tenderness for a moment and then answers,

"Well, they are people who struggle with life. Who try. Who trust each other—sometimes. Who have survived trage-dies. Who care for each other as best as they can. They are folks who are busy, who work hard, who are sick, . . . and tired. They are the sons and daughters of God who have said, 'Yes, we want to be in God's Kingdom. We believe Christ's promise of love and we want to go where we'll receive it.' "

The sunlight coming through the window of the restaurant hits the Wise Old Woman's sweatshirt in such a way that the reflection off the WOW sheds an even further insight in the pastor's mind.

"Ah, I see. We church folk have already said, 'Yes,' like the second son. A question to consider is, 'Are we or are we not at work in God's vineyard? Are we or are we not in God's presence?' "

The Wise Old Woman nods and gently says, "And, who did Christ say was getting in *first?*"

"The tax collectors and prostitutes," quickly answered the pastor, hoping that the Wise Old Woman wouldn't ask her about the behavior of the folks gathered on Sunday morning.

But instead, the Wise Old Woman acted as if the behavior wasn't the issue at all. She asked,

"Why did Jesus say those folks get in first?" And, the Wise Old Woman answered her own question, her initials gleaming silver and gold,

"Jesus didn't say they'd get in *because* of their behavior. He said they'd get in because they knew they weren't perfect and knew how desperately they needed God. They knew how much they longed to be in the vineyard. What does that say to you, honey? You—who comes to me afraid and broken, too?"

Now the pastor is feeling like a child. She listens as the Wise Old Woman loves her and gives *her* Good News:

"It's not the folks like the pharisees who are in God's presence. It's not the folks who think they know all the right words or how to do the right sermon. It's not the folks who think they know the religious rules and are rigidly and self-righteously and *joylessly* living them out.

"The folks who get into God's Kingdom vineyard are the folks who know they're not perfect. The folks who are afraid, the folks who are hurt, the folks who feel guilt, who agonize over broken relationships . . . the folks who are sick . . . and tired . . . and sick and tired. The folks who are acutely aware of their separation from God. It's the folks who say, 'Yes. I'll go into the vineyard and work with God. There's *nothing* which could keep me away!'

"It's the folks who not only go, but while they're there, they are the folks who will be making wine and when the work is done, they'll drink that sweet flowing wine with their brothers and sisters . . . communion."

The pastor, subdued, was barely able to let herself breathe and barely able to let herself feel the love this Wise Old Woman offered.

"So," she whispered, "What should I say on Sunday morning?"

"Just remind folks of the choice they have. They've already said one 'Yes.' Ask them to consider prayerfully if they have said or are saying the second 'Yes.' If they're not sure, simply invite them to do so."

The pastor, lost in thought still trying to figure out *how* to tell Jesus' story, didn't notice the Wise Old Woman was gone until the waitress came to fill her coffee cup. Seeing the waitress, reminded the pastor of her dream, the outrageous tip she had given to Spiceina—a waitress working hard at low pay to raise four kids.

The pastor got up. Figuring that any waitress who would keep the coffee cups of two weird women filled was worth a lot of money, left an outrageous tip on the table and headed to her office to figure out *how* to preach the parable on Sunday morning.

# Index of Contributors

# Index of Sermon Titles

# Index of Scriptural Texts

P9-DIJ-211

Dancing the Breeze

# Dancing the Breeze

BY GEORGE SHANNON

PICTURES BY JACQUELINE ROGERS

BRADBURY PRESS
NEW YORK

COLLIER MACMILLAN CANADA/TORONTO
MAXWELL MACMILLAN INTERNATIONAL PUBLISHING GROUP
NEW YORK • OXFORD • SINGAPORE • SYDNEY

*Bradbury Press*
*Macmillan Publishing Company*
*866 Third Avenue, New York, NY 10022*

*Collier Macmillan Canada, Inc.*
*1200 Eglinton Avenue East*
*Suite 200*
*Don Mills, Ontario M3C 3N1*

*The text of this book is set in ITC Modern Light No. 216.*
*The illustrations are rendered in watercolor highlighted by colored pencil.*
*Calligraphy by John Stevens*
*Book design by Julie Quan*

*Printed and bound in Singapore*
*First American Edition*
*10  9  8  7  6  5  4  3  2  1*

LIBRARY OF CONGRESS CATALOGING-IN-PUBLICATION DATA

*Shannon, George.*
*Dancing the breeze/by George Shannon: illustrated by Jacqueline Rogers.*
*p.    cm.*
*Summary: Lyrically describes Papa, young daughter, and*
*the evening breeze as they dance among the flowers in the front yard*
*while the moon rises.*
*ISBN 0-02-782190-0*
*[1. Fathers and daughers—Fiction. 2. Dancing—Fiction.]*
*I. Rogers, Jacqueline, ill.   II. Title.*
*PZ7.S5288Dao 1991*
*[E]—dc19     88-37598  CIP  AC*

*To Virginia and Carol*
— G.S.

*To the Dugway Gang*
— J.R.

Rocking and waiting
to see the moon
both of us suddenly
turn and smile.

Both of us hear it—
in soft notes of leaves
twisting green-silver-green,
and old dry leaves
scratching
over the grass.

We feel the breeze, too,
and smile again
as it slowly begins
to swirl in our hair,
then billows our robes
as we quietly stand
and join with the flowers
that dance the breeze dance.

Long steps with lupines,
and short ones with phlox,

the breeze leads us gently around the front yard.

Big steps with allium,
small steps with chives,

we dance all around,
we partners three—
papa and baby
and the evening breeze.

Quick steps with poppies,
slow steps with pinks.
Tiptoe steps, too,
with the sneaky ol' weeds.

Turning and bowing,
again and again,
we sing with the breeze
as it hums on our skin.

Songs of soft petals,
and songs of leaves,
we dance all the blooms
in our breeze bouquet.

Laughing and singing,
we keep dancing on

with fancy fern turns
and forget-me-not steps.

Turning and turning,

around and around, when,
just as suddenly as it began,

the breeze stops,
the music fades...

Our dance is done
'til another night
when the leaves will sing
our partner back
and feeling as light
as the rising moon

we'll dance again,
with the evening breeze.